In the Name of the Child

A Developmental Approach to Understanding and Helping Children of Conflicted and Violent Divorce

JANET R. JOHNSTON, PH.D.
VIVIENNE ROSEBY, PH.D.

THE FREE PRESS

New York   London   Toronto   Sidney   Singapore

THE FREE PRESS
A Division of Simon & Schuster Inc.
1230 Avenue of the Americas
New York, NY 10020

THE FREE PRESS and colophon are trademarks
of Simon & Schuster Inc.

Designed by Carla Bolte

Manufactured in the United States of America

10   9   8   7   6   5   4   3   2

Library of Congress Cataloging-in-Publication Data

Johnston, Janet R.
  In the name of the child : a developmental approach to
understanding and helping children of conflicted and violent divorce
/ Janet R. Johnston and Vivienne Roseby.
    p.   cm.
  Includes bibliographical references and index.
  ISBN 0–684–82771–9
  1. Children of divorced parents—Mental health.   I. Roseby,
Vivienne, 1951–   .   II. Title.
RJ507.D59J64   1997
618.92′89—dc21   97-3295
                                                    CIP

To

MALCOLM, KATHRYN, BENJAMIN

SARAH, NOAH, DAVID, KAREN, STEWART, ZOEY T.

Contents

Preface

*I*n the wake of a generation of high rates of divorce, an accumulating subgroup of separating and divorced families in our communities are now designated as "high conflict" by mental health and legal professionals and by the parents themselves. This fast-growing minority of divorced families poses serious social policy problems. They clog the family courts, requiring an inordinate share of access to the justice system. Many of their children are suffering emotional problems of clinically significant levels and consequently consume a disproportionate share of the community's precious mental health resources. Ironically, as the drama of the interparental struggle assumes center stage, the children's plight is often thrust into the background and awareness of their pressing needs becomes lost in the heat of the battle conducted in their name.

This book represents almost two decades of work with distressed families drawn from this subpopulation, all of whom were referred to our various counseling projects by family courts of the San Francisco Bay Area. We have learned, in a nutshell, that a protective nurturing environment for the child in the fractured family can be cultivated only when the child can be seen and understood as an individual separate from the parental conflict, and when the parents can be helped to reframe their agendas in terms of the child's developmental concerns and preoccupations.

The more we understand these children, the more questions we ask, especially questions about the damage being done to their capacity to form trusting, authentic, emotionally gratifying and moral relationships as they grow older. We offer our clinical observations and preliminary research findings as a work in progress, hoping to inspire more systematic research into this caldron of relationship failures. We confess our concern at the enormity of the task remaining for professional leaders and social policy makers who must respond to the fallout from parental separations and divorces that neither remedy the misery of parents nor relieve the suffering of children.

This book seeks to share practical strategies and policies for preventing or intervening early on with children at risk in highly conflictual divorces. Basing our findings on individual assessment of the developing child within his or her family, we propose criteria for day-to-day decision making about custody, visitation, and parenting plans and we describe treatment strategies. The book is organized into three parts:

Part I provides an overview of the dynamics of high-conflict and violent divorced families as they affect children. It is of relevance to a general, multidisciplinary audience concerned about the broad social consequences of the problem. More specifically, chapter 1 describes and illustrates the multilayers of typical divorce impasses between parents and how professionals and the courts can inadvertently escalate custody disputes. Contributors to these impasses may include tribal warfare generated among the extended families, new partners, misguided professionals, and inflexible courts, all of which may exacerbate interparental disputes that evolve out of traumatic and ambivalent separations and the psychological conflicts embedded in the vulnerability of men and women to the loss and rejection inherent in the divorce experience.

Chapter 2 presents a typology of interparental violence that we have observed in custody-disputing families: ongoing and episodic battering, female-initiated violence, male-controlling abuse, separation-induced trauma, and paranoid-psychotic reactions. How girls and boys relate to their violent and victimized parents within each of these patterns is described, together with guidelines for custody, visitation, and interventions with all family members. Chapter 3 describes how parent-child relationships become distorted and transformed by interparental conflict, family violence, and the parents' own psychopathologies, which in turn endanger the child's normal personality development. We submit that children exposed to scenes of severe family conflict and violence will attempt to make sense of what is happening and to control their unsafe world by forming defensive scripts of family relationships that mitigate against their capacity to trust and to tolerate intimacy with others.

Part II describes and illustrates common developmental threats to boys and girls of different ages and stages, together with criteria for therapeutic intervention and principles for developing parenting plans. This section is of most interest to those who help parents make decisions on behalf of children during and after divorce (mediators, custody evaluators, and judges) and to counselors who intervene directly with children and parents (attorneys and psychotherapists). Chapter 4 identifies the psychological separation-individuation of infants and toddlers from their primary care-givers as the crucial blueprint of personality formation and the developmental task that is most likely to be disrupted by parents' distress and dysfunction. Cumulatively, as children enter the oedipal stage, chapter 5 shows how incomplete psychological differentiation from their distressed parents is likely to lead to a rise in children's sexualized anxiety, difficulty in modulating aggression, and problems in consolidating gender roles and the foundations of sexuality for preschool boys and girls.

Chapter 6 describes how children during the school-age years find it difficult to trust other people and to feel sufficiently competent, lovable, and good. They increasingly rely on distorted and constricted unconscious scripts, derived from their chronically conflicted families, to understand, predict, and control interpersonal relationships. Their reliance on inner scripts and avoidance of real intimacy preclude their ability to benefit from the kinds of friendships and experiences that might help them to mature and bind them all the more tightly to distortion and defense. We postulate in chapter 7 that because earlier psychological conflicts are typically revisited during adolescence, there is an opportunity for resolution as well as the threat of stalemate at this time. Case illustrations show how problems in separating from parents, achieving stable, realistic self-esteem, feeling comfortable about one's gender and sexuality, and becoming capable, autonomous, trusting, and moral in the world are likely to resurface, making adolescence a particularly painful experience for these children and their families. Parental alienation and "unholy alliances" are the subjects of chapter 8. The disturbing dynamic in which children stridently reject one parent and align with the other may be a normal and expectable reaction, or it may be a pathological outcome of early and sustained damage of a vulnerable child exposed to chronic family conflict. The many threads of alienation are examined separately and then woven together in our case illustrations.

Part III focuses on interventions on behalf of children of high-conflict divorce. Chapter 9 provides an overview of emerging social policy and service programs in the courts and communities designed to address parents' legitimate concerns and to prevent or macro-manage ongoing disputes; it is of special interest to policy mmakers, administrators, and program developers. Alternative methods of dispute resolution (other than litigation) are described: divorce education, collaborative law, issue-focused mediation, therapeutic mediation, child-focused custody evaluation, coparenting counseling and arbitration, and supervised visitation. We suggest criteria for determining which kind of family benefits from which kind of approach, and at what stage in the process.

Chapter 10 describes and illustrates therapeutic mediation and the phases of long-term coparenting counseling with families in seriously entrenched disputes; that is, it shows how to micro-manage parental and family conflicts to protect the children. Finally, Chapter 11 presents a group treatment model that we developed for school-age children in highly conflicted and violent divorced families. Many of the therapeutic exercises described here can be adapted for individual work with children of this age. Group treatment strategies for preschool children are also described. These last two chapters are most relevant to mental health counselors who intervene directly with children and parents of high-conflict divorce.

This book is one of a series of related works, all of which have been published by the Free Press. Specifically, it is a sequel to *Impasses of Divorce: The Dynamics and Resolution of Family Conflict* (1988) by J. R. Johnston and L. E. G. Campbell, which details the individual family/wider social system factors that contribute to divorce disputes. Published simultaneously with the present volume is a curriculum for group interventions with children entitled *High-conflict, Violent and Separating Families: A Group Treatment Manual for School-age Children* by V. Roseby and J. R. Johnston, and a book of children's stories called *Through the Eyes of Children: Healing Stories for Children of Divorce* by J. R. Johnston, K. Breunig, C. Garrity, and M. A. Baris.

ACKNOWLEDGMENTS

The clinical work reported in this book was largely undertaken during our tenure at the Judith Wallerstein Center for the Family in Transition, Corte Madera, California. We are most grateful to Judith Wallerstein, Ph.D., founder and senior consultant of the center, for her vision, inspirational leadership, and encouragement. We acknowledge the collegial support of the members of the Center, and specifically thank the special clinical research teams that worked on the Protecting Children from Conflict projects during 1989-96, with sites at the Center in Corte Madera and the Mid-Peninsula Family Service Agency in Palo Alto, California. We appreciate the referrals from, and the collegial consultations with, the staffs of Family Court Services throughout the Bay Area—in Alameda, Contra Costa, Marin, Napa, San Francisco, San Mateo, Santa Clara, Santa Cruz, and Sonoma counties. We wish to thank the children and families who participated in the Protecting Children from Conflict projects, without whom none of this research would have been possible. Special thanks are due to a former colleague, Linda Campbell, Ph.D., for her earlier contribution to our understanding of high-conflict and violent families. We are most grateful for the sensitive and painstaking word processing and copy editing skills of Barbara Lehman. Finally, our thanks to Philip Rappaport, our editor at The Free Press, for his support.

Funds for the series of studies that contributed to the clinical findings in this volume were provided by the Gerbode Foundation, the Marin Community Foundation, the Morris Stulsaft Foundation, the Office of Juvenile Justice and Delinquency Prevention, the San Francisco Foundation, the State-Wide Office of Family Court Services (Administrative Offices of the Court), Judicial Council of California, and the Van Loben Sels Foundation. Most important, we wish to acknowledge and thank the Zellerbach Family Fund and its former executive director, Edward Nathan, for continuous encouragement and funding to explore creative solutions to the problems of violence and hate in families and neighborhoods. While we are greatly indebted to each of these private charities and public institutions for their financial support, the opinions, findings, and conclusions in this book are wholly those of the authors and not necessarily those of our sponsors.

Parts of this work have been published elsewhere in somewhat different form. Chapter 1 provides a synopsis of the earlier book in this series by J. R. Johnston and L. E. G. Campbell, *Impasses of Divorce: The Dynamics and Resolution of Family Conflict* (New York: Free Press, 1988). Chapter 2 is a composite of two papers by J. R. Johnston and L. E. G. Campbell, "A Clinical Typology of Interparental Violence in Disputed Custody Divorces," reprinted with permission from the *American Journal of Orthopsychiatry* (1993, *63:* 190-199), copyright 1993 by the American Orthopsychiatric Association, Inc.; and "Parent-Child Relationships in Domestic Violence Families Disputing Custody," *Family & Conciliation Courts Review* (1933, *31*(3): 282-298), copyright 1993 by Sage Publications, Inc., and reprinted with permission. Parts of chapter 3 and chapter 11 previously appeared in a paper by V. Roseby and J. R. Johnston entitled "Clinical Interventions with Children of High Conflict and Violence," reprinted with permission from the *American Journal of Orthopsychiatry* (1995, *65*: 48-59), copyright 1995 by the American Orthopsychiatric Association, Inc. Parts of chapter 6 previously appeared in a paper by V. Roseby entitled "Uses of Psychological Testing in a Child-Focused Approach to Child-Custody Evaluations," reprinted with permission from the *Family Law Quarterly* (1995, *29*(1): 97-110), copyright 1995 by the American Bar Association. Chapter 8 is partly drawn from a paper by J. R. Johnston entitled "Children Who Refuse Visitation," which appeared in C. E. Depner and J. H. Bray (editors), *Nonresidential Parenting: New Vistas in Family Living*, pp. 109-135 (Newbury Park, Calif.: Sage Publications, 1993), copyright 1993 by Sage Publications, Inc., and reprinted with permission. Finally, extracts for chapter 9 derive from J. R. Johnston's article "High-Conflict Divorce," in *The Future of Children* (1994, *4*: 165-185), adapted with permission of the Center for the Future of Children of the David and Lucile Packard Foundation. We express our appreciation to these publishing companies and journals for allowing this material to be adapted and reprinted.

Janet R. Johnston	Vivienne Roseby
Menlo Park, California	Davis, California
April 1997	April 1997

PART I

THE PROBLEM AND THE CHALLENGE

Chapter 1

The Family Crucible of High-Conflict Divorce and Entrenched Custody Disputes

*J*ust as a marriage can be deemed as more or less successful or as having failed, so can a divorce be seen as being more or less successful or as having failed to accomplish its purpose. In a successful divorce, the adults are able to work through their anger, disappointment, and loss in a timely manner and terminate their spousal relationship with each other (legally and emotionally), while at the same time retaining or rebuilding their parental alliance with and commitment to their children. A successful divorce can relieve children of the daily stress of overt parental conflict and associated anger and depression. Fortunately, the majority of couples appear to achieve this kind of transition relatively successfully. Charts and markers for their voyage have been well described elsewhere (Ahrons, 1994; Hodges, 1991; Kalter, 1990; Ricci, 1997). This transition is not easy; there is extensive evidence that it constitutes one of the most difficult challenges and painful experiences that can confront children and adults throughout their lives (Wallerstein & Blakeslee, 1989; Wallerstein & Kelly, 1980). Moreover, this task takes time. On average, conflict and turmoil continue for two to three years following separation, although there can be great variation: some relationships take many years to terminate, and some may never be resolved (Hetherington et al., 1982; Wallerstein & Kelly, 1980).

THE FAILED DIVORCE

About one fourth to one third of divorcing couples report high degrees of hostility and discord over the daily care of their children many years after separation and well beyond the expectable time for them to settle their differences (Ahrons, 1981; Maccoby & Mnookin, 1992; Wallerstein & Kelly, 1980). For about one tenth of all divorcing couples, the unremitting animosity will shadow the entire growing-up years of the children. This means that an accumulating subgroup of children are caught in these family situations. Since approximately one million children each year experience their parents' divorce in the United States, over a span of two decades more than five million children will be affected by ongoing parental conflict; for two million children, this condition may well be permanent (Glick, 1988; Maccoby & Mnookin, 1992).

Frequently, although not always, these parents take their disputes with each other to family court. Current estimates are that about one fourth of all divorcing couples with children have considerable difficulty completing the legal divorce without extensive litigation (Maccoby & Mnookin, 1992). Re-litigation about custody matters following the final divorce decree occurs with a smaller proportion of families (less than one fifth), but these legal disputes are often perceived to be the more intractable ones (Ash & Guyer, 1986b; Depner et al. 1994; Duryee, 1992; Hauser & Straus, 1991). Interestingly, ex-spouses who are highly litigious tend to be, but are not necessarily, the same group who are very hostile and highly discordant in coparenting their children (Maccoby & Mnookin, 1992).

Outside the court, highly conflictual divorced parents engage in frequent arguments, and undermine and sabotage each other's role as parents. This can involve talking negatively about the other parent in front of the child or having the child pass messages including insults and threats to the other parent. Some studies have shown that the children of these parents are witness to considerable verbal abuse (on the average about once weekly) and physical aggression between their parents (on the average once monthly), usually at the time of transfer from one home to the other (Johnston, 1992a; Johnston & Campbell, 1988). Parents can refuse to communicate and assiduously avoid each other; they can take unilateral actions with respect to their children, refusing to coordinate child care arrangements, transferring the child to another school or doctor without notice, refusing visitation, and even snatching and hiding their children from the other parent (Greif & Hegar, 1993; Johnston & Campbell, 1988).

In sum, high-conflict parents are identified by multiple, overlapping criteria: high rates of litigation and relitigation, high degrees of anger and distrust, incidents of verbal abuse, intermittent physical aggression, and ongoing difficulty in communicating about and cooperating over the care of their children at least two to three years following their separation. Probably most characteristic of this population of "failed divorces" is that these parents have difficulty focusing on their children's needs as separate from their own and cannot protect their children from their own emotional distress and anger, or from their ongoing disputes with each other.

Children who are the subject of chronic postseparation disputes between their parents have now been identified as one of the most "at-risk" groups among the divorcing population. For this group, the major benefit of the divorce—the cessation of parental hostilities—does not accrue. Many of these children have been embroiled for years in parental conflicts that predate the separation and continue afterwards (Emery, 1988; Kline et al., 1991; Tschann et al., 1989). For others, the separation itself focused the disputes on them (Hetherington et al., 1982; Johnston, 1993b). The most serious threat, however, is one we will argue within this book—that these children bear an acutely heightened risk of repeating the cycle of conflicted and abusive relationships as they grow up and try to form families of their own.

DIVORCE IMPASSE

Our thesis is that the outcome of a marital separation has much to do with the manner in which it is undertaken. A successful divorce largely depends on how well the stormy waters of the divorce transition have been navigated by the entire family and what help or hindrance the family got during their perilous crossing. In the remainder of this chapter we briefly review the anatomy of high-conflict divorces and entrenched postdivorce disputes over children to show how family members, friends, mental health and legal professionals, and family courts may inadvertently contribute to the creation of pitfalls that trap family members in a divorce impasse, where they can neither remain married nor psychologically disengage from each other.

This chapter is a brief overview of the previous book about the dynamics of high-conflict families that is the foundation for the present work: *Impasses of Divorce*, by J. R. Johnston and L. E. G. Campbell (New York, Free Press, 1988). At the same time, this review sets the stage for suggestions as to how our communities and courts can provide better support, more humane institutions, more responsive legal procedures, and better skilled mental health and legal professionals for the children and families of divorce.

Divorce impasse refers to whatever factors are blocking the divorcing family from resolving expectable separation conflicts and making the transition from an intact to a postdivorce family structure. Typically a divorce-transition impasse is a complex phenomenon, with elements that hold the dispute in place occurring at three levels: the *internal* level of individual psychological dynamics, the *interactional* level of couple and family dynamics, and the *external* level of the dynamics of the wider social system. The important point is that family members can become stuck at any or all three levels simultaneously, and the elements of each level can coalesce, locking the dispute into a mutually reinforcing pattern of entanglement.

The External Components of the Impasse

TRIBAL WARFARE. The external level of the divorce impasse is often not recognized by the disputing parties and their helpers, but it is not difficult to understand, once recognized. The main point is that divorce disputes can quickly spread and encompass the social networks of the couple, resulting in a modern form of "tribal warfare" where significant others, including extended kin, new partners, mental health professionals, attorneys, and even judges, become a part of the tangle of disputing relations and serve to entrench the fight.

Mrs. J left her husband after a secret affair with another man, when her children were 3 and 4 years old, respectively. By mutual agreement she kept custody. For the next seven years, the children enjoyed summer vacations and brief visits with their father, who flew in from another state on a wave of gifts and excitement. When the mother and her new husband fell on hard times financially, they began a series of lawsuits demanding increased child support from the wealthy father. Now Mr. J. had been greatly humiliated by the separation, but the new financial demands on him were the last straw. He hired what he considered the best attorney (i.e., the most aggressive one) and filed for custody of the children, now ages 10 and 11 years. In a bitter, escalating court trial, the mother wrote, and encouraged the children to write, angry letters about the father to the judge. The judge, who had recently experienced his own divorce, became incensed and, buttressed by a psychologist's evaluation that the children were being alienated from their father, he ordered a precipitous change in custody. The mother's close-knit extended family, local community, church, and the children's school became enraged. Fund-raising efforts and letters to newspapers and local politicians all resulted in the formation of an unholy alliance: the community against the outsiders (that is, the father, judge, attorney, and psychologist). The children became local celebrities. Despite the father's efforts to woo them, they spent a miserable two years as martyrs, living with their father, who found himself doing battle both with the children and with the medley of voices raised in support of them. The mother felt saddened and guilty about what had happened. With great bitterness, the father was forced to relinquish custody and withdraw (Johnston & Campbell, 1988).

As illustrated in this unhappy situation, with the deterioration of the marriage, the norm of privacy that governs the sanctity of the family breaks down. Separating spouses then may turn to others in their extended family and community for practical advice and emotional support and encouragement. Hearing only the one negatively biased version of the divorce situation, these significant others become outraged and seek to right the wrong and help the "victim." They can form alliances with and fight on behalf of the aggrieved party and in so doing unwittingly confirm negative, polarized, and often distorted views of the other spouse. Members of these alliances tend to claim the moral high ground by attempting to protect the children from the now demonized ex-spouse. This sets the stage for long-term disputes over the children.

It is perhaps expectable that extended families will stand behind and support their own family members during a divorce. However, this support often comes with a price: obligations, interference, and counterdemands that provoke stress and fuel disputes. For example, when a young divorced mother becomes financially dependent upon her own parents, she may be unable to resist when they agitate for her return to court to demand a decrease in the father's visits. In those more unusual cases where grandparents turn against their own offspring in favor of a daughter- or son-in-law during the divorce dispute, the conflict is compounded by a painful sense of betrayal on one side and obligation on the other. In these situations, unresolved conflicts and latent resentments within the larger kinship network can be easily displaced onto or incorporated into the custody dispute. Likewise new partners can activate custody disputes. For example, shortly after a man's remarriage, the new stepmother may agitate to "save" the children from their "neglectful" mother. On closer scrutiny, however, the real problem may be the new wife's anxiety about securing her role in a marriage that she fears is being threatened by the man's ties to his first family; hence the first wife is scapegoated.

A particular subgroup of external-level disputes are those conducted in the name of cultural and religious differences between parents as to how their children should be raised. Although these value differences may be hotly disputed and appear unresolvable, rarely are they the basic issues driving the conflict. Most couples of mixed racial-ethnic background who have given birth to children have already come to some kind of resolution or acceptance of their differences and need to be reminded of that understanding. The problem is that this acceptance of each other's differences is often recanted upon separation and divorce because of other factors that drive the conflict. For example, a divorcing man or woman may have an internal need, or experience pressure from extended kin, to return to his or her racial-ethnic or religious origins. In other cases, a parent may react to the pain of feeling discarded as a spouse by insisting on his or her religious values or cultural identity being given preeminent status in the child's upbringing. Alternatively, having lost a sense of their identity in being cast adrift from the marriage, parents may embrace a new faith or lifestyle for the first time, become an evangelist for the cause, and insist that their child become part of it.

In identifying external elements of the impasse, it is important to discover who appears to have instigated the custody dispute, what triggered its onset, and which coalitions are in support of each opposing party. In particular, it is important to distinguish potentially bogus custody disputes (those driven by external forces) from bonafide ones (those having to do with genuine concerns about the child). Furthermore, legal and mental health counselors need to focus their clients' concerns and energies on the crux of the problem; otherwise, an initially bogus custody dispute may evolve into a bonafide one. In the above examples, this may involve talking to the young mother about her feelings of obligation to her own parents or to the man about his new wife's anxiety over securing her role. Where religious and cultural differences are a cloak for other conflicts, these underlying dynamics need to be dealt with in counseling for parents to value their child's opportunity to experience multiple perspectives and to help their child become proud of his or her mixed racial identity.

THE ROLE OF ATTORNEYS. The traditional adversarial court system has long been criticized for the polarization of the parties' positions and the escalation of family conflict. The institutionalized polemics between attorneys, the established procedures for fact finding and assembling of evidence, and the costly, cumbersome, and often lengthy procedures involved in custody litigation appear to fashion the ideal social environment for escalating divisiveness and blaming between parents. Attorneys in particular have long been implicated for contributing to rather than resolving disputes, because of their advocacy role within an adversarial judicial system. Advising their clients not to talk to the other spouse, making extreme demands to increase the bargaining advantage, and filing motions that characterize the other parent in a negative light are all typical examples. Needing to show evidence of neglect, abuse, physical violence, or emotional or mental incompetence to win their client's case, attorneys compose documents that are a public record of charges and countercharges, citing the unhappy incidents and separation-engendered desperate behaviors of the emotionally vulnerable parties, often out of context. The consequent public shame, guilt, and fury at being so *mis*represented motivates the other party's compelling need to set the record straight in costly litigation.

The zeal with which some lawyers pursue a case at times has little to do with the client's needs or even the merits of the case. Ambitious attorneys, wishing to make a name for themselves in the legal community, may take advantage of an angry client's wish to punish and seize on a case because it provides a means to challenge the constitutionality of a new law or the legality of a procedure. Others may pursue litigation because of long-standing rivalries with the opposing counsel, or because they are misdirecting personal anger associated with their own divorce. In fact, attorneys are traditionally defined as both *counselors* and *advocates*, although the former function is often neglected in favor of the latter. When the required counseling goes beyond legal expertise, a referral to mental health professionals can protect both the clients and the attorneys from becoming entrenched in debilitating conflict and litigation.

THE ROLE OF MENTAL HEALTH PROFESSIONALS. The role of mental health professionals in fueling conflict has been less clearly acknowledged. Some therapists, who see only one of the parties to the divorce conflict, encourage uncompromising stands, reify distorted views of the other parent, write recommendations, and even testify on behalf of their adult client with little or no understanding of the child's needs, the other parent's position, or the couple and family dynamics. Unfortunately, some courts are willing to give credence to this kind of "expert testimony." In some high-profile cases, the parents' mental health therapists squabble among themselves, playing out the parental dispute in a community or court arena.

Among the most negative influences of mental health professionals are their written evaluations of the parents during the upheaval of the separation, which explain the situation solely in terms of the individual psychopathology of the separating spouses. Psychodiagnostic terms, such as *paranoid, alcoholic, narcissistic, sociopathic, violent,* or *battered woman's syndrome,* reduce the explanation of complex marital dynamics to the emotional (or so-called moral) capacities of the individual parents, clearly placing all blame and responsibility on one or the other. These psychodiagnostic terms have special technical meaning within the mental health professions. When used in public or in court, they can become pejorative labels strategically employed to degrade or destroy the reputation of one parent and to "win" custody for the other. If shared with the divorcing parties or their legal counsel, these authoritative declarations as to the character of the divorcing spouses solidify negative, polarized views, which then become as though "written in stone," ensuring that the dispute will continue. An alternative, conflict-reducing approach would be for mental health professionals' testimonies and custody evaluations to pay more attention to prescribing how the family can resolve their impasse and how the children's development can be protected, rather than assessing who is and who is not emotionally disturbed, and who is and who is not the better parent (Roseby, 1995).

In perhaps no other area of practice are legal and mental health professionals so much at risk for losing their professional objectivity, and becoming entangled with their clients, as in these high-conflict family situations. Some try to rescue the client in ways that are not possible or take on the fight as their own personal crusade. It is common for counselors and advocates to become ambivalent, covertly hostile, and personally involved in dealing with and representing their clients. These powerful and compelling responses to the pain and suffering of divorcing individuals (called countertransference reactions) are important signals to the professional involved to regain his or her balance and perspective in the case. This might involve taking a step back to review the basis for these reactions or seeking out another professional for consultation.

When the parental conflict has expanded and incorporated outside parties, especially other professionals, the intervention of choice is to call a strategy conference with all players of the disputing network, preferably before their respective positions have hardened. Sometimes the court is the only agent with the authority to bring the parties to the negotiating table via a status conference. This meeting can be used to design a strategy for case management or resolution and is often the first order of business in a custody dispute that appears out of control.

THE ROLE OF THE COURT. The court itself can trap a family in a divorce time warp, not so much because of unwise decisions but rather because of the manner in which it renders its decisions. In practice, the modern day family court views itself more simply as a forum for dispute resolution with a paucity of laws to guide it (Mnookin, 1985; Mnookin & Kornhauser, 1979). Its authority and judgment, however, can have powerful symbolic meaning for clients who are emotionally distressed and dependent on others for their self-esteem. Not only is the court considered by many as a forum where the private marital fight is exposed to humiliating public scrutiny, but it is potentially invested by its clients with a quasi-divine moral authority.

From the client's perspective, the judge's decrees become dramatizations of who is right and who is wrong. For example, the court may intervene to stabilize a child's living situation immediately after the separation, granting temporary custody to the father until the mother is better able to handle her own affairs. This is interpreted by the parents as a ruling that the mother is "unfit." Or a substantial financial settlement awarded to a wife may be seen by her as retribution for the wrongs perpetrated by her "unfaithful husband." It is especially important, if legal counsel or the judge suspects the parents are in court with a psychological agenda of obtaining a moral judgment, that court orders be clear and precise as to the basis for the decision. If they are unclear, they may constitute a permanent public record of inordinate shame and condemnation for some people. For example, the tragic suicide of a father in one of our studies could have been prevented if the court had taken the trouble to tell him that its decision to give him once-a-month visitation with his daughter, when he was asking for joint custody, was not based on his capacity to be a loving father to his little girl but on the needs of a very vulnerable toddler to have protection from horrendous on-going disputes that neither he nor his wife could control. This socially iso-lated, emotionally troubled man, whose entire identity hinged upon his fatherhood, clearly interpreted the court's judgment as a devastating indict-ment of his worth as a parent and a human being. Courts need to exercise special care when issuing dwelling exclusion orders or emergency ex parte orders of any kind, for these have the potential to elicit inordinate shame, helplessness, and a sense of injustice, which can result in child abductions or even homicidal revenge in vulnerable people (Greif & Hegar, 1993; John-ston, 1994b; Sagatun & Barrett, 1990).

Interactional Components of the Impasse

IDEALIZED IMAGES AND SHATTERED DREAMS. At the interactional level of the impasse, disputes are broadly of two kinds: the legacy of a destructive mar-ital relationship and the product of traumatic or ambivalent separations. In the first kind, which is well documented in the marital therapy literature, the divorce quarrels are a continuation of the marital feud, in which the spouses have deftly learned to provoke each other in a series of stereotypi-cal, mutually destructive transactions over their years together. Perhaps the second kind is more important; it relates to the manner in which the cou-ple came together (the courtship) and the manner in which they parted (the separation). Both these transitions, often dramatic occasions, have im-port for how the couple negotiate the divorce transition.

Couples who are extremely ambivalent about separation have long been recognized as among those who fail to settle their divorce. This subgroup of divorcing spouses basically hold onto idealized views of one another—romantic illusions—and are engaged in a never-ending search for ways of holding together their shattered dreams. It is hypothesized that their ideal-ization of each other is connected to their courtship. Many first met at a highly significant time in their lives—for example, as teenagers escaping from unhappy, inattentive families; when critically ill or greatly in need of help; or when in places of danger, such as war zones. For others, this first relationship was experienced as an "earth-shattering," highly erotic love experience. Individuals or couples with these kinds of courtship histo-ries tend to feel they have a special mission to accomplish with each other, and that a part of their very identity has been discovered and nurtured in collaboration with each other. In leaving the marriage, they are leaving behind significant parts of themselves, forsaking images and dreams for which they continually yearn. These couples can live neither together nor apart, so their relationship is contorted by repeated separations and unfulfilling reunions, by alternating periods of intimacy and outrage.

Ms. S was driving a car with a boyfriend of whom she wished to rid herself, when she had a terrible accident. They were both critically injured and she felt guilty and responsible. During the weeks when she was semiconscious and he hung between life and death, in her guilt she promised herself and God that if they survived, she would devote her life to this man. They married, and eight years later, though he had periodically abandoned her and had transmitted a venereal disease to her, she continued to cling to the marriage.

There are special therapeutic strategies for working with couples in this kind of divorce impasse, which involve giving them insight into the meaning of their courtship, confronting them gently with the realities of their present situation, and helping them mourn the loss of their illusions. It is especially important for them to identify within themselves qualities that they thought were in the relationship or within the other, so they feel they can leave as a "whole person." Couples who have ambivalent separations can have long-standing problems with shared parenting after divorce because their need to work together on behalf of their children often triggers their smoldering passions and their reengagement. These parents need special help to establish a businesslike, rule-governed coparenting relationship in which they take care not to seduce each other; for example, they are encouraged to meet and discuss their children in a neutral public place—not over a candlelit dinner! Custody and visitation arrangements that bring the parents into frequent, intimate contact should be avoided.

TRAUMATIC SEPARATIONS AND NEGATIVE IMAGES. There are kind and humane ways to end a relationship. There are also particularly brutal and traumatic ways to part. In our society a not unusual way of leaving gently is to enter into marriage therapy with one's partner, with the ostensible purpose of trying to fix the marriage but with the unconscious knowledge that one has reached the point of no return and only wants out. After several interviews with the family therapist, the partner who wants out declares that there is no hope for the marriage and then quietly withdraws, leaving the spouse in the care of a supportive therapist.

Contrast this to other ways of separating that are particularly unexpected and traumatic: a sudden desertion, the humiliating discovery of a lover, uncharacteristic violence, secret plotting and planning. One man took his wife to dinner for their twentieth wedding anniversary and gave her his gift: a petition for a divorce. A man returning from overseas military service at Christmas was greeted by a tape recorded message from his wife saying she'd fallen in love with another man. A grieving woman returned from her father's funeral to find that her husband had stripped the house of all their possessions and left with the children. An older man walked out for a pack of cigarettes and never came back. A young woman missed the last bus home from work and decided then and there she could never return. While recovering from emergency surgery for breast cancer, a woman was informed by her husband that he wanted a divorce.

Those who flee the marriage with no discussion or explanation often provoke desperate reactions in their mates (hysterical outbursts, physical struggles, child and possession snatching, suicidal or homicidal threats), which in turn may provoke outrageous counterreactions by the partner left behind.

In the ordinary course of events among divorces of all kinds, couples, at the time of separation, begin to do a great deal of soul searching and redefinition of themselves and their hopes and goals. They also make fairly fundamental redefinitions of their spouses. In cases of traumatic separation, there is an enormous betrayal of trust. This violation of the very cornerstone of the marriage, together with the desperate reactions and counterreactions, forms the basis for the redefinitions the spouses make of each other. The history of the marriage and the identity of the ex-spouse are negatively revised, often with the help of loyal family and friends. There is a sense of discovery as to who the ex-spouse *really* is and has been all along—that she or he is in fact "dangerous, crazy, bad, fundamentally untrustworthy." Without corrective feedback, these new "understandings" set in motion long-term disputes over the children, as each parent now feels compelled to fight consciously and self-righteously to protect the children from the "bad, immoral, or neglectful influence" of the other. Months or years later, each ex-spouse may well have regained individual psychological balance, but the negatively reconstructed image of the other remains fixed, still provoking defensive avoidance of each other and periodic quarrels over the children.

This process is well illustrated by Mrs. M, who explained that she had a dream in which she had to get not one divorce but two: one from her husband and one from a man she did not know. She went on to explain that her marriage had been romantic but she and her husband had recently been stressed by financial worries. When her husband obtained a job across the country, they agreed she would follow him. A month later she opened a letter, expecting it to contain her airplane tickets. Instead, she found a petition for divorce. Her shock was compounded when she later discovered that he had taken along a friend of hers to live with him. Not surprisingly, she felt she was divorcing a man she did not know. Perhaps more important, she also felt she was entrusting her children to a stranger. She now characterizes this man as "an unconscionable s.o.b." from whom her children required protection.

Traumatic separations can precipitate impasses and long-term disputes if mishandled by professionals. Attorneys need to beware of taking legal advantage of the sometimes desperately distressed couple by filing claims implying that an acutely traumatized party is chronically violent, dangerous, and mentally unstable. It is especially important for mental health professionals to recognize and intervene in traumatic separations early on, before the desperate acting-out escalates and during the "meaning-making" stage, when each party is trying to put together a story of why the divorce occurred. This is the optimal time to help both construct a more positive account that will help them regain self-esteem, a sense of efficacy and control, and a measured view of each other. Their account, or story, of the divorce should also allow them to coparent their children.

If the traumatic separation is long past but still clouded by defensive reconstruction and years of confirming hostile exchanges with each other, a different set of interventions is needed. Briefly, this requires attorneys and mental health professionals to collaborate on an explicit behavioral contract or parenting plan between the disputing parties that will be monitored

closely over time to gradually reestablish trust and a working coparental relationship—a process that typically takes from one to two years of engineering.

Internal Components of the Impasse

Although the psychological state of the divorcing individuals is acknowledged as important, it is often the least-well-understood element of the divorce impasse. Consequently, it is often mismanaged by helping professionals. At first glance, the behavior of most distraught divorcing couples
evokes the diagnosis of personality disorders. Indeed, psychological assessments of those who are the most entrenched in custody disputes confirm
characterological difficulties: compared with the norm, these individuals
lack a firm approach to problem solving, are more likely to perceive inac-
curately, reason idiosyncratically, and cognitively simplify their world.
Moreover, they are hypersensitive to criticism and inordinately concerned
about their own needs and perspectives (Ehrenberg et al., 1996; Hoppe &
Kenney, 1994; Walters et al., 1995). Further observation, however, usually
identifies a high degree of external stress that is associated with the divorce
and the custody dispute. Moreover, the individual's compromised functioning is often limited to difficulties in specific intimate relationships and
does not necessarily disrupt other aspects of work and social life. There is
some emerging evidence that those with histories of early loss and trauma,
in combination with unhappy marriages and stressful separations, are more
likely to have difficulty with divorce- and custody-related matters (Johnston, 1994b; McClenney et al., 1994). Accordingly, a more adequate and
useful orientation begins with the premise that high-conflict divorcing parents are, to varying degrees and in special ways, psychologically vulnerable,
and that a particular kind of stress or divorce crisis interacts with these vulnerabilities to provoke regression and to produce more rigid defensive
styles that look like or exacerbate personality disorders.

DIVORCE AS LOSS. Divorce is a voluntary leave-taking and as such is usually
experienced as both loss and rejection. One of the parties (rarely both at
the same time) wants out of the marriage. Loss—whether of a loved one,
the marriage, the intact family, cherished hopes and dreams, or the threatened loss of one's children—evokes powerful feelings of anxiety, sadness,
and fear of being abandoned and alone. Rejection, on the other hand,
evokes feelings of inadequacy, failure, shame, and humiliation. While these

responses are expectable, divorcing individuals differ in their capacity to manage and integrate these separation-engendered feelings.

With respect to loss, some people have difficulty acknowledging their feelings of sadness and mourning the end of the marriage. Instead, they seal over their grief with anger and try to prevent the inevitable separation by embroiling their spouse in unending disputes. Fighting and arguing are ways of maintaining contact (albeit of a negative kind), and even throughout all the fighting, these same individuals harbor reconciliation fantasies. For example, one woman disclosed that she had really wanted her husband to take her in his arms when she smashed dinnerware in the restaurant where they met to discuss their divorce settlement. Another man broke into his wife's home, violating a restraining order so he could leave her flowers.

In general, there are two main reasons for attempting to ward off loss by holding on to anger. First, many divorcing individuals have suffered a specific traumatic loss in their past (the death of a parent or sibling; the previous loss of a child by adoption, abortion, or death; the loss of the extended family through migration or political asylum). The divorce is likely to reactivate these earlier unresolved traumas, making the person fearful of letting go, in special ways.

Mrs. S lost her first baby through a sudden, inexplicable crib death. She now wanted to be in total control of her new child's physical environment. Any slight fever or illness in the child activated overwhelming concern for the child's survival, and she would cancel the father's visits, leaving him furious. To resolve this impasse, during counseling it was important to show Mrs. S that she was trying to "prevent the unpreventable," the potential loss of this child, because she was still trying to undo the unbearable loss of her previous daughter.

Second, other individuals may have had early childhoods that were ungratifying, unsupported, or neglectful (such as being children of alcoholic or mentally ill parents). Their trauma was so early, so pervasive, and so lacking in basic emotional resources that they failed to build any stable or autonomous sense of self. In marriage, they merged with their partners. With the divorce, these people do not experience sadness over the loss of a distinct other, as do those with a reactivated trauma; rather, they experience panic or intense feelings of being abandoned, cut off without hope of ever being reconnected to another. They may feel insignificant, overwhelmingly helpless, and unable to survive on their own. Here is a case in point.

"My husband left and Peter is all I have left, and now he's trying to take him too!" Mrs. R cried. Claiming that she was "slowly dying inside, a plant without roots and water," Mrs. R depended on 8-year-old Peter for survival. She became depressed and extremely panicky when he was not in the house and often asked him to sleep with her, much to his embarrassment. She could not permit him to spend more than one night away from her, so that visits to his father were constrained by her neediness.

In general, such persons respond to their anxiety about separation and their terror of abandonment in three ways. First, some remain diffusely dependent and actively cling to the spouse or their child as a substitute for the spouse. To feel less helpless and more independent, these men and women are likely to need a great deal of support from friends, family, and counselors, including encouragement to reach out to others at work and at church, and perhaps to begin dating again. Second, others defend against the threat of abandonment by adopting a pseudoautonomous stance, aggressively protecting themselves and their children, refusing to capitulate to anything lest they lose part of themselves. These individuals can become negativistic and oppositional, and insist on making unilateral decisions. Basically, friends and professionals need to applaud their efforts to be independent and stand on their own, while showing them that real power and control come from knowing when and how to say "yes" as well as "no." Third, perhaps the most confusing and difficult of all, are those who alternately cling and distance themselves in abrupt contradictory shifts:

Mrs. O demanded that her ex-spouse pick up their child from school. The following week, when he complied, she alleged that he had kidnapped the child from school. Mr. P, in turn, demanded visitation with his child in court but then failed to comply with the court order that allowed visits.

These people appear to use the interparental struggle over their children in part to create an existential sense of purpose and meaning out of the void that threatens to engulf them when separated from their family. In other words, they seem to be attempting to stave off psychological fragmentation with the maxim "I fight, therefore I am." This third subgroup usually need therapeutic management and the stabilizing influence of an extended family or social network to protect the child from the chaos that is generated.

DIVORCE AS HUMILIATION. The central internal struggle inherent in high-conflict divorces and entrenched custody disputes involves a high degree of humiliation and shame engendered by the divorce and the capacity of the individual to manage those feelings without losing face or an integrated, viable sense of self. This is referred to as *narcissistic vulnerability*. Vulnerability to shame can range from mild to moderate to severe, with corresponding distinctive clinical profiles. When there is a mild degree of shame, people often seek the support of friends, family, and professionals to assuage the feelings of inadequacy and rejection inherent in a marital separation. Often they seek to have acknowledged a specific, vulnerable aspect of themselves. For example, after a miserable, lonely marriage with a poor sexual relationship, a man may seek to have his physical attractiveness and sexual prowess acknowledged through a series of brief affairs. In the same way, a woman who has felt particularly criticized about her mothering capacity may wage a custody dispute and seek the support of the judge to have herself acknowledged as the "good" or "better" parent, who does not deserve her spouse's criticism.

Other people, with more wounded self-esteem, seek to rid themselves of any vestige of blame by actively proving that the other spouse is totally "inadequate," "irresponsible," or "bad for the child." This kind of vulnerability to shame is evident when people who divorce make exaggerated claims about their own capabilities and thoroughly denigrate the ex-spouse. These more vulnerable individuals have difficulty maintaining a positive, cohesive, and realistic self-identity. It is not simply an aspect of themselves they need to have acknowledged; rather, they seek total validation. In such cases, the divorce triggers an exaggerated sense of failure, which in turn provokes intolerable feelings of great anxiety and confusion. Their fragile sense of self-esteem depends on keeping all sense of failure outside the self, in the other or in the situation. So in an effort to defend themselves and protect against intense shame, they present themselves with a self-righteous air of angry superiority and entitlement (Lewis, 1992).

They view themselves as the "good, morally superior one," "the responsible and nurturant parent," in stark contrast to the ex-spouse, who is viewed as "irresponsible, unavailable, and psychologically and morally inferior."

Unfortunately, these individuals enter into mediation or the court with such an attitude of entitlement, such a refusal to own any responsibility for the problem, and with the apparent single-minded purpose of demeaning the other spouse that they tend to make quite unreasonable demands on their attorneys. They also annoy or anger the mediator or judge, who in turn may dismiss their claims or confront them in a way that furthers their humiliation and their need to project blame defensively.

Mr. A's wife quit their marriage (and returned to live with her own family) while he was recuperating from a back injury that left him unemployed, on disability, and unsure of his future. With great bravado, Mr. A took a very condescending, critical attitude toward his wife. He went to court repeatedly to prove that she was "incompetent, unable to care for the child or to live independently." Hence he projected his own sense of weakness onto his wife. He was further humiliated, however, when the judge publicly drew attention to his own inadequacy and called him a "vexatious litigant." Years later, this man is still obsessed with anger and bitterness at his ex-wife and at the legal system for his public shaming.

In cases of more extreme vulnerability, a divorcing man or woman may experience the spouse's desertion as a total, devastating attack. In defense, the abandoned partner may develop paranoid ideas of betrayal, exploitation, and conspiracy. As these spouses survey the rubble of their marriage, they begin to rewrite history and perceive their partner as having intentionally plotted and planned, from the outset, to exploit and cast them off:

Mr. J explained, when his wife left him for another man, "I was once naive and trusting but now my eyes are opened. Her loving femininity was all a sham. She's absolutely evil and untrustworthy. When I first met her, she played a sweet, innocent, feminine, dependent child, but when no one was looking she turned diabolical. It was all an act. She had this planned all along. She took my money, my house, my son, and left me nothing! She has everyone fooled, even the judge." Mr. J was currently accusing his wife of child abuse.

Feeling betrayed and weakened by the perceived assault, paranoid spouses respond aggressively with a counterattack that often becomes the central obsession in their lives. The other spouse, along with any allies, is viewed as dangerous, aggressive, and persecutory. Having been wronged, these people feel justified in seeking retaliation, or, more urgently, they believe in launching a preemptive strike—"attack before being attacked."

If humiliation is the predominant motivation for the custody dispute, tremendous care needs to be taken by friends, family, and all professionals involved with the case to assuage the deep feeling of shame and to help the person save face and regain a viable sense of self. It is also essential not to challenge or wound that vulnerable person any further, especially in such a public arena as the court. In cases of mild vulnerability to humiliation, one can clarify and offer insight to the client ("You were angry when you were made to feel like a fool!"), whereas in more severe cases of vulnerability, this same statement will be perceived as another intolerable attack. The client's degree of vulnerability also determines when and how to support his or her perceptions. In instances of mild vulnerability to shame, one needs to acknowledge and support the client's strengths ("You are a good father"). In cases of greater vulnerability to humiliation, one runs the risk that support will be construed as total validation of the client's distorted views ("You agree that I am a good father and my wife is a bad mother"). In extreme cases of vulnerability, support, to a man or woman with paranoid preoccupations, may be viewed suspiciously as a seductive trap ("You're saying that I am a good father just to get me to agree to X"). Careful assessment of the vulnerability to shame and the extent of narcissistic injury also indicates when one needs to restrain spouses (through legal orders and police action) to protect the targets of their paranoid ideas against potentially dangerous consequences.

It is often puzzling that many people going through divorce function relatively free from serious psychological disturbance in other areas of their life. In their jobs or with friends and associates, they appear to cope adequately, think rationally, and behave in a civil manner. In the realm of their relationship with their ex-spouse, however, and especially during significant events (court dates, anniversaries, holidays), these same people can look, think, and act in a manner that is quite emotionally and behaviorally disturbed, even psychotic. To this extent, the psychological disturbance is not clearly indicative of ongoing pathology; rather, it is situational and re-lational. Under such conditions, it is probable that the elements of these intrapsychic conflicts surface to varying degrees and need to be recognized and managed.

Impasse Dynamics and Intervention Strategy

The utility of an in-depth understanding of the multilevels and interlocking elements of the divorce-transition impasse is that it not only shows how to avoid compounding the problem but it also guides a strategic, focused, and minimally intrusive intervention into the family. Most difficult divorces have multiple elements of impasse that interlock, as illustrated by the following example.

As is typical for violence-prone men, Mr. R had serious self-esteem problems, so that he felt the rejection inherent in his marital separation as deeply humiliating. When his wife secretly planned her escape and abandoned the marriage without warning, this vulnerable man was acutely traumatized, mentally "rewrote" their marital history to reflect his sense of betrayal, and became paranoid. Meanwhile, with the support of family and attorney, his wife took action against him in court, where he was further humiliated by accusations of battering, and a court order that evicted him from his home and severely limited his contact with his children. Then he became acutely dangerous. The 4-year-old daughter became anxious about separating from her mother, was phobic about her father, and refused to visit at all. The distressed 12-year-old son fought with his mother and made an alliance with his "unjustly treated" father.

It is apparent in a case like this that the dysfunctional family relationships that are a product of these interlocking elements of the impasse can result in parent alienation as well as emotional and behavioral symptomatology in children. Identifying the multiple levels and multiple elements of the impasse in a case such as this allows one to assess which interventions are likely to be feasible and strategic ones. For example, the psychological vulnerability of the man is often the least amenable element to change. But given the systemic nature of the divorce impasse, well-focused interventions at one level can have ramifying effects elsewhere.

Protection of the wife and children in this case was, of course, the first priority. This involved providing her with emergency shelter and legal help (i.e., restraining orders and financial relief). Furthermore, in intervening, the court did not minimize, deny, or excuse the man's behavior; rather, it emphasized that domestic violence is a criminal act. However, it was also important to provide the man with a humane forum for dealing with his pain and to frame the court's intervention as a compassionate as well as a just one. This was demonstrated by the judge in his declaration from the bench:

"Mr. R, what you have done to your wife is a criminal act under the laws of this state, regardless of what you say she did or said to provoke you, and there are consequences that the Court is bound to impose. What you did to your wife is also psychologically very harmful to your children, whether they actually witnessed the event or not. Living in a violent home is bad for children. Mr. R, I hear you when you say you love your wife and children, that you are sorry for what you did, and that you have promised not to do that again. The Court is going to help you keep that promise to yourself and your family by doing three things: first, by providing your family with protection until it can be sure that you are no longer a danger, and you can show that you are no longer a danger; second, by providing you an opportunity to manage your anger better and to solve conflict in a nonviolent way; and third, by providing you and your children a safe place to visit together, where they will not be afraid, and you will be given an opportunity to show that you have a loving relationship with your son and daughter."

This way of framing the court intervention set the stage for the long-term intervention this man and his family desperately needed.

In sum, when the community is less confrontational and more supportive, and takes care not to unhinge a parent's vulnerable defenses, that parent will feel less humiliated, less afraid of loss, and more able to let go of the fight and the marriage. With careful intervention, a badly injured parent then has less need to seek revenge or to cling to the child or children for protection and refuge.

Underneath all the anger and bitterness of high-conflict divorce lie disillusionment and shame; deeper still lie sadness and loss. What are needed are more compassionate understanding, better therapeutic skills, and more humane institutional policies and legal procedures to provide divorcing couples and their children with access to their deeply buried feelings or, at the very least, prevent further infliction of emotional wounds that will not heal. The divorcing process within an adversarial legal system too often becomes a ceremony of degradation and shame. The challenge is to provide alternative forums—responsive to the diversity of families in our communities—that can promote mutual respect and help parents make a solemn redefinition of their rights and a serious commitment to their responsibilities within the postdivorce family. Within these forums, it then becomes possible to go beyond the legal rights of the adults involved to give a voice to the needs of those who have none—the children.

Chapter 2

Domestic Violence and Parent-Child
Relationships in Families Disputing Custody

$\mathcal{T}$he purpose of this chapter is to help parents and mental health and legal professionals understand that domestic violence includes a range of patterns. Within each type, the balance of power between the spouses, the sources of the violence, the frequency and extent of abuse, and the parent-child relationships that result are different. This understanding can lead to more informed decision making about the care and custody of children who live in families where domestic violence has occurred. Domestic violence is defined here as the use of physical restraint, force, or threats of force by one parent to compel the other parent to do something against his or her will. It includes assault (pushing, slapping, choking, hitting, biting, etc.), use of or threat to use a weapon, sexual assault, unlawful entry, destruction of property, infliction of physical injury, suicide, and murder. It also includes psychological intimidation and control, which may be maintained through such means as stalking, threats to hurt children or others, violence against pets, or destruction of property. Although emotional abuse (the range of psychologically damaging acts inflicted within relationships) is often more pervasive and possibly more psychologically damaging than physical abuse, it is not included in this definition. This analysis is limited to situations of physical violence, as defined, with the awareness that emotional abuse usually precedes, accompanies, and follows the cessation of physically violent incidents.

During the past several decades, an ongoing debate about which conditions precipitate or compound domestic violence has raged alongside the increasing social awareness of the magnitude of the problem. Psychodynamic theorists have speculated about psychological motivations within the abuser to act violently and have noted pathological needs within the victim to accept the abuse. Early theorists, for instance, argued about whether women are "normally" masochistic and therefore inclined to remain in abusive relationships (Deutsch, 1945; Horney, 1967). More recent psychodynamic and object-relations theories tend to interpret violence and victimization as evidence of personality disorders, especially borderline and sociopathic conditions, which have largely developed as a consequence of abusive childhood experiences (Gilman, 1980; McCord, 1988).

Social cognitive researchers attribute aggressive behavior to perceptual distortions and attributional biases (Dodge et al., 1990). Biological studies identify brain dysfunctions, hormonal irregularities or excesses, and the chemical effects of drugs and alcohol to explain violence (Bushman & Cooper, 1990; Lewis et al., 1989; Silver & Yudofsky, 1987). Family theorists view the problem from a systemic perspective and see violence as the product of the interaction between the spouses and children—in essence, a family affair (Dell, 1989; Giles-Sims, 1983). They suggest that there is a kind of circular causality in which violence can be provoked by the victim, and that mutual abuse occurs.

Most feminists advocates view domestic violence, and the failure of social institutions to respond to it, as an extension of the economic and political power disparity between men and women in the larger society. They advance socioeconomic explanations that stress the manner in which men are socialized to wield power and women to submit (Dobash & Dobash, 1979; Grillo, 1991; Lerman, 1984; Martin, 1987). Women's advocates object to explanations that interpret the victim's behavior as evidence of prior pathology rather than as the result of being abused (Walker, 1984). They also argue that focusing on the psychological motivations of the perpetrator allows men to rationalize and excuse their violence. Furthermore, feminists state that the idea of "mutual battering" implied by family therapists amounts to "blaming the victim," or at least creates prejudice against her because of her attempts to defend herself or to control an abusive situation (Berk et al., 1983).

The debate about the causes of family violence continues among psycho-dynamic, biological, family systems, sociopolitical, and social-psychological theorists, as though their theories represent competing and incompatible in-terpretations. By contrast, our clinical observations of high-conflict families during separation and after divorce have led us to view domestic violence not as a unitary syndrome with a single underlying cause but rather as a set of behaviors arising from multiple sources, which may follow different pat-terns in different families. Specifically, although we recognize the classic bat-terer/victim relationship identified by Walker (1984), we were motivated to examine this problem because we have also encountered a range of domes-tic violence situations that do not fit this profile.

There are, of course, multiple ways to categorize the phenomenon of family violence. From our viewpoint, the origin of or propensity for vio-lence can have one or more of three primary sources: within the person who initiates a violent act (the intrapsychic level), within the set of expec-tations and often unspoken rules that govern the relationship between per-sons (the interactional level), or within unusually potent stressors of the situation (the external level).

At the intrapsychic level, violence can function to relieve intolerable in-ternal tension, stress, or conflict. These unbearable states may be induced by drug and alcohol abuse, paranoid or psychotic ideation, or the vulnera-bilities of individuals with certain kinds of personality or impulse-control disorders (especially borderline, narcissistic, and sociopathic disorders). Both men and women are likely to experience internal states of distress of this magnitude.

At the interactional level, violence is a way to obtain or regain interper-sonal control in the event of a conflict of interest between family members. Many men are socialized to believe they have the legitimate authority, if not the duty, to exercise physical control over women (and many women concur with this belief). This is true in a number of societies, including our own, although there are cultural, religious, ethnic, and class differences with respect to this matter.

At the external level, violence can be evoked by a perception of danger from outside. Here, violence is a situationally specific response to a per-ceived threat to the integrity and survival of oneself, one's children, or other loved ones. In this respect, an aggressive or violent response is ac-knowledged as a basic human potential in anyone sufficiently provoked or threatened. It is possible that acutely stressful or traumatic events, including certain separation and divorce experiences, can precipitate aggression in both men and women who would not otherwise be violent.

Five basic types of interparental violence among divorcing families disputing custody can be identified according to the source of the violence, using this three-factor schema. (See Johnston and Campbell, 1993a and 1993b, for further details about theoretical possibilities and empirical findings.) The five types are (1) *ongoing/episodic male battering*, (2) *female-initiated violence*, (3) *male-controlling interactive violence*, (4) *separation-engendered or post-divorce trauma*, and (5) *psychotic and paranoid reactions*.

These five types of violence were identified in two qualitative studies of a total of 140 custody-disputing couples with 175 children, referred to different agencies from the San Francisco Bay Area Family Courts, who were diverse in socioeconomic and ethnic status (Johnston & Campbell, 1993a, b). In all cases, both disputing parents were interviewed separately to obtain details of violent incidents between them in the context of the history of their relationship and the custody dispute. Generally they described the first, worst, and last incident. They also completed the Conflict Tactics Scale (CTS) (Straus, 1979), which measures the frequency with which each spouse perpetrated specific acts of physical aggression. Reports on these measures indicated that three fourths of these separating/divorced couples had a history of physical aggression. On average, 26% had never been violent; 10% reported *low violence* (threw or smashed objects, and pushed, grabbed, or shoved the other spouse); 23% reported *moderate violence* (slapped, kicked, bit, or hit the other); and 41% admitted to *high violence* (beating up the other and threats of or actual use of a weapon).

The qualitative data describing the violent incidents within each couple's relationship were used to classify the primary instigator of physical aggression according to one of the major profiles in the typology described above. At least two clinicians made consensual judgments about the assignment of each family to a category. Each profile of violence was then completed by describing the typical precursor or buildup to the violent episode, the spouse who initiated the physical attack, the reaction of the victim(s), the severity and frequency of abuse, the amount of restraint exercised by the parties, and the extent to which the perpetrator accepted responsibility for his or her behavior. In addition, the balance of power between males and females was assessed, and the interactional styles of the spouses that either precipitated or resulted from the violence were described.

Before describing the different profiles of violence and parent-child relationships within each type, a caution: These studies were preliminary and exploratory; the results reported below are largely based on clinical inference, not on tests of statistical significance (Johnston & Campbell, 1993a, b). On the other hand, another researcher (Hanks, 1992), working with maritally violent couples, derived a very similar typology quite independently of the one we have developed, hence contributing to its validity.

PROFILE 1: ONGOING/EPISODIC MALE BATTERING

This category most closely resembles the battering spouse/battered wife syndrome, which has been well described in the literature (e.g., Walker, 1984). In these cases violence seems to originate from two sources—intolerable tension states within the man and his chauvinistic attitudes. These men are almost always the initiators of the attack, which had everything to do with their low tolerance for frustration, their problems with impulse control, and their angry, possessive, or jealous reactions to any perceived threat to their potency, masculinity, and "proprietary male rights." In our studies, drug and alcohol abuse by these men was a major precipitant and compounded the violence in about half the cases. The women who are victims of this type of chronic battering do not generally provoke, initiate, or escalate the physical abuse, at least not intentionally, and indeed they often do not know when the next attack might occur. Some women, however, are at times caught up in the fight and try to defend themselves.

The attacks in this category are the most frightening and severe, rising to dangerous, life-threatening levels. The batterer shows little or no restraint: he can beat or pummel the woman with a closed fist, throw her about, threaten with or use a weapon, while at the same time verbally demeaning and abusing her. His aim seems to be to inflict hurt and relieve tension as much as it is to control. These men are prone to blatantly deny or minimize violent incidents or project the blame onto the victim woman. For many, abuse begins in the courtship or during the wife's pregnancy and continues to be episodic or ongoing throughout the couple's marriage. Alternatively, the abusive man can so terrorize a woman with one acute incident early in the relationship that he maintains ongoing control of her through threat of its recurrence.

Being highly vulnerable to humiliation and often very dependent upon the women they abuse, these men generally increase the intensity of the violence at the threat of separation. If the separation is sudden or traumatic,

it is not uncommon for the man to stalk the woman, to alternately terrorize her with ominous threats and plead with her to return. In extreme
cases, there are threats or attempts at murder or suicide. While most of
these men, over time, are able to emotionally disengage, some remain obsessed with the woman who left them. In general, the potential for violence remains high long after the actual separation.

The psychological profiles of batterers indicate that these men tend to
be insecure, hypersensitive to others' opinions, and vulnerable to poor self-
esteem. Their bullying and aggressive posturings are attempts to compensate for feelings of emotional dependency and inadequacy. They have low
thresholds of stress tolerance and respond to everyday hassles with eruptions of anger and blame toward their wives and children, which quickly
turn into physical abuse. In addition, they tend to have traditional male
chauvinistic attitudes and an exaggerated concept of their own masculinity,
for which they need and demand acknowledgment and reassurance. Their
neediness quickly turns into uncontrollable jealousy and demands that can
result in marital rape.

In terms of the power dynamics in the couple, the women are intimidated and cowed both physically and psychologically by the men, who use
the threat of violence to control and dominate them. If the women have
remained in the abusive relationship for many years, they usually present as
fearful and chronically depressed, with low self-esteem. Uncertain about
themselves, they often seem hypersuggestible, submissive, and overly dependent upon their husbands and others, and tend to construe the situation
so as to blame themselves for their abuse. These women often deny or diminish the extent to which they are in mortal danger from their former
spouses and will not take measures to protect themselves, or their children,
without a great deal of support and help from others.

However, in our studies, not all the women from episodic or ongoing
battering relationships suffered from the "battered wife syndrome." A subgroup of women in this category of violence did not tolerate the abuse. Instead, they left the marital relationship early, soon after the abuse was first
manifest. These were assertive women with high self-esteem and good reality testing.

Mrs. A left the marital home precipitously after a friend gave her the encouragement to rouse herself from her depression and end her marriage to

a violent, jealous, controlling, and dependent husband. Pregnancy had precipitated this marriage between teenagers; afterward, the young woman worked as the principal financial provider for the family. Her husband contributed to their support by occasional drug dealing. Although Mr. A had liaisons with other women, he jealously guarded his wife's fidelity, even following her when she shopped or went to work. During counseling, Mrs. A recounted numerous instances when, after drinking, he bullied or beat her, destroyed furniture, and trashed the home, ostensibly because of her "failures" as a wife or mother. The police were called several times to disarm him and quell his violence. Mr. A vaguely dismissed the idea that he was abusive. In response to his wife's desertion, this man was distraught and alternated childlike pleas for her to return with bribes of expensive presents, promises that he would change, and ominous threats of murder and suicide if she did not comply with his wishes. His plan to take his wife hostage at her workplace was intercepted when he was arrested for carrying a gun.

Parent-Child Relationships

In families classified in the episodic or ongoing male battering category, younger daughters (under 7 or 8 years) are typically very passive and constricted children, with a high degree of underlying fearfulness and insecurity in relation to both parents. Younger girls especially feel unprotected by the mother; some have difficulty separating from the mother and react to separations with whiny, regressed behavior. They can have repressed or intrusive memories of violent incidents, which are the basis for their realistic fears and phobic avoidance of the father. At the same time, many of these fathers intermittently lavish attention on their daughters. At other times they remain preoccupied with their own needs. These unpredictable shifts in mood and availability can result in a great deal of confusion for the child. Many of these girls seem to have a double image of the father, viewing him both as a loving suitor and as a scary, dangerous man. In general, these men, especially substance abusers, have poor boundaries with their daughters, which involve reciprocal seductiveness and provocation of the father's aggression. These fathers need validation of their masculinity and attractiveness; they pull for this affirmation from their little daughters, who become watchful and oriented toward attempting to manage the father's equilibrium and anger.

Older girls (8 to 14 years) are more prone to angrily reject, avoid, or take a stand against the violent father and align with the mother. Some of them feel it is their job to take care of the mother by directly or indirectly managing the father. At the same time, older girls may become upset with the mother for tolerating the victim role and sometimes focus their irritation and anger upon her. Many of these mothers are too oppressed and depressed to be sufficiently emotionally available and supportive of their daughters.

Younger boys are typically difficult, oppositional, and aggressive; they are sometimes manipulative and controlling, especially with the mother. At the same time, they can become confused and anxious when fragmented memories of abusive incidents surface, and they worry about the mother's safety. Older, early-adolescent boys in this category typically explode in rageful attacks on the mother (reminiscent of those they witnessed in the father). The mothers, in response, are often passive and ineffectual, unable to control these growing boys. These women almost invariably end up becoming submissive to their aggressive sons, as they have been to their abusive husbands. The less conscious wish of these boys is for a close relationship with the mother, but they fear becoming like the mother—passive, weak, and victimized, all of which they equate with being feminine.

Both the younger and older boys are typically afraid of the father and constricted and obedient in his presence; at the same time, they are attracted to him because of his power. The violent father is often preoccupied with his own needs and inconsistently available to his son. These fathers tend to give contradictory messages about aggression to their sons. They may, for example, punish the boy's aggressiveness in an abusive manner, so that the father's verbal expectations belie the behavior he models. Boys who experience this treatment can long for the father's approval; they are fearful of being shamed by him and are covertly angry with him.

Children, both boys and girls, who have little or no contact with the violent father tend to repress their memories of violent incidents and to idealize him. They long for contact with him and blame themselves or the mother for his absence. Their behavior is often difficult and aggressive, which suggests a strong identification with the father, who, in these cases, is both the aggressor and the lost love object. In our studies, where a few violent fathers had major child care responsibilities, the father's low tolerance for stress, his need to assert power and control, and his hypersensitivity to slights resulted in episodic deterioration of the father-child relationship and the possibility of child abuse.

PROFILE 2: FEMALE-INITIATED VIOLENCE

In this category, the women *always* initiate the physical attack. This seems to result from their own intolerable internal states of tension and stress. Typically, these women become furiously angry, even hysterical, in response to the spouse's passivity or failure to provide for them in some way. They will nag, badger, and eventually throw objects at or pummel the husband in the hope of provoking some action that will result in having their expectations met and gratifying their needs. In the early stages of their relationship, the husband often tries to prevent or contain the fight, passively fending off the wife or holding her in check. These explosive temper outbursts by the woman are repetitive during the marriage and often become more intense at the time of separation and afterward. This is especially so if the woman feels she is not getting what is rightfully hers (with respect to a financial settlement, custody of the children, etc.). In some cases, the man loses control at some point and no longer seeks to placate or prevent the outbursts, especially during the separation period, and eventually responds in kind to the woman's attacks. The fallout from these physical exchanges is not minor; the majority escalate to high levels of severe violence.

In these types of relationships, however, the power dynamics remain more balanced. On the one hand, the women are active, demanding, and emotionally intimidating to their husbands; on the other hand, when really provoked, the men can exert greater physical control. The wives in these cases are assertive, willful women who neither look nor describe themselves as fearful. We found that substance abuse by the women compounded the problem in a significant minority of cases. Few of these women do much physical damage with their violence: broken cups, torn clothing, scratched faces are common. However, in some cases the woman can use a weapon such as ramming her car into her spouse's car or threatening him with a knife or a gun. Interestingly, these women generally admit their violent acts but blame the frustrating behavior of their partners.

The men are characteristically passive-aggressive, sometimes depressed, often obsessive and intellectualizing. They are sometimes too inhibited to act or communicate clearly with their wives. Indeed, many of these men are frightened of their wife's violence and extremely distressed and ashamed about being pulled into the fight and provoked into aggression. Some men who find it difficult to be directly angry themselves seem to gain considerable vicarious gratification from the partner's anger.

Mrs. B was an emotionally volatile, dependent woman married to a staid, intellectualizing professor. Initially, Dr. B adored her and left a previous wife and children to live with her. Mrs. B's dramatic emotional outbursts somehow gratified him and complemented his rational, obsessive style. However, when he became absorbed in his work or spent time with his children, she would become resentful and demanding. Dr. B would passively avoid her demands, and her rages would escalate to the point where she would throw objects, destroy his possessions, or lunge at him, scratching his face or breaking his eyeglasses. He would fend her off in self-protection or restrain her until she calmed. Mrs. B had a blatant affair, which finally ruptured the marriage. After the separation, this man's passive aggressiveness was expressed through custody litigation and financial withholding. In a fury one night, she sideswiped his car.

Parent-Child Relationships

These women's relationships with their children are erratic and unpredictable: alternately very loving and nurturing, and then explosive, angry, and rejecting, especially with their sons. Both boys and girls can be emotionally paralyzed by the mother's angry attacks. Typically, the young girls become timid and cringing, and withdraw in order not to be the object of the mother's wrath. Alternately, some girls assume a role reversal in the face of the mother's emotional tirades, taking care of her or temporarily assuming parenting and household tasks. This strategy often works more effectively to protect the girls from the mother's rages than the boys. The girls also tend to be supported by a warmer, more protective relationship with the father, who covertly indulges and idealizes them as the "good girl," in contrast to his view of his wife. As these girls grow older, they are likely to become more demanding, have temper outbursts, and get into power struggles with both parents, suggesting an identification with the aggressive female adult.

By contrast, boys in these families evidence a more passive-aggressive stance; a layer of sadness, inhibition, and depression suppresses their rage at the mother. In general, the boys engage in overt power struggles with the mother and are more openly abusive of her only to the extent that the father models this kind of counterreaction. The younger, preschool boys have more ambivalent relationships with their capricious mothers and seem unable to separate emotionally. They are simultaneously needy of her intermittent nurturance, covertly angry in response to her punitiveness and unavailability, and fearful of her anger and rejection if they act independently of her wishes. To the extent that fathers are passive and themselves intimidated by their ex-wives, they can neither easily protect nor rescue their sons, especially the younger ones, from the ambivalent mother-son bond; nor are they able to provide an effective model for dealing with the mother.

PROFILE 3: MALE-CONTROLLING INTERACTIVE VIOLENCE

In this category, the domestic violence is seen as arising primarily out of a conflict of interest or disagreement between the spouses, which escalates from mutual verbal provocation and insults into physical struggles. Although the man or the woman might initiate the physical aggression, the overriding response by the man is to assert control and prevail by physically dominating and overpowering the woman. The exercise of physical control is seen as legitimate by the male: he feels he had the right, if not the duty, to put the woman in her place and to manage the situation in this way. Physical aggression is an accepted way of resolving interpersonal conflict and of doing everyday business, and in this sense it is often rule-governed (i.e., the perpetrators are explicit about what are, to them, acceptable and unacceptable ways of hitting; for example, one should not attack from behind; one should look where one hits; hitting is OK in response to certain kinds of verbal abuse).

These men do not beat up their spouse and in general do not use more force than needed to gain her compliance. In this respect, the man exercises varying amounts of restraint in his violence, depending upon how much she resists his efforts to control. In our studies, alcohol use, but not necessarily its abuse, by either or both partners was a feature in slightly less than half of these cases. When alcohol was involved, the violence tended to be more severe and the memory of the incident clouded.

Generally, the conflict starts with a fairly minor altercation and becomes more and more serious, sometimes culminating in a terribly violent scene. The woman commonly ends up screaming or trying to leave the area. If she starts screaming, her spouse may slap her in a misguided effort to quell her "hysteria." In this sense, he tends to see her as a child who needs to be disciplined or controlled "for her own good." If she tries to leave or refuses to communicate with him, this triggers his attempts to control her by pinning her down or blocking her exit. By virtue of their superior strength, these men essentially coerce and dominate their mates, and they are more likely to inflict injury, whereupon the women truly become their victims.

In some cases the woman submits in passive fury. If she continues to struggle and counterattack (by hitting, kicking, biting, etc.), the violence can escalate to dangerous levels. Neither the woman nor the man appears fearful of the other spouse in this latter situation, and, in fact, both are assertive, feisty, and quick to respond to a perceived confrontation with a counterattack. Interestingly, in a subgroup of this profile of violence, there seems to be a degree of sexual excitement generated by these mutual brawls. This is not obviously true for any of the other types of violence.

Violence in these families is repetitive over the duration of the marriage, often increasing in frequency and severity as the relationship deteriorates. Once the couple separates, and if they are no longer interacting and unable to provoke one another, the violence is likely to cease, though it can reappear in other similar relationships.

Mr. and Mrs. C had a mutually demeaning relationship marked by continuous verbal assaults and frequent refusals to give in to each other. In an escalating interaction, he would call her names ("conniving bitch"), and she would call him names ("sadistic brute"), each goading the other on. She would wave a finger in his face, and he would stab the air in front of her. Both seemed to derive erotic pleasure from their verbal bantering and sniping. However, at some point, they would become physically abusive. She would make a particularly offensive remark, then push or poke at him. Mr. C had an especially macho self-image and was concerned about appearing weak and letting himself be pushed around by a woman. When his wife's provocation became physical, he would decide she needed to be put in her place. If she did not accede to his attempts to control or restrain her, he would take a swing at her or slap her. Both would then become increasingly angry, and the physical abuse would escalate to acutely dangerous levels, where she was at great risk.

Parent-Child Relationships

Because male-controlling abuse often coexists with female violence, the children in this category show mixed reactions, with predominant responses being aggressiveness and passive-aggressiveness in both boys and girls. Because violence is seen as acceptable in these families, both parents are poor models of ego control and anger management. Parents model fighting and arguing, rather than reasoning, as a means of settling disputes. Hence the children are caught between two warring figures, neither of whom can consistently control his or her own temper, set and enforce reasonable limits, provide clear direction, or take responsibility with the other or with the children. Nor are parents able to support each other's position with the children; rather, they tend to openly sabotage each other's authority. Inconsistent family rules, contradictory messages, unreliable discipline, and tension characterize these families. It is therefore not surprising that there is a great deal of factioning among the family members, and that the children's alliances keep shifting from one parent to the other. Power struggles and mutual coercion between parents and children are common. Physically punitive child rearing practices and physical fights between siblings are common.

These children develop an array of relationships with their parents. Some of the girls are assertive, strong-willed, and demanding, ready to jump into the vacuum left by the shifting power structure; other girls can passively retreat or become covertly defiant. Over time, they may switch back and forth from a passive to an aggressive stance. The younger boys are difficult to discipline and control—there is an element of excitement about their minor delinquencies that has a counterphobic flavor. Older boys tend to show little respect for authority. Some become belligerent and disobedient, refusing to listen to either parent, particularly the mother. Fathers often have peerlike relationships with their sons, especially as they grow older. These boys enjoy a kind of "we're men together" camaraderie that increases their self-esteem but also gives them permission to use aggression and coercion to get what they want, especially from their mothers and sisters. Fathers are inclined to admire their son's toughness and acting-out. Some of the mothers also foster the son's acting-out, as the son replaces the father around the house. The men tend to be more controlling and puni-tive with their daughters, as compared with their sons, and mothers have problems managing both their boys and their girls.

PROFILE 4: SEPARATION-ENGENDERED AND POSTDIVORCE TRAUMA

In general, this group is marked by uncharacteristic acts of violence, which are precipitated by the separation or are reactions to stressful postdivorce events (e.g., custody litigation and disputes over money and access to chil-dren that occur in the aftermath of the final decree). In these cases, vio-lence and the exercise of control occur only during or after the separation period but are not present within the marriage itself.

For some spouses, separation is particularly traumatic, a complete assault on their universe (e.g., the discovery of a new lover in bed with one's spouse or a sudden desertion). In response, they feel desperate, helpless, abandoned, and outraged. Threatened by intolerable loss, they try to hold on to and physically prevent the other from leaving, or scare the other into staying. These incidents usually involve a sudden lashing out (slapping the other across the face), throwing something, or destroying property (a cher-ished keepsake or heirloom). Some women take desperate steps such as ramming the spouse's car, cutting up his clothes, and throwing his furniture into the street. Some men physically restrain their wives from leaving. Times at which either spouse might be particularly vulnerable are events having symbolic meaning (the final settlement, the loss of the house, changes in custody, seeing the ex-spouse with a new partner) or special times of the year (anniversaries and holidays).

Usually, the partner who feels abandoned is the one who becomes vio-lent; this can be either the man or the woman. When this happens, the vic-tim partner is shocked and frightened by the uncharacteristic violent behavior of the mate, feeling that the other has "gone crazy." This unex-pected violence and the counterreactions form the basis for the spouses to negatively reconstruct their earlier perceptions of each other, casting a long shadow over the postdivorce relationship of these couples; that is, a new negative image of each spouse is crystallized out of these desperate behav-iors and has enormous significance in limiting the partners' trust and will-ingness to cooperate in the future with respect to their children.

In this category, the violence is not ongoing or repetitive. In fact, it is limited to one, two, or several incidents, albeit sometimes very serious ones, around the time of the separation or divorce. The perpetrators of violence in these cases, both men and women, are usually fairly frank about the incident and quite embarrassed and ashamed of their behavior afterward (i.e., the violence is perceived as unacceptable in these families). With respect to the power dynamics, the violence changes the balance dramatically, making the victim of the violence very frightened of the partner. As a result, the offending party gains significantly more psychological leverage. In this way, either the man or the woman might become empowered and gain more control by the violence.

Mr. D walked into his home one day to find his wife in bed with his friend. He stood there, shocked, sick to his stomach. In stony silence, he then left the room. During the next several days, as his rage mounted, he stripped the house of his possessions and left. When his wife came by his workplace to talk with him, he suddenly grabbed her by the throat and tried to strangle her, yelling at her in a strange voice to "get out of [his] life and never be seen again." She had to be rescued by his co-workers. On another occasion, he attacked her when they were arguing about the custody of their daughter. Later, in counseling, they both described a marriage that had initially been a loving companionship in which they never argued or fought. However, trying to survive without vocational skills or experience and the early arrival of a baby had taxed their ability to cope. Both became emotionally distant and withdrawn; they worked separate shifts and no longer slept together. Without communicating her conclusion to her husband, the wife determined that the marriage had effectively ended and began to date casually. Her husband ignored these telltale signs, thinking she would return to him, until the day he found her in bed with his friend.

Parent-Child Relationships

Both boys and girls who have witnessed separation violence are noticeably inhibited and constricted, and often have symptoms typical of posttraumatic stress. They are anxious, fearful, and unable to concentrate, and they avoid talking or thinking about the violent incident. Some of these children, especially the younger ones, have intrusive memories, nightmares, regressive clinging, and somatic symptoms (such as headaches or stomachaches). Occasionally a child may show a temporary phobic avoidance of the parent who is perceived to be violent.

In our studies we noted that mothers were likely to be more warmly supportive of their daughters and fathers of their sons in these cases of traumatic separation. In most respects, however, the diminished parenting is likely to be limited to the time of separation or postdivorce trauma, when parents are more vulnerable and violence is most likely to occur. In general, these parents expect and model good ego control and anger management. There is a good prognosis for reconstituting positive parent-child relationships in these cases, often with the help of therapy to resolve the anxieties and fears created by the traumatic events.

PROFILE 5: PSYCHOTIC AND PARANOID REACTIONS

For a very small proportion of custody-disputing families, violence is generated by disordered thinking and serious distortions of reality that involve paranoid conspiracy theories. For some, this is part of a psychosis; for others, it is a drug-induced dementia. In all such cases, the separation itself triggers an acute phase of danger.

The men and women in this category believe that the former spouse intends to and can harm or exploit them. Disturbed spouses perceive the ex-spouse as an aggressive, persecutory figure and see the ex-spouse's actions in the separation and the request for custody as deeply humiliating attacks. Hence they have an urgent need to counter the perceived hostility, danger, and victimization they anticipate from the ex-mate. Expecting trickery and deceit, they have a policy of attacking before being attacked. Feeling wronged, they feel justified in seeking revenge. There is little conscious shame in their assaultive behavior, and they can violate the ex-spouse while simultaneously maintaining a sense of righteousness. In their own view, they are forced to protect themselves from the other's malevolence.

In these cases, as with ongoing battering, there is little buildup to an attack within the relationship, nor does the victim (consciously) provoke it. The level of violence during these episodes ranges from moderate to severe. However, these persons are most frightening because they are so unpredictable. Paranoids who have organized, logical, and coherent delusional systems tend to hide their conspiracy theories, so that no one knows what they are thinking. Others, who are rambling, incoherent, and more diffusely disturbed, have correspondingly poor impulse control and can become agitated and physically abusive with no warning. It is evident in these cases that the violence is largely internally generated by the abuser's disordered and paranoid thinking and difficulties with impulse control.

The spouse victims in these cases are understandably very frightened because of the apparent irrationality and unpredictability of the attacks. They are relatively powerless in the relationship and have psychological profiles that suggest the battered spouse syndrome. Some seem oblivious to the acute danger they are in and need special encouragement to take measures to protect themselves and their children. Those who seek to help these victims of domestic violence need to take precautions also, because the paranoid conspiracy theories are often expanded to include them, so that they, too, may become the targets of violence, which may include the threat of homicide.

Mr. E filed for divorce after severe financial problems in the family culminated in his bankruptcy. Mrs. E felt extremely betrayed by his decision to abandon her, especially at this time, and developed clearly paranoid delusions about her husband. They included accusations that he had poisoned the family cat, that he was sending his (nonexistent) girlfriend to the son's school to harass and frighten the child, and that he was molesting her mother. As the litigation over custody of their son intensified, Mrs. E became highly agitated, claiming that the father was "an evil, dangerous man, and extremely cunning." She likened him to a recently convicted mass murderer who had massacred his family. In actuality, Mr. E was a shy, quiet, nonassertive man who was quite frightened of his wife's rages and nonplussed by her allegations. He commented, however, that she had always been "a little strange" and "often had it in for someone," but that he had not previously been the target of her hostility. Mrs. E physically attacked him on a number of occasions and then claimed he had attacked her. Finally, she accused him of molesting their child and fled with the boy "in order to protect my son."

Parent-Child Relationships

In our studies, there were too few children in this category to make generalizations; yet we did observe widely diverse functioning among these children. The most important issue appears to be the extent to which children are caught up in the parent's psychotic delusions (i.e., in a folie à deux with the parent), in contrast to being psychologically separated from the disturbed parent. If enmeshed with the parent, youngsters are likely to present as psychotic-like children who are strongly identified with the disturbed parent's distorted thinking and emotional state. If psychologically more separated, they appear like children who have been acutely or chronically traumatized (as with the separation trauma or battering categories).

IMPLICATIONS FOR INTERVENTION AND CUSTODY DECISION MAKING

The patterns described above suggest that the propensity for domestic violence derives from multiple sources and follows different patterns in different families, rather than being a syndrome with a single underlying cause. This being the case, there is a need for differential clinical diagnosis of the violent incidents *within the context* of the marital relationship and the divorce process. In counseling settings, the history of actual incidents needs to be elicited separately from each party. Such a history should include the precipitating factors, who initiates violence and who responds with violence, the frequency and severity of abuse and its patterns over time, and the emotional and physical sequelae for both victim and perpetrator.

The use of mediation with domestic violence cases has been a hotly debated topic (Germane et al., 1985; Girdner, 1990; Grillo, 1991; Lerman, 1984; Newman et al., 1995). Initial screening measures could help discriminate among various types of violence and suggest for whom and what kind of mediation may be appropriate. First and foremost, battering men and psychotic-paranoid persons are primarily unsuited for confidential mediation. Mediation can be dangerous because these clients can hide behind the confidentiality of the process and manipulate, control, and even terrorize the other parties, including the mediator, to achieve their own ends. Moreover, unless it suits the batterer's own purposes, agreements made in such a forum are unlikely to be accorded any respect. Instead, the victims need the authority and protection of the court.

With the other profiles of violence, mediation and family counseling methods need to be adapted to ensure physical safety, rebuild trust, and seek a balance of power between the divorcing parties (Duryee, 1995; Magana & Taylor, 1993). First, there needs to be a clear understanding that the clients' rights to confidentiality in mediation/counseling will be waived without consent of the parties if there are further threats or violent incidents (i.e., the court will be informed). In addition, enforceable stay-away or restraining orders need to be in place. The victim may need a support person to guide her through the process. Separate mediation and counseling sessions can be used to develop custody and access plans. Courthouse security and escort services to ensure safety on the premises should be provided. Referrals to community services for ongoing help and support of the family members can be made available.

Other factors being equal, sole or joint residential arrangements for children are contraindicated with a father who has engaged in ongoing or episodic battering, as they are with any parent who is psychotic or has paranoid delusions. In fact, in these cases visitation with the violent parent may need to be supervised or even suspended, especially if the threat of violence is current or ongoing. Children of these violent parents can be retraumatized if compelled to visit against their wishes. They often need treatment for posttraumatic symptoms of stress that are a consequence of their exposure as witness to chronic abuse, before they can reengage (Pynoos & Eth, 1986).

Resumption of unsupervised visits should be contingent upon the abusive parent's complete cessation of violence and threats of abuse, as well as his or her successful completion of a program designed for batterers and/or appropriate psychiatric or substance abuse treatment. Unsupervised visits should be structured according to what makes the child feel safe, and they should be governed by extremely explicit court orders with respect to dates, times, and places of transfer that can be easily interpreted by police officers and the court. The exchange of the child may need to be supervised by a neutral third party. Restraining orders need to be in place that will make the victim parent feel safer, even long after the cessation of abuse. The court needs to act swiftly and forcefully in response to any contempt of these orders.

Furthermore, tremendous care needs to be taken so as not to jeopardize the victim parent's safety as a consequence of the children's access plan. It is important to note, however, that spouses who have left a battering relationship or a psychotically disturbed mate are likely to have diminished capacity to parent as a function of their victimization, and they may need considerable help and support in reestablishing their competence with their children. This may include professional counseling or peer group support for their parenting (Walker & Edwall, 1987).

When a violent parent is believed to be psychotically disturbed, a psychiatric evaluation is needed and should include a risk assessment for homicide and suicide. This evaluation may need to include both parents and children so as not to exacerbate the disturbed parent's paranoid concerns. When a child shares the paranoid delusions of the psychotic custodial parent, custody may need to be removed from that parent within the protective confines of a psychiatric treatment facility to prevent dangerous acting-out.

A careful assessment of the parenting capacity of a woman who typically initiates violence is needed before placing children primarily in her care. It may be that her mate is a more appropriate residential parent. Unfortunately, many of these fathers are too passive and unavailable; they need much encouragement if they are to take primary responsibility and protect their children from the mother's volatile behavior. A psychological evaluation of these women may be needed with a special focus on their parenting practices. Custodial mothers in this category may need to be cautioned that their volatile behavior, which results in abusing, neglecting, or frightening their children, might also result in a change of custody to the father. Women can be offered counseling; unfortunately, as of this date, few group programs are designed specifically for abusive women.

A variety of time-sharing arrangements can be appropriate in the remainder of categories. However, in cases of male-controlling interactive abuse, fathers especially, and sometimes both parents, need education in parenting skills to manage their children assertively and flexibly, without resorting to coercion and physical altercations. If there is no current threat of violence, unsupervised visits may be appropriate, provided that their terms are explicitly stated in court orders with respect to dates, times, and places of exchange. It is important that clear, structured arrangements for transferring children from one home to the other be provided to preempt power struggles between these parents that might erupt into physical fights. A neutral exchange venue that is comfortable for the child, or supervision of the transfer, may be best.

The best prognosis for a shared parenting arrangement, in general, lies with those family situations where there has been no history of physical abuse within the marriage. Parents who have experienced acute incidents of violence only around the time of their separation or during the divorce process are the most likely to be able to reconstitute their coparenting capacities, provided they are given time and, often, therapeutic help to resolve the anxieties and fears created by the traumatic events. Brief, crisis-oriented family counseling and mediation may be needed that will include an exchange of explanations for the couple's unexpected or untoward behavior; apologies can be offered for the violations of civility; promises and commitments can be made regarding their future treatment of one another; and symbolic protections and real barriers can be put in place that help the family members feel safe again. Children need to be part of this healing process. This kind of intervention is usually willingly accepted, informally or by stipulation of the parties, obviating the necessity of a court order.

In conclusion, there is no single, simple policy recommendation, nor one procedural method, nor one treatment intervention that is suited for all domestic violence families. Differential assessment of domestic violence is necessary when helping parents make postdivorce plans for the custody of their children. Parent-child relationships are likely to vary with the different patterns of violence, and children of different ages and gender are affected differently. There are also several trajectories for recovery and reconstitution of family relationships, making a variety of custody and visitation plans suitable. The potential for future violence and the conditions under which it is likely to recur also vary among these patterns. These need to be considered in determining a custody plan to reduce the possibility of exposing children and victim parents to continued abuse.

Chapter 3

The Prism and the Prison of the Child

How Children Defend and Cope

*T*he family environment of highly conflicted, separated spouses or partners is typified by their mutual distrust, fear, anger, bitterness, and projection of blame onto the other, the ex-partner. The shadow of past domestic violence and the threat of its recurrence are common. As shown in chapters 1 and 2, there are internal psychological and interactional family dynamics as well as external-social explanations for how and why former lovers reconstrue each other's identity in this polarized, negative light. Of course, in some cases these negative views will have a basis in the facts of a spouse's violent, neglectful, substance abusing, or criminal behavior. More-over, these may have been dysfunctional families long before the couples separated, in which the children were subjected to ongoing marital con-flict and erratic or emotionally abusive care by their personality-disordered parents.

More commonly, however, these extremely negative views are an exag-gerated response to the humiliation of rejection inherent in the divorce and the individual's defensive need to project all sense of failure and badness onto the ex-spouse. Alternatively, such negative views may derive from a traumatic separation experience that has shattered the couple's previous sense of mutual trust and shared reality. Or they may have been wittingly or unwittingly constructed and confirmed by others in a social world now split by new partners, kin, and professionals, whose colliding agendas escalate and entrench the polarized positions. The adversarial legal system provides a particularly fertile environment for these unrealistic perceptions, fostering the projection of blame and entrenching the disputes by reframing facts and sharply focusing on who is right, competent, and good, and who is wrong, incompetent, and bad.

Whatever the origin of their highly negative views, the consequence is that these parents provide a frightening, fragmented, contradictory, and profoundly confusing family experience for their children. In this chapter, we consider this experience from the perspective of the children, describing their typical concerns and attempts to manage.

PARENT-CHILD RELATIONSHIPS
WITHIN A RANGE OF VULNERABILITY

Unfortunately, ongoing postdivorce conflict and litigation erode whatever potential these divorcing spouses do have for effective parenting. Parents who are moderately humiliated (narcissistically wounded) by the divorce, and those who have experienced traumatic separations, tend to develop more or less fixed beliefs (confirmed by their social world) that the other parent is "bad, dangerous, and irresponsible," and that they, by contrast, are the "good, safe, and responsible" caretaker. It is not surprising, then, that both parents are likely to selectively perceive and distort the child's concerns regarding the other parent. Indeed, it is common for the couple's expressed disappointments with each other to be mirrored in their concerns for how the other parent will treat the child. For example, if a woman has experienced her ex-spouse as emotionally neglectful, she expects him to be neglectful of her child. If the child then comes back upset or depressed after spending time with his dad, the mother attributes the difficulty solely to the father's lack of care. At the same time, other, more positive aspects of the father-child relationship are ignored or denied (i.e., the fact that this father and child have a lot of fun together and that the child feels a painful loss each time they part). In responding sympathetically to her child on his return home, the mother incorrectly interprets and then amplifies the child's sadness and anxiety. As a result, the child's emerging reality testing about his own feelings and ideas are ever so slightly and insidiously distorted. Furthermore, the mother's own anxiety and distress about her child's sadness are intensified because she is not able to communicate and clarify with her ex-husband about why the child might be upset. She is left feeling helpless about protecting her child.

In other words, vulnerable parents can overidentify with elements of the child's own emotional response, when it reminds them of their own experience with the ex-spouse, and ignore or deny other aspects of the child's experience that are contrary to their own. Anxiety between the distressed parent and child over certain issues is shared and amplified and is usually triggered by symbolic actions of the ex-spouse or symptomatic behavior in the child. An illustration:

———————

In the G family, the parents endured years of bitter, silent anger before the separation. As the father had increasingly failed in his professional life, the mother unwillingly assumed the role of provider. This dynamic was a formula for the man's shame and the woman's resentment. When the mother took their children, a boy and a girl, to another state to find work closer to her family of origin, the father experienced the loss of his children as another insult. The following year, the children returned to spend the summer with their father. When it was time for them to go back to their mother, the father refused to release his son. He explained his refusal to us in the following way: "I was standing in the backyard with Carl [the son] when we heard his mother's footsteps coming up the path, and I saw a look in my son's eyes that I knew so well. I guess, looking back, I always knew it was there. . . . He looked terrified! . . . like she would flatten him . . . castrate him . . . run over him like a steamroller, because she's always hated men. He could never feel safe being a boy, growing up around her. I ask him . . . not directly, of course, but just, you know, 'Is Mom yelling a lot? Is she picking on you more than your sister?' At first he used to just shrug, but he's starting to tell me more and more!"

The insidious consequence of this projection is that Carl experiences his father's empathic attunement most fully when he shares in this distorted perception of his mother. Integrity, reality testing, and even the child's emerging sense of morality are sacrificed, in these accumulating moments, to the child's hunger for the parent's empathy.

———————

Eight-year-old Becky was delivered home late by her noncustodial mother after a most exciting visit, during which she didn't want to stop to eat. She felt apprehensive about coming home late and guilty for having enjoyed herself hugely. As she entered the door of her father's home, the stepmother's fuming turned to fury when she found out the child had not been fed her dinner. Anxious to placate her stepmother and redirect the mounting fear of her anger, Becky cried that she had "begged" her mother to feed her but her mother "couldn't be bothered." What is more, she complained that she had spent a "horrible" day with her mother. Immediately, her stepmother quieted down; she soothed and fed the fretting child, agreeing that the mother had been "outrageously neglectful!"

When parents feel severely humiliated by the divorce (have greater narcissistic vulnerability), one spouse may experience the other's rejection, custody demands, or accusations as a total, devastating attack, and, in defense, may develop paranoid ideas of betrayal, conspiracy, and exploitation. In these more extreme cases, the ex-spouse and his or her allies are perceived as dangerous, aggressive, and persecutory figures.

As Mr. J began to piece together the rubble from his marriage, he began to rewrite history and to perceive his partner as having intentionally plotted and planned to exploit and cast him off: "I gave her everything . . . backed her up with every penny, and she took it all until there was nothing left and then spit me out like a piece of deadweight. She and her boyfriend set me up. Now, he's living in my house and abusing my child!"

In cases such as these, where the divorce represents a severe injury to self-esteem, parents have a more generalized inability to appreciate (or mirror) the child's experience of the other parent. They are intermittently depriving or punishing the child, if he or she is perceived to have defected to the other parent. Severely narcissistically injured parents cannot accurately enter into or reflect the child's unique experience of the other parent because of their own intense pain and the defensive need to view themselves as "all good" and the ex-spouse as "all bad" or even persecutory. These parents expect and need the child to reflect their own polarized negative views. Indeed, it is not uncommon for them to harbor distorted or exaggerated convictions that their child is being emotionally or physically abused by the other parent or his associates.

These parents are likely to place the child intermittently in an untenable double bind, such that to please or gratify one parent will displease and hurt the other. Any spontaneous, autonomous expressions of the child's feelings or needs tend to be ignored, denied, or experienced as a burdensome demand, or as a pernicious attack upon the parent, especially if these feelings and needs seem to be related to the phobic object, the other parent.

———————

When 5-year-old Sally expressed a wish to call her father on the phone and tell him how she learned to jump rope that day, her mother withdrew into sullen anger. Inexplicably, to Sally, her mother was "too tired" to read her usual bedtime story that evening.

———————

As shown here, these parents can become emotionally abandoning, rejecting, or even vengeful toward the child who expresses his or her own individual needs (individuates), especially the need to move toward the other parent. As in Sally's case, the punishing message is typically unspoken and is therefore impossible to be spoken about, which makes it even more pernicious. In some cases, however, the rejection is not at all subtle.

———————

Mrs. P was enraged when her 9-year-old son posed for a photograph with his father and new stepmother at his school's awards ceremony. Peter had protested to his father at the time, because he knew full well what might happen. Sure enough, when they went home afterward, his mother threw Peter's belongings out onto the street and screamed at him to "Get out! Go live with that jerk and his whore!"

———————

Sometimes the mere presence of the child, or the child's physical resemblance to the ex-spouse, produces a toxic, phobic reaction in the parent. The mannerisms or typical expressions of the other parent, when seen in the child, can activate resentment, even rage, toward the child, who at that moment is undifferentiated from the hated or feared ex-partner.

Mr. S described his daughter as follows: "She's kinda got a bad attitude, she's uppity like her mother. When she comes to my house she's surly and rude . . . they have brainwashed her. She's like a little mimic of her mother. . . . I have spanked her for it . . . I have to make her shape up. Finally, by the end of the weekend, she's like my little girl again!"

It is not surprising that children subjected to this kind of perverse conditioning can have serious difficulties discriminating their own feelings from those of their parents. They can also remain profoundly confused because, in most cases, the parents are verbally denying what their body language and actions are clearly expressing: "Of course I want her to see her mother and have a good relationship with her mother!" Mr. S declared.

Many parents in high-conflict divorces are especially vulnerable to separation and loss. One or both spouses may experience severe separation or abandonment anxiety as a consequence of the divorce. In some cases (as explained in chapter 1), their vulnerability is the result of previous traumatic losses. Others have experienced emotionally deprived childhoods and have failed to achieve complete separation from their early caregivers. Hence, for such persons, the marital separation triggers panic, intense fears of being abandoned, and the inability to survive on their own. Parent-child relationships in these cases are usually characterized by the parent's clinging dependency, as the parent attempts to undo the loss of the marriage by holding on to the child.

When her husband left, Mrs. L felt extreme panic. "It is like someone took a shotgun and blasted a hole right through me, and the wind is whistling right through!" she said with a shiver. For months, this pervasive sense of damage and hollowness caused her to wake fitfully from her sleep with anxiety attacks. The comfort of her small daughter's body snuggling next to her was the only thing that seemed to calm her. During the day, she found reasons to keep Laura home from nursery school because she couldn't bear to be alone in the house. Laura, who felt upset, did not understand the panic but clung to her mother and resisted visiting her father.

The parent is likely to experience a renewed threat of abandonment by the child, whenever he or she leaves for visitation. This provokes both intense anxiety and covert hostility toward the child, who is not, then, available to take care of the parent's needs. Not surprisingly, these children themselves then become ambivalent about separating. Alternatively, some children, sensing their apparent omnipotence in caring for a distressed parent, react as if the parent's very survival depends on their constant vigilance and caretaking.

Some parents defend against their fears of abandonment by taking a pseudo-autonomous stance and rigidly insist on making unilateral decisions on behalf of their children and refusing to cooperate with the other parent. This can result in inflexible, authoritarian parenting that is governed by one parent's need to be in control, rather than being firm, empathic, and independent in his or her judgment. Eventually, such rigidity can evolve into power struggles with the child, especially during adolescence, which in turn can precipitate the child's sudden defection to the other parent.

Parents with severe borderline, sociopathic, and narcissistic personality disorders are particularly vulnerable to both loss and shame, and are likely to view the child as a material possession that they can use as a weapon, vehicle, or conduit to the ex-spouse. In such situations, the child is little more than a means of punishment, a trophy, or a bargaining chip. Children consistently treated as an inanimate object, with only a kind of functional or symbolic value (vis-à-vis the dispute with the other parent), are at risk of developing a surreal sense of not existing—feeling and acting as though they are nonpersons.

———————

For weeks after his wife left the marriage, Mr. L kept Lisa home from school to keep him company, to comfort him. Later, when the mother recovered custody of the child, this man lavished bribes and promises of exciting outings on the little girl, but then failed to turn up for the scheduled visits. When his wife refused to talk with him, he would tearfully tell the distraught child good-bye, that he would never see her again—and then he would return the next day to renew his pleadings. Whenever his wife left the child in the care of the grandmother, he would take the little girl away with him, claiming she had been deserted; then he would drop her off with sundry acquaintances for her care. The child was constantly asked to plead the father's case with the mother: "Ask her, 'Where do you belong?' Tell her I love her and want her back!" When first seen in counseling, Lisa was a dazed, flaccid child. She lacked spontaneity and seemed vacant, joyless, and withdrawn. She made no demands and waited uncomplainingly for someone to attend to her needs, as if she had entirely given up any sense of herself as a viable person.

WHY SOME CHILDREN COPE BETTER THAN OTHERS

The kinds of disturbed family dynamics described above may have been operative throughout this marriage, or they may have been set in motion only at the time of the parents' separation, or after the divorce. When working with these families, it is important to obtain a detailed marital history, which will suggest how early and how pervasive the psychic damage is likely to have been to the child, who may have been exposed to varying degrees of disturbance in the parent-child relationship over time. In some cases, one or both parents may be characterologically disturbed in a more generalized way. The children may have been further stressed by abusive, neglectful, and impoverished environments—both before and after the divorce—derivatives of domestic violence, substance abuse by parents, poverty, and dislocation from school and community.

Before concluding on a definitive gloomy prognosis for all these children, a cautionary note: Researchers are still in the midst of the complex task of trying to understand how children of different developmental stages, both boys and girls, are affected by protracted and severe parental conflict. Systematic studies over these children's growing-up years are sorely needed. Overall, we are impressed by the range of outcomes in our clinical observations of these children over more than a decade. In general, the more severe, more protracted, and earlier the onset of the parental conflict in the child's life, the more disturbed the child becomes; but this is not always so. Some children, despite extreme family conflict and disturbed parenting, appear to be relatively well adjusted, while others with less family stress appear to become enmeshed and emotionally and behaviorally disturbed.

There are many possible reasons for these different outcomes (Anthony & Cohler, 1987; Rutter, 1987). Some children have access to other people who can support them (grandparents, a special teacher, a nanny). The presence of siblings, especially older ones, can act as a buffer. A few have benefited from effective psychotherapy. Children also differ in their personal coping resources: those with more adaptable temperaments, those who are more attractive, more intellectually gifted, more athletically or artistically skilled—all have alternative domains within which to achieve a viable sense of themselves and their place in the world. All these factors can vary the prognosis and outcome for any individual child. This great variability should be kept in mind as we consider next some of the common core concerns of these children, how they typically try to cope, and the possible threats to the development of a positive sense of themselves and their capacity for healthy relationships.

THE CHILDREN'S CORE CONCERNS

We have identified four central concerns of children when they live with divorced and disputing parents: What is true and what is false? How can I keep myself and my parents safe? Who is responsible for the conflict? Am I like the good parent or the bad parent? For these children, the answers to these dilemmas have to do with their profound fears about their ability to survive, both psychologically and physically.

We assert that the various ways by which children attempt to cope with these core concerns, and defend against their fears, are likely to result in entrenched patterns of feeling, perceiving reality, solving problems, relating to other people, and dealing with emotions. Each of these central concerns will be examined together with preliminary evidence from psychological testing that suggests how personality disorders may be shaping up in these children. (The psychological tests briefly referred to here are primarily Rorschach protocols [Exner & Weiner, 1982], data that will be discussed more fully in chapter 6 [Roseby et al., 1995]).

First, depending on their age or cognitive stage of development, children struggle with the puzzle of their parents' conflicting claims (What is true and what is not?). Some of the possibilities from the child's viewpoint are truly frightening. For example, children have brought the following questions to us: "Did Daddy throw Mommy out of the house, or did another man steal Mommy from Daddy?" "Is Daddy's new girlfriend really a witch?" "Dad made Mom have an abortion—does that mean he made her kill my little brother?" "My dad told me that when my mom was pregnant with me, she was also sleeping with a dirty crack cocaine dealer—so is he, or my dad, my father?" Hence, the child's ability to perceive and evaluate real-life events is distorted.

Ordinarily, children use their parents as a social reference for what is safe and trustworthy. These children, however, have the profound dilemma of making sense out of vastly contradictory views communicated through the hostility, fear, and distrust of their opposing parents (Who is safe? Who is dangerous? Whom can you trust?). At times, children's own fantasies are projected into the situation, increasing their fright.

Tears rolled down the face of 5-year-old Tony, as he told his counselor how scared he always was when the door of his father's car slammed shut behind him, out on the street, and he made the long trek up the walkway to his mother's front door, which would crack open barely wide enough to admit him. Tony was too young to talk about his role as psychological double agent in this cold war between his parents. He could tell us, however, how afraid he was—afraid that a large black bird would swoop down and attack him during his perilous transition, and that neither parent would rescue him.

All things considered, it is not surprising that psychological testing indicates the following about these youngsters as a group: they are likely to be hypervigilant and distrusting of others, and they do not expect the world to be a cooperative or protective place. Unlike typically developing children, who tend to turn to others, especially adults, for their needs, these children turn inward, unto themselves, to figure out how to solve problems and interpret social reality. Unfortunately their inner resources are likely to be meager, because these children defend against the double-binding inconsistency of their most significant relationships by avoiding complexity, ambiguity, and spontaneity. In the service of this essential need for predictability and control, their perceptions, feelings, and ideas remain simple, concrete, and utilitarian. The bind is that, as children turn inward, they must rely on an increasingly impoverished and distorted understanding of the nature of reality. Paradoxically, their path to safety leads them further and further away from new self-realizing possibilities.

Second, because of the profound neediness of their distressed parents, these children can become urgently concerned about the emotional and physical well-being of a parent (Will my mother be sad and cry if she is left on her own while I visit my father?). Convinced that somehow their own emotional survival depends upon keeping their parents safe, these worries about the well-being of a parent are often fused with nagging fears about their own vulnerability to being abandoned, lost, ignored, or even destroyed in the parental fight. (If I visit my father, will my mother be there when I get back; will her fury be aimed at me?) Consequently, these children are often highly attuned to managing their own as well as their parents' emotional states. Psychological testing confirms the pervasive emotional constriction that results when children inhibit and monitor the natural exuberance of childhood in this way. Their significantly low egocentricity scores (i.e., their meager sense of importance in relation to others) also point up how atypically "other-focused" these children need to be to maintain their parents' equilibrium.

Third, since they are often the centerpiece of the parents' fight, these children typically feel responsible for the outcome of the disputes. Yet most feel helpless to control or stop the conflict. While the younger ones believe they cause the fighting, the older ones feel the fights occur simply because they exist: "If I were dead, they wouldn't need to fight anymore" is a tragically self-blaming, depressive fantasy that is not uncommon. Feelings of great power and importance are juxtaposed, therefore, with paradoxical feelings of being overwhelmingly inadequate in the face of the parents' intractable anger. Hence the child's sense of agency, competence, or power is undermined. It follows that these children often have trouble directly asserting their own needs and wishes. Instead, they are likely to maintain an underlying oppositional and alienated stance masked by a compliant eagerness to please others. This facade can be maintained only until the children become overwhelmed by their own neediness, at which time they regress or explode into irritable-distressed or demanding-aggressive behavior.

These findings fit with the somewhat paradoxical results of the psychological testing, which suggest that, as a group, these youngsters tend to score unusually high on levels of self-esteem, using self-report measures, but reveal their preoccupation with being bad, damaged, nonviable, and inadequate on projective measures that bypass the child's observing ego (Johnston et al., 1987; Roseby et al., 1995). The tests capture both the confusing sense of importance and the underlying sense of insignificance and helplessness.

Finally, given their parents' continual denigration of each other, these children are clearly concerned with the problem of who is good and who is bad and with whom to identify.

Four-year-old Andy's sandtray play captured the predicament of a small child (himself) who was in the center of a battlefield. He commented, "But the good people wore bad masks and the bad people wore good masks. I wasn't sure which to follow!"

Like Andy, many children become confused, feel shame, or denigrate themselves if they feel they have become like the "bad parent." Hence the child's developmental task of acknowledging, tolerating, and integrating the "bad" with the "good" into a more realistic view of each parent (whole object representation) and, at the same time, forming a cohesive, integrated sense of the "good" and the "bad" in him- or herself (self-constancy) is made extremely difficult:

———————

Eight-year-old Allan could be alternately boastful and grandiose, until he was disciplined, and then he was totally deflated—he became self-flagellating and defeated. Fourteen-year-old Ian was perfectionistic with his schoolwork; if he didn't get it one hundred percent correct, he felt horribly dumb, like his "stupid father."

———————

When children maintain this kind of rigid separation between good and bad, they are bound to strive for an impossible perfection in themselves and other people. Each failure represents an intolerable fall from grace. This most fundamental failure (i.e., to achieve self- and object constancy) is reflected in the pervasive absence of basic trust that testing reveals in these children. It is not difficult to imagine that these polarized shifts from perfectly good to perfectly bad make trusting oneself or others, from moment to moment, a virtually impossible task.

TRAUMATIC SCENES OF VIOLENCE
AND THE FORMATION OF SCRIPTS

As shown in previous chapters, a large proportion of children of entrenched custody disputes will have experienced their parents' violence in the past. Moreover, many will continue to witness ongoing verbal abuse (spiteful comments, put-downs, threats, name-calling) and intermittent physical violence (pushing, shoving, hitting, even battering). Studies have shown that children do not need to be directly abused to be hurt by this manifest conflict and violence between their parents (Jaffe et al., 1990). Our clinical observations lead us to propose that such traumatic scenes can form indelible sensory metaphors in children's memory. The sparse coping skills and defensive postures children employ to try to manage the terrible threat these scenes pose are likely to become organized into patterns and form defensive scripts that undergird their unconscious expectations about how family relationships work. Under certain conditions, this interior script can organize the child's constricted, hypervigilant, rigid, and distrustful view of human relationships in general.

When we first saw him, 12-year-old Isaac could not remember any of the frightening scenes of marital violence that occurred prior to his parents' separation, when his father would chase his mother around the house, beating her. The memory of those violent scenes suddenly returned to him years later, as a teenager, when he had an altercation with his father. In a halting voice he described a series of visual and auditory images to his counselor: father crashing through the door, loud, angry voices, contorted angry faces, father stomping on his mother, who was flailing on the floor, mother crying, mother's face bleeding, himself frozen in the doorway watching, the police arriving, the police arresting his father, the police forbidding him to hug his dad good-bye.

He then went on to describe flashbacks and fragments of other scenes of severe family conflict, intermingled with horrifying nightmares of mayhem that often disturbed his sleep. This boy's repressed rage and utter shame at his helplessness during those childhood events, when he witnessed his father abuse his mother, undergirded his alienated oppositional stance and highly distrustful (paranoid) personality style. At age 15, he is a careful, guarded boy, passive and emotionally expressionless much of the time, especially when conflict threatens. Intermittently, this boy is prone to aggressive outbursts, at which time he hits his mother and sister. In this respect, Isaac shows that he has "turned passive into active" and has identified with his abusive father.

In the remainder of this chapter, the process by which emotionally highly charged family scenes (like those that Isaac experienced) form internal scripts and structure personality pathologies is described and illustrated in detail.

HOW DEFENSIVE SCRIPTS ARE FORMED IN EARLY CHILDHOOD

Incidents of severe family conflict and violence are believed to threaten children's emotional security in a very fundamental sense (Davies & Cummings,

1994). To understand this, we draw upon social cognitive theory about family scenes and scripts (or expectations) to explain how these incidents are stored in children's memory (Berger, 1988; Carlson, 1984; Schank & Abelson, 1977; Tomkins, 1978). Developmental theory about children's social cognition (Flavell et al., 1968; Kegan, 1982; Selman, 1980) and object relations (Mahler et al., 1975; Kohut, 1977; Kohut & Wolf, 1978; Winnicott, 1965, 1971) will complement this understanding and show how internal models of family relationship (Bretherton et al., 1990; Main et al., 1985) are shaped and distorted by repeated incidences of parental conflict, and how the distortions are defensively maintained to manage feelings of helplessness, shame, and rage. Furthermore, it will be shown how all this can inhibit the children's capacity for understanding themselves and other people, for tolerating the expression of the full range of feelings, for empathy, and for moral thought and action (Kagan & Lamb, 1987).

Traumatic scenes of family violence are now known to impact very young children, even infants and toddlers. A primitive script (or inchoate expectation) can initially be formed from schema of preverbal sensory and perceptual experience during infancy, long before the child has access to language to encode the experience. For babies and toddlers, then, frightening scenes of family conflict and violence may never be available for cognitive recall but can continue to manifest themselves in scary dreams and in diffusely anxious feelings. Two examples follow.

———————

Twelve-year-old Katie recalled a repeated dream from which she invariably woke up crying. It was of two disembodied voices shouting, at first faintly, from a distance, and then increasing in volume and proximity to a deafening roar. At the age of two, this child had been witness to the scene when her father discovered her mother with a lover.

When Tom was 2 years old, his father murdered his mother. After his mother was repeatedly stabbed in a nearby room, she struggled to the side of her son's crib, where she died. Tom has no memory of the event, and the facts were kept secret from him until he was a young adult. However, from the time he can first remember, he has suffered from repeated diffuse and overwhelming anxiety attacks, wherein he feels that some unknown, dreadful thing is happening.

———————

By the time the young child has achieved representational capacity (indicated by the capacity for language and symbolic play), the script has become a pattern that organizes children's largely unself-conscious "rules" for predicting, interpreting, responding to, and controlling their experiences within their families. Scripts derived from emotionally charged scenes tend to be conflated in memory and psychologically magnified. For pleasurable scenes, the script is generally magnified by the production of variants; that is, the child who has previously been gratified by a particular scene tends to innovate by producing variations on the theme inherent within the script. For example, an infant who receives a rewarding response for cooing is encouraged to experiment with other forms of vocalization. A child given warm appreciation for being helpful seeks new ways to please.

Negative scenes, on the other hand, tend to be magnified by the formation of analogs; that is, the child seeks to find and then to defend against similarities as new scenes are scanned for old dangers and previous disappointments. For example, a toddler who associates mother's angry expression with a punishing slap freezes when a caretaker seems disapproving. A youngster who associates his father's arrival to pick him up for visits with another parental fight becomes immobilized when his father calls him on the phone. Hence, scripts derived from highly negative family scenes generate more constriction and invariant coping responses. Children who experience particularly negative scenes tend to incorporate a greater number of previously unrelated scenes into forming and maintaining the negative script, thus minimizing creative new ways of coping and simplifying their perception of the world.

The intolerable feelings aroused by scenes of severe conflict and violence between parents result in memories that are defensively encapsulated and not easily recalled by the child. Moreover, parents commonly avoid, deny, or defensively distort incidents about which they are ashamed: they hope the child does not remember or did not understand what happened. Some adults think they are protecting their child by not talking about the event. As a result, the memory of the scene remains essentially private, fragmented, and embedded in the idiosyncratic experience of the child, and not easily talked about with others. This "conspiracy of silence" within the family prevents the reparative work of talking-through and emotional abreaction, which would enable the child to assimilate and master the traumatic episode. When this is not done, there is a heightened risk that the child will reenact the traumatic scene (sometimes compulsively) in nightmares or destructive play, alone or with peers (Terr, 1988).

Traumatic scenes may become psychologically magnified when memories are intermingled, confused with one another, and reorganized around the common denominator of the internal script that governs them. The following example illustrates.

Six-year-old Jennifer fell from a tree and broke both her wrists while camping on vacation with her noncustodial father. Though he was a loving father, he was angry and bitter with his ex-wife. The child's mother, angry and distraught over the accident, rushed to the father's house to take the child home. In a physical struggle in the child's presence, when the father tried to explain the prescribed medications, he grabbed the mother's wrist and flung her from him. She fell down the stairs and broke her arm, leaving Jennifer screaming in fright.

Most interestingly, during her counseling session, the child described the accident and the violent incident briefly and rather blandly, then appeared to distract from the topic by drawing a picture of a crying baby standing in water with a life jacket around its waist. When asked to describe the picture, Jennifer recalled that when she was "a baby" (a toddler), her father made her wear a life jacket despite her protests. She then fell over in her wading pool, was unable to right herself, and feared she was going to drown.

This child appeared to have conjoined three traumatic experiences: the pool incident, the tree accident, and the parental fight when her mother was injured. The common denominator of these three events was Jennifer's script of a father who tried to be protective and helpful (i.e., he made her wear a life jacket; he demanded the right use of the prescribed medications) but was likely to become angry and vengeful if resisted, even potentially lethal, toward her and her mother.

Often the original traumatic scenes have been completely repressed, with only fragmented images or other sensory memories available for conscious recall. Children appear to react with indifference to these fragments that, though remaining ultra-clear in their memories, are typically reported with bland or commonplace affect. This is similar to what has been referred to as *screen memory* in the psychoanalytic literature (Spero, 1990). There is also a tendency for these memory fragments to be activated in response to any new negative experience or threat of trauma. We hypothesize that in actuality, the memory fragments are likely to be linked by virtue of the script, which conjoins several traumatic scenes. Ironically, this process provides the child with a kind of negative sense of predictability.

Alicia's mother was severely depressed, angry, and resentful about having to care for her baby daughter during the first two years of the child's life. She harbored frightening fantasies of hurting or abandoning her baby. Gradually, her depression eased. At 7 years, the child suffered a ruptured appendix and was rushed to the hospital for emergency surgery. She spent several uncomfortable days there, reacting poorly to the medical procedures, with her mother constantly at her side. Later, when she was 10 years old, her parents separated. At that time, Alicia was exposed to many highly conflictual scenes, which involved her mother's becoming uncontrollably angry and physically attacking her father.

In the two years following the divorce, prominent among this child's symptoms of anxiety and distress were frequent somatic complaints, especially pain in her left lower abdomen. She feared she was going to die and became excessively dependent upon and unable to separate from her mother. In therapy, Alicia was highly anxious and unable to talk about the divorce situation. She did, however, recall quite vividly, though with astonishing indifference, being in the hospital as well as other seemingly mundane scenes in a day-care center as a preschooler. Those scenes were actually fragments of memories from times when she had been highly distressed about being left by her mother.

This child had evolved a script wherein the threat was abandonment and destruction by her mother. She tried to manage this threat by retreating into somatic symptoms and clinging dependency, because these behaviors would evoke her mother's caretaking response. It is interesting that the specific fears Alicia was trying to ward off by her scripted symptoms were also evident in repetitive terrifying nightmares, in which the symbolism of the angry mother and her unsafe world were barely disguised.

The script produced from a traumatic scene (or scenes) will probably depend on a number of factors: the child's limited perceptual opportunities and cognitive capacities, the current emotional-developmental issues that concern the child, and the effectiveness of the child's coping efforts in any attempt to master or control the threat inherent in the situation. How might each of these factors help structure the particular script likely to be formed?

Cognitive Capacities

Children often witness only part of a parental fight. For instance, a child may hear screaming or thumps through the bedroom walls or overhear threats and accusations from one side of a telephone conversation, or, in the aftermath of a fight, may see broken furniture or a blackened eye, or hear helpless sobbing. The child is then left to surmise the whole of the scene from these fragments. The meaning the child constructs is partly influenced by his or her cognitive capacity for perspective taking. According to social cognitive theory, this capacity provides a foundation for the development of interpersonal understanding, defined as the way children understand and reason about themselves, other people, and the interactions between them (Flavell et al., 1968; Selman, 1980).

The development of interpersonal understanding parallels the child's increasing ability to move beyond the boundaries of his or her own point of view in order to understand, maintain, and differentiate that point of view from the perspectives of others. A preschool child with an egocentric perspective and intuitive logic may form primitive scripts based on magical thinking that does not grasp the existence of any other point of view. For example, 5-year-old Amy explained that she was magic, "'cause when I come into the room, my mom and dad stop fighting." She went on to explain, "When I go to bed, I leave my magic by the door and it stops them fighting in the night!"

The younger school-age child who has developed the capacity to grasp another's perspective (as well as his or her own) but can keep in mind only one perspective at a time (unilateral perspective taking) will typically experience incidents of conflict from only one parent's point of view, and will then develop scripts for understanding herself, and relationships, that involve simple, concrete, one-way interactions: "My mom is mean, she yelled at my dad and he was sad. I make him happy!"

The older school-age child, who can now begin to hold in mind two other perspectives simultaneously (bilateral perspective taking), views the scene in a more complex way: "My dad hurt my mom's feelings. He said she was fat. She yelled at him and called him bad words. Then he hit her. After, I talked to her and she feels better."

The adolescent, with the capacity to hold everyone's perspective in mind as he or she scans the various possible outcomes of different actions (third-person perspective capability), can recall the same scene with more detachment. In this case, the script that evolves is likely to be more abstract and general, and involve a transaction between family members: "My parents are always cursing each other and calling each other bad names, and then they start hitting. If they've been drinking, there's not much I can do. I just leave."

The thesis proposed here, which is supported by our clinical observations, is that the complexity of the script (i.e., the extent to which it includes, differentiates, and integrates different viewpoints and hence corresponds to good reality testing) depends upon the perspective-taking capability of the child when the script was formed. Furthermore, it is hypothesized that once the script is formed, the unself-conscious injunctions embedded in it can, in turn, delimit further development of the child's perspective-taking ability under conditions that signal the threat. For example, children whose scripts dictate that they remain aligned (or, more primitively, merged) with one parent against the other are severely limited in their ability to take the first step beyond egocentrism toward differentiation of self and other. When this first social cognitive achievement is disrupted, further growth toward an increasingly differentiated, reality-based appraisal of self and others cannot proceed normally, unless the script can be made conscious and available for revision.

During her preschool years, Jane was exposed to frequent terrifying scenes in which her parents would get into a brawl late at night. Her hysterical mother would pull her out of bed and literally hold her as a shield against the angry father. The father would then back off. Years later, at crisis periods during the protracted, bitter litigation over property and child custody, Jane suddenly became inexplicably phobic and angry toward her loving father. She merged completely with her mother's negative views and refused to visit him. She could not remember anything about the good times she had had with him, and construed all of his attempts to invite her back to him as dangerous. It was not until those early memories were reviewed and reworked in therapy that she was able to tolerate her mother's periodic rages against the father, without making this irrational alignment.

Emotional Issues

The thematic content of a script derived from a traumatic scene may be determined in part by the emotional issues being confronted by the child at that particular stage of his or her development (Erikson, 1963; Mahler et al., 1975). For example, consider a situation in which three boys from the same family witness their father hitting their mother. The 2-year-old, who is normally preoccupied with concerns about separation, will be the most anxious about the emotional unavailability of his mother to comfort him during the stressful experience. The script he develops for understanding and managing his relationships is likely to have a theme of separation and abandonment. The 5-year-old will probably focus on the father's wrath, seeing it as a potential attack upon himself because of his oedipal fantasies (i.e., his eroticized longing for exclusive possession of the mother and her resources). The thematic content of his script will probably reflect issues of competition and revenge. The attention of the 8-year-old, who is concerned about mastery, will more likely be captured by the exercise of power and control by the aggressive father and the induction of submission in the victimized mother. If so, the thematic content of his script will be about maintaining superiority and control and avoiding inferiority and helplessness.

There are indications from longitudinal observations (Terr, 1988, 1990) that the original traumatic scene can be reworked in the child's memory so that, as the child's central concerns shift over time, the content of the script reflects new developmental themes. Scripts can also be surfaced and reworked by children in conversation and play with their parents and peers, or they may be reconstituted within therapy. It is possible, however, for the script to remain fixed at its point of origin. This underscores the need to take a careful history about traumatic scenes witnessed at early ages and at critical developmental stages.

The Effectiveness of the Child's Coping Responses

The ways in which the child and the child's caretakers respond to violent scenes are likely to have profound effects on the kinds of scripts or expectations developed by the child. Typical primary responses (i.e., responses not mediated by cognitive processing) to acutely threatening scenes are freezing, flight, or fight. In younger children, freezing is the most common response, immediately followed by signs of distress such as crying and clinging. If these responses relieve the child's initial anxiety, they are likely to be reinforced and become a part of the child's script. Other, more complex defenses may be used, including dissociation, denial, repression, somatic responses, and splitting. An example is Jason, who typically hyperventilated in response to his mother's screaming tirades; this immediately quieted her and induced her solicitous concern for him. Another example is Brenda, a product of a bitterly feuding divorce, who appeared to block out the visual image of her beloved father and denied that she could see him when she happened to meet him on the street while she was in the company of her angry mother.

An episode of intense parental conflict or a scene of domestic violence usually produces a flood of negative emotions that the script serves to ward off or manage. These include primary affective responses such as fright or helplessness, and secondary emotions such as shame, guilt, a sense of injustice, or a wish for revenge. These negative feelings can be overwhelming, especially when amplified by the child's own aggressive fantasies (unconscious rivalries or destructive wishes).

Watching her parents argue through a barely opened door, 7-year-old Ricki clenched her fists and prayed to God to stop her father from killing her mother. In actuality, her father had done no more than slap her mother, and that only once; but Ricki, at the time, was furiously angry because her mother was abusive toward her. Her unconscious, angry wish—and her terrifying fear—was that her mother would be murdered.

Children's unconscious rules for how to defend against intolerable feelings—anxiety, fearfulness, shame, blame, helplessness, badness—will probably become embedded in their scripts. As will be shown in the following chapters, the complexity of their defenses and the coping skills available to them depend partly upon their developmental stage. Some children repress their intolerable feelings from conscious awareness. Repression of emotion inhibits children's capacity to perceive, understand, and tolerate their own and other's feelings. As a result, their interpersonal understanding may have a mechanistic quality in which behavior is detached from emotional motivation and is frighteningly difficult to predict or manage outside the confines of the script.

Children who are more primitively organized may cope, for example, by being aggressive, grandiose, and defiant with their peers at school but will be constricted, robotic, and defeated with their embittered and intermittently violent parents. These children do not subjectively experience the extruded feelings of fear and helplessness when they become aggressive and grandiose. Therefore, they cannot perceive or empathically understand the fear and helplessness their behavior evokes in their peers. Clearly, this coping style not only mitigates against basic self-integration but also disrupts the achievement of empathy, the basis for interpersonal morality.

More sophisticated coping responses (i.e., responses mediated by cognitive processing and complex emotional reactions) may be employed and incorporated into the script, especially by older children. These include throwing oneself between the fighting parents; distracting them by being naughty, charming, or seductive; having an "accident"; actively avoiding the situation by retreating from the scene; or engaging in different kinds of role reversal (e.g., taking care of siblings or performing special chores and services for the distressed parent).

Over time, these increasingly consolidated coping responses define a scripted role for the child that becomes embedded in his or her internal working model of family relationships. These specific responses to their parents tend to generalize into their other relationships. The mechanisms by which this occurs continue to be the subject of ongoing study. Here are two examples of this kind of generalization.

Four-year-old Emma typically curled up and went to sleep in the back seat of her mother's car whenever her father and mother started violently fighting over her at the time of her exchange for visitation. Three years later, her parents had settled their disputes, but in altercations with her peers, Emma was noted to become extremely passive, languid, almost somnolent.

Eight-year-old Michael, who had long managed his parents' frequent fighting, was typically controlling with his peers. When minor disputes arose on the playground, he would interfere and "supervise," much to the resentment of his classmates.

Sometimes these scripts appear to lie dormant for years, until the young person tries to form intimate relationships or becomes a parent (Egeland et al., 1987; 1988). When observing these disturbing, even tragic cases, however, it is important to remember that, fortunately, these are not the outcomes for the majority of children who have witnessed violence (Kalmuss, 1984; Kaufman & Zigler, 1987; Widom, 1989; Zeanah & Zeanah, 1989). Lacking good long-term studies, we do not yet fully understand why many children grow up without repeating these early patterns, while a significant and disturbing minority, like Carrie and Jose, described below, become victims or victimizers.

Carrie's parents' violent marriage ended in divorce when she was in preschool. Never again did she witness her father hit her mother. In her late teens, however, she began living with an abusive young man. When asked why she tolerated his violence, she answered simply, "Because he loves me—I know he loves me because he hits me!" (Wallerstein & Blakeslee, 1989).

Ten-year-old Jose witnessed his drunken, jealous father beat up his mother on several occasions. Each time the boy tried to throw himself between his parents to protect his mother, he himself was hit, which made him feel small, helpless, and ashamed. This boy grew up with a seething rage at his father and intermittently suffered a brooding depression. At age 17, Jose fell in love for the first time and quickly became intensely possessive of his girlfriend. Then she broke off the relationship. Feeling again powerless and shamed, he took a gun and threatened to kill her.

IMPLICATIONS

Whereas highly significant scenes (in these cases, incidents of frightening conflict and violence) originally create the script (with its rules and expectations about relationships), the script itself tends to guide the child's appraisal, emotions, and management of subsequent interpersonal events (Dodge & Somberg, 1987; Dodge et al., 1990). When the child is confronted with a threat of repeated conflict or violence, the script, or expectation, is quickly activated in response. In fact, in these highly vigilant children, defenses and coping responses embedded in the script can be triggered by minimal cues or enacted to preempt confrontation and conflict.

In summary, children exposed to distressing scenes of interparental conflict, especially those that include violence, manage their distress, make sense of what is happening, and control their world by forming a defensive script of family relationships, which then becomes the prism through which they view the world. In other words, when danger is perceived where refuge should be, children tend to cope by developing increasingly rigid and constricted patterns of feeling, thought, perception, attention, and memory, which become organized as largely unconscious "rules" for scanning and controlling interpersonal contact.

Without intervention, these patterns, or scripts, form a prism that allows in signals of interpersonal threat while more benign information is filtered out. As a result, such children feel, paradoxically, both confirmed in their view of the interpersonal world as dangerous and yet safe, because they can scan for and control the threat. As these patterns consolidate, they mitigate against the child's capacity to trust others and to tolerate intimacy with others. The *prism* therefore becomes a *prison*, as children's opportunities for cognitive and emotional growth are limited to the confines of the script. The result, to varying degrees, is emotional constriction, avoidance of feelings and genuine interpersonal contact, difficulty experiencing empathy with others, and distortions in moral reasoning and conduct.

Children show a wide range of adaptations, depending upon individual temperament and other buffering resources available within the family and community. In the following chapters, we show how children at each developmental stage are affected differently. Those who are younger tend toward the more severe forms of developmental distortion and arrest but seem more amenable to change when their family situation improves. Older children often appear to be more resilient to the acute stress associated with divorce conflict, but if given no relief from chronic conflict, they are likely to show consolidated disturbances that are more resistant to intervention.

PART II

THE DEVELOPMENT OF CHILDREN IN HIGH-CONFLICT FAMILIES

INTRODUCTION TO PART II

*W*hen parents in a conflicted divorce seek mediation, evaluation, or psychotherapy services from mental health professionals, they are likely to approach the process with an agenda that can be understood at two levels. Fundamentally, the agenda of each parent is to solicit the professional's alliance. Although the parent may not acknowledge or even be conscious of this covert intent, it is likely to be experienced quite forcefully by the professional. The pressure on the consultant is to unilaterally support one parent as being entirely good and to see the other parent as entirely bad. For example, one mother (Mrs. H) described herself as the loving, primary parent. She described the children's father, on the other hand, as "a manipulative liar whose only interest was in the appearance of being a perfect father." The vehemence of the parent's presentation alone is likely to elicit a degree of empathy from the professional, if not outright suspicion toward the other parent. In the first meeting with the other parent, however, the professional is likely to experience an initial feeling of confusion, as that parent also emerges as a person with an understandable set of concerns and point of view. In Mr. H's first meeting, for example, he described himself as "the only safe harbor the children have ever had," because the mother was "a self-involved depressed woman whose own history makes it impossible for her to really parent her children." This covert pressure to solicit an alignment on the side of one parent against the other tends to be articulated as a concrete and particular intention to change the children's custody or visitation plan. Parents tend to justify the changes they request as the solution to difficulties their child is experiencing.

For younger children, these difficulties may involve unusually aggressive or regressive behaviors before or after visitation. Others experience physical complaints such as stomachaches, headaches, or asthma. Some parents observe sexualized behavior in their children. When this happens, one parent may conclude, all too quickly, that this symptom is proof that the other parent is molesting the child. Parents of older children often worry about signs of school failure or breakdowns in the child's social or extracurricular life. In a highly conflictual situation, each parent is likely to believe that these types of difficulties are the direct result of the other parent's harmful or subversive influence. Mrs. H complained that her 7-year-old son, Jason, was "hyped up after visits with his father and exhausted from all the crap they do together. . . . His father can't sit still for a minute. And Jason won't listen to me for a second when he gets home. . . . Next thing I know, he's crawling in my bed at night because he can't sleep alone. He needs a break from this . . . he's worn out from trying to keep up with his father. They have no real relationship, it's all just this running around!" Mr. H agreed that his son seemed agitated at the end of visits but felt that "he gets kind of hyper when he has to go back. . . . I can tell that he doesn't really want to leave me. I don't see why he has to either . . . and neither does he. What am I supposed to tell him!?"

The parents' views of themselves, of each other, and of the situation seem unconnected, and their ideas about what is best for the children are similarly polarized. Often, the visitation schedule becomes the focal issue, because it is here that the child's contact with the other parent can be regulated. The professional, in turn, may become overly involved with the minutiae of the scheduling disagreements and begin to shift support back and forth from one parent's perspective to the other. When this happens, a sense of clarity and position is lost. The result can be feelings of confusion, dissonance, and futility in the face of very real pressure from each parent. These feelings can serve as a window into the child's experience. It is the child's experience and point of view that are elucidated in Part II. It is the child's perspective that can create a fragile path through the quicksand of the parents' conundrum. Only when the child can be seen and understood as an individual separate from the parental conflict, and when the parents can be helped to reframe their agendas in terms of the child's concerns and preoccupations, can the professional then define his or her own position and advocate effectively for the child.

A SPECIAL NOTE TO THE READER

The following chapters are arranged in developmental sequence and are best understood as a hierarchical treatment of issues that will become layered within the child as he or she grows. For example, if the child is being seen for the first time at age 9, it will not be enough to read the school-age chapter (chapter 6). Rather, it will be important for anyone who wants to understand that 9-year-old to read the chapters that address the stage of life when that child was first exposed to parental conflict or violence. If the child was aged 2 at the marital separation (or was exposed to high levels of conflict or violence in the marriage at that time), it will also be important to read the chapters that discuss the developmental risks for toddlers and preschoolers (chapters 4 and 5).

When the details of the child's history are not clear, or when there are concerns that one or both parents may have a long-standing history of emotional vulnerability, we strongly recommend a careful reading about separation-individuation (in chapter 4), because it presents the organizing foundation of many subsequent difficulties and intervention strategies. What we are stressing here is that a child's history lives on within him or her. We cannot understand that inner landscape without knowing all the forces, past and present, that have contributed to its shape.

Chapter 4

Infants, Toddlers, and Preschoolers

Problems in Separation-Individuation

*W*hen very young children are exposed to chronic conflict between their divorced parents, their anxieties tend to become manifest as they transition back and forth from one parent's home to the other's. Their difficulties may include a range of behaviors such as crankiness, irritability, clinging to one parent, and physical resistance to the other parent. These problems often escalate when the child returns from a visit. Commonly described patterns include a period of defiance or irritability that the parent cannot soothe. This resistance is likely to be followed by signs of regression. The child may have difficulty sleeping alone at night, wake with nightmares, have toileting difficulties, or want a bottle that had been previously relinquished. Outside the home, youngsters may become unpredictably volatile with peers or controlling in their play. One mother described as follows her 2½-year-old's behavior when she returned from visits.

"She screams and cries for hours when she comes home. She won't let me touch her. The only thing that works is to talk about when she was a baby—that's how I have to seduce her back to me. I talk to her about what a great dad she has—but obviously he's not returning the favor! He's trying to turn her against me and show her what a crummy parent I am!" The father of this little girl, on the other hand, felt she was having tantrums because she did not want to return to her mother and should have more time with him.

Although the parents' individual concerns must be carefully considered, it is essential to understand what conflicts and anxieties the child may be trying to express or manage by means of these symptomatic behaviors. When the behavior can be understood from the child's point of view, both parents and professionals can respond more empathically and effectively. This chapter describes the developmental processes that ordinarily preoccupy young children and the ways in which parents' psychological vulnerabilities and bitter conflicts can distort these processes, generating insoluble internal conflicts and intolerable anxiety. It is these inner dilemmas that are expressed in behavior.

THE NORMATIVE PROCESS OF SEPARATION-INDIVIDUATION

To understand the young child's difficulties, it is useful to begin with a basic understanding of the normal developmental processes that may be disrupted by the parental conflict. To simplify the following discussion, we will mostly refer to the primary parent as the mother, though we do not assume this is necessarily the case. Sometimes the primary parent is the father, and sometimes both parents share primary caretaking responsibilities.

In the first three years of life, the child's most fundamental developmental achievement is to establish an authentic sense of self as a person physically and psychologically separate from the mother (or primary parent). If the child succeeds in this, the authentic self will fuel the child's sense of wholeness, inner vibrancy, and self-direction throughout life. Mahler and her colleagues (Mahler et al., 1975) referred to this process as *separation-individuation*. Mastery of this profoundly important process begins in infancy and depends upon the mother's fairly constant and empathic responsiveness to the child as a separate person. Take, for example, the mother's ordinary preoccupation with her baby's every coo and cry as she says, with a sort of weary pride, "That's just his little trying-to-settle-down noises." Or, "I'd better go up, she sounds like she's hungry." If the parent is accurately attuned to the child in a predictable way, a pattern of signaling and response develops between them. The mother may, for example, stay and rub her baby's back until he shifts from an agitated cry to his "settling-down noises," which she recognizes as the signal that her baby is now soothed and ready to sleep. Alternatively, the mother responds to cries that she identifies as hunger by scooping the baby up and feeding her. These accumulating moments form a pattern that help the child to feel he or she is a separate person in a responsive, predictable world. Over time, that pattern and the mothering functions embedded in it (acknowledging, soothing, and protecting) become part of the child's own inner repertoire for coping.

In optimal situations, this pattern of responsiveness is "good enough" (Winnicott, 1960); it need not be perfect. The best intentioned mother does not, nor should she, always understand her child with perfect empathy. As the child learns to master disruptions in the familiar patterns of care, he or she matures. In the early phases of the separation–individuation stage, the infant normally experiences these expectable variations in the patterns of care as actual changes in the mother's identity (Mahler et al., 1975); therefore, the child's sense of self in mother's care shifts responsively as well; that is, when the infant experiences the mother as empathically available and responsive, she is the *good-mother,* and the self in her care is the *good-mother-me.* When she is not available and responsive, she is the *bad-mother,* and the self in her care is the *bad-mother-me.* If the mother's response range is reasonably steady, the young child learns to trust that these seemingly separate or split self/other states will shift in predictable ways, because they are inseparable parts of an immutable whole.

When, for example, the young child drops his cup from his high-chair for the first time, the mother may smilingly bring it back to him. She may do this several times. After the tenth time, however, she may reasonably feel irritated and decide to take the cup away. For the child, she is, at that moment, the bad-mother, who is angry and uncomprehending. The child is likely to protest loudly when this unsettling event occurs. In his rudimentary way, he is disappointed, because the good-mother (who gratified by steadily replacing the cup and appreciating his play) has gone away and he does not like the bad-mother, who has taken her place. In this moment, the child experiences himself as the bad–mother–me, who has lost his milk and his play and who made the good-mother go away.

If the mother can create a reasonable and predictable balance between frustration and gratification, then the child grows in his capacity for integration. If, for example, she tolerates his loud protests or his tantrum about the lost cup without withdrawing, punishing, or capitulating, the child learns that no part of the self is so incomprehensible, intolerable, or overwhelming that it makes the good–mother go away forever. Over time, the mother's steadiness and predictability help the child to understand that the good–mother and the bad–mother are one and the same person. Similarly, the child learns that the good–mother–me and the bad–mother–me are aspects of one self.

This integration of contradictory feelings and experiences represents a major developmental achievement that has been referred to in both the psychological and the psychoanalytic literature as *object constancy* (McDevitt, 1975). This essential capacity allows the child to maintain a positive emotional attachment to another person, even in moments when that person is frustrating or ungratifying; that is, the child who has achieved object constancy can tolerate ambivalent feelings toward the same person and still value her or him for qualities not connected with need satisfaction (Burgner & Edgcombe, 1972). When this developmental achievement is in place, the child can learn to accept his or her whole self as a person who, like mother, has a shadow side. This unfolding tolerance supports the child's capacity for constant, realistic relationships that can survive frustration and ambivalence because they are founded on basic trust in the self and in others.

The Internalized Good-Mother

By toddlerhood, the child exploring physical separateness is increasingly practicing psychological autonomy as well. She borrows from patterns of responsiveness learned in infancy (the internalized good–mother) to feel reassured, to figure out feelings, and to calm down. The child uses the real mother for refueling when these efforts to fly solo are unsuccessful or overwhelming. For instance, 2-year-old Sara might trip while she is running gleefully away from her mother. She tries to soothe herself, whispering, "Sara fall down, kiss the booboo, all better." But if the sting is too much to bear, she will run to her mother for help. As the mother comforts her daughter, she helps her determine what is safe in the world beyond mother's orbit and supports her pleasure in "doing it myself." She may say, "Go ahead, Sara, you can run ahead, but when you get to the bricks you can walk slowly or wait for Mommy, because there are cracks that make you trip." This refueling and support of the child's mastery, in turn, becomes part of the internalized good–mother. The child can then continue to feel loved and protected not only by the real mother but also by the mother's internalized representation when she is absent. In the foregoing example, Sara may remind herself to stop when she gets to the brick part, just as her mother told her to do. In so doing, she calls upon memories and images of her mother's support and protection to take care of herself.

The Role of the Father in Supporting Individuation

The father has an increasingly central role to play as he excites and invites the young child to venture forth into the wider world. In a family with normally loving spouses, the mother will likely show much pleasure as the child relates to the father. She may say, for example, "Look, Daddy's home!" and smile as the child runs happily into his waiting arms. These separations from mother to father bring feelings of pleasure and excitement. The child is venturing out but not too far, using the father as a transitional person. Likewise, when the child can be in contact with the father without losing contact with the mother—when a little boy can wrestle with his father and still hear mother's laughter as she watches them together—then growing up and becoming separate need not cost him her love. The child learns he can find connections in other relationships and need not lose his mother in the process, that feelings of dependence can coexist with feelings of independence. This kind of integration is a blueprint for healthy intimacy, and intimacy is the cutting edge of maturation and the lifelong process of learning about the self, other people, and relationships.

DISRUPTIONS IN SEPARATION-INDIVIDUATION IN THE HIGH-CONFLICT DIVORCED FAMILY

In the high-conflict family, one or both parents tend to be psychologically fragile. This vulnerability may be due to the failure to achieve complete separation from the parents' own early caregivers, unresolved past experiences of traumatic loss, or the cumulative wearing down of psychological resources that characterizes the end of a failed marriage. These vulnerable parents struggle with a chronic sense of emptiness and remain dependent on others to help them fend off fears of abandonment and maintain a positive sense of self. Not surprisingly, they tend to see others as quite powerful, and they are highly vulnerable to loss, rejection, intrusion, or demands. Vulnerabilities in the parent are likely to disrupt the infant's and young child's separation-individuation process long before the marital separation occurs.

Predivorce Disruptions of the Separation-Individuation Process

The fragile primary parent's responses to the infant or young child are likely to be determined by how that parent feels at any given moment, rather than by the child's separate needs and experiences. Furthermore, the mother (usually the primary parent) may jealously guard the child's affections so that the father is marginalized. These combined circumstances leave the child particularly isolated and vulnerable to unpredictable shifts in one parent's emotional availability. The fragile mother may, for example, be able to comfort her young child when the mother herself is feeling calm and supported. In these moments, the child experiences her as the good-mother and the self as the good-mother-me that is part of her. On the other hand, if the mother is feeling particularly vulnerable, she may experience the child's cries as unreasonable demands that conspire to deepen her sense of helplessness and angrily refuse to help him. In these moments she is the bad-mother and the child in her care feels himself to be the bad-mother-me.

Because the mother's responses vary more with her own needs than with the child's, they do not cohere into a pattern the child can predict. As a result, the child lacks a foundation upon which to build an inner repertoire for coping. Instead, the child internalizes and maintains a split representation of the good-mother and the bad-mother, who come and go in ways that seem frighteningly random. In the face of this unpredictability, the child is likely to remain vigilantly focused on the parent, unconsciously learning how to keep the good-mother from disappearing. In a sense, the child becomes the soothing good-mother for the parent but cannot internalize a constant good-mother for him- or herself. Nurturing continues to come from outside the self but can never be taken for granted. Not surprisingly, separations are frightening for these ill-equipped children.

The dangers of individuation are further confirmed if the fragile primary parent feels shamed and rejected by the child's natural strivings for separateness and self-expression, and responds by becoming emotionally unavailable or punitive. In this situation, the child's inner fragmentation becomes intensified. The good-mother-me is increasingly experienced as the part of the self that does not separate but instead soothes, supports, and evokes the good-mother. The bad-mother-me is then associated with the child's normal strivings for autonomy, as well as with feelings that support these strivings, such as anger, power, and pleasure in mastery. In the context of this kind of relationship, the child's normal maturational impulses begin to arouse intense anxiety, because they make the good-mother go away, leaving the bad-mother in her place. The child's experience is paradoxically both powerful and frightening. He feels powerful enough to soothe the good-mother or to make her go away; at the same time, he is helplessly and unbearably vulnerable without her. Abandonment and engulfment are the twin fears that haunt these children.

Parents' Clinging Dependence at the Marital Separation

The child's developmental difficulties may intensify when the marriage ends, because the marital separation often evokes overwhelming terrors of abandonment within the fragile parent. These terrors may belong not only to the present but also to unresolved past experiences of rejection and loss. The parent is likely to cope by clinging desperately to the child. One mother, for example, described how, after meetings with her ex-husband, she would sit and rock her silent, compliant 2-year-old as she wept out her grief and rage. She said with a helpless shrug, "I know I shouldn't, but I have to depend on someone!" In such situations, it seems to the child as if the parent really might disappear or die without her. The power associated with the child's position can neither be realized nor relinquished. Instead, it binds the child to the fragile parent in a posture that shifts endlessly between helplessness and omnipotence. At the same time, the child's inner resources are consistently used to fend off abandonment rather than to support the emerging self.

The Father as a Toxic Figure

The child's difficulties with individuation are further heightened in the high-conflict situation when she tries to use the mother to figure out what is safe in the world beyond the mother's orbit. In the ordinary way of things, the mother signals not only that the father is safe but also that she derives pleasure from the child's contact with him. In the high-conflict situation, on the other hand, the mother is likely to signal (often nonverbally) that the father is toxic and potentially dangerous in ways that may have been foreshadowed before the separation by her repeated signals that the father was ineffective or irrelevant. The child's own experiences with the father may not confirm these signals, and so she becomes confused about what is real. Compounding the child's confusion is the fact that the mother is likely to draw comfort from believing that the child's experience of the father is just as negative as her own. The distressed mother and young child draw closer together as they share in a distorted view of the father. The double bind is that the availability of the good-mother depends upon the child's relinquishing her real feelings, memories, and perceptions associated with a positive connection to father. This bind is profoundly serious because father represents not only himself but also a bridge to the world beyond the primary relationship.

Exposure to Parental Violence

If the child is exposed to interparental violence, his fears of the bad-mother and confusion about the father's possible dangerousness are dramatically heightened. Separation becomes associated with brutality and victimization that is not only imagined but acted out in real life as well.

One 5-year-old boy described his memory, from age 3, of watching his father beat his mother: "I was closing my eyes really tight. I was trying to plug my ears. I didn't want to see the fight . . . he was gonna kick in the window. He was yelling at her, 'You little bitch, give me back my television.' I was thinking they'd just stop fighting . . . they'd notice I was there . . . I felt so scared they might hit me." Later, this boy made a drawing of the fighting. When asked why he made the people without faces, he said, "I didn't put any faces because . . . they didn't notice I was there."

These kinds of experiences clearly rub salt into the child's earliest wounds, heightening his fantasies about the potential of the unintegrated shadow side of himself and his parents, and compounding the feelings of helplessness and nonbeing that have already become associated with any stirrings of the autonomous self.

The Child's Hostile Dependent Bind

The hostile dependent bind that results from the young child's difficulties with separation-individuation is likely to affect the developmental course over the long term, as illustrated in the following projective story told by a 9-year-old girl named Tess.

In her first sandtray scene, Tess placed a mother doll in one corner with a girl doll at her side. She placed a father doll in the other corner. Tess began the play by picking up the mother doll and setting her down in a scrunched-up position. She then commented, "She's mad, she's always mad and sad. Let's leave her outside in the rain!" Tess became absorbed in pouring sand on the mother doll and was silent until she buried her. She then said with a kind of grim satisfaction, "We'll leave her there for 24 hours . . . we'll just leave her there!" At this point, Tess settled the girl doll down next to the buried mother doll. The counselor asked, "Is the girl staying then?" Tess responded, "Yeah." The counselor asked, "Won't she be hungry or thirsty or anything?" Tess answered, "Yeah, I guess . . . she'll go to the dad's and get food, and then she'll come right back and wait in the rain."

Here, Tess communicates clearly her inability to find gratification anywhere but within the unbreakable tie with her mother. It is a tie braided of helplessness, longing, and anger.

The Case of Frances J

How do these young children cope with the intolerable anxiety and confusion associated with separation from a fragile mother to a somehow dangerous father? The following case material describes the transition behavior of a 2½-year-old girl named Frances. Her parents, Mr. and Mrs. J, endured a brief but bitter marriage, which deteriorated into battles that were both verbally and physically abusive. When first seen at our service, they had just finalized a protracted court battle during which Mrs. J had sought and been refused the right to take her daughter back to live in Texas with the mother's family of origin. The parents continued to disagree about their time-sharing arrangement, and both justified their positions by complaining that Frances was having difficulty with transitions between the parents' houses. According to Mrs. J, "Frances is impossible at exchanges; she throws tantrums, she's obnoxious, and she can't seem to handle anything." Mr. J's description of Frances's difficulties was similar: "She just gets really quiet when I pick her up, and when I take her back she cries . . . she has this major tantrum, she slaps her mother, and she's like deaf to me."

Frances had been seen on previous occasions and had impressed the interviewer as a very self-contained little girl who looked older than her years, enjoyed showing the way to the playroom, and apologized if she dropped a marker on the floor. This impression of Frances's pseudomaturity was deepened when Mrs. J made a two-hour appointment to see a counselor at our service. When the counselor explained that she would need to see the mother alone, Mrs. J said that was fine, because Frances could play by herself in the playroom with no trouble. In fact, Frances did sit in the playroom for over two hours, without once disturbing the interview or straying from the little pile of toys and snacks her mother had provided. Mrs. J did not find this behavior in any way remarkable. Frances's good-mother-me posture disintegrated, however, at transitions, as illustrated by the following incident.

Transition from Mother to Father

Mr. J arrived at the prearranged time and sat in the corner of the waiting room in a chair to the left of the door. He did not speak but tapped his fingers anxiously as he waited for Mrs. J to arrive with Frances. Mrs. J arrived some five minutes later and approached the front door of the center with Frances molded to her hip. As soon as the front door opened, Frances caught sight of her father and scrambled to get down from her mother. It is not difficult to understand that Frances was beginning to anticipate this transition with a sense of danger. She was being helplessly propelled toward the bad-mother-me state (the visit with her father), risking the loss of the good-mother. Frances also knew there was a danger that the violence between her parents could happen again. This little girl's anxiety was further heightened by the fact that she understood, from her mother's signals, that she was approaching a parent who was bad, in a way that she could not completely comprehend. Frances stood silently, turning neither to her father nor to her mother for comfort. Mrs. J remained standing in the doorway, vibrating with rigid indignation.

Frances then walked to the center of the waiting room, about three feet from both parents. She seemed to be at a loss. In this moment, the loneliness of her double-binding situation was painfully apparent. She turned toward her father and opened her mouth wide, so he could see that she was eating something. It was a distant effort at contact and a test of her mother's mood. Mr. J asked Frances what she was doing, and Mrs. J hissed, her voice seething with impatience, "She's showing you she has candy in her mouth!" The epithet "You fool!" went unsaid but was hanging in the air. Frances clearly received the signal: neither separation from mother nor approach to father was safe. She began to twirl her hair around her fingers, then walked over and sat on the floor next to a small table where crayons and paper were spread out. She picked up the crayons, one at a time, without purpose.

It is important to emphasize here that neither parent moved to comfort or direct this child in any way. Frances's fears of abandonment were being realized as she attempted to navigate helplessly within the force field of her parents' mutual antagonism. For a child who was often omnipotently in charge of her parents' well-being, her present helplessness was all the more intolerable. After three or four silent and excruciating minutes, this undemanding, pseudocompetent child put her head down and began to whine, as she rubbed her face back and forth on the rug. Again, neither parent stepped in to comfort her—just as neither parent would later recall that Frances showed much difficulty with this transition. Finally, Mrs. J said, "Good-bye Frances, I'll see you when I get back," and left. Frances stayed where she was for several seconds; then when it was clear her mother had gone, she got up and climbed into her father's lap. Outwardly, she betrayed little of the panic and longing for the good-mother without which she was left to manage in her mother's absence.

Transition from Father to Mother

After two hours with her father, Frances came back to the waiting room, bearing the burden of her anxiety about her mother's very existence: Would Mother be there? Had she died or fallen apart without Frances? Would Mother still want her after she had consorted with the enemy? Would she accept the bad-mother-me, and could the good-mother somehow be evoked once again? As soon as she saw Mrs. J in the waiting room, Frances ran to her and began to whine and demand that she be taken out to buy a salad. It was an unusual choice for a 2½-year-old but effective in winning her mother's approbation. Mrs. J smiled in recognition. "This is something she likes to do just with me!" she confided to the counselor. Frances's panic and longing became apparent as she focused entirely on her mother, behaving as if Mr. J had disappeared. But Mr. J lingered on and asked Frances for a hug. She obliged, stiffly and with minimal contact, while Mrs. J stood by, barely tolerating the interaction. Frances immediately returned to Mrs. J and began to show signs of a tantrum. She became increasingly whiny, demanded to be picked up, to look in her mother's purse, to take off her glasses, and so on. She would not listen to her mother but badgered her angrily. It is not unusual for young children to express their frustration and rage in this way, resisting the mother's unspoken demand to relinquish their own autonomy and their connection to the father.

Some children feel angry with the mother for lying, because, after all, father was really nice and not bad as she said. The child's anger may also be fueled more or less consciously by the father. Mr. J, for example, exhorted Frances to behave. He reminded her not to have any more tantrums "when Daddy drops you off," because "it's hard for Mommy to manage." The unspoken message was that Frances had better take care of her mother, partly because he, too, was afraid of a scene. Frances dissolved into tears and arched her back as she was carried out to the parking lot by her mother, with father pacing along beside them. As she was put into the car, Mr. J asked for one more hug, all the while reminding Frances to be a good girl for her mother. Again, Frances was placed in an untenable double bind. The hug for her father in her mother's presence was emblematic of her dilemma: If Frances did not hug her father, he would be hurt. If she did hug her father, she risked her mother's rage and bad feelings. For Frances, being good meant being in the good-mother-me posture in which she nurtured, soothed, and avoided making demands. Frances might just be able to manage this posture with each of her parents separately; to do so with both simultaneously presented an insoluble conundrum.

Discussion of Frances's Family

The difficulties that Frances expressed in her transition behavior had their origins in the beginning of her parents' relationship. Mrs. J was a psychologically fragile woman, who had failed to achieve a complete sense of psychological separation from her own mother. Like many fragile parents, Mrs. J had also experienced a traumatic loss, in this case the unexpected death of an older sibling. This event resulted in the more subtle loss of her mother's emotional availability: "I never got my mom back after my sister died and I still feel that loss."

Mr. J presented himself as a passive man who believed he could handle almost anything. His mother died precipitously when he was 3. He said, "After that, Dad and I were always close . . . I was more passive, like him, but I was strong . . . I felt I had to lead my stepbrother and my brother, and they followed me like sheep." Early in his relationship with Mrs. J, he again felt he had to be strong. He said, "I view her as always making herself dependent on other people and expecting other people to solve things for her . . . I was her white knight." A relationship pattern developed in which Mrs. J controlled by being needy and demanding, and Mr. J acquiesced in the angry hope of satisfying his wife. This pattern was recapitulated when Frances was conceived. Mrs. J said about the pregnancy, "We planned her . . . I had been off the pill exactly a year and I decided we'd be careless." The pregnancy came as a surprise to Mr. J. He said, "I didn't feel ready, you know, to be a father, but I knew it was what she really wanted and I thought that the baby would keep her happy." In a sense, Frances came into the world with a mission, "to keep her mother happy," which was unconsciously assigned to her by both parents.

For a while, the infant fulfilled her parents' hopes. As Mrs. J said, "I loved it at home with Frances. I was happier than I'd ever been." Mrs. J described her husband's involvement as marginal. As a result, Frances was left to cope alone with her mother's frightening and unpredictable emotional shifts. Her father, in the meantime, became increasingly withdrawn and essentially "tiptoed away" from any involvement in the family. Like many infants and young children in these situations, Frances was symptomatic at bedtime, when she needed to be able to separate and soothe herself. As Mrs. J remembered it, "Even when she was really little, getting her down at night was like putting her on the rack . . . sheer hell!"

When Frances was 6 months old, her father became involved in an extramarital affair. In recalling this period in the marriage, Mrs. J said, "I had no idea what was going on. I just spent all my time with Frances. I was breastfeeding her, and I swear, with how I was feeling, my milk should have gone sour!" Mrs. J's comments about her breast milk provided a stunningly accurate metaphor. Her increasingly anxious and angry dependence on Frances did produce a kind of toxic nurturing, which could not support the emergence of this child's authentic self. Many children with separation-individuation difficulties express this experience of toxic nurturing in their play as unpredictable shifts in being given food that is sometimes good and sometimes poison. Older children with separation-individuation difficulties tend to use the same metaphor to describe their own ambivalence in the relationship. As one 8-year-old girl played out over and over again, "She's feeding the mom sweet milk—No, it's really poop, but the mom doesn't know that!"

When Frances was 11 months old, Mr. J left the marriage. Mrs. J felt abandoned and helpless in ways that she had spent a lifetime trying to avoid. Mr. J, on the other hand, felt guilty and ashamed that he had failed to be "the white knight" for either his wife or his daughter and was humiliated by his own passivity. Not surprisingly, each parent became entrenched in familiar styles of coping. Mrs. J turned immediately to her family of origin and made plans to move back to Texas with her daughter as soon as possible. Mr. J sought to repair the shame about his passivity in the marriage by becoming a "white knight" for his daughter. Using his father's financial and emotional support, he legally opposed Mrs. J's decision to move. As he described this decision, he said, "I've accepted that she [Mrs. J] is not going to change but I've built my resolve to remain a person in Frances's life."

The legal dispute regarding Frances's custody and her mother's relocation went on for 22 months, until Frances's age of 2½. During that time, Mrs. J became increasingly depressed and entrenched in her conviction that moving back to Texas was the only course of action that could make life tolerable for her and her daughter. She said, "I have trouble getting out of bed, I don't balance my checkbook, I can't concentrate, and I repeat myself all the time. . . . Nothing's working!" During this time Frances was essentially left in the care of a mother who was apparently determined to become dysfunctional (unless and until the court would allow her to leave), and who obsessively focused on her need for time with her daughter: "All I want is more time with Frances! I feel like her day-care provider is her real mother!"

Frances felt increasingly isolated and, at the same time, incomprehensibly responsible for helping her mother to feel better. At the same time, her ideas about her father became more and more frightening as she overheard her mother's anguished nightly phone calls to Texas about what was being done to her by her ex-spouse. Frances had little opportunity to resolve her fears and fantasies about her father, as her contact with him was limited to brief midweek visits.

Transitions between parents encapsulated all of Frances's anxieties. According to Mr. J, his ex-wife used transitions to vent her anxiety and frustration: "Pick-up times are used as a forum for her to tell me what a son-of-a-bitch I am." Mrs. J concurred that transitions throughout the time of the court trial, and after, were conducted in an atmosphere of intense hostility that was barely contained. She said that Frances "senses my sadness and frustration when he comes to the door for her . . . like I'll say stuff to her like, 'Don't let Daddy steal you away.' I can't help it, I cry and I know she sees it. When she leaves it's like entering a black hole for me!"

It is difficult to imagine the fears of loss and abandonment that Frances endured during such separations. During one particularly traumatic episode, at her age of 15 months, Mr. J had gone to Mrs. J's home to pick up Frances for a visit. Mrs. J refused to let him take Frances, and Mr. J called the police to enforce the court order. A screaming exchange of obscenities ensued. When Mr. J tried to carry Frances to the door, Mrs. J kicked him in the groin. Mr. J put Frances down and "just managed to basically stagger out of the house!" Exposure to this type of violence naturally resulted in increased levels of tension and hyperalertness, which Frances would bring to all future transitions that involved both her parents. The fear she carried was that they might fight and hurt each other. And mother might fall apart or become violent with Frances in the same way that she was violent with father. This could happen if Frances tried to leave her, the same way father had done. At the same time, father might indeed "steal her away," because clearly he must be a bad man for mother to be so angry with him.

Frances's current difficulties were not limited exclusively to the transitions between her parents. She continued to have trouble sleeping separately from either parent. Mrs. J pronounced herself exhausted by Frances's nighttime demands, which she believed resulted from Mr. J's insensitive handling of the child's worries. For his part, Mr. J said, "She has scenes with me about sleeping by herself. She wants me to leave the lights on, and I just feel that someone has to be firm with her and she'll come around. She wraps her mother around her little finger!" Each parent attributed Frances's difficulties to some aspect of his or her own conflict and managed them accordingly: Mrs. J would not support Frances's capacity to master sleeping alone, and Mr. J ignored her very real terrors.

Mr. J's inability to empathize with Frances contributed to her sense of loss and abandonment whenever she separated from her mother to visit her father. It should be remembered that this was a child who likely had little opportunity to internalize a good-mother that she could draw upon for comfort in times of stress. Her capacity for self-soothing was therefore very limited and her dependence on others extreme. When Mr. J would not comfort her during their visits, she was indeed lost in a void. Not surprisingly, Frances expressed ambivalence toward her father. According to Mr. J, she would literally grit her teeth together while saying "I love you." Frances both longed for her father and at the same time felt furious with him for hurting her mother. She would ask him, "Why do you take me away from Mommy? . . . Why do you make Mommy sad?" In a less conscious way, Frances was also angry with her father for abandoning her to the job of caring for her mother.

With her mother, Frances was at times undemanding and pseudomature (her good-mother-me stance), and at other times bossy and manipulative (her bad-mother-me presentation), shifting between feelings of helplessness and omnipotence. Mrs. J described her as "The Littlest Tyrant." She depended on Frances utterly, and Frances, in turn, had little choice but to cling to her. In her relationships with both parents, Frances's angry feelings were often expressed but never acknowledged. In day care, Frances's feelings could not be contained; they escaped from her in ways that seemed to lack rhyme or reason, because they could not be directed to their real objects. As the day-care provider described Frances, "She's got aggression in her. She'll just go up to kids and push them in the face—pinching, scratching, and hair-pulling, out of the blue. . . . She wants discipline; she can be really testy and I don't give in to her, but I think her parents probably do."

IMPLICATIONS FOR INTERVENTION

What interventions are the most likely to soothe young children like Frances, calm their symptomatic behaviors, and protect their developmental progress? Ask the parents and their answers are likely to point to the visitation schedule, because the schedule determines who is going to be the primary player and receive the "good parent seal of approval." In the first available research of its kind, Solomon and George (1996) evaluated the effects of various custody arrangements and levels of conflict in divorced families on the adjustment patterns of infants and toddlers up to 3 years of age. These researchers concluded that infants and toddlers in low-conflict situations, although expectably stressed by overnight visitations, were likely to remain securely adjusted in a wide range of scheduling arrangements. Low-conflict situations allowed the parents to have ongoing and detailed communication that supported the abilities of each to respond empathically to her or his child. In contrast, infants and toddlers making transitions between highly conflicted parents, who could not communicate about their child in this way, appeared to be insecure, disorganized, and anxious regardless of the schedule. Under either condition, it is clear that the schedule alone does not account for differences in young children's adjustment and cannot substitute for the kind of working relationship that parents must develop. This reframing of the agenda—that is, focusing on the parents' communication rather than on the schedule—is the first order of business when beginning an intervention with highly conflicted parents of infants and young children. In this approach, the schedule is defined as an important buffer that may be necessary but is certainly not sufficient to ensure the well-being of the young child. To address the schedule only is like providing a paper parasol in a hurricane. As might be expected, the parasol constantly has to be taped up or replaced.

Parenting Interventions

When the child is struggling with separation-individuation in a high-conflict situation, there are two focal points in the therapeutic work with parents: first, to address the panic of separation in the mother (or primary parent), and second, to heighten the father's (or nonprimary parent's) attunement to the child in areas where empathic understanding is truly lacking. This process requires the mental health professional to function as a neutral figure who can maintain a reasonably accurate and compassionate representation of the child's experiences and concerns. In this role, it is essential to assess each parent's capacities as fully as possible. This cannot be done without taking a thorough history of each parent in his or her own nuclear family. Without an understanding of the parents' own issues and conflicts, it becomes impossible to identify their effects on the present crisis. The history may indicate, for example, that one or both parents may themselves have failed to achieve a complete separation from a primary parent, leaving them dependent and lacking in inner resources. When the marital separation occurs, such parents experience a sense of panic that cannot be fully appreciated without an understanding of its earliest origins. The marital separation (as well as the child's attempts at individuation) may also evoke feelings connected to previous losses that remain unresolved. Vulnerable parents often cope with these stresses in inflexible ways that are difficult to modify. In the case of Mrs. J, for example, the early loss of her sibling (as well as her mother's subsequent withdrawal) left her vulnerable to fears of abandonment and feelings of helplessness. She tried to avoid these feelings by controlling her present-time relationships as much as possible. Not surprisingly, Mr. J's withdrawal and her subsequent loss of control over her marriage and exclusive relationship with Frances were intolerable. Mrs. J responded by becoming all the more intractable and controlling in the postdivorce situation. Mr. J had learned to manage the loss of his mother (at his age of 3) by avoiding his own emotional needs, while stoically taking on practical care of himself and his siblings. Mr. J tended to recapitulate this role in his adult relationships. When their histories can be understood, the depth of each parent's intransigence in the face of his or her current crisis can be also understood more empathically.

When the parents have some capacity for self-reflection, the mental health professional can begin to help them differentiate those aspects of their responses that belong to the present from those that belong to previous trauma. Mr. J, for example, had been able to make use of psychotherapy since his divorce and was beginning to understand aspects of the passive-aggressive style that propelled him into the position of an ambivalent and resentful caretaker. This insight was essential in getting him to acknowledge his current confusion about his role in Frances's life; that is, he wanted more time with his daughter, but he was afraid that Mrs. J would fall apart without her. As a result, he blocked the move to Texas but did not insist on the kind of time with Frances that he wanted or felt she needed. As Mr. J began to come to terms with his ambivalence and to see that he had essentially placed Frances in the role of her mother's caretaker, he became more specific about the kind of time-sharing arrangement he wanted. When he was able to be clearer about what he really wanted, Mrs. J was able to calm her fears that he was planning to take Frances away from her forever.

Careful assessment of the parents' histories and present functioning can also help the mental health professional to evaluate their capacity to be empathic with their child. This essential quality depends on the parents' ability to tolerate a full range of feelings in themselves and to understand that the child also has a range of feelings that are separate and distinct from their own. Evaluation of this capacity occurs naturally as the therapist attempts to heighten each parent's empathic understanding and, in the process, discovers her or his degree of openness and flexibility. For example, when the therapist reviewed with the parents her written description of Frances's transition, she was attempting to counteract their denial of their daughter's helplessness and isolation and to provide instead a compassionate interpretation of the child's experience. Mr. J used the interpretation to think about changes in his parenting behavior that could more effectively support Frances's needs. Mrs. J, on the other hand, understood the interpretation but could not hold on to it. As a result, part of the work in each session was to help this mother recall her understanding of Frances's experience and separate it from her own. When this kind of groundwork has been done successfully, each parent will begin to think differently about the child or at least be able to tolerate the therapist's point of view about the child as a separate person.

Addressing the Panic of Separation in the Anxious Parent

At this point, the therapist can begin to sort out the anxious parent's realistic concerns about the child's separations from those that are distorted by his or her own needs. When this sorting-out process occurs in the presence of an empathic and respectful other, the anxious parent has the opportunity (often for the first time) to fully articulate his or her worries without being dismissed as hysterical, hypersensitive, or overcontrolling. Mrs. J, for example, was realistically concerned about Frances's safety with Mr. J because he frequently took her on visits to his parents' home, which had an unfenced swimming pool. No matter how much Mr. J reassured his former wife that he would watch Frances at every step, Mrs. J did not feel comfortable with the situation. Mr. J tended to dismiss her concerns as one more example of her need to control every move he made. The therapist, however, supported Mrs. J's concerns and asked Mr. J to arrange for the use of a temporary fence. At the same time, Mrs. J was equally concerned that Frances should not be exposed to Mr. J's girlfriend, claiming that the child would be confused about who her real mother was. This issue reflected Mrs. J's own worries about her capacities to be a competent and nurturing parent, because she herself lacked an internalized good-mother. Mrs. J's anxiety about her capacity to be a good mother was a real concern that required careful attention. However, it could not be resolved by erasing Mr. J's girlfriend from Frances's life but rather by focusing on Mrs. J's own parenting skills and supporting her as she struggled to find a way to be more nurturing and less demanding of her daughter. The therapist's sorting-out process was framed by a pragmatic consideration of the child's safety and emotional well-being. Once Mr. J understood this and could see that Mrs. J's panic about Frances would not automatically translate into full control of his every move, he became more cooperative. Mrs. J was soothed enough by the concrete validation of some of her concerns that she was able to tolerate the redirection of others. Optimally, in families like this one, each parent begins to internalize this sorting-out process on the child's behalf, again, depending on his or her capacities.

Addressing the Attunement of an Excluded Parent

Often, the primary parent in a highly conflictual situation will communicate realistic concerns about the nonprimary parent's ability to be appropriately responsive and nurturing with the infant or young child. These concerns commonly arise when the father has been excluded from involvement with the child during the marriage. When the marriage ends, the continuing exclusion of the father may be justified by the mother's now legitimate concerns that he cannot parent adequately, because "he never has." The father may heighten the child's and the anxious parent's fears by treating the child's very real terrors about separations as if they have been swallowed whole from the mother and can be dismissed once the child is with him. In these situations, the father may attempt to reassert control by dealing insensitively or even harshly with the frightened child.

For example, as noted earlier, Mr. J tended to be dogmatic and impatient when Frances had difficulty sleeping alone, and his unsympathetic response left Frances feeling panicked and helpless. In the parenting intervention, it was useful to help Mr. J acknowledge that he had missed many opportunities to get to know his daughter during the marriage. In fact, Mr. J felt very angry as well as guilty about his passive acceptance of a marginal parenting role. Once these feelings could be discussed, Mr. J began to think about working more actively toward understanding and supporting Frances in the present. As the work with Mr. J progressed, the counselor, in turn, was able to reassure Mrs. J that Frances was now getting more of the kind of support she needed when she was in her father's care. Again, this reasonable consideration of her concerns helped Mrs. J trust the therapist to provide a "reality check" whenever she began to worry about Frances.

ACTIVE STRATEGIES FOR SOOTHING THE CHILD

Verbal and Nonverbal Transition Rituals

The work described above sets the stage for the parents to begin developing collaborative strategies that will actively help their child to master separations. They start by learning to pay careful attention to what they communicate to the child verbally (intentionally) and nonverbally (unintentionally) at transitions. One need only sit with highly conflicted parents in the same room (before either has spoken a word) to understand how easily their hostility and tension can be absorbed from the atmosphere alone. Physical communications and facial expressions can easily heighten the tension. An infant (particularly the infant already hypersensitive to mood states in her caretakers) can become anxiously disorganized when she sees the mother's face grimace with worry or feels the father's tight grip on her arm. After all, it is these proprioceptive and physical cues, rather than verbal information, that regularly guide the infant's experience of relationships (Stern, 1985). Reassurance to the infant or young child depends upon the parent's heightened awareness and willingness to control these nonverbal communications.

Infants' and young children's anxieties can also be calmed when parents establish rituals that support the child's capacity to tolerate the back-and-forth separations. For the preverbal child, such rituals largely depend on concrete activities and rhythms that help to signal the transition in a predictable way. An example might be when transitions are scheduled to take place shortly after a predictably occurring activity in the child's day, such as lunch or a nap. Some aspect of the activity can be used to signal the upcoming transition (i.e., use of a particular plate at lunch or blanket for the nap). Parents may also develop gestures that communicate a visit is soon to begin. Recent developmental research (Acredolo & Goodwyn, 1996) has indicated that preverbal toddlers can make highly effective use of gesturing with their parents and other caregivers to communicate and receive information. This signaling may be followed by any number of rituals intended to reassure the child of the parent's calm support of the impending separation. For example, the parent and child may sing a familiar song together as they gather up the child's belongings and transitional objects. For the young child faltering in the process of internalizing the good-mother, transitional objects that represent her and calm the child become powerfully important. Some transitional objects may already be in place and readily identifiable—blankets, stuffed animals, a favorite sweater (no matter how ratty and old). For other children, transitional objects need to be identified, or created, with more conscious effort: a photograph of each parent, a tape recording of the parent's voice, or even a pet. This ritualized gathering up of the child's things is like putting together the resources that he or she will need to "make the crossing." It takes on particular importance when the child makes the transition alone, without, say, a sibling to buffer the stress of separation. As the mother helps the child to "gather herself" in this way, she is actively supporting the child's separation. The ritual may be repeated when the child arrives at the home of the father, as they carefully unpack the child's bag and identify the contents one by one. Creating a special place for the child to keep his or her belongings can further help the child to feel anchored when making transitions.

Contrast this ritualized soothing process with Frances's experience as both her parents, struggling to tolerate the presence of each other, remained frankly unaware of their daughter's solitary struggle. We have seen parents in similarly conflicted situations fight over their child's transitional objects or refuse to allow the child to take these symbolic possessions from one home to the other. Some completely strip the child of clothing at the exchange or return the child in dirty, torn attire because of disputes over ownership of the "good" clothes. One man took the photo of her mother that his 2-year-old daughter was clutching and threw it on the street, declaring to the mother, "She doesn't want a picture of your ugly old mug!" Many parents refuse to acknowledge the existence of the other parent when the child is with them. "We never talk about you . . . we have better things to talk about!" one man snickered to his ex-wife. Others unilaterally refuse to allow the child to talk on the telephone to the absent parent or even to provide a phone number where the other parent can be reached, "because it intrudes on my time with my child." All such experiences disrupt the child's sense that the self is a constant—across time, settings, and relationships.

As the young child becomes more verbal, the parents can also begin to talk him or her through the anticipated transition sequence. The parent may say, for example, "Today is Friday. You see your dad today. We will do what we always do. You will come home from the baby-sitter's and we will pack your bag. You can pick out what you want to take [this may include any number of transitional objects]. I will read our special book [see below for an example] . . . then Daddy will come. You will say good-bye and give Mom a hug and a kiss, and then you will go in the car to Daddy's house. When you go, I'll work for a while, and then I'm planning a hike with Mathilda. I'll miss you on the hike because I love doing the long trails with you, but you'll have a good time with your dad, and we'll do a long trail together next week. When you get to Daddy's, you will unpack like you always do and put your things in their special place. Then you will go to McDonald's like you always do . . . then it will be time for a bath . . . just like at Mommy's. Then Daddy will read the special book to you as well." A similar variant can then be used by the father when the child is preparing to leave and return to mother. (The "special book" that is referred to here may be *The Runaway Bunny* [Brown, 1942] or *Love You Forever* [Munsch, 1986]. Both books tell stories that reassure very young children about the constancy of their parents' love.)

The "talking-through" process can be accomplished during appropriate windows of opportunity (i.e., when bathing or traveling in the car), and the essential portions can be repeated during the actual transition. This kind of communication contains several messages to the anxiously separating child. First, that she is held lovingly in mind while absent (i.e., the child does not disappear into the void of the bad-mother-me). Second, that the parent can be self-supporting in the child's absence. Third, that the parent will welcome the child back upon her return (i.e., the good-mother will be constant).

The more concrete and detailed these recitations, the more reassured the child will be. It is useful, for example, for one parent to know enough about the other parent's plans to talk about them out loud. This not only helps the child to feel more in control as he anticipates the transition and the activities that will follow, but it also represents the parent's acknowledgment of the child's reality with the other parent. This acknowledgment can actively counter the fragile parent's tendency to treat the child as if he essentially ceases to exist until it is time to return.

Many variants of these transition rituals can be developed, depending on what is familiar and soothing to the individual child. In some respects they are identical to the type of ritual that most parents would ordinarily use to help their child anticipate any difficult separation, such as going to a babysitter, entering preschool, or going to play at a new friend's house. Ironically, the young child's needs for exactly this type of anticipatory preparation and calming are the most intense yet the least recognized within the high-conflict transition.

ACTIVE COPING STRATEGIES FOR THE CHILD

In addition to transition rituals, parents can actively teach their children coping strategies. These suggestions can provide a means of relief for parents who have been repeatedly told what they should not do but have not been helped to develop practical alternatives. For example, the parent and child may draw a picture of the child's space or room at the other parent's house. The parent need not have seen the room to elicit the child's description by asking, "Where shall we put the bed? the dresser?" and so on. The child can then be helped to draw in where the transitional objects, clothes, and other items will be placed when they are unpacked. Some children may need to place the actual objects on the drawing. Each moment that the parent can remain calm and interested in the child's experience with the other parent is a moment in which the child feels reassured that the separation can be tolerated. Additionally, the parent may use role playing and puppets or other representational toys to act out the transition with the young child. When the transition is acted out, the verbal child may volunteer (or the parent may suggest) feelings or worries associated with the transition.

Parents can also be helped to develop stories that communicate understanding and reassurance to the child. These often involve animal characters who represent identifiable qualities in each parent and in the child. These stories essentially communicate to the child, "I understand how it is for you. I know that it is hard. Your reality (which I know is separate from mine) makes sense to me, and I will support you as best I can." They can be told in moments of stress and are particularly soothing at bedtime, when anxious children are particularly vulnerable. (Examples of these types of stories may be found in a companion volume, *Through the Eyes of Children: Healing Stories for Children of Divorce,* Johnston et al., 1997, New York: Free Press).

Bedtime rituals that are an orderly and predictable progression of events leading to sleep can be very important for highly anxious children. Mr. and Mrs. J were helped to develop such a ritual for Frances's bedtime. It began soon after dinner and involved the kind of step-by-step preparation common in many households (i.e., bath, brushing teeth, reading a story, etc.).

In working with highly conflicted parents, the difference is simply that the elements of the ritual are consciously identified and used as tools to support the child's separation. In addition to the bedtime ritual and a mutually agreed upon time for going to bed, Frances had charge of the lights in her bedroom. She was also allowed free access to a range of transitional objects, which began with a torn and dirty blue blanket and eventually (as the parents began to understand their daughter's needs with increasing empathy) came to include her dog. Large "watch-bears" were a later addition. These stuffed animals were set up at either end of Frances's bed, and she was continually reassured they would stay awake all night to guard her. Frances took particular delight in listening to each parent's stern instructions to these bears to "watch over Frances all night long and don't you dare take a wink of sleep!" Frances was also given a child's tape recorder at bedtime, with which she listened to story and singing tapes as well as poems that her mother and father had recorded. Finally, if all her other efforts to sleep failed, Frances was occasionally allowed to bring a sleeping bag into her mother's or father's room.

As these strategies were being established, the therapist worked separately with each parent to help both actively encourage Frances's mastery of sleeping separately and to monitor any nonverbal communications that may have countered their verbal encouragement. From Mr. J's point of view, these strategies were consistent with his intention to help Frances feel more independent. Mrs. J, however, did not respond so readily at first. She worried that Frances would feel unloved if she were not comforted and cuddled enough. Unconsciously, she felt shut out by these efforts to help Frances toward greater autonomy. It was important to help her understand that good mothering includes protecting but also supporting, so that "Frances can feel proud of herself." As these strategies took hold and Frances became less symptomatic, Mrs. J's confidence increased and she began to feel like the capable and good mother that she longed to be. More pragmatically, she was exhausted by her daughter's nighttime difficulties, and she was relieved when their efforts began to help Frances soothe herself to sleep.

NEUTRAL TRANSITIONS

The child's feelings of safety during transitions can be heightened by the presence of a benign third party, in the presence of whom both parents feel constrained to behave well. This is particularly true if the child has been exposed to verbal hostility or violence in the past. When a neutral third party is not available, and parents cannot manage their feelings in the presence of each other, the child may be best protected if transitions occur in a neutral setting and do not involve both parents at the same time. Often the neutral setting is at the child's day-care center or baby-sitter's home.

When the young child makes transitions from a setting other than home, it is especially important that the care provider be fully informed of the schedule and alerted on a daily basis about who will be picking up. With this information, the care provider can help the child to anticipate the transition positively and to feel that the grown-ups are in charge of an orderly world. Parents can help the care provider develop a modified transition ritual to assist the child in that setting. In these situations, the use of weekly calendars with stickers for mom days and dad days, different-colored lunch boxes for mom days and dad days, and special clothing are all concrete ways to help the child anticipate and master the transition. On a practical note, any relevant court papers should be left on file with the baby-sitter or day-care provider, in the event that one or the other parent claims a schedule change that must be verified.

THE NEED FOR THERAPEUTIC CONSTANCY

In working with highly conflicted divorced parents, it is essential to understand that many of these strategies will not be easily received or readily implemented. Often the work proceeds in the "two-steps-forward, one-step-back" style. There is a natural reluctance in parents to relinquish behaviors and attitudes that help them to manage their own anxieties. It is also difficult for parents who have felt intolerably injured by each other to shift focus away from repairing the injustice and toward what is necessary for the child. Often the therapist takes on the role of a constant, caring figure who tolerates the parent's ambivalence and remains available to repeatedly reframe the issues from the child's point of view. The more fragile the parent, the more frequent the need to reframe. The work can be demanding and at times tedious. Nevertheless, in our experience it is the therapist's ability to remain constant, neutral, and child-focused—in spite of the seemingly endless ups and downs—that often becomes the essential ingredient in bringing about a reasonable level of stability and protection for the child.

USE OF THE SCHEDULE TO BUFFER THE CHILD

Preliminary evidence from the work of Solomon and George (1996) indicates that infants and toddlers appear to be relatively secure and well-adjusted in a variety of scheduling arrangements, if the level of parental conflict is low and communication and collaboration regarding the child are high. This finding is not surprising, as the child in such cases is likely to feel supported by each parent during transitions, as well as by the familiar routines and response patterns that parental communication and collaboration make possible. For example, if an infant cannot be soothed after he wakes from a nap, one parent may call the other for suggestions. The call may yield commonplace communications such as, "Have you tried holding him across your lap and rubbing his back? . . . Have you tried Sesame Street? . . . he loves to watch it after his nap."

Parents also need to help each other as the child's language emerges. For example, when a child plaintively and repeatedly calls for "Be-Be" and the parent does not know that this is her new word for her favorite bear, then both parent and child become upset. If, on the other hand, the parents have communicated about this new development, then the child can be reassured that her language works in both homes, and that she will be acknowledged and understood in this new way by both parents. This reassurance, in turn, represents one more way to support the child's continuity of experience. Moreover, these crucial communications can enhance both parents' feelings of competence, as they begin to function in the role of single parent and help the child to feel soothed in familiar ways.

Until these buffering conditions can be achieved in the work with highly conflicted parents, however, the schedule itself can serve as a protective function, if it is developed with the child's needs in mind. It is from this perspective that we consider the parameters of time-sharing.

Time-Sharing Parameters

In conflictual situations, very young children appear to benefit the most from schedules that resemble their preseparation patterns of contact with each parent. This approach to scheduling is essentially empirical and does not presuppose primacy of either parent; it simply allows the child to rely on the predictability of events and the familiarity of physical surroundings until parents can provide support in more flexible and cooperative ways. It represents a conservative baseline from which the parents' work proceeds and is designed to minimize the child's level of stress.

A second consideration that must be weighed very seriously is the number of transitions the schedule will impose on the child. The goal is to create analogs of the preseparation patterns of contact, which will provide enough time with each parent to support a relationship while limiting the number of transitions. For infants and toddlers, relationship building requires fairly frequent contact, because very young children cannot hold other people in mind when they are apart from them for very long. The need for limited transitions is dictated by the traumatic nature of such separations in a highly conflictual situation. To use a concrete example: Frances's typical pattern of contact with her father during the marriage was the time they shared, most evenings, from 6:00 P.M. until her bedtime. Continuing this pattern on a daily basis, however, would have provoked intolerable anxiety in Frances as well as in her parents, who became upset and disorganized in each other's presence. Shifting to the time-honored "every-other-weekend" visits, on the other hand, would make the time away from her father feel like forever to this very young child. A reasonable, age-appropriate analog might involve contact with Mr. J from late afternoon until bedtime two (later on, three) times a week. Balancing familiarity of routine with limited transitions is a process that cannot be reduced to a formula. If Frances continued to be symptomatic within that arrangement, the number of transitions could be further reduced and the number of hours per visit increased, so that actual amounts of time with father need not be compromised.

At times, the scheduling decision may require a choice between the need to protect the child's familiarity of routine (such as timing Frances's visits to resemble her pre-bedtime patterns with Mr. J) with the need to conduct transitions in a neutral place. The importance of setting up neutral transitions depends on a review of the historical information to determine the child's previous exposure to episodes of verbal or physical conflict as well as parents' current abilities to control this type of acting-out. If this consideration is significant and a neutral person cannot be present in the home of one or the other parent, then the possibility of using a neutral place of transition might take precedence over familiarity of routine. For example, visits before bedtime would require that Frances be passed back and forth between father and mother at home. In the past, this resulted in her exposure to frightening arguments and physical fights. Observations of transitions from mother directly to father indicated that they continued to be highly stress-inducing. In this case, therefore, the counselor recommended that Frances be picked up at her baby-sitter's home by father and returned to the baby-sitter, where she could spend a neutral hour or so before mother picked her up. This arrangement was put in place two days a week. The counselor also suggested additional time for father during one weekend day to be structured in a similar fashion, if possible.

The question of overnight visits often demands the lion's share of attention and concern in divorce situations involving young children. Currently available evidence with regard to this issue suggests that when parents remain in high conflict, when they cannot be helped to resolve their own separation panic and continually fail to empathically understand their child's experience, and when they are unable to collaboratively establish predictable routines and rituals, then the young child's tolerance for overnight separations is likely to be compromised. Optimally, therefore, the parents' separation panic and capacity for attunement to their child should be attended to with some degree of success before overnights are established. This is particularly but not exclusively true for children under about 3 years of age, who are particularly vulnerable to separation difficulties.

When the child has experienced very few separations from a vulnerable primary parent (particularly when the other parent has been excluded), the scheduling goal is to gradually limit the number of transitions and, just as gradually, increase the time of each separation from the primary parent. The criterion for graduated change is always the child's tolerance, which can be assessed after a brief adjustment period. When parent reports are discrepant or otherwise unreliable, the mental health professional needs to consult with others who know the child and, perhaps as well, directly observe a transition.

The final configuration in this graduated approach varies, to a large extent, according to the success of the parenting intervention. When parents can be helped to actively support and protect their child, then the final configuration may comprise considerable time sharing and overnights. If not, the configuration is more likely to include reasonably frequent blocks of time (typically within a range of one to three times a week), without overnights.

Parents excluded from overnight visitation often express fears that if they do not have overnights, they will not develop a "real" relationship with their child. In such cases, the parents need to understand that the security of their child's primary relationship is the essential basis for his or her sense of security in other relationships, both now and in the future. That security depends on protection from traumatic separations that is best achieved by the parents' willingness to collaborate on behalf of the child. It is particularly important for the excluded parent to understand that without collaboration there can be no trust. Without trust, the anxious parent will not support the child's separation. Without that support, the child's separation will be traumatic, and the excluded parent will bring anxiety rather than comfort to the child. At the same time, the anxious parent needs to understand that a child who cannot separate is a child who cannot mature. This long-term view is a useful frame for helping parents to anticipate how their child's need for each of them will keep shifting over time, and how they will both need to develop a tolerance for these shifts if their child is to feel supported as he or she grows and changes.

The child's need for predictability is the final and essential consideration; it requires that the schedule determined at the conclusion of the parenting work represent a practical arrangement to which the parents can commit for a reasonable period of time. Barring this outcome, a highly specific court order may be needed to ensure a protective baseline for the child. The schedule, of course, needs to be altered over time, as the child's needs and circumstances change. These revisions may be made by the parents, a coparenting arbitrator (see chapter 9), or further order of the court.

Chapter 5

The Preschool Years

Separation, Gender, and Sexualized Anxiety

*A*s young children emerge from toddlerhood into the preschool years, they confront new developmental concerns that focus on gender and sexuality. Earlier preoccupations with becoming a separate person now shift and extend to concerns about becoming a separate, *gendered* person who is a boy or a girl.

Gender: The Preoedipal Phase

The process of becoming identified as essentially a boy or a girl represents a narrowing of possibilities that earlier seemed boundless (Coates, 1990; Fast, 1984). For boys and girls between the ages of approximately 12 to 30 months, who once believed they possessed both the powers of having a penis and of giving birth, the reality slowly dawns that one attribute makes the other impossible. In addition to these biological realities, the child has to come to terms with other limitations, as well as possibilities, that are defined by his or her family within the context of a larger culture. In rigidly male-dominated families, for example, a girl may feel diminished as she recognizes her gender, particularly if women are not especially valued. Alternatively, in some families, a boy may become highly anxious if being male means being different from a mother who rejects his maleness, particularly if he cannot find worth in the eyes of his father (Fast, 1990).

Sexuality: The Oedipal Phase

If all goes well, by approximately age 3, the child will have come to terms with the fact that he is, and will remain, a boy; that she is, and will remain, a girl. On the heels of this achievement, children begin to consolidate the meaning of their gender in sexual terms (Fast, 1979; Mächtlinger, 1981). This new developmental focus marks the beginning of the oedipal passage. During this phase, children typically experience a rise in erotic and aggressive impulses. These feelings, and the fantasies associated with them, ordinarily become focused on the opposite-sex parent. The girl now longs to be exclusively valued as the most powerful and attractive female in the world. She wants this affirmation from the most powerful and attractive male she knows—her father. A similar longing ordinarily draws a boy to his mother. These early explorations of sexuality seem to be organized around the child's egocentric belief that his or her powers of attraction are unique and so deeply compelling that all other contenders (i.e., the same-sex parent) will fade in comparison. Not surprisingly, the oedipal child's fantasies are tinged with rivalrous wishes as well as vague notions about adult sexuality in relation to the opposite-sex parent. For a boy, these oedipal wishes (as well as his sense of what it means to be a sexual male) may be expressed when he asserts that he will marry his mother and make her proud of him. A girl's sense of herself as a sexual female, on the other hand, may be communicated by her expressed intent to marry her father and take much better care of him than her mother ever did.

A successful consolidation of gender identity and sexuality requires that the child come to terms with the realistic limits of his oedipal fantasies. Those limits are provided by the parental relationship. The child is not allowed to vanquish the same-gender parent with the power of her rivalrous aggression and become the oedipal victor. This is because the parents' mutuality does not ordinarily falter at this time. They continue to be "in possession of" each other and to provide consistent limits that contain the child's aggressive urges to take possession instead.

As parents stand firm in this way, the child must come to terms with the reality that he cannot, by the force of his own demands or wishes, reconfigure the oedipal triangle. Instead, the child must find solace in identifying with the gifts and capacities of the same-sex parent and in the delayed fulfillment of sexual wishes (Ross, 1982). A boy no longer expects to marry his mother but hopes to grow up and marry someone just like her. A girl will consolidate her identification with her mother in a similar way. With this success, the child begins to internalize the parents' jointly held standards for being good (i.e., controlling aggressive and sexual impulses) and is diverted from courting the exclusive acknowledgment of the opposite-sex parent. Instead, she becomes focused on learning how to earn acknowledgment in the world of peers. The new competencies that result can then help the child feel able and entitled to achieve his or her delayed wishes and fantasies in the future (Erikson, 1963; Fast, 1990).

VULNERABILITIES IN OEDIPAL CHILDREN IN THE HIGH-CONFLICT FAMILY

In high-conflict families, the child's normal rivalries with the opposite-gender parent are often seen as pawn's moves conceived by one parent to undermine the other. As a result, vulnerable parents tend to feel attacked or betrayed as their child begins to change and grow. They may respond by becoming anxious, withholding, or punitive toward the child. For children in such a situation, it is not difficult to imagine that ordinary maturational impulses can begin to feel dangerous. There is no safe way forward, and no real way back.

Children caught in this kind of untenable bind tend to become symptomatic. Mothers of boys as young as 2½ describe feeling confused and angry when their sons begin to oppose them, to imitate their fathers, to distance themselves, and to reject their mothers. Typically, this oedipal behavior is followed by renewed signs of separation panic, as these boys become overwhelmed by the fear of losing their mothers forever. Little girls, on the other hand, often seem less overtly troubled as they confront issues of gender and sexuality. A closer look, however, suggests that girls in high-conflict families maintain a connection to their mothers by withdrawing from their own emerging power and sexuality. Some little girls, fueled by their rivalrous feelings, become oppositional with their mothers, while others reject whatever they perceive to be feminine in themselves and in their mothers.

In the endless spiral of the parental conflict, these new symptoms in the children, in turn, provide further ammunition for the battle. Increases in masturbation and sexualized play, which are particularly but not exclusively observed in boys in highly conflicted families, are perhaps the overt symptoms most likely to escalate the conflict. It is not uncommon for these symptomatic behaviors to trigger accusations of child molestation by one parent against the other. Such concerns about child sexual abuse should no more be automatically dismissed because of the presence of parental conflict than they should be automatically believed. Rather, we suggest here that it is the child's experience, including the developmental meaning of sexualized behavior and erotic play, as well as the possibility of actual abuse, that should be explored and understood.

BOYS IN HIGH-CONFLICT FAMILIES

Vulnerabilities in the Formation of Gender Identity in Preoedipal Boys

When little boys recognize that they are male, they also recognize that they are different from their mothers, to whom they are usually primarily attached. Therefore, consolidating his gender identity represents a significant step toward becoming an autonomous person. When separating from a fragile mother in a conflicted relationship feels dangerous, the additional step of consolidating gender identity can feel dangerous as well. The boy in this situation must contend with already entrenched fears that his mother will disintegrate in his absence or abandon him as punishment for leaving her, as well as with new fears that he will drive her away by becoming just like his father, who is toxic to her. The bind is that to become separate and male is to be abandoned by his mother, while staying merged with her is to risk emasculation.

This conundrum invites a kind of split that is organized around gender. In this defensive solution, boys appear to experience their maleness and their sexuality as a fragmented part of the self, the bad-mother-me, who makes the good-mother go away by striving toward separateness and the toxic father. The connection to mother (as well as the longing for intimacy and nurturance that is part of that connection) becomes associated with the good-mother-me, who keeps the good-mother satisfied and close. Unfortunately, this good-mother tends to threaten rather than embrace masculinity. What is disturbing here is that this kind of splitting works against the normal integrations of the period, when children ordinarily begin to weave together the bad and good in themselves and others, as well as the parts of themselves that feel identified with and connected to mother and father. This blending that creates a foundation for gender identity that is both nurturing and strong is placed at considerable risk when children find safety in fragmentation rather than integration.

Mothers in highly conflicted divorce situations encourage this type of gendered splitting when they respond with fear, anger, or withdrawal to behaviors in their sons that remind them of the loathed former spouse. Although they may refrain from denigrating their sons directly, they freely insult the father and, in the process, the male-identified aspects of these boys. One mother described her struggles with her 3-year-old son as follows: "He won't accept what I say, he gets halfway between yelling and crying, and the issues he chooses are totally ludicrous! Like, I try to get him to take a bath and he won't—so I lose it and call him a pig, just like his father."

In a high-conflict situation, the boy's defiance may literally mimic the father's behavior toward the mother. A father may tolerate if not cultivate these behaviors because they help him to feel acknowledged and supported by his son in the parental conflict. The father of the 3-year-old whose mother called him "a pig, just like your father" often encouraged his son to tell him all about the mother's "bossiness." After he heard his son's complaints, this father enjoyed explaining to his little boy, "You're getting too big to be bossed around! We don't do it that way, do we? We talk it out man to man." In this way, the father encouraged his son to defy the mother and subtly suggested that not doing so was effeminate.

Vulnerabilities in the Development of Sexuality in Oedipal Boys

When sexuality becomes linked to gender identity during the oedipal period, a boy's sense of conflict and danger is likely to be exacerbated. New erotic urges toward his mother can heighten a son's fears of being literally swallowed up by her, with no hope of separation. These anxieties are particularly troubling if the boy has failed to achieve a solid sense of his own physical and psychological separateness during earlier phases of his development. A boy's vulnerability may be further intensified by fears of reprisal if, by virtue of his father's absence, the son emerges as the oedipal victor. Fantasies of oedipal victory are often evoked when mothers try to reestablish a sense of intimacy with their sons in ways that violate appropriate physical boundaries. One mother, for example, acknowledged that she did not really want to help her son master sleeping alone because she felt reassured by his regressive longing to curl up next to her at night. Other mothers literally will not relinquish control of their son's bodies, remaining intrusive in toileting and hygiene long after the child could be taught to take responsibility for himself.

With this loss of boundaries, boys are likely to feel erotically stimulated in ways that deepen their fears of mother's engulfment and father's aggression. If the father has actually been physically violent in the past, the boy's fantasies about the father's rivalrous aggression have a terrifying basis in reality. For oedipal boys in a high-conflict situation, then, the dilemma is to remain emasculated, impotent, and connected to mother (and devalued or abandoned by the father) or to become male, sexual, and separate like father (and devalued or abandoned by the mother).

Oppositional Symptoms

The way in which this conundrum ultimately shapes the boy's emerging sense of self, gender, and sexuality depends in large part on the availability and relative power of each parent. If the father is available, the boy may solve his dilemma by taking on the father's characteristics, thoughts, and feelings as if they were his own. All connections to the potentially engulfing mother and the good-mother-me aspects of the self that were connected to her are severed. The short-term risk is that these little boys may become imprisoned behind a wall of opposition toward their mothers, which cuts them off from her nurturing as well as from their own capacities for gentleness and intimacy. Over the long term, the risk is that boys in these situations may consolidate a kind of impersonal masculinity defined by an absence of these nurturing qualities. Furthermore, that impersonal masculinity may be affirmed by violence, if the boy has understood violence to be an essential aspect of being male and an instrument of power and separateness.

If the father cannot be available, or if the mother is so powerful that the risks of separating are too great, then boys are at risk of becoming immobilized, depressed, and confused about their masculinity and of remaining merged with the mother. For these boys, there seems to be no safe way forward into manhood.

Sexualized Symptoms

Sexualized behaviors can be deeply compelling for boys caught in the web of these dilemmas. This may be, in part, because such behaviors affirm the presence of the penis and its functions. This validation of a boy's sexuality reaffirms his masculinity as well as his existence as a separate person (Kirkpatrick, 1990), or, as Eissler (1958) suggested in describing older boys, "I come, therefore I am." When a boy's individuation from his mother is fragile, these new feelings can be particularly comforting; that is, when a boy cannot find within himself a reliable sense of his mother's acknowledgment that he is separate from her, then his sexual feelings can take on these reassuring functions instead. They provide a vulnerable boy with newly autonomous ways of feeling independently alive and comforted that were not available before. On the other hand, *because* these feelings awaken a new surge of independence, a boy may experience them as dangerous new aspects of the bad-mother-me that further heighten the risk of abandonment by his mother (Roseby, 1995). A self-perpetuating cycle can develop in which a boy's heightened anxiety about separation can deepen his need for the existential soothing of his sexually arousing play. The following case material illustrates how the changing dynamics of a parental conflict produced shifts from oppositional to anxiously sexualized symptoms in a 5-year-old boy.

The Case of Nathan M

The Family History

Mr. and Mrs. M had a bitterly conflictual marriage that ended when Nathan was 2½ years old. They continued to be embroiled in conflict and multiple litigations after the separation. They first came for counseling when their son was 5 years old. Mr. M was a very self-centered and immature man who saw himself as his son's primary parent and protector from a "tyrannical and controlling" mother. He felt, for example, that Mrs. M's efforts to get Nathan to clean his room were tyrannical: "She tells him if he does, she'll take him out for a treat! Isn't that just like saying that if he doesn't do it, she won't get him a treat! It's a real abuse of power!" Mr. M believed, with absolute conviction, that his son was struggling under the weight of Mrs. M's oppression in precisely the same way that he had felt himself to be oppressed by her. In actuality, Mr. M. had trouble distinguishing feelings of rage and helplessness that belonged to his own past relationships from those that belonged to relationships in the present—his father had been oppressive and his mother unprotective. More significantly, he could not differentiate his own feelings and experiences from those of his young son. Mr. M was often visibly upset and would cry or rant angrily during counseling sessions (mainly about how he had been cheated out of time with Nathan), often appearing as if he were on the verge of losing control. When asked whether he thought these displays were frightening for Nathan, Mr. M said, "It is a hundred times more frightening for him to get double messages that he can't understand than to just see the feelings and know what's going on!" He said that masking his feelings would be like lying to his son. Although Mr. M could be nurturing, he more often relied on Nathan for reassurance, telling him after an outburst, "Daddy needs a hug."

Mrs. M seemed both depressed and exhausted when she was first seen. She said, "I've just about had it on all fronts. I feel totally depressed and hopeless. I wish I could just go away and leave everything and everybody." Mrs. M had very little experience of being mothered herself and was especially vulnerable to feeling overwhelmed, helpless, and ashamed when she could not handle her son. "I feel like a bad mother. I can't figure out what to do. . . . Sometimes we're just as close as we ever were and then . . . I don't know . . . he sees his father and he comes home and I swear, it's like looking at his father! He bosses me around, he talks to me as if I were dirt . . . he has tantrums. I can't stand it. . . . Sometimes I feel like I want a divorce from my son!" At these times, Mrs. M would withdraw from Nathan because she could not bear the way she felt when he was so ambivalent about her. She could not see the vulnerable side of her little son at all.

Nathan himself had been encopretic since the age of 3. Mrs. M understood the encopresis to be a response to Mr. M's "crazy and unpredictable behavior," while Mr. M felt that Nathan was just trying to achieve control in relation to a mother who "wants to be in charge of his every move." In spite of both parents' failure to see their son as a person separate from themselves and their bitter conflict, Nathan was struggling toward a fragile individuation. In this distorted process, Nathan's encopretic symptoms appeared to provide him with an oppositional sense of having a separate existence.

In addition to his struggles with separation, Nathan needed to define and anchor his masculinity. His efforts in this direction resembled a kind of merging with his father, imitating him and taking on his thoughts and feelings as if they were his own. Not incidentally, this merger was likely the only solution that could gratify Mr. M and ensure his continuing availability to his son. From this position, which felt like the kind of masculine separation he was longing for, Nathan attempted to see his mother through his father's eyes. This difficult stance was made clear as Nathan struggled to recount a violent argument he had witnessed at age 2½. During the argument, Mr. M broke his wife's wrist. In retelling the incident, Nathan carefully said, "My dad broke . . . no, no, my mom *made* my dad break her wrist!"

Nathan's Troll Story

During his initial play session, Nathan told the following story. "Once upon a time, there was boy at a wedding. This boy didn't stay long at the wedding. He tricked the bride and walked away from the wedding and went for a long walk. Then he fell into a deep troll hole where there was a girl troll looking for a boy to marry. He tried to get out of the troll hole but he couldn't because the Troll King comes along and says, 'You must stay and marry the girl troll because she wants to marry you and you will stay and marry her. You will wear the troll tail and eat troll food.' The boy doesn't want to marry the girl troll, so he tries to run away but they hold his feet, and then he gets out by himself!"

The story suggests that Nathan was angry with both his parents, who had turned into trolls. The change from bride (good-mother) to girl troll (bad-mother) indicates Nathan's continuing inability to integrate the good and bad aspects of other people and himself. In the story, the good-mother was someone else's bride, whom he tricked and left. Nathan's choice of the word *tricked* suggests that he felt ashamed and secretive both about his sexual feelings toward his mother and his need to separate from her. Immediately upon leaving the good-mother, the boy encountered the bad-mother in the form of the female troll who wanted to marry him and make him eat troll food. Because he fears that her possessiveness toward him is sexual, this troll is not only the bad-mother but the bad *oedipal* mother as well. Nathan's story communicates his strong need to separate from her erotic and suffocating presence. Even clearer is the sense that Nathan has no refuge. His story seems to define the father exclusively in terms of his role in this distorted oedipal triangle. He is the Troll King, who *wants* Nathan to marry the girl troll. In other words, the father has abdicated, leaving Nathan to take his place, to wear the tail and eat the troll food. Nathan has been sacrificed to the devouring, sexual longings of the bad-mother so that the father can escape. At the end of the story, Nathan confronts his choices. He may remain as the terrified and shamed oedipal victor, or he may scramble away, unaided and alone.

Nathan's Oppositional Symptoms

The struggle to establish his masculinity was fraught with danger for this child. Earlier difficulties with separation from his mother were now compounded by the regressive pull of his oedipal attraction to her and the frightening injunction from his father to "be male in my place, to take over as the consort of the bad-mother." In spite of father's seeming invitation for the son to become the oedipal victor, Nathan still had to worry: Will his father become angry, jealous, and vengeful anyway?

Nathan attempted to manage these myriad anxieties by merging with his father and opposing his mother, that is, by becoming the bad-mother-me. This defensive solution solved some of his difficulties. Becoming one with his father and rival discouraged further rivalry and protected Nathan from his mother's engulfing presence. However, there were new difficulties. Nathan was now doomed to oppose and reject his mother while longing for her at the same time. There was no model in Nathan's fragmented family, or in his split inner life, for achieving separation from his mother and maintaining connection to his father. Clearly, this boy was caught in a powerful dilemma; to feel separate and masculine, he must also feel and be bad. In reality, Nathan's dilemma was apparent in his swings between compliance and opposition in relation to his mother, swings that seemed to escalate before and after visits with his father.

Nathan's Sexualized Symptoms

The nature of Nathan's symptomatic struggles altered about two weeks after the family was first seen. At that time, Mr. M became verbally abusive and threatening with his former wife. Mrs. M was very frightened. Her attorney was successful in having visitation suspended for a time, "until it could be determined that Mr. M was able to take responsibility for his behavior when he was with his son." The threat of losing all contact with his "male anchor" seriously disrupted Nathan's efforts to consolidate his separateness and his masculinity. He became noticeably more compliant with his mother and with the behavioral regime she had instituted to manage his encopresis.

Nathan's therapist commented on the change in Nathan's oppositional behavior in the following way: "He's really much more compliant, he's cut down on his anger, and he's easier for his mom to manage. On the surface it looks good, but his mother reported to me that he's been drawing pictures of graveyards—and in the sandtray he's doing a lot of burying." When Nathan was seen by a counselor in our service during this time, he was asked to identify three wishes, but he insisted that he wanted only one: "If I could just die, die in my sleep." In his preoccupation with death, Nathan seemed to communicate both a longing to be free of the paradoxical binds of his life and a wish to be rid of his separate masculine self.

In an effort to manage his pain, as well as to assuage his increasingly potent mother (who could banish his father), Nathan behaved as if his father had never existed. Mrs. M described with satisfaction how, when the father telephoned, Nathan seemed to forget about him as soon as he hung up the phone.

It is noteworthy that Nathan was also left with no real way to express his anger. He clearly imagined that his rage (and the autonomy it represented) had somehow made his father abandon him and might have a similar effect on his mother. In therapy sessions, Nathan spanked a "bad" baby doll over and over for pooping on the father doll, while the mother doll looked on. Nathan then had the father doll say to the baby, "I'm not living with you now." Next, Nathan spanked the baby doll over and over again for pooping on both parents' faces and for crying. He then put the "bad baby" in "jail" in a closet and calmly resumed his play. At one point, Nathan described a brother named Eric, who was "a very angry boy, a bad boy" who lived with his father. When the therapist referred to this comment in a later session, Nathan denied the statement and said indignantly that if he had a brother, he certainly would not be named Eric! As Nathan capitulated to the perceived demands of his powerful mother and increasingly relinquished his efforts to separate from her and connect with his father, he became overtly confused about his masculinity. In therapy group, he presented his bottom to the other children, asking to be spanked and chanting, "I'm a boy, I'm a girl."

For this oedipal child, the symptoms of gender confusion suggested that his loss of a sense of a separate self was inextricably associated with the loss of his masculine, sexual self as well. Here, Nathan's symptoms were particularly telling. He began to masturbate publicly and often. His behavior now represented the separating bad-mother-me and became a substitute for the encopresis and noncompliance that had fueled his separation heretofore. It was as if this behavior alone could now soothe Nathan and reassure him that he still existed. Most telling is the fact that this oedipal boy's sense of vitality and realness became anchored in his maleness and his sexuality. This connection between feeling alive and feeling masculine indicates how a boy's inability to establish a firm sense of his gender and sexuality can feel life threatening to him.

Perhaps most instructive is the postscript to this case, which occurred when Mr. M's visits were reinstated. Within a brief space of time, mother and therapist, each with a different interpretation, described a behavioral reversal in which Nathan became once again emotionally labile, oppositional, and difficult for his mother to manage. At the same time, the school reported that his masturbation had diminished and become negligible.

The Case of Dante P

Dante's Early Struggles

It is not uncommon for boys caught in the web of an oedipal dilemma to display a range of sexualized symptoms that are not limited to masturbation. Four-year-old Dante P, for example, had been enmeshed in his parents' conflict since his age of 18 months. Mrs. P was a highly anxious woman who lived in terror that her ex-spouse would molest or abuse Dante, as he had abused her. Mr. P was an emotionally needy man who was deeply humiliated by his former wife's accusations. To compensate for his vulnerability, he was intermittently controlling and intrusive with both Mrs. P and his son. Mr. P tended to idealize his son, as he once idealized his wife. Dante's early struggles with separation were apparent in his mother's descriptions of transitions to preschool or visits. He would "totally fall apart" and become hysterical, clinging to, clawing, and attacking his mother. His acute fears were also apparent in his asthma attacks and chronic enuresis. Like Nathan, Dante symptomatically attempted to establish a boundary by controlling his body functions, in his case, by refusing to eat.

As Dante outgrew toddlerhood and began to struggle with issues of gender as well as separateness, he showed the characteristic swings between opposition and compliance with his mother. In the good-mother-me state, he clung to her. As he tried to separate and establish his masculinity, he shifted to an oppositional bad-mother-me position and hit her. However, Dante experienced his father as equally demanding and engulfing. In this family, as in Nathan's, the oedipal triangle was distorted. Not, in this case, because Dante was the oedipal victor, but because the child perceived himself to be the prize that both parents longed for and sought after.

Dante's Oedipal Dilemma

In the sandtray, Dante tended to repeat a particular play involving a special dinosaur, who seemed to represent him, and two gender-diffuse superheroes, who seemed to represent his parents. In the play, the special dinosaur was the desired prize, and the two supermen fought for possession of him. The dinosaur would say, "Which one loves me the best? You can keep me . . . and the other one can visit me. And then the superman, who got to keep the dinosaur because he loved him best, pats him and says, 'You're a good boy' . . . and then [the father] superman wanted to kill the [m]other superman cos he doesn't want him any more." Dante then indicated that the mother superman was blown up and destroyed in a volcano, with the help of the dinosaur.

In this play Dante passively achieved a kind of separation by virtue of the fact that the father chose him. After having chosen him and praised him for being good, Dante's father blows the mother up. Dante seemed to believe that only by destroying the mother could he achieve separation from her. His total powerlessness in relation to her, however, did not shift to annihilating rage until he became merged with his father. The oedipal twist here is that in that merged relationship, Dante felt as if he had become the object of his father's oedipal desire. To please his father (who worried about his finicky eating), Dante would stuff his mouth with food until he gagged. This kind of intrusion by the oedipal father bears a haunting resemblance to Nathan's worries about being intruded upon by the oedipal mother and "forced to eat troll food." Naturally, this dynamic with his father, as well as his difficulties with separation from his mother, raised worrisome questions in Dante's mind about his masculinity.

Dante's Sexualized Symptoms

Not surprisingly, Dante's play suggested a marked gender confusion (throughout his therapy sessions, Dante identified women dolls as men and girl dolls as boys), as well as a compulsive curiosity about sexuality. His stories often included sexually explicit play in which he had the supermen insert their guns into the anus of a doll he had undressed. During this same period, Dante's mother reported that he was engaging in overt sexual play with peers that involved undressing and inspecting little girls and trying to insert an object into the anus of a boy peer. As might be expected, the therapist raised the question of possible sexual abuse in this child's history. Although the mother was concerned about this possibility, neither the parents nor other professionals who had been involved with this family presented evidence of any such history. Rather, it was suggested that this sexualized play (like Nathan's) surfaced because it served particular needs in Dante. It seemed to be both self-stimulating and self-soothing, enabling him to explore his own confusion about gender as well as his normal developmental curiosity about the specifics of sexual behavior. At the same time, these activities (in which he engaged with compulsive furtiveness) seemed to support a pleasurable sense of autonomy from his relatively unbounded and intrusive parents.

GIRLS IN THE HIGH-CONFLICT FAMILY

The Defensive Consolidation of Gender Identity

For girls in high-conflict families, consolidating femininity and sexuality during the oedipal passage is likely to progress somewhat differently. Even if a girl is faltering in the process of separating from her mother, the recognition of her own gender need not provoke fears of abandonment and loss, because the recognition is one of being like rather than different from her mother (Kirkpatrick, 1990). The risk is that girls might soothe their worries about separation by establishing a particular version of femaleness, a good-mother-me kind that does not strive for authenticity or autonomy but remains in undemanding connection to mother.

Oedipal Conflicts in Sexuality for Girls

During the oedipal phase, her burgeoning sexual impulses fuel a daughter's longing to be admired and valued as a female by her father, as distinct from her mother. This acknowledgment requires a degree of separation from the oedipal mother and inevitably results in rivalrous feelings toward her. In high-conflict situations, daughters may experience these new feelings as too dangerous to express at all. When girls inhibit these feelings in themselves, parents tend to see them as asymptomatic, and it is often assumed that they have comfortably shelved their oedipal issues until adolescence. In fact, these little girls communicate in their stories and projective play that they have unconsciously split off these new developmental impulses, because they feel like shameful and bad aspects of themselves.

The problem here is that when girls disown their sexuality, they remain fully confirmed in their identity as females who are not separate from their mothers. What then remains is a sweetly feminine and asexual facade that is not regarded as problematic until adolescence. At that time, the absence of inner resources and conflicts about autonomy and authenticity tend to be expressed in a range of widely reported problematic behaviors, including precocious sexual activity and substance abuse, as well as early, unsuccessful marriages to emotionally unstable or much older men (Hetherington, 1972; Kalter, 1977; Kalter et al., 1985; Mueller & Pope, 1977; Pope & Mueller, 1976; Schwartzberg, 1980; Wallerstein & Kelly, 1980).

In some high-conflict families, girls do attempt to achieve a measure of separation from their mothers during the oedipal period. Their efforts tend to be expressed in newly oppositional behavior toward their mothers. Perhaps not surprisingly, this new defiance often has a rivalrous quality. The mother of one 4-year-old girl, for example, complained that her daughter had begun to challenge her authority in a very demeaning way, while demanding to be allowed to telephone her father at all hours.

A more limited number of girls seem to invite their father's acknowledgment and admiration during the oedipal period by attempting to merge with him. When this happens, girls may reject their mother and whatever they believe to be feminine in themselves. One 5-year-old girl, for example, had been seen in individual therapy for some time before coming to group. In her individual work, this little girl had been struggling with her father's marked preference for her older brother. When she came into a group therapy session for the first time, she was sporting a new boyish haircut, boys' clothes and shoes, and an unusually husky voice. One child in the group asked her, in some confusion, "Are you a boy or a girl?" and she responded, "Go figure!" This kind of process may occur when the daughter seeks acknowledgment from a father who rejects her femininity. In other cases, this kind of deliberate boyishness represents an identification with a mother perceived to possess more masculine power than the father.

In high-conflict families a daughter's efforts to separate from her mother during the oedipal period may or may not survive the dangers she associates with them. First among these dangers is that her mother will abandon her if she becomes attached to her father, in reality or even in fantasy. This concern becomes particularly potent during the oedipal period because a girl's longing for her father at this time is likely to represent, both to her and to her mother, not only a separation but a rivalrous betrayal as well.

The Dangers of Oedipal Victory

In a high-conflict divorce situation, a daughter who wins the kind of attention she longs for from her father, but without the tempering presence of her mother, is likely to feel she has unwittingly become the oedipal victor. When this happens, the daughter must contend with unconscious fears about her mother's vengeful rage. These dangers are compounded if the father is consciously or unconsciously seductive with his daughter. This can occur when fathers become exhibitionistic about their masculinity and sexuality. One father, who had recently remarried, began to walk around the house naked in his children's presence. He claimed that this was part of his new sense of freedom and urged everyone in his family to join him. Fathers may also become more or less consciously careless about protecting the privacy of their sexual relations with new partners. In another case, two sisters (5 and 3 years old) described to their therapist, with breathless excitement and confusion, having seen their father engaged in sexual intercourse with his girlfriend in a sleeping bag in the living room, shortly after the girls had been put to bed. In other situations, daughters become the exclusive focus of their father's life. In a sense their relationship becomes a substitute for the marriage, meeting the father's (and sometimes the daughter's) needs for intimacy.

In these types of relationship, the boundaries between father and daughter are not always maintained. Sleeping and showering together, for example, may become commonplace. Visits often feel like dates. These situations can stimulate erotic feelings and fantasies, which both disturb and attract these vulnerable girls. When the daughters return to their mothers after visits, they carry with them a sense of shame and secrecy that is more or less consciously associated with their fathers and their own sexuality. The mother, in her turn, may unconsciously add to the shame by treating her daughter as a soiled concubine of the father. One mother, horrified by her daughter's newly flirtatious behavior toward her father, described how she set limits with her daughter when she returned from the father's house: "I just tell her very plainly, 'You can't twist me 'round your little finger like you do with your father, little missy. Your curlicues and flounces don't impress me one way or the other!'" Another mother called the therapist, in acute distress and anger, because her daughter had accompanied her father and his girlfriend on a date. In her rivalrous rage, this mother essentially fused her two rivals—the daughter and the girl-friend—into one entity: "God knows what else she's been exposed to and has her little fingers in! If this goes on she'll get AIDS! You know, when I called over there he was in the bathroom washing her hair—God knows what else they do in there!"

The Oedipal Retreat

When these girls attempt some exploration of their oedipal impulses, they often end up retreating from this new terrain (Edgecombe, 1976). This can occur because their fears and fantasies about mother's anger and revenge, as well as their shame about their own emerging sexuality, become over-whelming. The need to retreat is compounded if fathers, for whatever reason, are not available to their daughters in a reliable way or if fathers are consciously or unconsciously seductive. As girls back away from their own autonomy and sexuality, they seem to adopt a relatively docile stance in re-lation to their mothers. This compliant stance often masks a deeper am-bivalence about separation that is intermittently expressed in covertly defiant or hostile ways.

In the service of their retreat, many girls begin to actively resist visiting their father, often mimicking their mother's demeaning words and attitudes about him, as if they feel compelled to reassure themselves and their moth-ers they have returned to the fold, divested themselves of their oedipal as-pects, and are once again purified as the good-mother-me. At the same time, the bad-mother-me, who is separate, sexual, and connected to father, cannot be entirely disowned but seems to hover at the periphery of con-sciousness. In their projective play, their stories, and their dreams, these girls continue to represent the oedipal aspects of themselves and their fa-thers as deceitful, shadowy figures who must hide their shameful connec-tion from the powerful mother.

In the two cases that follow, these issues were played out in more dra-matic ways than most. Because of this very lack of subtlety, these cases lend clarity to the conflicts about power and sexuality that girls in high-conflict families often manage in relatively asymptomatic ways.

The Case of Isobelle G

The Parents

Isobelle G was 4 years old when her parents, who had been involved in endless bouts of failed mediation, were referred to our counseling services. Mrs. G was a talented artist who tended to become overwhelmed with helpless anger whenever she felt misunderstood. Although she expressed these feelings very forcefully, she did not expect them to have any impact. Because of this, she had a very difficult time understanding that her daughter might be frightened of her unpredictable rages.

Mr. G was a rather immature and self-involved man. He maintained a very close relationship with both his parents, to the apparent exclusion of any other social connections. Mr. G was an airline pilot by profession. Because of this, he frequently changed the visitation schedule at short notice and repeatedly disappointed his little daughter. He had difficulty accepting that Isobelle was having a hard time with this unpredictability, because he always explained to her why he needed to change his plans. He felt that Mrs. G's concerns about Isobelle's disappointments were just irrational efforts to malign him as a father. He could not see that Isobelle herself needed to be able to count on him.

Isobelle

When first seen at age 4, Isobelle was a solemn and timid little girl who had noticeable difficulty allowing her mother to leave the playroom at any point during the session. In fact, separations from her mother were a struggle for Isobelle in all situations. Her mother said, "She'll cry, yell, claw at my leg," at school, at bedtime, and at transitions for visits to her father. In fact, when she was first seen, Isobelle was refusing to visit Mr. G most of the time. Isobelle's separation difficulties were no doubt exacerbated by a congenital digestive defect that required several surgeries to correct. Although fully recovered, Isobelle was left with a residual vulnerability to infection that required, according to her pediatrician, a "mostly common sense" approach. To Mrs. G, however, this meant being in total control of Isobelle's environment at all times. She was sure Mr. G was incapable of taking care of their daughter properly, and she could not be convinced otherwise. She felt that he was "a Disneyland dad. . . . He'll have all the fun with her, and I'll have to pick up the pieces." Although her concern was ostensibly about Isobelle's health, Mrs. G was also anxious about losing the competition for her daughter's affection and loyalty. As she said, "Isobelle and I were so close we were famous for it. Now I'm afraid she's going to pull away." Mr. G's behavior contributed to his ex-wife's worries. He seemed to have difficulty trusting his own judgment as a parent and generally called on Mrs. G when Isobelle became upset or ill.

Over the next few months, Isobelle's resistance to visits diminished as she began her own individual therapy, and Mr. and Mrs. G (with the help of the project counselor) began to support their daughter's efforts to separate. One day during this period, Isobelle came to therapy carrying a bag of paints. She said excitedly, "My mom says I can take these to my dad's house! And my dad will make a special place so I can take some of my old toys too!" Permission to use her toys as transitional objects was new and appealing to Isobelle, and Mrs. G, in particular, was initially reassured by her daughter's eager response.

The Emergence of Oedipal Themes

Isobelle's oedipal fantasies, no doubt loosened by her mother's support of her increasing attachment to her father, came into rather dramatic focus approximately six months into treatment. The shift began when Isobelle told her therapist that she and her father had seen the movie *Hook*, which features a grown-up Peter Pan who can fly. A series of sessions followed (lasting several months) in which Isobelle became increasingly preoccupied with a male and female doll that "danced beautifully together all the time and then flew away to get married." The similarities between the grown-up Peter Pan character and Isobelle's father were difficult to overlook. Mr. G was, after all, an exciting, grown-up play companion who came and went in his daughter's life as magically and unpredictably as Peter Pan, after flying here and there (albeit by plane) to places Isobelle could only imagine. In his Peter Pan fashion, he also tended to shun the more responsible aspects of fatherhood by turning to Isobelle's mother when parenting decisions were required. The Peter Pan image captured the essence of Mr. G for his daughter, and she seemed to fall in love with the fantasy as much as with the father.

When Isobelle's infatuation first became apparent outside her therapy sessions, Mrs. G made a panicked phone call to the therapist. "Isobelle is acting like she's going to die if she doesn't get more time with her dad!

When the slightest little thing goes wrong she collapses in a heap and says 'I want my dad, I want my dad,' over and over and over. . . . I can't stand this!" Mrs. G was upset and confused by her daughter's behavior but worried that, if she refused her demands to be with her father, Isobelle would become stressed and ill. Over the next 12 months, Isobelle saw her father more and more frequently, though she was often upset and confused by the continuing unpredictability of his schedule.

The Oedipal Conflict

For several months of her therapy, Isobelle was exclusively preoccupied with the dancing couple who could fly. After a trip out of town with her father, her play was expanded to include a Batmobile, which Isobelle imbued with great vitality and aggressive power as she zoomed it around the playroom. A mother doll, however, hated the Batmobile, and the little girl doll resorted to a range of tricks to get her to like it, to "feel how smooth it is!" Invariably, the mother doll would recoil, and then Isobelle would bury the Batmobile in the sand and say, "The mom doesn't like it, it's mean!" She followed this by hissing and spitting at the mother doll. This play, coming on the heels of a trip with her father, suggests that oedipal victory and its attendant dangers were looming too close for Isobelle. She repeatedly invites the mother to reclaim her rightful place vis-à-vis father and restore her daughter to a safe position in the oedipal triangle.

The Oedipal Retreat

Toward the end of this approximately 12-month span of play, Isobelle began to worry openly about her relationship with her mother. During one session, for example, after the doll mother once again rejected the Batmobile, Isobelle said, "The girl hurt the mom's feelings." When the therapist asked how this had happened, Isobelle replied directly, "I didn't want to come home . . . and then my mom hurt my feelings. . . . She made me keep the [bedroom] door closed and I thought a monster would come." At the same time, Mrs. G began to complain that she was being thrust into the role of disciplinarian "mean mom," while Mr. G continued to be irresponsible and unpredictable. Mrs. G was also justifiably furious about having to comfort her heartbroken daughter whenever Mr. G failed to keep to the schedule.

With the conflict once again heating up around her, Isobelle's pleasure in the dancing couple who could fly and her fascination with the powerful Batmobile gradually diminished. As these themes began to fade from her play, Isobelle again began to resist visits with her father. She increasingly resembled the timid 4-year-old who had actively resisted separation from her mother. Her attempted journey through the oedipal terrain seemed to have failed in the face of overwhelming risks: that she might be abandoned by a mother who felt betrayed, and that she would then be left to the care of an unpredictable father who was more consort than parent.

The Enduring Nature of Unresolved Oedipal Themes

What is perhaps most striking here is the way in which these unresolved oedipal issues continued to preoccupy this child over time. When Isobelle was re-evaluated at almost 9 years of age, she repeatedly played out her struggle for separation from her mother. For example, in sandtray play, Isobelle represented herself as a trickster named Sly Wolf, who regularly deceived her mother (Mother Wolf) to pal around with a capricious father character named Snake Butt. It is no surprise that Isobelle represented herself in her story as a "sly wolf." The name captures her split sense of self as a deceiver who lacked integrity and could not be fully real with anyone. In the play, Sly Wolf would pretend to go off and play alone, when in fact she was meeting Snake Butt, her "best pal." When Mother Wolf called, Sly Wolf would return, bringing her mother a "treat" (though Isobelle commented to the evaluator, "It's part poop and part sweet. . . . pretend the Mother Wolf eats the poop part!"). This play was periodically interrupted by Snake Butt's hostile phone calls to Mother Wolf. When this happened, "The Mother Wolf gets a headache and has to go to her room." In response, Sly Wolf would throw Snake Butt out of the play and soothe her mother back to feeling better.

Isobelle remained enmeshed in a relationship with her mother that was both hostile and dependent. Her father abetted her occasional acts of defiance toward her mother and was sometimes hostile himself. In the final analysis, however, Isobelle painted him as a vaguely laughable figure who could be disposed of when necessary and had little power to affect the central struggle between mother and daughter. From her immobilized position, Isobelle could not safely move toward a fully autonomous or sexually realized womanhood. She was locked instead into a kind of hyperfeminine dependency that provided a fragile mask for her underlying rage and disappointment.

The Case of Tanya P

The Parents

Tanya P was 7 years old when she was first brought to our counseling services by her father. He said Tanya had been raised by her mother until her age of 5, but that she had been living with him for the past two years. He also said that Mrs. P was unstable and could not protect Tanya, because she continually drifted into relationships with violent men.

In her first interview, Mrs. P agreed she had been involved with a number of physically abusive men in the past, Mr. P among them. She described her former husband, during their brief marriage, as emotionally dependent and violently explosive whenever he felt abandoned or rejected: "He would break things . . . push me around . . . beat me up." When this happened, Mrs. P said that "Tanya would scream, cry, or hang on my leg . . . or else wrap herself in the drapes." She also described herself as "very needy" and told us Tanya was her "only real reason for caring at all about my life."

Mrs. P tried to be protective of her daughter, but she seemed to have little real insight into Tanya's needs and feelings. In fact, she precipitously took Tanya to live with Mr. P in the middle of the night, after she received a particularly violent beating from her boyfriend. As she described this critical event, she said, "I just wanted a safe place for her until I could get things worked out with this guy. . . . It was never supposed to be a permanent thing!" While this mother had tried to keep her daughter safe, she had difficulty seeing the event from her daughter's point of view. She could not really understand that Tanya felt abandoned, "because . . . she knew I was doing it for her, and that I was coming back!"

Shortly after Tanya came to live with her father, he became involved with a very straight-laced girlfriend. This young woman took a dim view of the way Mrs. P had raised Tanya and insisted that Mr. P petition the court for sole custody. Mr. P and his girlfriend prevailed in this litigation, in part because Mrs. P either could not or would not organize an effective response. Things quickly changed for Tanya at this time. Lacking any real experience of being parented himself, Mr. P quickly relinquished the job to his girlfriend. As a result, the relationship between father and daughter changed from one of playful flirtatiousness to one in which he essentially became the anchor of his girlfriend's well-meant but overly strict efforts to establish a sense of order, discipline, and routine in Tanya's life. Mrs. P continued to be marginally involved with Tanya but felt too overwhelmed to challenge what she felt to be an unfair and punitive decision by the court. Any subsequent discussions of scheduling were accompanied by expressions of explosive anger by both Mr. and Mrs. P, to which Tanya was regularly exposed.

Tanya

When we first met Tanya, she was a giddy, smiling 7-year-old with darting eyes that checked constantly to see whether she was pleasing and holding adult attention. Her teacher described her as "very bright, but socially inappropriate. She constantly needs to be the center of attention. She flirts, chases the boys on the playground. . . . She'll toss up her skirts in the boys' faces . . . and really this is to be expected in kindergarten, but not at this age. In a way, she's very immature, but in another way she acts like a teenager." At the same time Mr. P confided, in a tone that was both horrified and disgusted, that he had found Tanya's diary, in which she had lovingly described how good it felt to touch and play with her "packet," the word she used for her genitals. "She's going to grow up to be just like her mother. . . . I don't know what the hell we're going to do when she's a teenager. . . . she'll be pregnant by the time she's 14!"

This 7-year-old girl seemed to be playing out oedipal issues that remained unresolved and continued to preoccupy her. She spent many sessions in the first six months of her treatment breathlessly unburdening herself of a seemingly endless supply of stories, memories, and impressions. In doing so, she seemed to be disclosing without feeling, as well as entertaining and testing the therapist: Would she listen? Would she pay attention? Would she judge?

As Tanya slowly began to open up, her unresolved oedipal issues began to surface. The terrors of being abandoned by her mother to her oedipal father were dramatically re-created in the following story she told: "One night, in the middle of the night, the little girl is sleeping and the mother comes and wakes her up and takes her to a beauty parlor. It's all light and bright and she puts on makeup and gets beautiful and she says 'Oh, you're going to be so beautiful and everything will change now' but then really the mother is plotting to take the girl to the children's adoption center. It's near the dog pound. If the children don't get adopted, they get killed."

In fact, as another of Tanya's stories suggests, the parents seem to have united in their abandonment of Tanya: "One day, a little homeless girl was lost in the forest with no place to go. She met a handsome king and he said 'Oh you are so beautiful and you are homeless, come to the palace and marry me.' The little girl did not know what to do, so she went to the palace. (At this point in the play the king kisses the little girl passionately.) The king says, 'Come with me and we'll sleep together in the same bed because we love each other. . . . And the king gave her beautiful clothes and she didn't look like a little homeless girl anymore . . . she was so lovely . . . but then the beautiful good fairy appears and she's yelling 'What are you doing here?! *I'm* the king's wife, how dare you? Get into the basement! Guards, murder her!' And the king said he was sorry to the beautiful good fairy . . . and put the little girl in the basement." Tanya's short-lived oedipal victory evokes the rivalrous rage of the true queen (who most likely represents combined elements of the mother and the father's girlfriend) and ends in a life-threatening betrayal by the father.

This child was caught in the web of an oedipal conflict that allowed no resolution. She could not really become "purified" by denying her father and retreating to her mother in the good-mother-me position, first because Tanya spent very little predictable time with her mother. Perhaps more important, Tanya seemed to feel that the connection with her mother was irretrievably broken. Whether or not retreat was possible, Tanya seemed to need her oedipal feelings. This was likely because, as her history and her stories suggested, Tanya had felt most fully acknowledged and valued as an oedipal rival or an oedipal prize in her short and somewhat chaotic life. To relinquish her oedipal self, her sexuality, and her separateness would be to lose that validation and risk disappearing entirely. But becoming fully oedipal and separate from her mother was not a supportable solution either. In this position, Tanya had contended with the terrors of ocdipal victory and a new rivalry with her father's girlfriend. The result had been betrayal and a second abandonment, this time by her father. Deepening the dilemma was the fact that Tanya's anxiety about this entrenched oedipal conflict was likely soothed by sexual feelings aroused during masturbation. These feelings, aspects of her oedipal self, were kept as a shameful secret. In this endless dilemma, Tanya literally had no safe way to be. With peers, she had only her "performances" and her sexuality to offer, and this she did with the manic effort of one who fears she might disappear at any moment.

IMPLICATIONS FOR INTERVENTION

Helping Parents to Focus on the Child's Needs

The concerns that naturally preoccupy an oedipal child are likely to alter his or her relationship with each parent in more or less subtle ways. In the war zone of a high-conflict divorce, these changes tend to be interpreted by the parents as shifts in the child's allegiance. These interpretations evoke intense reactions in the parents that are frightening and confusing for the child. A mother, for example, may become angry and withholding in response to her son's new bravado. Her reaction occurs because the change represents not only a loss of intimacy with the son but a defection to the father. The resulting anxiety can disrupt the mother's ability to provide the calm and reassuring presence her son needs. Similarly, a father may be delighted by his daughter's new interest in him because it signals a small victory. He may readily believe she is moving toward him because her mother is really not parenting her as well as he is.

In these situations, mental health intervention can help parents to understand that these shifts represent the child's normal developmental repositioning, in which both parents are essential although their roles shift in salience. When this understanding is in place, the child's needs and experiences become the focus of concern and the parental conflict (and the allegiances associated with it) recedes from consideration.

Intervention with the Family of Nathan M

In the case of Nathan M (whom we met earlier in this chapter), Mrs. M became overwhelmed and essentially abandoning when her son came home from visits acting like a miniature replication of his father. However, like most parents who want to do the best they can, she was ashamed of her behavior toward Nathan at these times and tended to gloss over the details. These were elicited only after careful and painstaking requests from the therapist, such as "Please forgive me for being so simple-minded about this, but if I'm going to really understand how hard this is for you, you have to tell me as if I am a fly on the wall, moment by moment." In this slow unfolding, Mrs. M was able to describe how she dreaded Nathan's homecoming. As soon as he came in the door, she would placate him with treats and television, and then become suffused with helplessness, followed by fury, when he stubbornly rejected her efforts to reestablish a connection. In her dilemma, the mother would then make a demand that she knew Nathan would not obey—for example, that he unpack his things immediately or take a shower. When he refused to comply, she would end up dragging him bodily to his room and leave him there to sob and rage, until he came out and begged her forgiveness. In this humiliating way Mrs. M regained intimacy with her son. As she shared these details, Mrs. M began to understand that provoking Nathan was a way to justify her own need to terrorize him back into submission and to vent her rage at him for leaving her. Like many mothers in high-conflict situations, Mrs. M also feared that if she were unable to manage her son, she would have to give him up entirely to his father. Sometimes, she confessed, she felt so overwhelmed that she wished this would happen.

As Mrs. M began to understand that Nathan's behaviors reflected a normal developmental struggle toward separation and boyhood, she could also begin to see that her own fears were placing her son in an insoluble bind: "Be with me, or be a man." At this point, Mrs. M's questions shifted away from the conflict—"How can I stop his father from encouraging this behavior?"—and began to focus on her own parenting:"How can I understand this new maturity in Nathan, and make room for him to be a boy in our relationship, so that he does not have to pull away from me?" This perspective represents an essential reframing of the dilemma, which is often central to the work with highly conflicted parents. Here, parenting is defined less in terms of providing a perpetual rescue from the other parent and more in terms of actively parenting to support the child's capacities. This notion is best introduced after the parent has had the opportunity to talk about the sense of helplessness and despair that comes from trying to control the other parent. The therapist can then empathically help the parent to understand that continuing to hope for change in the other parent is truly the path to helplessness. Such interventions, of course, are not appropriate if the other parent in fact presents real dangers to the child's health or well-being.

Supporting Nathan's Identification with Father

It was important for the therapist to help Mrs. M find ways in which she could actively support Nathan's identification with his father. She balked at first, saying, "Now why should I give him the idea that I approve of that lying son of a bitch? He certainly is not doing the same for me . . . and besides why can't Nathan just take James [her lover] as a role model!" In response, the therapist explained that Nathan felt himself to be a part of his biological father. The qualities in his biological father that his mother *could* accept represented the basis upon which Nathan would be able to weave together the mother/father identified parts of himself. The therapist emphasized that if Mrs. M could not provide this kind of support, Nathan would likely try to preserve his relationship to his father and his masculinity by pulling away from her completely. Although Mrs. M could not identify any qualities that she currently appreciated in Nathan's father, she was able to recall qualities in the man as she had known him when they married. It was these memories that she began to impart to her son.

SETTING RULES AND EXPECTATIONS

When parents can cooperate about rules and limit setting, the child derives comfort from the resulting clarity about how to be good. This consistency, over time, becomes internalized as the child's own moral standard. When parents cannot explicitly support each other by sharing the same rules, they can work toward communicating a general expectation that the child will abide by the authority of the adults in charge, even if the specific rules are different; that is, one parent may say, "You will do it this way in my house, and I don't care if you do it differently at your [other parent's] house. When you are here, you follow my rules, whatever they are!"

For Nathan, neither the attempt to support his identification with his father nor the attempt at parental cooperation proved to be effective. In spite of the therapist's efforts, Mr. M continued to actively encourage Nathan's opposition in relationships with most authority figures, including Mrs. M. He was convinced that his son's defiance of her was an appropriate reaction to her toxic and overcontrolling parenting. Similarly, when Nathan was expelled from a summer camp for repeatedly throwing food in the dining hall, Mr. M was outraged that the camp director did not sit down with Nathan to hear his views on the topic. He felt the camp director was dictatorial and told Nathan so.

When the parents' disparate expectations continue to confuse and double-bind the child, a shift from joint to sole legal custody may be appropriate. In Nathan's case, joint legal custody was too well entrenched to shift without significant emotional and financial cost. Instead, Mrs. M's attorney successfully petitioned the court to issue a set of orders that limited each parent's ability to intrude into Nathan's life when he was in the care of the other. The court also specified a highly detailed visitation schedule that provided for uninterrupted blocks of time with each parent. This time frame allowed Nathan to orient himself in each home, without having to manage disorganizing interruptions. The court also issued orders that explicitly required both parents' cooperation with Nathan's therapy and both parents' consent prior to termination. In cases like Nathan's, which are managed by legally imposed boundaries rather than parental cooperation, therapy for the child (with an experienced professional) should be seriously considered, as it may afford the child his or her only opportunity to find a way toward integration.

SETTING APPROPRIATE BOUNDARIES

Controlling the Child's Exposure to Adult Sexuality

When children are developmentally preoccupied with their sexuality, they may easily become overwhelmed by the power of their own impulses. This is a particular risk when vulnerable parents become focused on establishing new sexual relationships. These are often conducted in an erotically charged and exhibitionistic atmosphere. Children naturally respond with strong feelings of anxiety and excitement, which are often managed with sexualized play and masturbation. In high-conflict situations, these behaviors may easily trigger the abuse alarm. Clearly, it is important to help parents understand these risks and act preventively by setting and maintaining appropriate boundaries with their children. These matters need to be addressed in a firm and practical manner that focuses on the child's developmental needs and experiences, and avoids shaming the parents.

This strategy framed the intervention with the father of 4-year-old Steven. This child, who had recently developed an anxiously aggressive swagger, confided to his maternal grandmother that he had seen his father "with no clothes on with [his girlfriend] and then he hurt her." At about this time, Steven began wearing a belt and refused to take it off, even for sleeping. When his anxious mother brought him to our services to be evaluated, Steven took the clothes off the Ken and Barbie dolls, and had them kiss and lie upon each other. He said, "Then, there's a big explosion . . . and he jumps up and down on top of her." Steven repeated these themes compulsively over the course of several sessions. He also begged to be allowed to wear his cowboy chaps so that the evaluator could see them and demanded that she act as if she were afraid of his large size. In one session, he confided that he wanted to own a wild bull he could ride whenever he wished. Steven's play indicated that he was preoccupied with and confused by whatever he had seen or overheard, and that he felt ambivalent about being able to do what Daddy could do: he was both attracted to and afraid of his father's power. In light of this, his efforts to manage did not lack a certain 4-year-old logic, as he tried to stem the tide of newly aroused sexual feelings by the simple expedient of wearing a belt.

Steven's father denied that his son had seen anything at all. The therapist avoided the trap of challenging what could not be proved. She said that, of course, she was sure that this man had acted with utmost caution, as any sensible father would. Instead, she focused on Steven, explaining how sensitized and curious he was likely to be about sexual matters at this stage in his life, and that no matter how cautious a parent might be, it was difficult to control what children hear or imagine. She said that children at this stage of development can confuse sexuality and aggression very easily, and Steven seemed to have done that. The therapist spoke to the father as if his understanding of the need for appropriate privacy was a given. In this way, she could avoid shaming him and still provide him with information, without appearing to lecture.

Because the parents had in fact had a violent marriage, it was entirely possible that Steven had seen both sex and violence. The focus, however, was not on proving facts but on gaining the father's compliance in protecting Steven from further exposure. To accomplish this, the therapist suggested that the simplest way to settle Steven down and prevent any further difficulties was to keep the father's time with Steven separate from time with his girlfriend. In particular, she advised him not to allow his girlfriend to sleep over when Steven was in his custody. She empathically reminded him that his ex-wife was somewhat impulsive, and she could not guarantee that future episodes would not result in a Child Protective Services investigation. The therapist took the position that such an investigation would be upsetting for everyone, but most particularly for Steven, and would best be avoided for all concerned. Likely because he felt neither challenged nor shamed, and because he knew that other adults were now alerted, Steven's father was able to follow through on the therapist's suggestions. At the same time, both parents were helped to consider their child's developmental needs in a more focused and protective way.

Maintaining Appropriate Physical Boundaries Between Parent and Child

Sometimes physical boundaries between parents and children are violated in ways that can be both arousing and shaming to the child. These situations require a forthright explanation of the child's increasing need for privacy and physical integrity. When Jacob, for example, experienced a period of enuresis at age 4, his mother insisted on checking his underwear at regular intervals to see whether he was dry. She did not understand that his vigorous resistance represented a healthy effort to preserve his dignity and avoid her potentially arousing intrusions. Instead, she felt that it was one more instance of oppositional behavior instigated by his father. She believed that establishing compliance in this matter represented her son's return to her fold, as if Jacob could have no resistance to her that was meaningful or valuable in its own right. The therapist countered this belief by offering developmental information that helped the mother to understand that the problem was about her son's integrity and not about her former husband. This understanding countered the mother's helplessness and helped her to focus on her own parenting.

By contrast, in Isobelle G's family discussed earlier in this chapter, the father was not particularly intrusive with his daughter. However, he capitulated to her demands to sleep with him, because "Mommy won't let me sleep with her at her house." Mr. G allowed this sleeping pattern to become established because, to him, it was one way in which he, and not the mother, could meet Isobelle's needs. He did not consider that the situation reinforced Isobelle's oedipal fantasies in ways that would ultimately become too frightening for her to tolerate. The pattern was already well established when it came to the therapist's attention and consequently required a series of slow but firm approximations toward the goal of helping Isobelle to sleep alone.

When parents become conscious of the need to make changes, they often do so in ways that feel abrupt and rejecting to the child. This possibility can be headed off if the therapist reviews the actual words the parents plan to use. The concreteness of this approach can circumvent any misinterpretation of the therapist's suggestions.

WHEN THE SEXUAL ABUSE ALARM SOUNDS

Unfortunately, the issue of boundaries often does not come to the fore until the possibility of child sexual abuse has been raised. Without evidence or admission on the part of the accused perpetrator, it is extremely difficult to establish the meaning of the child's behaviors, feelings, and fantasies and to determine which of these represent a response to an eroticized boundary failure and which represent a response to a sexual intrusion that is physical. Although Child Protective Services investigations tend to focus on the distinctions, for the child either scenario will inflict its own kind of developmental damage.

The Value of a Timely and Rational Response

When one parent raises charges of child sexual abuse against the other, it is essential to respond actively and immediately. An active response is preferable to tactics that delay because of the belief that the charge is one more in an endless series of variants and will eventually die down from lack of attention. Inappropriate delay often leaves the child to cope alone with the onslaught of a parent's panic and anger. It is usually more effective (and ethically defensible) to respond as one would to any potential psychological emergency. Here, the goal is to provide a response designed to calm the parent's panic and contain the acting-out. Generally, the first order of business is the child's well-being. The counselor needs to review in a concrete and detailed way what has been said to the child and what can now be communicated that will soothe him or her. Next, the counselor will plan to communicate immediately and rationally with the accused parent. In some situations, this kind of facilitated communication resolves the issue. In others, the counselor needs to interview the child as soon as possible.

Follow-Up and Collaborative Evaluation

If the therapist concludes there are no grounds for a child abuse report, the situation may still require a follow-up plan for prevention and periodic assessment. This would include working with both parents to identify and control factors that might be contributing to the child's behavior. Specifically, the parents will need some help in setting clear boundaries, controlling exposure to sexual activity in movies and on television, and setting explicit rules and standards to help the child understand that sexual activity is for private enjoyment only.

When the child's presentation during the evaluation is ambiguous, the therapist may request a consultation from an expert in the assessment and treatment of child sexual abuse. It is important to stress here that the therapist's expert understanding of the effects of the parents' conflict on the child should not be confused with, or used as a substitute for, expertise in the area of child sexual abuse. Neither specialty has developed a foolproof assessment strategy that can reliably sort out the difference between a sexualized response to a boundary failure and a symptomatic indication of direct sexual abuse. What both experts can offer, when they work together, is a framework for understanding the child, the child's history, and the parents, as fully as possible. Finally, when the evidence warrants a reasonable suspicion of sexual abuse, the therapist may decide to make an immediate referral to Child Protective Services.

Unresolved Charges of Child Sexual Abuse

When allegations of child sexual abuse can neither be substantiated nor put to rest, the child typically continues to visit the accused parent in an atmosphere of intensely magnified mistrust and anger. In these cases, the family needs therapeutic management that provides some possibility for protection, if not healing. Hewitt (1991) described a case management strategy for handling these types of situations that, in essence, involves helping the child to develop a list of the kinds of touching that he or she does not like. The child then shares this list with each parent, in separate meetings, and each parent is asked, in the presence of the therapist, to agree to abide by it. Both parents are also asked to affirm to the child, in the presence of the therapist, the child's right to disclosure. This affirmation can serve as a protection, and as a warning, for the accused parent. If the parent has been wrongly accused, then the concreteness of the parameters can prevent further accusations. If, on the other hand, the parent has in fact molested the child, he or she cannot very well refuse to publicly affirm the child's right to tell other trusted adults.

Protecting the Child's Relationships with Trusted Adults

Finally, children caught in this shaming and confusing web of fear and suspicion may benefit from ongoing individual therapy. Aside from the obvious potential support to the child, the very fact of the child's treatment can have an impact on the conflicted parents. Specifically, both parents will know that a child in treatment is being continually assessed and in regular contact with a safe person in a private setting. If the abuse is nothing more than a false allegation, both parents may feel reassured by this knowledge. If abuse has occurred, the perpetrator's concern that the child may now disclose the facts in treatment can limit further incidents. When therapy for the child is not practical or financially feasible, it can be especially important to facilitate the child's access to ongoing relationships with trusted adults such as grandparents, school counselors, neighbors, coaches, or a volunteer big brother or sister.

Chapter 6

School-Age Children

The Struggle to Feel Lovable, Good, and Competent

*I*n the ordinary way of things, the school-age child is focused on mastering a variety of physical, intellectual, and social challenges in the world beyond the family. Peer relationships, as well as relationships with adults other than parents, become vital anchors along the way. To a large extent the child's progress depends upon the continuing support of his or her family and the strength of internal resources achieved in preceding developmental stages. In particular, the well-functioning child draws on a steady sense of self-worth and trust. This foundation can help the school-age child to tolerate learning from failure as well as from success. In addition, children rely on an inner standard of right and wrong to guide their participation in the larger community. When these achievements are in place, "the inner stage is set for entrance into life" (Erikson, 1963), and the child can use the grade-school years to braid together what Bibring (1961) identified as the essential component of enduring self-esteem: the capacity to feel lovable, good, and competent.

BASIC TRUST AND THE CAPACITY TO FEEL LOVABLE

If the child's earliest relationships have provided a predictable supply of empathic nurturing and support, then he or she is likely to develop the basic trust that is rooted in a reasonably constant sense of being lovable. Basic trust allows the child to turn to others without fear of becoming infantilized or disappointed when life's demands threaten to undermine this sense of self-worth. When basic trust is in place, the school-age child expects that adults—such as teachers, coaches, troop leaders, other parents— will provide the same kind of empathic support that his or her own parents have consistently provided. In fact, these very expectations, in turn, tend to engage the adults' support and affirm the child's original trust.

The Growth of Relationships and Social Understanding

When 7-year-old Rose was in second grade, her best friend was a popular, willful little girl named Gillian. Rose, who tended to form intense connections with one friend at a time, was devastated when Gillian began to pal around with two other girls, who were the "princesses" of grade three. Although Gillian still wanted to be her friend as well, Rose was too resentful for compromise. She was preoccupied with feeling sad and angry about Gillian's betrayal and was disappointed when she tried to make new friends who did not seem to be nearly as much fun as Gillian. In her after-school program, Rose became noticeably bored and sometimes rude to the other children. After one such episode, she confided crabbily to a teacher, whom she had known since kindergarten, "No one's fun like Gillian. I hate her . . . and I try to make new friends but nothing works . . . It's not the same, Gillian felt like my family, my sister! No one else feels that way."

At that point, the teacher wisely suggested that friends do not always feel like family. She told Rose, who played soccer, that friendships are like sport; they require practice and even coaching. After mulling over this new idea for a bit, Rose asked who could coach her. The teacher volunteered to do so, when Rose was in the after-school program. She said, "When you start to get cranky or bossy with your playmates, I'll remind you. We'll have a signal. Pretty soon, you will have some new friends." Although Rose progressed in a "two steps forward, one step backward" style, she eventually tipped the balance in favor of tolerance. After several months of coaching, Rose told her teacher she had invited Gillian and another friend to play at her house the day before. The teacher asked how things went and Rose replied, "It was good. . . . I told my mom how to coach me and it really worked!" In this situation, Rose was not questioning whether she was lovable or good; instead, she was irritated by the loss of what she felt entitled to. Her steady ability to hold on to a positive sense of herself helped her to tolerate feeling mad, sad, and disappointed. Because Rose could tolerate her own feelings and trust that others would too, she was able to reach out for help. In so doing, she found solutions that enhanced her competence.

Relationships and the Potential for New Mastery

During the grade-school years, this type of learning about relationships is increasingly characterized by an emerging ability to see oneself from the point of view of another person (Selman, 1980). This developmental shift allows children to see themselves more objectively and realistically, and fuels their desires to become masters of their own feelings and behaviors. The preschooler, for example, may allow himself a good cry in the first few days of nursery school, whereas the first or second grader will bite her lip as she fights for control in front of her classmates. Similarly, older grade-schoolers strive for an increasingly "cool" and unfazed appearance. Because other people can now be understood to have their own point of view, they are seen less as an extension of the self and more as fully real and separate. Children understand with growing clarity that their actions affect other people and shape others' perceptions of them. Naturally, school-age children are more self-conscious than ever before. Ten-year-old Charles, for example, had been swimming with a city team for over two years when his coach insisted that he enter a championship meet for the first time. Charles agreed, although he was both excited and nervous. When the coach asked him why he was so nervous, Charles answered querulously, "What if I just can't finish a race? Everyone will make fun of me at practice after that. . . . It'll be so humiliating!" Charles's concerns highlight the growing self-consciousness of the school-age child. This new awareness tends to redefine what it takes to feel lovable, which is often inextricably braided with what it takes to feel competent in the eyes of one's peers. If Charles has enough inner resources and can trust his parents or his coach for help when he needs it, his self-conscious fears can fuel new mastery. He may practice very hard to avoid humiliation and succeed at the championship. In that case, he will encounter new capacities that preserve his sense of being lovable and competent. Alternatively, he may fail at the championship, and learn (with support from those around him) that being lovable does not necessarily depend on being competent. Optimally, this realization will deepen his trust in relationships and diminish his fear of failure in the future.

WHEN BASIC TRUST FAILS AND
THE CAPACITY TO FEEL LOVABLE IS TENUOUS

For the youngster in an embattled divorced family, this type of progress through the grade-school years may be blocked as much by current conflicts as by compromised achievements in the preceding stages of development. If, for example, vulnerable parents were not able to be consistently and empathically responsive during the separation–individuation phase, the child will fail to completely internalize a steady and self-supporting sense of being lovable (see chapter 4). Lacking reliable inner resources, the child will continue to depend on emotional supplies that are unpredictably or only contingently available. A vulnerable parent may, for example, respond empathically only if she has access to some kind of emotional support herself. In this situation, the parent's availability is likely to seem entirely unpredictable to the child because it depends on unseen processes within the parent. The child remains preoccupied with figuring out how to control the parent's responsiveness because his or her survival and sense of self depend on it. In other situations, a vulnerable parent may be contingently responsive, often when the child is gratifying in a particular way. If these patterns persist, the child's sense of being lovable feels tenuous and hopelessly confused with being good. Being good becomes defined as being able to evoke the parental response that the child desperately needs but cannot trust, whereas being bad might result in a terrifying loss of the parent's physical or emotional presence, an abandonment.

The Child's Defensive Fragmentation

If early development has been disrupted in this way, the school-age child's "inner stage" is not set "for entrance into life." Instead, the child remains focused on the primary players in the first act (the parents) and the central question of whether he or she is lovable in their eyes. The child will unconsciously resolve the awful ambiguity of this question by developing an unconscious script for predicting his or her own part in the drama as well as those of parents. The script contains rules and expectations for understanding and controlling how to remain lovable and good and avoid being unlovable and bad. Typically the script is entirely unconscious. Its rigid shaping of thought, feeling, perception, and behavior is best detected in the repeated themes of children's projective play, stories, and role plays. It is important to note that this unconscious script is likely to depart significantly from the self-description that children borrow from family mythology and will readily articulate.

The child's preoccupation with how to remain "perfectly good" and therefore lovable can inhibit confident progress and result in a profound sense of shame and fragmentation. Eight-year-old Karen, for example, had been the subject of her parents' bitter and sometimes violent conflict since her age of 18 months. Now in third grade, this bright and verbal child described her sense of inner disconnection by explaining to her therapist that she had "good parts" to show to the world and "bad parts" that she could not show. When the therapist asked Karen what these different parts of herself were like, she carefully divided a piece of paper in half. On one side she made a list of perfect attributes, on the other a list of negations: "awesome" versus "totally dorky"; "popular . . . everybody loves me" versus "creepy . . . everybody hates me"; "smart" versus "retarded"; "beautiful" versus "really ugly."

Karen's struggle with this shifting sense of whether or not she was lovable and good left her feeling acutely vulnerable to the judgment of others. A central question in every interaction was whether others would see the "good Karen" or the "bad Karen."

How the Child's Defensive Fragmentation Can Undermine Relationships

Developmentally vulnerable children like Karen seem to understand other people in equally simplistic terms. Eleven-year-old Wendy, for example, explained that she was really good friends with her classmate Margaret at the beginning of the school year. "She was really nice to me, we were like friends . . . but then she wouldn't sit next to me at the assembly and now I know she's really mean. . . . She fakes it when she feels like it." Wendy could not explain what had gone wrong between herself and her classmate, nor was she willing to explore the topic. She dismissed Margaret and the relationship with a shrug, saying, "I don't know. I thought she was like this really neat person, but she's really a creep. Sometimes she's nice now, but I know she's a big liar." Wendy was not interested in any further explanation or exploration of her disappointment. From her point of view, she had solved the problem.

Like many of the school-age children in our project, Wendy seemed to have little capacity to tolerate fluctuations in her friend's attitude or behavior. Instead, unable to bear the threat of abandonment that Margaret's slight evoked, Wendy reverted to a scripted understanding of her friend's behavior. She decided that her friend had simply shifted from being "a really neat person" to being "a creep." This understanding was entirely consistent with Wendy's unintegrated experiences of other people and of herself. Ironically, Wendy's inability to stand the pain of her friend's inconstancy (without an immediate flight to the comforting confines of her inner script) robbed her of the chance to learn new ways of understanding relationships.

How Defensive Fragmentation Can Undermine Social Understanding and New Mastery

When children like Karen and Wendy fail to internalize a constant sense that they are lovable, they remain dependent on the reassurance and support of others to maintain a positive sense of themselves. Whenever that support is withdrawn, the child is left feeling unbearably unlovable, bad, and even nonexistent. Because of this, every interpersonal failure, from the mildest criticism to an imagined slight, tends to be experienced as a terrifying fall from grace. Parents in conflicted divorce situations are often baffled by their grade-school child's intense reactions to any type of confrontation or correction. Ten-year-old Karl's father, for example, described how he caught his son in a white lie and confronted him. He said, "Karl seemed to literally fall apart before my eyes . . . screaming and crying like I had accused him of murder! He totally denied it, like it couldn't possibly have happened, as if what I *knew* was true couldn't possibly have happened, had nothing to do with anything real. . . . I just could not bring it up again!" Karl's developmentally primitive belief, that bad and good are unconnected, can turn even the slightest human fault into unlovable "badness" without hope of redemption. This fragmented understanding of self and other, that tends to dominate these children's inner scripts, makes it impossible for them to acknowledge error. Their panicked flight into denial in turn robs them of the chance to learn more about how people see them and how to handle criticism more competently.

THE CAPACITY TO FEEL LIKE A GOOD CHILD

In most families, children learn "being good" requires following rules of conduct upheld by both parents in a fairly predictable way. Children enjoy their parents' approval and their own feelings of being "good" as they learn to use the rules to gain self-control. This kind of learning ordinarily peaks toward the end of the oedipal period, when "being good" increasingly involves learning to contain the rise in erotic, aggressive, and possessive impulses characteristic of this stage. If both parents honor and enforce a mutually held and reasonable set of rules and expectations during this critical passage, the child will likely acquire a useful moral foundation that comes increasingly from within.

The Growth of Moral Understanding and Behavior

The school-age years mark a significant period in the child's moral growth. During this time the child's motives for being good evolve beyond a wish to avoid punishment and toward a wish to preserve relationships (Gilligan, 1982; Kohlberg, 1981), that is, to balance being good in the eyes of another as well as in the eyes of oneself. As children struggle to achieve this kind of reciprocity, their capacity for moral reasoning and action tends to become more subtle and less absolute. Ten-year-old Oliver, for example, spent an entire summer wrestling with the question of whether and how to stay best friends with his classmate Scott, who had punched him in a fit of temper on the last day of school. Scott told Oliver that he didn't mean to hit him, so he should be forgiven. To Oliver, Scott's intention did not matter one way or the other; he was still faced with a moral dilemma: how to be good according to his own uncompromising standards, which dictated that you never hit a friend, and how to be good in the eyes of Scott, who seemed to think that he was entitled to be forgiven just because he "didn't mean to hit" Oliver. By the beginning of the next school year, however, his friendship with Scott was back on track. When his parents inquired, Oliver shrugged, saying, "Well, what I think is, he didn't really mean it so I guess it wasn't so bad. He just oughta control himself better."

In the course of his inner struggle, Oliver began to master the moral meaning of the difference between action and intent. As a result, his understanding of right and wrong became more flexible, complex, and realistic. Oliver was able to master these complexities, finally, because he was able to hold on to his affection for Scott in spite of his disappointment and confusion. This capacity to tolerate discomfort and ambivalence can catalyze new maturity.

How Defensive Fragmentation Can Undermine Moral Growth

When children cannot bear the natural ups and downs of friendship because they depend so completely on others to feel lovable and good, moral growth is sacrificed to the need for connection. When 10-year-old Leslie, for example, returned from a visit with her father and his girlfriend, Teresa, she confessed to her mother that she had spent her pocket money on a birthday card for Teresa. When Leslie saw that this news made her mother furious, she quickly added that her father had spanked her when she did not want to buy the card, so she felt she had no choice. In reality, Leslie's father was a passive man who never spanked his daughter; in fact, he had trouble getting her to do anything she didn't want to do. In addition, Leslie enjoyed a close relationship with Teresa and preferred visits that included her. Still, in that moment of confrontation, nothing else mattered to Leslie except the need to soothe her mother and restore the feelings of being lovable and good in her presence. All Leslie's other loyalties slipped away. It is difficult for children to follow any kind of moral standard when the need to feel loved, on any terms, is paramount.

How Defensive Fragmentation Can Disrupt the Capacity for Empathy

Sometimes when children succeed at being "good" (by meeting the exacting demands of the powerful other), they seem to feel almost superhumanly perfect. At these times, all frailties experienced as "bad" (unworthy and unlovable) are split off from consciousness. Empathy, the essential moral fiber of human relationships, cannot develop in this defensive fragmentation. When, for example, 9-year-old James ordered his 4-year-old stepsister to walk four blocks with him to the grocery store, she went. When he then insisted that she walk home alone (because he had met a friend at the store), the child wept and begged him to accompany her. James refused and walked away without a backward glance. When James's father learned about this, he was appalled by his son's coldness. Later, James told his counselor, with a shrug, "She's a stupid wimp. I would never beg like that. She could go home alone. Big deal!" James's harsh view came from the power he gained from feeling he was "perfectly good" because he needed nothing. He unconsciously split off from any feelings of vulnerability or neediness that might undermine this state of perceived perfection. As a result, he was unable to identify or acknowledge these feelings in his young stepsister. He turned his back on her weeping in precisely the same way he turned his back on his own pain, because it was unbearable.

This lack of fellow feeling stands in sharp contrast to the empathic powers of a typically developing school-age child. When 8-year-old Peter teased his little sister until she began to weep with helpless rage, he paused to notice that she was really distressed. Making a small crooning sound of comfort, he stooped and put his arms around her. Peter was able to perform this simple act of kindness because the part of him that felt powerful was not achieved by disowning the part of him that felt helpless. Even when he felt powerful, he could identify and empathize with his sister's vulnerability. Moral sensibility and action rest on this essential recognition of the humanity of the other.

How the Parental Conflict Can Undermine Moral Growth

The daily realities of the parental conflict may threaten the child's capacity to hold, with any integrity, to a consistent standard of right and wrong, even if development has been reasonably steady until that time. This is because, in a high-conflict situation, each parent is likely to explain to the child that he or she (in contrast to the other parent) is on the side of the angels. In fact, these conflicting messages tend to become more overt as children reach school age, because the parents tend to see the child's growing awareness and rationality as a new capacity to make judgments about the other parent. The child now has the potential to become an informed ally in the conflict. Parents often say that they need to fully explain the other parent's failings to their child to teach appropriate standards of right and wrong. This need for moral guidance, they say, now supersedes the child's need for protection from the conflict. As one father explained, in a tone that was both self-righteous and bewildered, "My kid's furious with me for pointing out bad things about her mom, but it's time she learned. How else do I help her know right from wrong, now that she's getting older? I'm like a mirror for both of them; they hear about their faults from me and they hate it, they prefer denial!"

The child's moral confusion is intensified when the parents' pressure to take sides feels like an invitation to lie and to believe lies. Soon no one can be believed, not even oneself. For example, when 9–year-old Benjamin's parents separated, he confided to a project counselor, with unusual perceptiveness, "I don't know, they say bad things about each other. I don't know who to believe. My mom says Dad's a cheat and she thinks I'm just lying if I defend him. She thinks he put me up to it. Dad says Mom's mean to me, when she's not. Dad thinks I'm just scared of her if I defend my mom!"

Over the next two years Benjamin's parents pursued an unrelenting series of court actions. Each parent sought to gain sole custody, and each was willing to believe that victory would reflect Benjamin's true needs and wishes. At the end of this period of time Mrs. T complained bitterly that Benjamin was "lying blatantly to anyone and everyone." When Benjamin was subsequently reevaluated, his projective stories communicated a pervasive sense of his own duplicity and loss of moral integrity. Each story was a variation on a theme in which the central figure was "a spy who lived in the attic at the mom's house and the dad's house. No one knew he was a spy, he kept it very secret, everyone thought he was just a nice kid." Clearly, when the child lacks a moral foundation, then the development of personal integrity and competence in the interpersonal world is likely to be seriously compromised.

THE CHILD'S CAPACITY TO FEEL COMPETENT

When children can draw on a steady inner confidence that they are both lovable and good, and if they have the continuing support of their families, they can learn from the challenges of the school-age years without becoming overwhelmed. Ups and downs may bring discomfort, ambivalence, and even temporary regression, but these setbacks can also catalyze new growth and competence in the classroom, in the neighborhood, and on the playing fields. When development is on track, this new mastery becomes the foundation for identity achievement in the future.

When the Child's Developmental Resources Fail to Support Competence

As described in chapters 4 and 5, many children in high-conflict families have compromised their capacity for trust and independence. As a result, any further exploration of their competence in the world beyond the family is likely to induce considerable ambivalence. Although mastering concrete skills on the playground or in the classroom can provide a welcome new sense of control and relief from the uncertainties of relationships, this progress toward self-sufficiency may also cause overwhelming anxiety about loss and abandonment.

In some children, this ambivalence about their own competence is readily apparent. For example, 9-year-old Benjamin (described earlier) did very well in class at the beginning of each school year and then seemed to trail off in a cloud of forgetfulness and distraction. His teacher noted, "The more I praise him, the more likely it is that he'll somehow forget or lose his homework the next day! I have never seen a kid so set against making it." Benjamin himself was acutely conscious of these patterns in his behavior, though he did not understand them. He explained sadly to his therapist, "Every morning I get up and I say to myself, today's gonna be a perfect day, no screw-ups . . . and every day I just don't make it."

Other children, girls in particular, manage their ambivalence by achieving competencies they do not truly seem to own (Roseby & Wallerstein, 1997). Ten-year-old Leslie (also described earlier) had a sometimes rageful mother who longed for her daughter to be recognized as gifted and successful. Leslie received excellent grades at school, danced well in ballet recitals, and rarely misbehaved. When asked to make three wishes for herself at age 21, she said, "I want my mother to never leave me, and I want to be a physicist." The resolution of her ambivalence was embedded in this strikingly polarized answer. While Leslie could plan to become a physicist and thus maintain the satisfying sense of control that her academic competence gave her, she had little sense that such achievements would lead to further autonomy. In fact, all Leslie's achievements seemed to be in the service of maintaining the connection with her fragile and demanding mother, rather than in the service of her own identity. There is an almost cardboard quality to the performances of pseudocompetent children like Leslie. Their achievements provide control and safety rather than vitality or joy. Their instrumental progress provides them with the capacity to work but not to love.

When the Parental Conflict Disrupts Competence

Chronic intrusion of the parental conflict tends to rob the child of familial as well as internal support. This is because parents who have become locked into battle position often have difficulty focusing on the concerns of their school-age child in any realistic way. Too often, any setback in the child is construed as a failure of the other parent while the child's needs are ignored. For example, when Karen (described earlier) was assigned to a program for gifted and talented students (on the basis of her outstanding test scores), she became overwhelmed by the amount of homework in her new classes. She frequently failed to turn in her assignments because she was ashamed if they were not completed on time. Karen's father panicked at first, then blamed his ex-wife in a fit of rage. He said she was not sufficiently supervising Karen's homework, because she was, in this as in all things, "completely irresponsible." Without further discussion, he concluded that the only solution was for him to sue for full custody of Karen. Although her father eventually calmed down, Karen had already been robbed of much needed guidance and support. Instead, she felt compelled to perform perfectly, without assistance, to prevent further eruptions of her parents' chronic conflict. School-age children become increasingly self-conscious about the lack of support in their families. They describe their experiences with phrases about feeling "torn in half," "fought over by a couple of mean dogs," and "being in the middle of a stupid tug-of-war." Children seem to use these words to convey their anger and disappointment as well as the dawning suspicion that other children's parents do not behave the way their own parents do. This kind of embarrassment comes up in treatment groups when the participants generate lists of "feeling words" that consistently include descriptors such as "embarrassed," "feeling weird about my family," and "scared to tell friends about what's going on." Similarly, children communicate a painful consciousness of their own fragmentation and loss of integrity when they describe themselves as "two-faced," "weird," "confused," "withdrawn," "sick," "left out," and "like an alien." Because these children feel ashamed of their own fragmentation and the lack of support in their families, they tend to avoid the kind of authentic contact with others that might make new learning and mastery possible. A self-destructive pattern emerges as children substitute scripted defensive strategies, which serve to maintain distance and the appearance of control, while undermining the kind of engagement with the demands of reality that would lead to new levels of competence and mastery.

PATTERNS OF DEFENSIVE FRAGMENTATION: RORSCHACH FINDINGS

This profound sense of mistrust and alienation is not always identifiable in children who tend to excel at picking up cues about what is expected of them and can mask their own vulnerabilities as a matter of survival. Not surprisingly, observational checklists and cursory interviews often indicate they are performing adequately in the classroom, in sports, or other areas of performance but fail to capture the fragile and layered quality of their competence. Their underlying vulnerability becomes apparent only when we attempt to initiate a treatment relationship or conduct a projective assessment.

The Rorschach projective test proved to be particularly useful in our attempts to evaluate and understand this group of children, for several reasons. First, the unstructured nature of this particular test tends to bypass the characteristic defensiveness of these acutely self-conscious children. Second, the Rorschach is a comprehensive personality instrument that can provide information about the child's psychological organization—that is, how internal processes work together to shape the child's way of understanding and responding to the interpersonal world. Third, the Exner comprehensive scoring system (Exner, 1990) allows for reliable comparisons of the scores of children in high-conflict families with normative samples of same-age children. Findings from the results of 21 boys and 27 girls, ages 6 to 13 (Roseby et al., 1995), provided a strikingly coherent pattern of psychological organization that differed markedly and consistently from the typically developing 9-year-olds who were selected as an average-age comparison group (Exner, 1990).

The Sense of Self

Specifically, the quantitative results of testing showed that, in a majority of cases, school-age children in high-conflict families lack basic trust in themselves and other people and do not feel particularly viable or important in relationships. In addition to showing a markedly limited capacity for trust and positive self-esteem in their quantitative scores, the content of the children's responses communicates a fragile and fragmented sense of self. For example: "This looks like a line in the middle of a person, pulling it apart, looks like being ripped apart." "This looks like two witches on top of a beast's head and the beast is on top of a fire and the beast's head is splitting." "A leaf, but cut off a little, as if cut in half." Other responses suggested the child's unconscious grief over the loss of the real and integrated self, which is sacrificed to the demands of the parental conflict. For example: "Someone that was flattened, run-over, a cat." "This one is of a rainbow being washed away by the morning breeze, 'cos you can see the colors are dripping and melting away." "A flower that is dying."

Rules and Expectations About Relationships

Additional findings indicated that by the time they reach school age (if not before), these children have consolidated a set of rules and expectations about relationships that protect, on the one hand, and isolate from corrective experience, on the other. Specifically, they tend to ignore intense or complex feelings and oversimplify their own and other people's ideas to the point of distortion. Rorschach testing showed that unusually high levels of unexpressed anger are central among the feelings these children try to avoid. While this shutting-down process works to reduce experience to patterns that can be predicted and controlled, it also closes children off from vast amounts of interpersonal learning that ordinarily occurs during the grade-school years.

In almost half the youngsters tested, their pervasive lack of basic trust, alienation from other people, and unexpressed anger accumulated to a level of clinically significant hypervigilance; that is, their psychological energy was devoted to vigilant scanning of interpersonal and intrapsychic experience. Again, the content of children's responses provides some insight into the substance of the quantitative deviations in the Rorschach test scores. Their responses communicate the kind of dangers that might erupt in themselves or others without this ceaseless hypervigilance. For example: "A monster. Right here are eyes, and he's really mad, eyebrows like this, and dots in eyes, his face, this is his mustache, my dad has a mustache." "Look at this demon . . . two legs . . . his head . . . a big roaring mouth . . . two eyes and he has spikes on top of his head." "Some kind of devil or a pirate with a big greedy mouth." Furthermore, responses frequently contain benign figures that have threatening elements, and vice versa. These suggest a world in which the split-off "shadow side" of human experience intrudes with terrifying unpredictability. For example: "Two clowns clapping hands and their heads just came off." "Santa Claus, the hat, beard, nose, tummy, and this pirate sword." "Frankenstein doing the splits."

Because they expect so little from others, these children seem to expect everything of themselves, inflexibly using their own thoughts and ideas as virtually their exclusive way of dealing with problems. Given the barren, almost mechanistic structure of their inner lives, this strategy is not likely to help these children to feel competent among their peers.

The defensive rules and expectations we infer from these Rorschach findings all limit the child's access to developmentally critical information. They lessen opportunities for talking through difficulties with other people, forestall engagement with new ideas and feelings, and ultimately restrict the child's contact with his or her own internal life and the present reality of interpersonal events. Not surprisingly, these factors create an idiosyncratic world view. Literally 100 percent of the children tested responded with a clinically significant level of unusual or frankly distorted perception and understanding of the interpersonal world, which further fueled their vigilant mistrust and undermined their competence.

PATTERNS OF ORGANIZED FRAGMENTATION: CLINICAL PRESENTATIONS

These disturbing test results suggest that children in high-conflict families are robbed of the kind of flexible access to an expanding range of inner experiences and interpersonal relationships that would ordinarily support maturation during the school-age years. Instead, these vulnerable children seem to manage the fragmenting pressures of their parents' conflict by developing increasingly inflexible and distorted patterns of understanding themselves and others. In some children, these patterns or scripts become organized around a core schema, in response to traumatic scenes of family violence and conflict (see chapter 3). In others, the patterns seem to provide ways of managing the more subtle and chronic stresses of family relationships that are inconsistent, contingent, and double-binding. Whatever their source, these patterns seem to serve a common purpose: to limit nuance and complexity and to reduce experiences to black-and-white terms, in which thoughts, feelings, and responses are rapidly screened and unconsciously classified as safe or dangerous. In general, whatever leads to feeling acknowledged, protected, or valued is safe, and whatever might lead to shame, loss, or abandonment is dangerous. Over time, the child's way of being in the world becomes increasingly limited to patterns that feel safe, while experiences that feel too dangerous become more and more inaccessible. This kind of fragmenting defense provides children with a sense of protection and control, but at the cost of their capacity to be spontaneous, flexible, and, ultimately, real.

The "Happy-Happy Joy-Joy" Mask

Some children find safety in patterns that limit their own awareness or expression of any authentic aspects of themselves. These children do not seem to be fully present as they relate to others. They appear instead to offer a kind of inflexible mask which screens them from any real contact. Some children maintain this kind of distance by pleasing and distracting with their smiling responses to the cues of others. In this presentation, any feelings of anger, sorrow, or opposition seem to have been erased from inner consciousness. Karen (described earlier), who saw her father assault her mother on several occasions, provides a case in point. When she was first seen, her counselor noted, "She talked without stopping, as if silence or stillness would be intolerable . . . hugging me tightly at the interview, saying, 'I like you soooo much." Karen's frenetic efforts to please and entertain seemed to be her way of managing the terrifying inconsistencies she described in the following story.

"This is the story of Little Red Riding Hood. She lives in a big dark forest. Sometimes she lives with the beautiful good fairy and sometimes she lives with the wolf. Sometimes the good fairy tells her, 'You are so good and so smart and so beautiful and so everything I always wanted you to be.' But some days Little Red Riding Hood forgot to bring the fairy fifty cents . . . then the fairy would yell and scream and say, 'Get out of here and go to the stupid wolf!' and she would wander off into the dark forest and get to the wolf's house. The wolf would say, 'Oh you are so beautiful and good and sweet my little puff ball . . . ' but sometimes he would roar, 'Where's my meat?' and Little Red Riding Hood forgot the meat and she was scared so she ran off into the forest until she got to her secret box of clothes and she put them on and turned back into a perfect princess."

Karen's longing for a protective state of perfection was also reflected in a drawing she completed during group work. The task was to draw a completely private room that contained anything that could be imagined. Karen's room contained only a magical dress-up box that could turn her into a fairy princess whenever she wanted. Later, in treatment, Karen began to refer to her inflexible sprightliness as her "happy-happy joy-joy mask." Children like Karen seem to consolidate this kind of artificial exterior when their experience of love and protection in primary relationships has been fundamentally unpredictable. As a result, they need to feel completely in control of themselves and their contact with others to feel real, protected, lovable, and good. In Karen's case, these feelings depended on an appearance of perfect responsiveness.

The Facade of Remote Self-Control

Other children achieve a kind of safety by refusing to be drawn into any interaction that might jar their self-control. In this presentation, spontaneity is cut off and replaced with a kind of impenetrable remoteness, which serves to mask the underlying vulnerability. For example, when Leslie (described earlier) was first seen, she marched, silent and unsmiling, into the counselor's office, where she sat down in the counselor's chair. She spoke very little and answered all direct questions with a shrug. After some coaxing, she approached the sandtray. In her first play, a baby dinosaur repeatedly teamed up with "its mother" to bury a third dinosaur "who was always trying to butt in and play with the baby." When asked if the third dinosaur belonged with the first two, Leslie said, "The baby's not sure, but the mother comes and fights it off." Leslie then anxiously dug out the buried dinosaur and began the play again. She masked her worries and ambivalence with an appearance of solemn, almost mechanical self-control. This outward presentation did not shift for many months. During the intervening period, Leslie seemed to hover at an invisible interpersonal boundary; that is, she was physically in the room but was emotionally unavailable. She spent hours sifting sand with her back to the counselor but checking periodically to see whether the counselor was still watching. Later, she would write messages in the sand and then challenge the counselor to decipher them. She responded to the counselor's inevitable failures with the resigned disappointment of a tired adult. In this way, Leslie managed to communicate how she felt as she repeatedly failed to solve the endless puzzle of her parents' paradoxical demands.

In this defensive configuration Leslie did not acknowledge her confusion or her helplessness in the face of her parent's conflict. These feelings were split off from her conscious awareness because they were unbearable. Instead, she presented as being fully in control, both rejecting and bored, while she induced feelings of helplessness and confusion in her counselor. It was the counselor who described session after session of feeling immobilized, distant, unable to figure out what was going on, and cut off from any possibility of connecting with Leslie. After an arduous number of these numbing sessions, the counselor began to talk to Leslie about the feelings that seemed "so big for you that they floated out for me [the counselor] to catch." Leslie at first resisted, then slowly began to tolerate this gentle but persistent acknowledgment. When this kind of tolerance develops (and there is no substitute for time and patience here), real contact in the treatment relationship may become possible.

Both Karen and Leslie achieved a measure of safety and distance by presenting a pleasing or controlled facade. This kind of presentation is consistent with girls' defensive tendencies to avoid separation and definition in high-conflict families. It also fits well with the kind of social expectations that confront girls in their school-age years, and it provides the appearance of 'fitting in.' In projective play, however, the underlying constriction is often represented as a kind of death.

Intermittent Explosiveness

Boys in high-conflict families often have a more difficult time organizing themselves quite so neatly. Areas of safety and danger seem to be more amorphous for them and less easily defined. Nine-year-old Kurt's mother, for example, described him as "trying very hard to take his dad's place. He helps me out with the kids, he's incredibly sweet . . . then he gets mouthy and goes into these tantrums like you would not believe . . . and I don't know what to do with him then." His parents' divorce and bitter conflict had robbed Kurt of any regular contact with the father whom he loved and blindly admired. He was furious with his father for leaving, and with his mother for banishing him. He could not acknowledge his anger toward his father for fear of hurting him. Nor did he feel safe expressing his anger toward his mother, because he knew she was his only real support in the world. At the same time, he could not relinquish these feelings. First of all, the anger was a tolerable way to mask his underlying pain and to set a boundary between himself and his mother. As Kurt's mother said, "He shows only the anger, not the hurt." The anger also represented a way for Kurt to maintain a kind of connection with his often explosive father. For

Kurt, it was not clear which felt more dangerous, having or not having anger. Because of his ambivalence, Kurt could not split off these feelings with any consistency. Kurt's teacher described him as "a really nice kid . . . but he has a lot of anger that often comes out inappropriately. He gets berserk . . . out of control . . . the other kids back away. It happens at least once a week. After the tantrum he won't communicate, he gets rigid and furious . . . he'll try to leave if I let him. He's trying very very hard not to let people know him. It's like he's scared about some part of himself that people shouldn't find out."

In an early session with his counselor, Kurt used a drawing to communicate the panic and despair he felt as he tried and failed to split off his anger. In the drawing, he outlined a bomb with a black center. Above the bomb, he wrote the words "I'm afraid I'm going to explode." When his counselor asked what other feelings might be in the bomb, Kurt pointed to the black center, saying, "I don't know, they're all in that middle." Kurt's unsuccessful struggle for control, so central to a school-age child, was seriously undermining his sense of being lovable, good, and competent. He made this clear one day when he wrote over and over on his homework, "I HATE ME . . . I HATE ME."

A Polarized Presentation: From Alignment to Alienation

Some school-age children, particularly as they move toward adolescence, seem to achieve a sense of safety and predictability by dividing themselves and their parents into polar opposites. In this presentation, the child identifies one parent as "perfectly good" and feels and behaves like a responsive, loyal, and "perfectly good" child in that parent's presence. The other parent is identified as "perfectly bad" and the child with that parent is as unresponsive, oppositional, and dissatisfied as he or she is good with the other.

In younger children, this organization can be quite fluid as the child finds safety and comfort in experiencing whichever parent she is with at the moment (and herself with that parent) as perfectly good. The absent parent (and the self with that parent) then becomes perfectly bad. Over time, however, this pattern tends to consolidate so that one parent is *consistently* identified as "good" and the other as "bad." The identified "good parent" tends to be the one who is most gratified and responsive to the "perfectly good" presentation in the child. In this way, the emotional supports that the child desperately needs become most predictably available. For school-age children, this compartmentalized distortion of themselves and their relationships can be particularly compelling. It resolves the uncomfortable ambivalence that develops with the child's maturing capacity to understand both sides of the conflict and provides relief from the parents' increasing pressure to align. The interpersonal world begins to make sense and the child feels less anxious. The following case traces the evolution of this kind of pattern from early ambivalence through consolidation, into parental alienation.

The Case of Belinda D

Eight-year-old Belinda D was first seen in the high-conflict project approximately one year after her parents separated. At that time, she described a world that was both bleak and chaotic. In the sandtray, she set up a scene in which her parents were off in separate corners "fighting on the phone," while her father's new lover, Miriam, was taking care of her own two children as well as Belinda. "Everyone's crying. I'm trying to talk to someone about my homework . . . no one can help!" At this point, Belinda introduced a dinosaur, who ate all the children and threatened her father's girlfriend. Belinda had her father attempt a rescue, but he saved only Miriam. When asked for an ending to this story, Belinda said, "Everybody died where they were—frozen in death like when Vesuvius exploded, only not hot lava, poison air." The sense one got was of Belinda's overwhelming vulnerability in a situation where invisible and uncontrollable dangers pervaded the atmosphere like "poison air." Even her father, who had always cast himself in the role of rescuer, was focused elsewhere.

Mr. D, a highly narcissistic man, was unaware of his daughter's disappointment in him. He continued to believe he was a kind of healing force for his child, in the same way that he had once been for his former wife, whom he believed was sadly inadequate. Mrs. D, in her interview, described how it felt to be seen as damaged and in need of perpetual rescue: "I was so confused, because I was so angry and yet I had this 'wonderful husband' who was also a 'wonderful father.' . . . I felt like a terrible mother. . . . I wasn't happy and I was emotionally and physically unavailable to Belinda." Eventually Mrs. D concluded that her options were either suicide or divorce. She chose divorce but felt so guilty and undeserving that she left Belinda in the family home, in the primary care of her father. After some months passed, Mr. D met Miriam and reconstituted a blended family, with Belinda and Miriam's two children. Mrs. D, who was also beginning to establish a separate life, began asking for more time with Belinda. The family came to the project at this point, because neither parent could agree on a schedule and the situation had become chaotic.

Quite early in the process it became clear that each parent had very different views of Belinda. Their views were dictated less by who their daughter really was than by their conflict. Mr. D frequently confused Belinda with her mother and tended to see them both as emotionally disturbed. He said, "Belinda could hardly relate to kids in her school when she was little. Even now she'll do anything for attention, including crawling in the garden and eating worms. She can't pay attention to the details of her life . . . she says she's stupid . . . terrible . . . wants to run away from both of us!" By focusing on Belinda's difficulties, Mr. D could continue to see her as the victim of his wife's damage and himself as the hero needed to rescue her. In contrast, Mrs. D could not acknowledge any difficulties in Belinda. She felt that doing so represented an intolerable capitulation to Mr. D's view of her poor mothering. She said, "Sometimes she's rude and naughty but basically she's fine. She's average. All the teachers say they're all just normal kids in her class." For Belinda, her parents' increasingly polarized views meant that, with her mother, she felt more real and understood when she was "good," and with her father, she felt more real and understood when she was "bad."

After two months in the project, the situation took a dramatic turn. Mrs. D attempted suicide and was hospitalized for several weeks. Mr. D disclosed the suicide attempt to Belinda because he felt "she really needs to understand about her mother at this point." The terror of losing her fragile connection with her mother was intolerable for this child. Belinda responded with a relatively swift consolidation of her previously shifting allegiances. While she had appeared confused and even dazed before this, now she became increasingly polarized in her behavior and her perceptions of each parent. Mr. D described these changes: "Now she gets very distant before she goes to visit her mother, she pulls away from me, gets ruder, defiant, just like her mother. It hurts me. . . . She says she wants to be with her mother all the time now." Note that Belinda had rejected any semblance of closeness to her father. In this way, Belinda's world continued to make sense and her allegiance to her mother remained intact. This increasingly merged alliance seemed to gather strength as mother and daughter shared a fused and distorted perception of the "bad" father. The mother

said, "Belinda and I had a conversation the other day where we were comparing experiences with her father . . . you know . . . that he's sweet and
nice with other people, but as soon as she's alone with him he'll talk in a
low voice and say mean things. She doesn't think he really loves her. . . .
He's all over her, but he doesn't really care about her. . . . It's so familiar!"

After six months, Belinda's behavior at her father's house had deteriorated so dramatically that Mr. D and Miriam agreed the custody arrangement should be reversed. Belinda would now spend most of her time with
her mother and visit her father on alternate weekends. According to the
mother, Belinda's misbehavior at her father's house was an understandable
response to his controlling personality. She said Belinda was always good at
her house. Belinda agreed. "I'm good at my mom's . . . she's totally great.
. . . Life would be perfect if I never had to see HIM [her father, to whom
she now referred by his first name] again."

Over the next two years, Belinda's alliance with her mother and rejection of her father became more and more entrenched. Mr. D insisted that
Belinda needed to be in treatment, but Mrs. D refused. She felt this was an
all-too-familiar repetition of his tendency to see pathology in everyone
around him. By age 12, Belinda was refusing all contact with her father,
and he was describing himself as a victim of parental alienation.

IMPLICATIONS FOR INTERVENTION

Perhaps the most disturbing feature in these defensive patterns is the degree
to which the child actively, if unconsciously, distorts his or her own experience to achieve a measure of safety and predictability. Over time, these distortions define the child's reality, define the self. Without intervention, these
children are at significant risk for developing entrenched character pathology.

In this section, we focus on the need to develop custody and access
schedules that protect the child's involvement in age-appropriate activities
and limit the intrusion of conflict into his or her concerns. Individual and
group treatment strategies for this age group will be discussed in chapters
10 and 11, respectively.

Psychological Test Results as Leverage

Conflicted parents often have a hard time recognizing vulnerability in their
school-age children, who tend to mask their underlying difficulties quite

convincingly. Rorschach testing, which can sensitively identify developmental lags and distortions in demonstrably objective terms, can be a useful way to heighten parents' understanding and concern (Roseby, 1995). Test scores can be treated as *findings* the evaluator shares with the parents, rather than as *clinical impressions,* which are all too easily perceived as judgments. As a result, the tone of the discussions tends to be less defensive and parents can focus clearly on their child's needs.

This therapeutic use of testing, to gain leverage on the child's behalf, can be incorporated into a range of case management strategies. For example, when the parents of 11-year-old John reached an impasse in their mediation, the mediator asked to have the child evaluated by another psychologist. The mediator explained that the evaluation would help them to define a child-focused direction in their work. When the evaluator completed her testing, she reviewed her findings with each parent and with the mediator, noting in particular that John's scores differed significantly from those of a typically developing 11-year-old. Once this information was available, the mediator openly revealed to the parents how worried she was about John's prognosis. This blend of objective data from the evaluator and real concern from the mediator helped the parents to accept that their son was really suffering because of their conflict. Their consciousness of his pain motivated them to work toward a highly detailed schedule that protected John's commitments as well as each parent's time with him. The schedule served as a baseline to follow when the parents were generally failing to cooperate or could not agree on a particular visitation issue.

Using the Schedule to Buffer the Child

During the school-age years, the child increasingly focuses his interests and concerns outside the family sphere. In the world of her peers the child practices independence and gains competence in the process. When parental conflict consistently intrudes, the child is preoccupied instead with the burden of practical concerns, such as whether and how the parents' fighting will disrupt the orderly conduct of his own academic and social affairs. Some children, like Belinda D, for example, struggle with chaotic schedules that make it impossible for them to know with any certainty which home they will be in and for what period of time. This uncertainty makes it difficult to organize homework, make plans with friends, or attend sports and other extracurricular activities with any consistency. Other children have more predictable schedules that change precipitously whenever the parents disagree or make agreements without considering the child's agenda. Many live with chronic uncertainty about where they will live and which school they will attend because their parents, like those of Leslie, are continually contesting these very issues. Such family circumstances feel more like quicksand, pulling the child back, than a safety net enabling the child to go confidently forward.

A Structured Schedule

In these situations, a structured schedule that takes into account mother's time, father's time, and the child's time can be an important and practical way of protecting the child's involvement in age-appropriate matters. This is particularly true when the child has been able to find relationships or activities outside the family that enhance her sense of competence in the world. The school-age child's involvement with these types of naturally occurring supports can be as valuable as psychotherapy. Clearly, the schedule should serve to protect that involvement as much as possible. A structured schedule, in which the child's time with each parent is relatively uninterrupted, also works with children's own defensive tendencies to keep their experiences with each parent separate. In general, such schedules work best when they contain a high level of detail and provide uninterrupted blocks of time that limit transitions between parents. These schedules need not limit the parents' ability to cooperate flexibly and responsively. Rather, they provide specific guidelines that can be used as a backup plan when parents fail to agree.

Specificity in the Agreement or Court Order

These kinds of stabilizing agreements or court orders often require a level of structure and specificity that may be difficult for mental health professionals, attorneys, and judges to anticipate or accept (Roseby, 1995). This can be particularly problematic in court. Some judges insist that so much detail and specificity is inappropriate, a kind of babying of parents who should "grow up" and start cooperating. When this happens, orders may be issued that require precisely the kind of negotiation that broke down before litigation and necessitated the order in the first place. In one such case, for example, two bitterly conflicted parents were seen in the high-conflict project because they could not cooperate on clauses in their order that stated the holiday rotations were "to be agreed upon between the parents." This order had been issued after two years of failed mediation and three prior hearings regarding scheduling disagreements. In such cases as this, specificity in the order or agreement can reduce the likelihood of misinterpretation, disagreement, and further conflict. Weekend and holiday visitation periods require precise definition, as do rotations from year to year and conditions for transfer of the child, as in the following example.

"Christmas vacation shall be divided such that during odd years (i.e., 1997, 1999, etc.), the child is with his mother from the time of release from school for that holiday (at the time specified by the school calendar) until 8 P.M. on December 24th, Christmas Eve. The child shall then be with his father from 8 P.M on December 24th, Christmas Eve, until his return to school at the end of that holiday (at the time specified by the school calendar). This schedule shall be exactly reversed during even years (i.e., 1996, 1998, etc.). Transfer of the child at 8 P.M. on December 24th shall occur by means of mother transporting the child to the home of the paternal grandparent at that time. If this transfer site is not available, father shall notify mother no later than noon on December 23rd, and father shall then pick the child up from the mother's home at 8 P.M on December 24th instead."

This kind of detail requires a significant level of parent involvement before any agreement or court order can be finalized. Opportunities for this kind of input are often denied, particularly when court orders are imposed. However, failure to allow for this kind of forethought can result in further disputes, which are time-consuming, costly, and damaging to the child. In such situations, judges may request that parents or their attorneys submit highly detailed proposals in writing. These could be reviewed in status conferences before the hearing. Alternatively, the judge may request additional mediation or evaluation for the sole purpose of obtaining very specific recommendations regarding the kind of schedule that would fit the realities of the individual family. This labor-intensive approach, in mediation and arbitration as well as in court, can maximize the potential for parental compliance and reduce the potential for conflict in the future.

Chapter 7

Early Adolescent Issues

Toward Resolution or Stalemate

$\mathcal{R}$isks to young adolescents in high-conflict families center around several themes that recapitulate strains and distortions from earlier stages. These take on special significance because of the unique developmental tasks of adolescence. Specifically, these several tasks include separating from a primary parent; forming a positive and stable sense of self; affirming one's gender and sexuality; feeling capable, autonomous, and trusting in work and play with peers; and establishing an internal sense of right and wrong. These renewed struggles can make for particularly tumultuous and painful early teenage years for these young persons and their highly conflicted families. Adolescence, however, affords some important opportunities. Precisely because this phase of development usually revisits earlier psychological conflicts, it provides these young people with the opportunity to achieve a new level of resolution, as well as psychological and physical emancipation from their enmeshed, conflicted families.

HOW ADOLESCENTS OF CONFLICTED DIVORCE ARE DIFFERENT

Emotional Lability

To provide a context for understanding the experience of the subgroup of older boys and older girls in highly conflicted divorced families, it is important to be reminded of what is expectable and normal about early adolescent development (Hauser, 1991; Schave & Schave, 1989). The adolescent years are not easy under the best of circumstances. Quantum changes are taking place internally and externally at this time. Physically, there are growth spurts and the maturation of secondary sex characteristics, which make coming to terms with one's own self-image all the more compelling. Concomitant increases in sexual and aggressive energies fuel young people's emotional lives, making them feel even more anxious and out of control. Emotional lability—that is, erratic periods of excitement alternating with feelings of agitation and depression—is relatively common (Blos, 1970; Anna Freud, 1958).

The presence of consistent, emotionally well-modulated parents and other adults who can be empathic and accepting of the youngster's tumultuous feeling states but constrain inappropriate acting-out is important. Unfortunately, these are not the ego-models available in high-conflict families, where parents are absorbed in their own cycles of rage and depression. Alternately, these vulnerable parents may have such permeable emotional boundaries with their youngsters that they can easily become caught up in and resonate with the youngster's emotional distress in an increasing crescendo that feels frighteningly out of control to both parent and child.

Adolescence as a Second Separation-Individuation Phase

It is developmentally expectable that young adolescents will begin to pull away from persons to whom they were primarily attached; in fact, they can often become unexpectedly hurtful and critical toward parents who were once unconditionally loved and uncritically valued. Normally, this distancing is halting and ambivalent. Moments of critical disdain can mingle with unusual insight, compassion, and maturity that, in turn, can give way to quite childish and dependent behavior. Intrapsychically, the internal representations of the adolescent's beloved parents and other important caregivers are being fundamentally altered, in a process that has been called "the second individuation phase," reminiscent of the 2-year-old toddler who practices separating physically and psychologically from her primary parent (Blos, 1967, 1970).

Unlike the earlier phase of separation-individuation, however, the adolescent process is intimately related to moral development, because it involves a de-idealization of the parent as guide and mentor, in the service of achieving autonomy. As adolescents de-idealize their parents and become more emotionally disengaged, there is typically a loss of some superego control, as the youngster becomes temporarily less influenced and grounded by parents' approval and censure. Consequently, uncharacteristic misbehavior and minor delinquencies can occur.

Parents typically need a great deal of self-confidence and support from each other to weather the storm of assaults that normal adolescents make on their self-esteem, judgment, and authority. Clear expectations, firm, consistent limits, and appropriate monitoring of the young person's whereabouts and behavior are important to sustain during this time. Young adolescents are particularly stabilized by the ability of parents to cooperate and provide a united front in their care and guidance. This kind of environment is not available in highly conflictual families where parents disrespect and denigrate each other.

As a consequence of divided parental authority and the competition for the youngster's affection and allegiance, adolescents can easily dismiss one or both of their disputing parents or manipulate them both to obtain special privileges and avoid responsibility. Moreover, because disputing parents are not able to communicate and coordinate with each other, monitoring the whereabouts of the elusive young teenager becomes almost impossible. It is not uncommon in high-conflict divorced families for young teenagers to precipitously reject, or be rejected from, the household of one parent as a consequence of fairly normal adolescent challenges to parental authority. This often happens when the acting-out becomes linked to the ongoing parental conflict. Of course, they are usually welcomed with open arms by the other parent, who is highly gratified by their defection from what is perceived to be "the enemy camp." In the ensuing struggle, the internal images of one or both parents are precipitously de-idealized, leaving the youngster without moorings. In this way, parents undermine not only each other's authority and status as an ego ideal but the adolescent's perception of what is fair, expectable, and responsible conduct as well. Hence conscience development is further eroded, and delinquent behavior may consolidate.

The costs of separating from a primary parent and becoming psychologically autonomous are too great for some young adolescents, and they do not dare attempt the enterprise. This is especially true for youngsters who have lived at the center of the marital battle for many years, as well as for those who have assumed the burden of sustaining an embittered, depressed, and emotionally dependent parent in the fight with the ex-spouse or with the world in general. As described earlier (chapters 4 and 5), the central developmental threat for very young children of high-conflict divorce is their difficulty separating from and inability to differentiate themselves from their primary caregivers. Now, during adolescence, this critical developmental task is revisited with renewed urgency and meaning. In this respect, these adolescents are challenged to do what they are least equipped to do. Thus, this recapitulation of developmental conflicts provides both the opportunity for resolution and the threat of stalemate.

Sexual Anxieties and Oedipal Conflicts Revisited

The vulnerable child's basic fears associated with being separate and autonomous from a parent—fears of being abandoned, annihilated, disappearing from view, and being bad—are compounded by the reactivation of oedipal issues during adolescence. The young adolescent girl within an entrenched custody battle, with newly awakened awareness of her sexuality, will find it hazardous to use her father as a stepping stone as she tries to extricate herself from an enmeshed relationship with her mother. This is especially true if there is no stepmother or woman friend who will dilute her father's emotional investment in her, and even more so if the father has a poor sense of appropriate boundaries with his daughter. Visits with the father become rife with situations that generate sexual anxiety: coping with the onset of her menstruation at her father's home; sleeping, bathing, and sharing space in his small apartment; even going out with him to the movies or dinner. Receiving her father's affection, time, and attention is highly gratifying but also seductive and can result in an alarming sense of discomfort. Feelings of anxiety can increase to overwhelming proportions when the young adolescent girl returns home to her mother, who, in these situations, is perceived to be the rejected and scorned "previous lover" of her father. Unconsciously sensing her mother's jealousy and fearing retribution, the daughter may seek to appease her by every possible means, including regressive dependency, somatic symptoms, defensive denial of her own femininity, or even refusal to subsequently separate from her mother to visit her father. Other young "oedipal victors," less intimidated by the mother, will come home as an emissary of their father and fight with their mothers.

The young adolescent boy's burgeoning sexual impulses more typically propel him to take some refuge in his father at this time, as a defense against the threat of a sexualized relationship with his mother. Unfortunately, this

move involves considerable costs for those in divorced families that are fractured by ongoing disputes over custody. Although many of these mothers
seem to have more understanding and acceptance of the boy's need for the
father (more than they do the girl's need for him), the boy's defection to his
father often results in the withdrawal of some of the loving support and allegiance of his mother. Stung by the loss, these boys can become depressed
and alternately angry, challenging, and attention-demanding of their
mothers. They, too, are prone to return to their mother, after visiting the
father, defensively swaggering and espousing the father's cause. Alternatively, for a minority of these boys, the regressive pull to the mother can be
too strong, sometimes because the father is too critical or emotionally disengaged, or has been thoroughly denigrated by the mother; the youngster
then may not be able to separate from her to go on visits at all. In these
cases, adolescent boys can experience considerable anxiety about their
oedipal victory and defensively avoid asserting their masculinity.

Experimenting with Personas and Ego Diffusion

In the normal course of development, disengagement and distancing from
primary caregivers allows young persons to reorganize and reintegrate their
images of parents and significant others at a moderate pace. In this process,
adolescents also rework their own self-image, forging a unique identity
gradually over the teenage years. In the early stages these adolescents identify with a series of other people or images (role models and mentors),
"trying on" other personalities (like that of a pop star or sport hero), and
acting "as if" they were someone else (perhaps an attractive peer). Ego diffusion and loss of a bounded sense of self are normal developmental threats
at this stage (Blos, 1970; Erikson, 1963).

It is reassuring and stabilizing for the young adolescent if his family can be
relatively tolerant and consistently responsive during this experimentation
phase. Parents locked in battle with each other, however, are usually hypersensitive and overreactive to their young teenager's posturing. Feeling
threatened as to how their child's behavior might reflect on them, parents
project blame onto the other spouse: "You're behaving like the twit your
mother is!" a father will declare, or a mother will shrug helplessly, "What
can I do, when his father encourages him to go around dressed like a punk!"

Moreover, as illustrated in the previous chapter, children of entrenched
disputes are likely to have entered adolescence with a fragmented sense of self.

For example, they can feel and behave, alternately, perfectly good and terribly bad; present a pleasing, compliant mask to others and defensively hide from their authentic feelings and perceptions; manage their interpersonal world by posturing in a defiant, angry manner; or withdraw within a constricted, inscrutable stance. These fragmented selves continue to be reinforced by the manner in which parents relate to them in their separate homes. In these cases, the expectable ego diffusion that is a minor digression from the quest for identity is so threatening that young adolescents may defensively stall and become arrested in their emotional development. Or they can become increasingly fragmented in their emotions and behavior. Symptomatically, they resemble borderline adolescents (Esman, 1989; Miller, 1978). It is not known to what extent these manifest difficulties foreshadow long-standing personality disorders. Extended follow-up studies of these youngsters into adulthood are very much needed (Masterson & Costello, 1980).

Perceptual and Judgmental Deficits

It is developmentally expectable for the young adolescent to display somewhat illogical thinking patterns (Elkind, 1967). First, young adolescents are typically egocentric and preoccupied with the belief, usually unfounded, that they are the primary object of other people's critical attention. This has been called the "imaginary audience" phenomenon and helps explain why they are so acutely self-conscious and easily mortified. Second, young adolescents have a tendency to construct fables about themselves with themes that stress their personal uniqueness, omnipotence, and invulnerability. They are inclined to believe that "no one else feels the way I do," "I'm never allowed to do anything!" "It won't happen to me," and "I can do anything I want." Called "personal fables," these beliefs may allow them to take risks and act in other ways that indicate poor judgment.

Interestingly, these characteristically adolescent ways of thinking probably help young people in the process of negotiating their separateness and connectedness to other important people, as they sort out who they are and what kind of person they want to be (Lapsley, 1993). Imagining how other people might perceive one (the imaginary audience) allows the teenager to experiment with relationships, while maintaining some distance and assimilating the emotional experience of being with peers and others in manageable doses. Similarly, poignant states of feeling unique and invulnerable (the personal fable) allow young people to protect the integrity and boundaries of their fragile, emerging sense of self against the intrusions and demands of others.

In the ordinary course of events, the faulty perceptions that can result from these kinds of attributional and judgmental biases are moderated when the young adolescent shares his thoughts and feelings with trusted others—especially friends. A shared view of the world more grounded in reality gradually emerges. As discussed in previous chapters, however, many children from families where there is ongoing conflict and intermittent violence have difficulty forming trusting, authentic connections with their peers. They feel increasingly like aliens during the acutely heightened self-consciousness of adolescence. In fact, they can feel not just foreign but peculiar, a mutant. In defense, some entertain grandiose beliefs about their own special capabilities and dismiss or diminish those of others. Hypervigilant, self-protective, and often harboring a "hostile world view," they do not turn to others to help solve problems but instead rely upon themselves. This means that their distorted perceptions are not temporary developmental phenomena that become increasingly more realistic by helpful exchanges with close confidants. Instead, they become consolidated as invariant ways of understanding themselves and the interpersonal world.

Diminished Capacity to Relate to Peers

It is well known that peers assume a great deal of importance in the normal course of adolescent development (Jordan, 1993). In fact, the peer group can function as a "transitional family" as ties are loosened with the family of origin. It is expectable that during early adolescence, the choice of friends and role models tends to be somewhat self-serving, and relationships tend to be held together by projections of young persons' separate, individual needs rather than by mutuality. In this sense, peers at this age are seen as extensions of oneself ("self-objects"), as parents once were, and also serve as a way point to more autonomous psychological functioning (Blos, 1970).

Peers, especially same-sex peers, typically provide social support, protection, and anonymity within the crowd. During the middle-school years, friends, especially those of the opposite sex, may be chosen for how they reflect on one's status and the adolescent fantasies they help create. It is expectable that during early adolescence, friendships tend to be relatively shallow and lacking in constancy. In the normal course of development, it is often not until the middle or later teenage years that friendships deepen and mutuality and intimacy become possible. It takes considerably more time for most normal young men and women to integrate sexuality and tenderness within a respectful and caring relationship.

Unfortunately, many of the adolescents who have experienced chronic family conflict do not have the basic interpersonal tools to begin to meet the challenge of these formidable tasks. A subgroup of these youngsters during junior high school withdraw into a lonely, passively observing stance at school and on the playground. Isolated from significant relationships that could repair their deeply embedded distrust and sense of shame, they are vulnerable to painful loneliness or even depression. Interestingly, some of them, especially the girls, invest themselves in their academic work. These achievements represent a refuge from their feelings and the need to relate to others. In this respect, they are often perceived to be progressing well. No one seems to notice that they eat lunch alone, escape to the library during recess, or hang at the perimeter of the group, where they are neither seen nor avoided. Their isolation cuts off access to the vitally important adolescent peer culture of relationships and seems to leave many of them in some kind of "never-never" land, suspended between childhood and adulthood with no passage from one to the other. The case of Susan, described later in this chapter, illustrates this kind of adolescent dilemma, together with treatment issues.

More likely to be noticed are those more "out-of-control" youngsters who act out fragmented aggressive and sexual aspects of themselves and others in ways that briefly focus the attention and admiration of their less adventurous peers. This subgroup seems to exaggerate all aspects of early adolescence. In school and on the street, they are rowdy, unruly, gross, exhibitionistic, sadistic, and volatile. During earlier years, these particular children may have been scapegoated or ignored by their classmates; now they are highly gratified by the amused envy of their peers for their "cool" and daring escapades. This might even ensure them a negative leadership role. They are inclined to take serious risks involving drugs, alcohol, and sexually promiscuous behavior. Unless they get some help, these young people may not progress to more mature peer relationships. Rather, they become caught in the whirlpool of an exaggerated early adolescence, where relationships remain utilitarian and exploitative, alternately victimizing and victimized. Sexual and aggressive impulses in the service of self-soothing and self-protection remain split off and unmodulated by loving, tender feelings. Mutually satisfying relationships, in which others are experienced as separate persons in their own right, are more difficult to develop. The case of Jason described later in this chapter illustrates this kind of problem, together with case management and family therapy issues that often arise.

Evolving Cognitive Capacity to Achieve Distance from Family Conflict

In the normal course of development, the wonderful and exciting project of creating a unique self and exploring relationships with others, especially peers, is helped during midadolescence by the evolving capacity to think and reason in abstract ways about a variety of hypothetical alternatives ("formal operational thought"). Introspection becomes more common as teenagers are able to think and reason about relationships from a third-person perspective. They are able simultaneously to hold a subjective point of view while coordinating other points of view. At the same time, the adolescent begins to apprehend the psychological attributes of other people, including personality dispositions that are more manifest and motivations that are more hidden (Piaget, 1979; Selman, 1980). Now having the capacity to recognize multiple perspectives, they are better able to understand more complex social interactions. Their cognitive advances enable them to achieve a more critical distance from their friends and family (Gordon, 1988).

Provided they are not too harshly driven by the press of their emotional needs, teenagers from enmeshed, conflicting families can draw upon these cognitive capacities to help them gain more perspective and independence, which in turn can provide considerable emotional relief. For this reason, the older, intellectually advanced teenagers more clearly benefit from counseling than do their younger counterparts. They have the capacity to use friends and other adult mentors to gain a greater critical distance from their disputing parents. Furthermore, using their superior capacities to reason, differentiate, and discriminate, older adolescents are better able to separate out the good or valued parts of parents (and significant others) from the parts perceived to be negative. This enables them to be more tolerant of the shortcomings of others and ultimately of their own. In the process, they can replace previous internalizations of their parents with an abstract internal ego ideal, which will help guide and stabilize their conscience development.

A significant proportion of teenagers in highly conflictual families, however, do not realistically differentiate the strengths and vulnerabilities of each of their disputing parents. Instead, the young person appears to become caught up in the interparental war and views one parent as the all good, perfect parent and the other as having no redeemable features. Their view of themselves is similarly polarized in that when joined with the "good" parent in a "holy crusade" against the "bad" parent, they are self-righteous and intolerant. In the most extreme cases, adolescents in these unshakable alliances with one of the disputing parents support the interparental feud by such means as spying, sabotage, and harassment, and stridently reject the other parent, refusing visits. These kinds of attitudes and behaviors have been referred to as "parental alienation syndrome" (Gardner, 1992).

It is perhaps not surprising that children who developed a fragmented sense of self during their earlier years, feeling perfectly good when joined with their primary parent and feeling bad when separated, are more likely to develop this extreme stance during adolescence. We have hypothesized that this kind of defensive splitting contributes to a concrete, simplistic, somewhat utilitarian and harsh view of interpersonal relations—a view without nuance, empathy, or compassion. Parental alienation is a troubling outcome of high-conflict divorce during early adolescence, because it can solidify a merged relationship with one parent and a fragmented sense of self, at a time when youngsters really need to begin to separate from both parents and consolidate a more realistic self-identity. The phenomenon also creates a great deal of consternation and frustration in family courts because it is so resistant to change.

CASE ILLUSTRATIONS OF INTERVENTIONS WITH ADOLESCENTS

In the balance of this chapter, we illustrate many of the common dilemmas discussed above by describing the difficult passage through adolescence of a young girl and a young boy, both of whom have lived in highly conflictual divorced families for years. These two cases also illustrate some of the treatment issues in individual psychotherapy with adolescents and in family mediation and counseling on their behalf. However, the subject of parent alienation is covered in detail in the following chapter, because it is a multidetermined problem not unique to adolescence.

Susan's Search for an Authentic Self

Susan was seen in therapy from age 12 until she was 15. She was the younger child in her family; her older brother, age 25, had left the home. Her parents had divorced when she was 7. An extremely acrimonious marital relationship preceded, and a bitter ongoing custody dispute followed, their separation. The mother had suffered intermittent bouts of anger and depression since Susan's birth. After years of fending off his wife's irate demands in a rather passive-avoidant manner, the father rallied and sought a divorce. In an avalanche of legal documents, he characterized the mother in an extremely derogatory light, citing her erratic emotional states to justify his leaving the marriage and to support his claim for custody. Feeling utterly betrayed and attacked, this vulnerable woman then projected onto him the hatred that had crystallized from her anger. As a result of this projection as well as the man's genuinely attacking behavior, she became phobic and paranoid about her ex-husband and sought to rescue her daughter from his "malevolent" influence. Since the divorce, Susan had been placed, by court order, in the joint care of her parents, who lived in adjacent communities, alternating nine days with her mother and five days with her father. This arrangement was continually challenged in court by the mother, who wanted sole physical custody and no more than every-other-weekend access for the father. In defense of his position, the father continued his vitriolic attacks upon the mother.

At the outset, in accord with a child who acts in ways that comply with others' needs and expectations, hiding her authentic feelings and perceptions, Susan behaved in a markedly different way with each parent. Not surprisingly, each parent viewed her very differently. Reflecting what her father wanted, Susan acted bright, chatty, "cutesy," and entertaining when she was with him. He was delighted with his attractive daughter, and she became his principal companion and playmate. The only problem he acknowledged was Susan's difficulties with sleeping and her frequent nightmares. When she returned to her mother, Susan typically "collapsed in an emotional heap." She was highly anxious and distressed; she talked obsessively for hours about her pervasive fears and often needed to sleep with her mother. In addition, she was lethargic, mildly but chronically depressed, complained a lot about diffuse aches and pains, and periodically resisted going to school.

During these times, her mother was exquisitely empathic to her daughter's every mood and her every concern. Overtly, the mother was highly gratified by the child's dependence on and closeness to her. Covertly, she felt burdened and resentful of the enormous demands the child made for her exclusive attention. She blamed the father for causing the child's distress through "his sheer carelessness, his emotional neglect, and his exploitation of the child for his own needs." On the other hand, the father perceived Susan as "happy and coping well," and dismissed the mother's concerns as evidence of her "craziness" and "unfitness as a parent."

Susan's transitions between parents were marked by severe, overt parental conflict. Susan dawdled whenever she packed to go to her father's, a job made monumental because she would insist on carrying many of her stuffed animals as well as her clothes and books. She could not leave anything of significance at either house, and many of her possessions seemed to represent transitional objects. Typically, her mother became enraged if the father made any attempt to talk with or even look at her at the time of the exchange. His audacity in driving into her driveway or piling Susan's possessions by her door sent her into a frenzied rage. She screamed at him, threatened to call the police, and on one occasion physically attacked him. The father, on the other hand, would provoke his ex-wife by hanging around and "spying" on her. He would smugly document her outbursts for another round of humiliating allegations in court.

Susan was marginal in her peer group, an observer from the sidelines, shy and reclusive. She was most uncomfortable with other adolescent girls' preoccupation with boys and clothes and was painfully sensitive to being different from them. Privately, she disparaged other girls for their "silliness." On weekends, she preferred to play alone with her large collection of stuffed animals and miniatures or read adventure books meant for much younger children, rather than spend time with peers. Later in the course of her therapy, she began to articulate a profound sense of loneliness and isolation from others and a growing hunger for friendships. At school, Susan achieved very well among a highly achieving class, but not without cost. She was anxious about her performance and tended to procrastinate and become overwhelmed by her assignments. She showed no interest in athletic or extracurricular activities.

Susan was brought to therapy at our center by court order. Though she was a pretty, well-proportioned girl with long, fair hair and a clear, pale complexion, her demeanor was generally constricted and depressed. While her mother insisted that Susan needed counseling, she questioned the therapist's allegiance in the custody dispute and was distrustful about the content of the sessions. The father, on the other hand, dismissed his daughter's need for any help. Not surprisingly, Susan too was distrustful. Her resistance took the form of controlling the agenda by talking nonstop in a monotone, almost compulsively, about mundane events in her day-to-day life.

She refused to talk about her parents or their divorce. She did, however, reveal her pervasive anxiety (about earthquakes, fires, and burglaries that might destroy both her homes), her obsessive worries (about sleeping, eating, minor aches and pains), as well as her specific fears (for instance, that she was intermittently terrified of her pet chihuahua).

For many months, Susan's obsessive enumeration of events in her daily life would take up the major portion of the therapy hour. Toward the end of the session, however, her thought associations would become looser and she would begin to reveal, in symbolic form, the dynamics of her central concerns. Typically, she would draw pictures, create a sandtray scene, or talk about some of the bad dreams she had, one after another. After she finished, she would allow the therapist several minutes to make comments or suggest interpretations. Any attempt to hurry this process would quickly stall it. Any premature interpretation made her angry and avoidant.

The initial themes in the repetitive nightmares Susan recounted suggested a terrifying world of fragmented, contradictory images of her parents. In some dreams, men (who reminded her of her father) were dangerous and out to exploit her for their own gratification. In other dreams, she watched in terror as a man who looked like her father dressed as a policeman was being attacked by a prehistoric lizard (who was later identified as her mother). In her dream, the lizard would invariably turn and pursue her; she would run for protection to her mother's house, only to be confronted with a skeleton that came out of her mother's closet. These split views of her parents as good/bad, protective/scary, and exploitative/nurturing indicated her basic developmental conflict as she tried to determine whom to trust and who was safe. Both of her doting, protective parents seemed to have a negative side that could be activated if she dared separate from one to go to the other.

Susan's guilt over being the oedipal victor, which heightened her anxiety about being destroyed in the parental fight, was apparent in another series of dreams. Here, she found herself sneaking into a home that looked like her mother's and stealing underwear, which she would then take to her father and an unknown woman (herself). Upon her return, she feared she might be killed by the wicked Queen of Hearts, who lived on her mother's street (the revengeful mother).

In the early stages of therapy, it was not possible to interpret for Susan the startlingly clear symbolism of these dreams—Susan, from age 12 to 13 years, was not ready to hear what they might mean. She continued to be extremely ambivalent and distrusting about the depths she was willing to plumb in working with the therapist. She revealed her ambivalence in a series of drawings that she made. In one, she drew a mother and baby owl in a nest and in a tree, then noted that a person walking underneath the tree threatened to disturb them. "The person was acting stupidly, clumsily!" Susan said disparagingly. In another drawing, she fantasied a dangerous household appliance (a hair drier) at her father's house, which would kill anybody who got too near it. Through these drawings and her continued resistance, Susan warned the therapist not to interfere with the cozy little bird nest (i.e., her relationship with her mother), nor should anyone get too near the electrical charge (her dangerous father and her own sexuality).

Taking the cue to be nonthreatening and supportive, the therapist waited during this early period of adolescence and spent the time playing in the sandtray with Susan, using the small collection of miniature animals that always traveled with the teenager wherever she went, stuffed in her pockets or her backpack. In these play sessions, Susan revealed an enormously vivid imagination, for she lived in a fantasy world more reminiscent of a preschool child's than a teenager's. The miniature animals all seemed to be imbued with personalities based on projections of Susan's own feelings and perceptions she could not otherwise own. In the presence of the empathic therapist, she was gradually allowing her own split-off, repressed feelings and ideas to emerge.

In the process, Susan tested to see whether the therapist could be safely used as a stepping stone to support her separation from her parents and their enmeshed conflict. This testing was revealed in a series of dreams she reported, one of which was about two tribes fighting and her being captured and held hostage. She found herself perched on a rock in the middle of a bog, with fast-moving water and swampy forest all around her. An old lady sitting next to her promised to keep her from slipping into the murky depths. But she did not know whether the old lady would be strong enough to keep her from falling or rescue her if she fell! This dream was directly interpreted to Susan as her distrust of whether the therapist was strong enough to help her. She seemed quite gratified at being understood.

Susan was almost 14 years old when she made her first move to separate from one of her parents (her father). Increasingly during the months that followed, she began to express irritability at him and tested his interest in and commitment to her. She demanded that he drive her places and buy her trinkets but then was scornful of his tastes, deriding him for being old-fashioned.

Her muted anger and derision also served to keep him more at a distance, protecting her against the sexual anxiety he engendered in her and against her related unconscious fear of her mother's retribution for stealing her husband.

During this process, the therapist had to work with the father to help him tolerate these challenges without becoming too angry, trivializing Susan's demands, or blaming the mother for his daughter's high-handed behavior. On those occasions when the father failed to be appropriately tolerant and empathic, Susan would telephone her mother to complain about him. Afterward, when she returned to "the sanctuary" of her mother's home, her mother would comfort the pale, exhausted-looking child, saying, "You've been through hell and now you've reached asylum!" These incidents refueled the mother's attempts to change the access schedule, citing the father's "selfish, mean, and cruel" treatment of Susan.

Interestingly, as Susan felt supported by the therapist in gaining some distance from her father while staying connected with him, her mother began to report, with mixed feelings, that Susan "has increasingly withdrawn from me. . . . She's taking possession of her life . . . is not so dependent upon me when she comes home." It appeared that the therapeutic transference at this point rested upon Susan's image of the mother (good-mother) who was supportive of her need to be assertive with her father. However, the fear of the scary, angry mother (bad-mother) lurked in the background. In addition, Susan continued to be distrustful of the therapist. This was revealed in a series of fantasies in her sandtray play in which she portrayed the therapist as potentially dangerous, having the capacity to destroy or exploit her in some way. In this respect, the therapy seemed caught in the double bind of the mother-transference that was operating. In short, Susan's core distrust and hypervigilance were at issue, and she indicated that she felt the therapy was like a gun held to her head. In reply, the therapist was warmly understanding about her distrust, communicating a tolerance for the girl's anger. Susan was then able to reveal her fantasy that if she continued with the therapy, she would become not only assertive and autonomous but would gain as well the capacity to destroy (her parents).

Shortly after telling this particular fantasy, Susan briefly recounted three nightmares and asked the therapist to help her interpret them. The theme of each of these frightening dreams incorporated her central fears about relationships with others: They indicated how careless and dangerous she felt her father was, her ominous feelings associated with her mother, and how cruel her peers seemed to her. The following three months of therapy were marked by her increasing irritability and complaints of boredom and frustration, which were interpreted as reflecting her continuing anxiety about exploring her relationship with her parents, her suppressed anger, and her ambivalence about asserting her needs in a more positive way.

An interesting change occurred in Susan's symptomatology at this point. She began to project menacing feelings and malicious intent onto her beloved dog. She reported scary dreams about his claws sticking into her and not being able to release herself from him. In her waking hours, she feared he was possessed and that he was dominating and controlling her. Curiously, this delusional thinking about the dog was shared by her mother. In fact, her mother felt compelled to allow the dog to be extremely demanding (of food, attention, to be let in and out of the house) and was greatly resentful of her servitude to him. Susan finally came to the realization that her mother would hold and stroke the dog on her lap with utmost hostility and rejection in her facial and body demeanor.

In actuality, the mother's treatment of the dog was a terrifying reminder of Susan's preverbal memories of her mother's parenting, memories that were linked to her early experience of an extremely depressed mother who compulsively nurtured her every need but had fantasies of both suicide and infanticide. To protect herself from this frightening revelation, Susan again merged with her mother, incorporating the mother's views of the dog and sharing her paranoid projections.

This problem was gradually dealt with over the months by clarification and interpretation along the following lines. The therapist explained that the dog was simply an animal with a small brain, that he had been "spoiled rotten" and conditioned to expect instant gratification. He was not capable of the malicious intent and demonlike qualities Susan attributed to him. She was encouraged to be directly assertive with the dog by putting him outside when he was a nuisance, which she began to do with some relief. At the same time, the therapist talked about how her and her mother's treatment of the dog was similar to her own experience of her mother's parenting. With Susan's permission, the therapist talked about her mother's depression when Susan was a baby and about some of the confused and conflicted feelings depressed moms can have at these times. Together, they discussed her mother's ongoing difficulty with depression and the stress of the custody litigation, and her tendency to take on too much responsibility—conscientiously doing everything herself and then feeling exploited and angry because her own needs were not met. This dynamic had probably developed first with her own family of origin, and later in the marriage, and now with her daughter. Shedding tears of sadness and relief, Susan readily identified these characteristics in mother's treatment of her.

From this point on in the therapy, Susan was usually able to consciously identify her mother's changing moods, describing them vividly in colorful, symbolic language. When her father acted to provoke her mother, when her parents had altercations about money or plans for vacation, or when they were forced to be in each other's presence at school events, Susan, although she found these occasions very anxiety provoking, was able to provide a detailed account of everyone's actions as well as her own constricted feelings.

Most interesting, after surfacing these primitive fears of abandonment, neglect, and destruction by her parents, Susan was able to access memories about the divorce and parental conflict that she had previously repressed or strongly resisted talking about. She began by voluntarily bringing in a diary that contained a mundane account of her life at the time of the divorce. A series of drawings she had made of monsters and dragons was even more revealing. There were crying dragons and a dragon trying to protect a baby bird in the nest from the hot sun after the mother bird abandoned it. There were strangely unintegrated, contorted monsters; monsters with spikes and teeth and eyes all over their bodies; anemic monsters; tiny, vulnerable creatures; dragons with chicken feet. Susan was able to talk about the symbolism of these drawings. She also explored much earlier memories of feeling abandoned at day care, getting lost in the woods, being made to swim in a pool where she felt very frightened of drowning, and an accident she had when she was 5 years old.

All these memories contained similar themes of fear of abandonment, being hurt, and dying. The therapist linked them to Susan's early attempts to separate and become autonomous from her parents, and Susan recognized that she had always been anxious about separating from her mother. In particular, she became aware that she used somatic symptoms to elicit her mother's nurturance and protection. She could not turn to her father, who had always been a shadowy, amorphous figure in her consciousness. As she struggled to understand her fears of separation if she asserted herself in any way, Susan recalled a repetitive dream: "There's this huge giant wooden door. Me and Mom are sitting on this wooden bench and her arm is around me. And the giant door creaks open . . . and there is something behind there! I have a scared, ominous feeling . . . " This was interpreted to signify her inchoate fears of the unexpected and the unknown, probably experienced very early in her life as a consequence of the unpredictability of her parents' emotional availability, in general, and her mother's angry, depressive bouts, in particular. Paradoxically, she had come to rely on her mother's fierce "protection" from the fears generated by none other than her protectors—her own mother and father.

These interpretations of her early experiences led to a series of dreams in which Susan seemed to express anxiety and guilt about experiencing pleasure in ways that her mother could not do herself. These dreams may have also indicated her fear of being like her mother, doomed not to expect joy. The symbolism of these dreams involved brightly colored feathers or gemstones that Susan coveted. She wanted to gather them up for herself but felt she did not deserve them, or did not have the right to take them, especially because, in her dreams, these treasures were often what remained of a scene of devastation (the rubble of her parents' marriage). In the discussion that followed her reporting these dreams, Susan articulated that she felt responsible for making her mother happy. In response, the therapist was frankly supportive of Susan's own right to happiness, asking her to give herself permission to have a happier life than her mother's, and giving her permission not to be responsible for her mother's unhappiness, and not to be her mother's only confidante and friend.

At this stage in the therapy, at age 15, Susan talked explicitly about getting some distance from both her parents, saying in a manner expectable of an adolescent, "I'm bored with my parents. I don't want to be around them!" However, she found herself ruminating excessively, which contributed to her indecisiveness and procrastination. She did not have the capacity to reach out to her peers as substitutes for her dependency on her parents. She remained essentially quite lonely. Her hunger for relationships was painful to watch. "I want to be noticed by teachers," she said, "but I don't know what to do to be special. I don't want to fade into anonymity!"

Play was no longer useful to Susan—she could not recapture her pleasure in her stuffed animals and miniatures: "I don't know what to do with my stuffed animals, they are overpopulating my bed. . . . I can't get fun out of them anymore. I keep trying to sort them out, and I throw out about two percent each time." In response, the therapist reminded her of the folk song "Puff the Magic Dragon" and talked about being sad about the loss of this special sanctuary of her childhood.

Susan approached her first year of high school with trepidation and some excitement. She was understandably anxious about the academic work it involved and the formidable task of relating to many new adolescents and teachers. She continued to work through her separation-individuation issues as she tentatively reached out to her peers. During this year, her father began dating again. Although Susan initially kept her distance from the woman, her hunger for companionship got the better of her, and she soon formed a warm relationship with her father's companion. Interestingly, this woman provided a buffer against Susan's sexual anxieties about her father, which allowed her to express closeness to him again.

In the final year of therapy, Susan was seen less frequently as she seemed to be developmentally back on track. She reported very few nightmares, and her somatic symptoms mostly disappeared. Her new dreams reflected mostly concerns about peers, school achievement, and sexuality. She discussed typical adolescent fears of awkwardness and self-consciousness. Periods of depression alternated with periods of optimism and excitement. Increasingly, she began reaching out to new girlfriends and expressed pleasure in peer activities; she began to enjoy movies, skating, and shopping on weekends. She even began to talk to boys, whom she insisted were "just friends."

Susan talked with a mix of compassion and frustration about both her parents. She was able to talk directly about their altercations and the fallout of their disputes with each other on her. She practiced asserting herself with both parents and her friends, having become aware that she had a strong proclivity to be passive, especially when anything threatened her or made her anxious. During one of her final therapy sessions, Susan articulated her defense against the terror of her parents' anger and her fundamental fear of losing herself: "I get real scared when my parents are mad. It's this deep anger, this revenge thing they have! I go into a coma thing . . . into slow motion! It's hard to assert myself. . . . I turn off everything except life support! I get really dull when that happens. . . . I turn off all the lights. So in new situations when I get scared, feel danger, I do the same thing. Now I am trying to do new stuff. I have to *make* myself do it consciously. After a while it will work and it will become second nature. I'm becoming more like myself now . . . more able to be myself."

Jason's Struggles with a Fragmented Self

Jason, at age 12, was the only child of divorced parents. Their extremely conflictual marriage of 13 years had escalated to violence on the father's part, which precipitated the separation. At the time of entry to our counseling service four years later, the mother had remarried and had a new baby, while the father lived with his widowed mother. An initial shared custody arrangement, recommended by a custody evaluator, rapidly broke down and was shifted by court order to give the mother primary care of Jason, who visited his father on alternate weekends and some holidays. The father was chagrined at this arrangement and continually agitated to have more time with his son.

Though an attractive and intellectually gifted woman, the mother was impulsive, emotionally labile, erratic, and unpredictable in relationships with others. She had a shifting view of relationships and was markedly lacking in self-confidence. In the ensuing custody dispute, she relied excessively on advice from a series of professionals, attorneys, and therapists, whom she initially hired and idealized, and then de-idealized and fired when they failed to meet her needs and expectations. The father, by contrast, was extremely interpersonally sensitive, quick to take offense, and easily humiliated. He was also intelligent, competitive, and ambitious in his work as a football coach at a prominent college. He was defensive and distrustful to the point of being paranoid about the series of therapists and evaluators that the mother involved in the ongoing custody litigation.

Both parents were highly vulnerable to criticism, to any sense of failure. Both were highly invested in Jason, whom they both perceived to be an extension of themselves whenever he was gratifying, good, and well achieving. He was perceived to be an extension of the other parent when he was ungratifying and underachieving. Sadly, Jason had a congenital deformation that left him slightly crippled. He also had some emotional and behavioral problems, largely as a consequence of the long-standing, entrenched parental disputes. Not surprisingly, the boy's problems were a constant source of narcissistic injury for both parents.

Typically, the mother became extremely anxious and disorganized, openly blaming the father whenever Jason was unhappy or difficult to manage. She usually did this to publicly humiliate the father among his prominent friends, family, and colleagues. The father felt that this was intolerable and typically became enraged. During the marriage, this kind of public criticism precipitated his controlling behavior and violence toward her. After the separation, it precipitated another round of litigation, in which the mother's requests were dismissed in court. (In the legal arena, she tended to make unrealistic requests, whereas he typically took a more rational and strategic stance.)

When first seen in family counseling, Jason was a sturdily built, dark-featured pubescent boy who was quite good-looking. He came compliantly to the court-ordered counseling sessions, and with a remarkable impassivity that belied his impatience and anger, he answered in monosyllables the therapist's questions about his family situation. Psychological testing corroborated the initial clinical impressions. This boy was hypervigilant, guarded, suspicious, and untrusting. His self-esteem was exceedingly fragile, especially as it related to his physical disability. He was quick to take offense and to see others as hostile and critical of him, before checking out the reality of the situation.

Defensively, Jason avoided emotionally charged situations and tried to be very good and conforming. However, he would become increasingly immobilized when stressed and then explode in anger. He also seemed depressed and confused, eliciting strong countertransference feelings from the family counselor, who wished to help him in his struggle to separate from and define a viable identity within the enmeshed family conflict. However, he seemed to get little emotional relief from talking. In fact, he had a very utilitarian attitude toward counseling: if it did not further his immediate goals to get something material from one of his parents, he saw no purpose in it.

Jason's school performance was marginal. He received extensive physical therapy for his disability. Until adolescence, he had been somewhat ignored and scapegoated by his classmates. Now in junior high school, he was fast achieving the reputation among his peers for being a "cool dude," a quick, witty, and rebellious leader to whom other young, like-minded adolescents gravitated. His prankish behavior bordered on the exploitative: he schemed to extort money from other boys and seemed to get a sense of power and pleasure from terrorizing female classmates. His mother alleged that he stole money and other objects from her quite frequently and then blatantly denied it. For some time, the father refused to acknowledge that Jason was at all responsible for the missing items at his own home.

A projective story that Jason told at the outset of counseling (using the sandtray materials) seemed to communicate his internal representations of himself in his family. He described a barren world covered with sand where there was an ongoing battle between two armies. His jaundiced view of the parental fights was symbolized by the fact that "the diseased combatants in this battle were *eating* one another!" His own omnipotent but depressive fantasies about his emancipation as an adolescent were portrayed in this story as "a lone, blind survivor of this battle . . . who had everlasting life . . . emerging from a coma a millennium after everyone else had perished." His feelings of alienation from custody evaluators, physicians, and physiotherapists were symbolized by "half-human people who capture and examine the survivor" to satisfy their curiosity rather than to help him. Again and again, as he told it, a weary battle was waged: "They kept fighting and fighting . . . they could never figure out they needed to live in peace!" The lack of internal or external superego controls in this barren world was evident in his comment, "Everyone was their own leader. When someone did something bad, there was no one to stop them. You had to be the strongest to win in the world." Jason ended this nightmarish story, however, with a glimmer of hope for a better world order—he indicated that a civilization ever so slowly emerges out of the chaos. Interestingly, this projective story turned out to be somewhat prophetic.

During early adolescence, as Jason attempted to separate and individuate from his disputing parents, a cyclical pattern of family pathology emerged that reinforced his internal good/bad split, further fragmented his tenuous ego integrity, and undermined his conscience development. The pathological cycle was repeated several times before effective intervention was possible. Each cycle was more intense than the previous one until, finally, the conflict escalated to an untenable, dangerous level. Only then was change possible. The third and most traumatic cycle is described here:

As is expectable with young adolescent boys who are increasingly aware of their masculinity and sexuality, Jason sought his father's interest and approval, and tried to distance himself from his mother by challenging her authority. However, he also remained ambivalently dependent on her to do things for him (she had a history of being somewhat overprotective because of his physical disability). During early adolescence, his oppositional and hostile behavior was extremely threatening to her, which could be anticipated in a mother who lacked confidence in her own judgment. She became anxious, disorganized, and defensively split off from Jason, as he was perceived to have become the "bad son" like the "bad, exploitative, manipulative father." Moreover, she told him this. Precipitously rejected by her, Jason was hurt and furious, and immediately took his father's side in the ongoing custody conflict, strongly identifying with his father's feelings and views. Verbal conflict and power struggles between mother and son escalated. On several occasions, Jason physically threatened her, destroyed objects, and even hit her, reminiscent of his father's violent attacks.

During this phase, Jason would call or visit his father and tell him long, sad, but distorted tales of his mother's abuse, which the father was only too willing to believe. In fact, these stories confirmed and validated the father's views of this "out-of-control woman who lies and manipulates to get whatever she wants." The father idealized his son—Jason became the "good boy" who had enormous potential. The father believed his ex-wife's maliciousness toward him was destroying Jason, and that his son had to be rescued from her. He was convinced that, if his son had any problems, they were "entirely due to her jerking the boy around, her inconsistency, her emotional tantrums."

At his mother's home, Jason's conduct was appalling; he was completely unmanageable. His mother's attempts to discipline him (by withdrawing privileges and refusing to cater to his demands) were quickly undermined by the father, who compensated for the mother's "poor treatment" of the boy by providing him with whatever he wanted. By contrast, in accord with his father's expectations, Jason became the "perfect son" in his father's home—he was described as "sweet, helpful, gentlemanly, and loving to everyone." In this respect, the defensive good/bad split within the young adolescent was confirmed and validated by both parents and acted out within the two households. At the same time, Jason was not made accountable for his difficult behavior; his distorted reality testing and projection of blame were not corrected. Each parent was being thoroughly denigrated by the other, contributing to Jason's precipitous de-idealization and rejection of, first, his mother and, later, his father. His painful sense of loss, disillusionment, isolation, rage, and depression was poignantly evident in some poetry Jason wrote at this time.

The situation exploded in mutual rejection by son and mother, and Jason came to live with his father. The father was gratified; he interpreted this as the mother having "kicked Jason out" of her home, and he was warmly empathic with the boy's feelings of being rejected by her. His own mother was induced to take on the role of the "good mother" to replace the defective "bad mother." Furthermore, brushing aside any evidence of imperfection in his son, he conceded to Jason's expressed wishes to play football on a competitive team, despite the boy's physical limitations. In this respect, Jason sought to become the perfect athlete that his father, the successful coach, had always wanted.

In the ensuing months, Jason struggled to maintain the "good self" and live up to his father's idealized views of him, but the facade of this fragile, split self began to crack. He became covertly more irritable and difficult with his grandmother, especially when his father was absent. He concealed evidence of poor grades at school and did not tell his father that he was sitting on the bench during most of the football games. He presented his father only with his successes. He became increasingly delinquent—drinking, experimenting with sex, and stealing small objects and money from his father's house. When indisputable evidence of this conduct came to light, his father began to question him and asked Jason to account for himself. As the father's idealization of the son began to crumble, so did the son's idealization of the father. Jason's fantasies of his own omnipotence, invulnerability, and authority to determine his own destiny rapidly increased: he felt he no longer had to answer to anyone! He began staying out late, did not turn up for football practice, canceled his physiotherapy, and began cutting classes at school.

When the father confronted his son about these infractions, Jason swore at him and tried to walk out of the room. This direct insult to his authority triggered the father's narcissistic vulnerability, and he became enraged. A horrible physical struggle erupted between father and son. With a look of hatred on his face that the father had never before seen, Jason screamed obscenities, accusing his father of being abusive—in language identical to that his mother had used. The father in turn ridiculed the boy, calling him "a cripple" and "a liar and a thief . . . just like your mother!" Each had triggered the flip side of the defensive split—the bad self and the bad other. Jason, who as a young boy had witnessed his father abuse his mother, was particularly terrified by what had been unleashed and literally felt he was fighting for his life. In desperation, he leaped out the window and ran away. He was picked up roaming the streets by a police officer who took him into protective custody. Child Protective Services workers investigated the incident and considered filing charges against the father for child abuse.

This incident precipitated another round of custody litigation and the most extreme levels of tension and conflict that either parent had ever experienced. The mother was infuriated that the professionals and the courts had not protected her son from "this abusive man." She considered her son entirely blameless in the matter. Undoubtedly, the incident had activated her traumatic experience of marital abuse by the father, and she identified strongly with her son from the position of victim. The father was enormously humiliated by the abuse allegations and the subsequent public air-ing of the incident among his friends and colleagues by the mother. He felt deeply wounded and betrayed by his son. Jason was extremely depressed, angry, and frightened, and refused any contact with his father.

Although a family counselor was in place 18 months before this traumatic incident, she could not find an effective way to provide insight into this pathological cycle of events or to stave off the inevitable crisis. Both parents allowed her only a limited role—helping them mediate their time-sharing arrangements. She was allowed access to Jason so that she could represent his wishes, in a very literal sense, in the mediation. Attempts to moderate the parents' extremely negative views of each other and to more realistically interpret for them the teenager's experience in each home were largely unsuccessful. Both parents felt the family counselor had been duped by the other spouse, and both were convinced they had been validated in their negative beliefs as Jason played out his split self in both homes.

Following this crisis, the family counselor collaborated with the parents' attorneys and the family court counselors in helping the parents come to an agreement to allow Jason, who was now 14 years old, to live with a mutual family friend, in another city, for a period of time, to give him some distance and relief from the enmeshed conflict. It was acknowledged that he could live in neither parent's home for the time being. Interestingly, Jason developed a surprisingly good relationship with this wise and grandfatherly man over the following six months. Both parents entered into a far more realistic phase of family counseling after this distressing incident.

Initially, the mother was highly agitated and trusted no one to help her. She spent her days calling her attorneys, various counselors, friends, and family members, and took many impulsive actions based on their sundry advice. The most effective strategy was for the family counselor to organize the mother's main support system, which included her new husband, her family attorney, and the foster father for her son, to provide a concerted, coordinated, and supportive response to her demands. The approach was to reassure the mother that Jason's behavior was normal adolescent rebellion that had escalated because the parents were not able to cooperate and present a united front for him. Most of the therapeutic work was done with the father, who entered into serious deliberations over what had gone wrong between himself and Jason. Beginning with tremendous compassion and empathy for the father's pain and confusion, and with respect for him as a man who wanted to be a good father, the therapist helped him analyze and understand the splitting that had occurred (the idealization and de–idealization) within Jason, which mirrored the negative projections of both parents. The therapist was firmly confrontive about the father's responsibility in the situation, the nature of his abuse of Jason, and his own vulnerability to being shamed that had triggered his rage.

With the help of his foster father, Jason was encouraged to contact his father within several months. In a series of emotionally powerful reunification sessions between Jason and his father, they reviewed together what had led up to their violent confrontation and what had actually happened during the incident. Apologies were offered and accepted, realistic expectations of each other as father and son were affirmed, and appropriate parental authority was acknowledged. Tears were shed and hugs were exchanged as they both voiced their remorse for the pain they had caused, and both father and son were able to talk about their residual feelings of tension, mistrust, anger, and sadness. These reunification interviews set in motion a gradual reestablishment of the father-son relationship over the next year, wherein each achieved more realistic views and expectations of the other.

When he was 15 years old, Jason asked to resume living with his father, under his sole care, and the mother conceded to this request. It was agreed that she could no longer manage Jason nor could the parents guarantee a cooperative stance on his behalf. The father was gratified by Jason's request but sober about the responsibility it entailed. He remained somewhat mistrustful of his son's motivations and his own judgment about the boy. In particular, he was apprehensive about possible alcohol and drug use by Jason. The father continued to use intermittent counseling to sort out appropriate management of his teenager. From time to time, Jason dropped by to visit his mother but did not care to stay too long because they quickly got into arguments and power struggles. He attended school regularly, but his academic performance continued to be marginal. Interestingly, Jason became an expert wrestler, a sport in which he was not limited by his physical disability. He soon had several friends who shared this passion.

SOME ISSUES IN WORKING WITH
YOUNG ADOLESCENTS AND THEIR PARENTS

Probably the major obstacle in working therapeutically with adolescents of highly conflictual and violent divorcing families is their fundamental distrust of relationships. Despite the startling differences in Susan's and Jason's experiences, this is what they had in common. While it is expectable for self-conscious young adolescents, ambivalently and awkwardly distancing themselves from their families, to be resistant to talking about their feelings in counseling, it is not normally expectable for them to resist forming warm, trusting relationships (Springer, 1991). By contrast, having close relationships and talking about feelings, for adolescents of highly conflictual families, are both longed for and perceived to be toxic and dangerous. Consequently, these youngsters devise myriad ways of controlling, avoiding, manipulating, and stalling therapeutic work. Yet improving their ability to access other empathic adults and to make meaningful connections with their peers is critical for the kind of self-repair necessary to restore their developmental stride.

A consistently empathic, patient stance on the part of the therapist is needed, along with utmost integrity of purpose. These youngsters are acutely aware of being exploited, betrayed, or used on behalf of someone else's agenda. The therapist needs to closely monitor countertransference reactions of boredom and frustration (which signal disappointment to the young person) and avoid being diverted or manipulated by the youngster (which caters to fantasies of omnipotence). On the other hand, premature interpretations or pushing the young person where she or he is not ready to go quickly stalls the process. Soliciting their agreement for counseling and getting their explicit permission to broach certain subjects helps adolescents feel respected and that they have some control over the process. Empathizing with their distrust and letting them know you understand and support their need for defensiveness is the next step. The critical task is then to empathically reflect their own experience within their families, mirroring what it feels like to be burdened by a needy parent or caught between warring parents.

However, in the quest to empathize with the untenable positions in which these young people find themselves, it is tempting to agree with them that parents are acting unfairly, irrationally, or outrageously. The danger here is that such confirmation can further undermine the adolescent's respect for his parents and their tenuous authority over him. Being suddenly confronted with the imperfections of a beloved parent can also be experienced as a depressing loss. There is a risk that the adolescent will perceive the therapist's empathy as a validation of her own distorted perceptions, in which she sees her parents in polarized terms—as being powerful or impotent, right or wrong, wise or stupid.

In general, the task is to help the youngster make more discriminating observations and judgments (e.g., determining when a parent is making a reasonable request and when it is unreasonable, or distinguishing how the parent might be trying to do the right thing in the wrong way). Young adolescents are often impatient with this kind of discussion. However, one can sometimes capture their imagination and attention by using humor, exaggeration, contradiction, or paradox to convey new perspectives. Playing a role-reversal game with young teenagers in which they take the part of the parent can help them gain more perspective and control. Calling upon adolescents' expanding cognitive capacities to have them devise rules or procedures to follow that are "fair" helps them to think more rationally. Using projective media—poetry, sculpture, music, stories, plays, artwork, rap—can bring to the surface more complex feelings and perspectives than they can, perhaps, consciously admit.

The crucial work with parents of adolescents in difficult divorces and conflictual families is preventive. It involves educating them about what are expectable, developmentally appropriate moves that their adolescents are likely to make and helping them tolerate the exploration, distancing, provocation, and ambivalence. These vulnerable parents need considerable reassurance and support to avoid overreaction or rejection when the young person makes a move to separate, especially a move toward the other parent. Ordinarily, teenagers like to make their own, more flexible visiting arrangements with parents that fit with their busy social schedules. Where parental conflict is extreme, the stakes are often too high for the young person to exercise this kind of initiative, and parents then need help in setting up more structured, even ritualistic access plans.

The most difficult and sometimes impossible task is to keep the parents' own emotional needs and their negative perceptions of each other from invading their views of their child and judgment of the child's needs. Helping these parents develop a coordinated, cooperative response to their youngster is optimal. However, when this is not feasible, clearly delineating who has decision-making responsibilities and establishing explicit time-sharing arrangements helps prevent the youngster from taking advantage of the parents' differences and mitigates against the parents' continuing to triangulate the teenager in their ongoing disputes.

Chapter 8

Parental Alignments and Alienation Among Children of High-Conflict Divorce

*M*ost children and adolescents of divorce are eager to have an ongoing relationship with both of their parents, and most are pained by loyalty conflicts and the fear that they might have to choose one parent and lose the other. A minority of children, however, will become enmeshed in the parental conflict to such a degree that they are said to be aligned with one parent and alienated from the other.

When this happens, rejected parents may give up and go away (thus contributing to the dropout rate of fathers after divorce). A small proportion of rejected parents, however, do not disappear from their children's lives without protest; instead, the matter becomes a subject of litigation in family court. In these cases, judges are called upon to arbitrate, while mediators and therapists are expected to resolve the problem through negotiation and counseling. Police may be asked to enforce court-ordered visitation between a reluctant child and the persistent parent. Within the polemics of court litigation, the aligned parent may be accused of aiding and abetting the child's noncompliance and of "brainwashing" the child on behalf of the parent's own agenda. This all results in a plethora of ethical, legal, and family dilemmas usually regarded as extremely difficult if not impossible to resolve to everyone's satisfaction (Lund, 1995; Turkat, 1994).

This chapter summarizes an array of etiological factors that contribute to children's alignments with one parent and rejection of the other and details the intervention implications for the courts and mental health professionals, especially in the most entrenched cases. The developmental appropriateness of the child's response, treatment measures, recommendations for custody and access, and the prognosis for each etiological factor are described (see Johnston, 1993a, for empirical findings). The first three of the etiological factors are developmentally appropriate responses of children. The remainder are related to more pathological processes within parents, family dynamics, and children.

The discerning reader will observe that this chapter recapitulates most of the themes in the previous developmental chapters (4 through 7). This is because parental alienation and the psychopathology it entails is an ever-present threat in chronically conflicted and violent families. It is a likely outcome brought about by a confluence of developmental and family processes that culminates during adolescence; that is, although indications of alienation can occur in much younger children, it is during adolescence that the phenomenon becomes the most pronounced. Unfortunately, at this stage it is particularly resistant to treatment.

NORMAL DEVELOPMENTAL FACTORS

Separation Anxiety in Young Children

Children under the age of 3 to 4 years commonly resist visitation and often become symptomatic at the time of transition from one parent's home to the other. They are generally more likely to whine, cry, verbally complain, and cling to one parent or the other, usually the mother. However, for most of these very young children, the resistance to visit is not usually accompanied by any sustained expression of dislike or discomfort with the other parent; they settle down fairly quickly once they have made the exchange. By itself, this kind of reluctance to visit should not be viewed as alienation. Young children are normally more likely to react with anxiety and to protest being separated from the parent with whom they have a primary psychological attachment, and that parent is likely to be the mother. The transition from one parent to the other commonly sets off developmentally expectable anxieties about safety and survival, especially among children younger than 3 or 4 years, who have not yet internalized an image of the primary figure (Bowlby, 1969, 1973, 1980); that is, they cannot for any length of time visualize or keep in mind a memory of the absent parent, so that visitation to the nonresidential parent creates separation or abandonment anxieties. These young children also have difficulty understanding the concept of time, cannot grasp the rhythm of the visitation schedule, and remain anxious about when they will be reunited with the primary parent.

Problems are likely to arise when the child's normal anxieties are not properly dealt with by both parents (as shown in chapter 4). Many high-conflict parents are ambivalent or skeptical about the value of visitation, especially when the child is symptomatic and resistant at transitions. Consequently, they are not adept at soothing the child and making the child feel safe and competent to handle the changes. Indeed, the parents' failure to deal with their child's anxieties, exacerbated by mounting conflict between the parents, can result in more serious developmental damage that may ultimately make the child vulnerable to alienation (as is shown later in this chapter). For this reason, preventive counseling is essential for these parents.

Consolidation of Gender and Sexuality

In the normal course of events, children's preferences for one parent over the other shift as they grow older and sort out their gender identity (Cath et al., 1982; Erikson, 1963; Blos, 1970). As described in chapter 5, the oedipal phase (among 3- to 6-year-olds) is characterized by boys being libidinally attracted to their mothers and girls to their fathers, and both boys and girls being competitive with and wanting to exclude the same-gender parent. Later on, especially during the early teen years (as shown in chapter 7), young people show more preference for the same-gender parent, a development thought to consolidate their gender role and protect against their mounting fears of a sexualized relationship with the opposite-gender parent. Of course, the many kinds of activities and discourse that children typically share with their same-gender parent and peer group also helps establish a secure gender role. Unfortunately, these expectable shifts in preference can become a major crisis in a divorced family, consolidating an alignment rather than resolving naturally over time.

Social-Cognitive Stage of Development

It is also developmentally expectable that children of different ages will have differing cognitive capacities to understand their parents' disputes with each other; therefore, depending on their developmental level, they will be more or less impacted by the logic of their parents' allegations and counterclaims. Social cognitive psychologists (Flavell et al., 1968; Selman, 1980) have shown that children have an evolving capacity to see events from another's perspective in addition to their own. They also have an advancing ability to differentiate self and others in increasingly psychological and less observably behavioral terms.

Very young children (3 to 5 years) make attributions about parental disputes from witnessing overt parental conflict. Hence, depending on what they observe, they will conclude that "Daddy hates Mommy 'cos he yelled"; and a little later they will note that "Daddy likes Mommy now 'cos he talks nice to her." From about 4 to 8 years of age, children have a budding capacity to see things from another person's viewpoint. They can take one parent's perspective at a time but not both simultaneously. At home with mother, they hear and believe one story, that "Daddy didn't pay Mommy any money"; but at father's home, they are quickly convinced that "Mommy wasted all the money." For these reasons, it is not uncommon for these younger children in high-conflict families to form unstable, shifting alliances. They become easily confused and can excite concern and chaos by telling different stories to each of their divorced parents.

From the time they are 7 to 9 years of age, children have begun to develop the capacity for self-reflexive thinking. They can simultaneously hold more than one perspective at a time and can begin to imagine how their parents view them. These new cognitive capacities mean that children of this age can experience cognitive dissonance and consciously feel acute loyalty conflicts, because they can comprehend the incompatibility of their parents' viewpoints. They are also more aware of inner feelings and mixed feelings, and now know that bad feelings between their parents can continue even though their behavior suggests otherwise.

Children cannot sustain these kinds of loyalty shifts in intensely disputing families for very long, however, probably because such ambivalence is too painful to bear. So, expectably, between the ages of 9 and 12 years, children begin to fix their alignment with one or the other parent and with varying degrees of intensity begin to exclude or reject the other parent. Having not yet developed the older adolescents' ability to critically distance themselves via the third-person perspective capacity, these children become stuck in the simplistic view that one parent is right and the other parent is wrong.

In sum, the alignments seen at this age appear to result from a convergence of developmental factors: the young child's capacity to apprehend both sides of the conflict, which results in intolerable loyalty conflicts, and the young adolescent's tendency to adopt a judgmental or moralistic view of the situation. In addition, as the child enters adolescence, there is typically greater pressure from family members to take a more active role in the parental fight, because the child is now perceived as being "old enough to take a stand." Parents need to be educated about these expectable shifts in attitudes and behavior, to see them as quite normal; otherwise, they can be exacerbated and intensified by parents' anxious, punitive responses to the child and the competition between the parents for the child's affection and allegiance.

PATHOLOGICAL FACTORS

The Chronicity of the Parental Conflict

In general, the more intense and prolonged the divorce conflict and the more exposed children are to parental disputes, the more likely the children will be drawn into an alignment with one parent and become alienated from the other. This is an expectable outcome, and parents should be warned of this possibility early on in counseling. Of course, the optimal goal is to have them cease fighting and cooperate in their parenting, but this is not always possible. Instead, the counselor can help parents to construct protocols for communication, barriers to constrain their interaction (e.g., no in-person contact), and buffer zones for the child (e.g., exchanges at a neutral, safe place). Antagonistic parents are encouraged to develop separate, parallel parenting relationships with their children, governed by an explicit court order that documents their access schedule, times, dates, and place of exchange for all occasions. The need for collaborative decision making should be kept to a minimum, with mediators or arbitrators used when necessary.

The Parents' Contribution to Alienation

THE ROLE OF THE ALIGNED PARENT. It is important to consider the psychological dynamics of each parent in creating and maintaining the aligned/alienation syndrome within the highly conflictual divorcing family. Both the covert and the overt tactics of the alienating parent have long been recognized and are well described elsewhere (Clewar & Riven, 1991;

Gardner, 1987). In general, the alienating parent has been portrayed more or less unsympathetically, as one who is primarily vengeful and malicious. From our perspective, separation and divorce for these parents is typically experienced as loss (with accompanying feelings of anxiety, sadness, and fear of being alone). It is also experienced as rejection (together with feelings of shame and failure). Consequently, these vulnerable people can become acutely or chronically distressed. For relief, some turn to their children for nurturance and companionship, as allies against the world and as the salve for their wounded self-esteem. Others, in an effort to defend themselves from the humiliation of rejection and failure, project all the blame onto their divorcing spouse, whom they now view as the bad parent: endangering, neglectful, and irresponsible. As a result, they feel self-righteously compelled to fight to protect their children from the other parent.

To have their own needs met, the children must reflect whatever the wounded parent needs and wants. Consequently, these children can become vigilant and highly attuned to the parent. The child fears that disappointing or abandoning the depressed or emotionally volatile parent (often the mother) may result in being ignored, rejected, punished, or even destroyed by that parent. Alternately, sensing an apparent omnipotence in caring for a distressed parent, the child acts as though the parent's survival depends on his or her constant vigilance and caretaking. For these reasons, the child may find it extremely difficult if not impossible to leave willingly for visits to the nonresidential parent, fearing what might happen to the left-behind parent during his or her absence, or out of anxiety at disappointing and betraying that parent by "going over to the other side."

Parents who wittingly or unwittingly fuel alienation in this manner need a combination of support (for their own distress) and counseling (to help them to relieve the burdens they are placing on their child). Many of these empathic children can also use a supportive counselor to help them withstand the pressure to rescue their parent and maintain their own integrity. This kind of intervention needs to be paired with gradually increased access arrangements at a rate tolerable to the child. In extremely rare cases, where the aligned parent is flagrantly psychotic or unremittingly sociopathic in the use of the child, a radical custody change may need to be effected to rescue the child.

THE ROLE OF THE REJECTED PARENT. The part played by the rejected parent in maintaining the child's alignment has received very little attention to date; hence, these parents have been viewed somewhat as passive victims of the other parent's vengeful rage. It is our observation that alienated parents are often rather inept and unempathic with their youngsters. While the aligned parent is fueling the child's alienation (either overtly or covertly), the rejected parent is often contributing to the alignment by a combination of counterhostility and dogged pursuit of the child (either overtly or covertly). Most rejected parents are not only hurt but highly affronted, even outraged, by the child's challenge to their authority and the lack of respect accorded them. Some try to reassert their parental position by force, which can end in physical struggles with the child. Other alienated parents pursue the child relentlessly with a barrage of phone calls, letters, unexpected appearances at the child's activities, all of which feel intrusive and even frightening to the young person. The child's negative reactions are denied, or are simply dismissed as "the other parent talking" and by declarations that the child has been "brainwashed." These declarations are especially infuriating to adolescents trying to hold on to their emerging autonomy. In fact, many rejected parents do not clearly distinguish their children as separate persons from the ex-spouse and attempt to carry on the marital dispute, in all of its primeval intensity, through the medium of the child. It is not surprising that such children feel utterly disempowered as a person in their own right.

What is often evident, however, is that beneath these children's strident anger is a pathetic longing for the rejected parent. They want to be rescued from their intolerable dilemma and seem to be continually testing, by more and more extreme, negative behaviors, how much the rejected parent does or does not care, and whether they exist for that parent in any other way than as a shadow of the adversary. In intervention, the first order of business is usually helping the rejected parent to reach out to the child in a nonintrusive and respectful manner, and to patiently tolerate the child's testing in a manner that sends the message that the parent does indeed care and can be trusted. Increased access to alienated parents should be contingent upon their capacity to provide this kind of empathic attunement and their capacity to acknowledge the child as a person separate from the ex-spouse.

The Family Dynamics

The family dynamics that produce alienated children are typified by extremely divergent parenting styles. Aligned parents are usually extraordinarily naive about their own psychological neediness and their confused emotional boundaries with their children (Lampel, 1996). They tend to relate to their children as equals, often speak of them as their "best friends," or, in a reversal of roles, rely on them for direction and nurturance. Hence, they are often permissive and undemanding as parents and give their children a great deal of authority to make their own decisions, including the resolution to have nothing to do with the other parent. Once the children voice their own views and feelings toward the rejected parent, aligned parents calmly and self-righteously declare their neutrality in the issue. They often justify their parenting style as "empowering the child" and point to the (pseudo)mature stance of the child as proof of its effectiveness.

By contrast and often in reaction to this emotional enmeshment and permissiveness, the rejected parent is likely to be overly autocratic, demanding, rigid, and punitive (i.e., their parenting style can be markedly authoritarian). As the conflict between the parents escalates, the child retreats back into the protection of the aligned parent, sharing that parent's distress and phobic reaction to the other, and will actually characterize the alienated parent as "mean" and "scary." Of course, this intensifies the humiliation and rage on the part of the rejected parent and the antagonism and avoidance on the part of the alienated child in a vicious cycle of self-fulfilling prophecy. When these disputes enter the courtroom, the traditional adversarial approach provides the ideal environment to reify the villain/victim dichotomy.

The Role of Domestic Violence in Alienation

Domestic violence is another etiological agent for parent alienation. Children of various ages who have witnessed incidents of violence between their parents are likely to have been severely frightened if not traumatized. In general, younger children are likely to suffer greater distress than older ones. As explained in chapters 2 and 3, from our perspective children who witness incidents of high conflict or violence between parents appear to exacerbate the defense mechanism of splitting, so that one parent (the abuser) is seen as either all bad or completely justified, and the other parent (the victim) is seen as either all good or totally deserving of the abuse. (Other interpretations have explained this process as identification with the aggressor or the victim.) As we have agreed in chapter 5, young boys who witness their father's powerful, aggressive posturing tend to manage their fears of him by merging with him and incorporating his disparaging view of the mother (and of women, in general). In this way, boys simultaneously affirm their "maleness" and confuse it with aggression. It is proposed that this kind of aggressive masculinity helps them to deal with their anxiety about separation from their mothers (and results in boys' eschewing the more feminine parts of themselves). Likewise, young girls are likely to merge with the mother, the perceived victim of aggression, affirming their "femaleness" but also confusing it with powerlessness in relation to men. These extreme identifications with the aggressor (usually the father) or the victim (usually the mother) can contribute to the kind of alignments that are formed and to the child's alienation from the other parent.

It is also important to understand that many of these children have realistic fears about the danger of a violent parent, particularly a battering father, and they resist visitation because they do not feel safe with that parent. Alternatively, they do not feel safe in leaving mother, home, siblings, or pets, perceiving them all to be vulnerable to attack by the violent parent. Resistance to visitation and parent alienation in cases of domestic violence are usually derived from a complex mix of the child's realistic and irrational fears (phobias) of a parent's dangerousness.

Children traumatized by witnessing family violence may need to be treated for posttraumatic stress syndrome, which involves recovering, abreacting, and working through the traumatic memories in a safe, supportive, therapeutic environment, before they can (re)engage in a more secure relationship with both the perpetrator and the victim of abuse (Pynoos & Eth, 1986; Schwarz et al., 1993). When there is an ongoing threat of violence by a parent, or when children have been directly physically abused or sexually molested by a parent (or believe that they have been abused, despite definitive proof to the contrary), they also need therapeutic support and the protection of supervised visits. When a parent continues to be abusive or violent, contact with the child may need to be suspended or terminated.

The Child's Contribution to Alienation

What is most notable and often surprising is that individual children and adolescents can respond very differently to the familial pressures of highly conflictual and violent parents. Some resist alignments; they maintain their own integrity and view of the situation and do not take sides despite the obvious attempts by a parent to influence them negatively. Others, with little or no encouragement, can become alienated. Some youngsters are most forgiving of a parent's ineptness and lack of empathic attunement; others are truly frightened and angered by the parent's lack of respect for their feelings or inability to make them feel safe. Both normal developmental factors within the child (described above) as well as pathological processes (described below) can contribute to these differences in susceptibility.

EARLY ORIGINS OF EXTREME PARENTAL ALIENATION. For most children who form alignments, their preference for one parent and dislike of the other is of moderate intensity, often kept covert or private and tempered by a wish not to hurt the feelings or raise the ire of the rejected parent. If it remains moderate, the alignment is not a cause for concern. A disturbing number of children, however (in excess of one fourth of the young adolescents in our samples of litigated divorces), make what we call "unholy alliances," these being overtly hostile, unshakable stances within which the child may stridently reject, refuse to visit, and even persecute one parent. In these cases, there is considerable distortion of reality as the child views one parent as "all good" and the other as "all bad." These more bizarre reactions are not developmentally expectable; rather, there are clearly more pathological individual and family dynamics at work.

These more extreme, distorted perceptions and behaviors of children have been labeled "parent alienation syndrome" by Gardner (1992). But rather than seeing this syndrome as being induced in the child by an alienating parent, as Gardner does, we propose that these "unholy alliances" are a later manifestation of the failed separation–individuation process in especially vulnerable children who have been exposed to disturbed family relationships during their early years. Having observed these children over more than a decade, we conclude that it is clearly those who have sustained these kinds of developmental difficulties (mostly as a consequence of interparental conflict and parental narcissistic disturbance as described in chapters 1 and 3) that are likely to present the more extreme forms of parent alienation during early adolescence.

In chapter 4, we drew from object relations theories, especially those of Mahler and associates (1975), to explain failures of separation–individuation during the very early years of a child's life. In the normal phases of the infant's and toddler's psychological separation and individuation, the parent's tolerant and constant attunement to the child's good and bad aspects allow the child to internalize a constant and whole sense of self. This developmental attunement, supported by the parents' mutuality, allows this constant sense of self to remain intact when the child separates from the primary parent (usually the mother) to go to the other (usually the father). Normally, the toddler uses the mother (or primary parent) to equilibrate his emotional distress: she is a "refueling station" and the social referent for what is safe and pleasurable outside the mother-child dyad. Normally loving spouses (and those divorced mothers who value the child's relationship with both parents) show much pleasure in encouraging the child to venture out to relate to the other parent (usually the father). In turn, the father excites and invites the young child to venture forth. The father is then used as a stepping stone to forming relationships in the outside world: he is a transitional person (Abelin, 1975; Cath et al., 1982).

Compare this normal situation of loving spouses with the experience of a child caught between highly conflictual parents (either within the marriage or after divorce). As discussed and illustrated in chapter 4, the mother in these cases is likely to express anxiety, panic, and rage or may have a phobic reaction to the father. At times of the child's transition from one parent to the other, the mother's feelings may be clearly visible in her face or are transmitted viscerally to the child in her arms as her body tenses. Acute states of anxiety and hostility in the mother can be provoked by repeated outbursts of anger or threats between parents, which may include actual violence.

For these children, the transition to the father not only signals an impending separation from the mother but also represents a transition to the bad-mother and the bad-mother-me state. In her perceived defection to the father, the child experiences a precipitous loss of attunement with and support from the mother, so that the young child's separations from mother to go to father become fraught with fear and anxiety about abandonment. The internal good-mother-me state is precipitously replaced by the bad-mother-me state. If this becomes an expectable part of the child's life, there is a threat that the young child will delay achieving or fail entirely to achieve what is called "self and object constancy" (Lax et al., 1986). Instead, the child retains a split sense of self (feeling alternately all good or all bad) and views others as what are called *part-objects* (i.e., others are also perceived as either all good or all bad, depending on whether those others are gratifying or frustrating the child's needs).

The repeated trauma associated with separations or transitions from mother to father prevents the child from having a steady and predictable access to the internal good-mother-me state that normally promotes self-soothing and helps to modulate anxiety. Moreover, this integration failure interferes with the child's ability to make use of the father as an alternative primary parenting figure. The child's perception of the father, then, remains a primitive projection of that which is potentially bad, frightening, and unsafe. For the child, this means not being able to integrate the sense of good and bad in the self, the mother, and the father in order to experience each as a separate, whole person.

In sum, children who have lived with chronic parental conflict since infancy or toddlerhood and those whose parents are inconsistently available to them emotionally are more likely to grow up highly dependent, with insecure attachments to both parents and ongoing difficulties with separation from the primary parent, usually the mother. These children are candidates for the more extreme forms of parent alienation. It is these children who are not able to differentiate their own feelings about the other parent from those of their primary parent.

The point we wish to emphasize is that parent alienation that derives from these very early developmental failures in the child is laid down in the preverbal memory banks of the child and is, therefore, largely unconscious and nonvolitional. The alienation involves very primitive psychological defenses not easily amenable to treatment. Removing the child precipitously from the aligned parent in these cases can be ineffective and even dangerous, unless it is done with extreme therapeutic care. (We are aware of one 10-year-old boy who hanged himself when he was court-ordered from his aligned mother into the custody of his father. Another child had an epileptic seizure, her first, when she was forcibly removed from her aligned father.) Parent alienation in these cases is not simply a matter of pernicious, conscious "brainwashing" by an embittered parent: the more important ingredient is a vulnerable, receptive child who has likely sustained early developmental damage.

The treatment of choice involves long-term therapy of the child with the goal of effecting a gradual separation in a supportive therapeutic environment. This therapy should include collateral counseling and support for both parents. When young adolescents struggle with their new, more complex cognitive understanding of their parents' conflicts at the same time they are renewing their attempts to separate from an ambivalent relationship with an aligned parent, the thought of reconciling with an alienated parent may be intolerable. Therapeutic efforts in this direction are likely to stall and may, in fact, be ill-advised. Efforts are better spent using the therapy to help these youngsters begin to separate from the primary (aligned) parent. In the most severe cases, when a child is caught in a folie à deux relationship (i.e., a shared paranoid psychosis) with an extremely mentally disturbed parent and the child is in danger, the separation of parent and child may need to be undertaken within the protective confines of an inpatient psychiatric unit or in a residential school for emotionally disturbed children.

CASE ILLUSTRATIONS OF INTERVENTIONS WITH ALIENATED CHILDREN

The treatment of alienation and refusal of visitation is illustrated here by two cases. In the first family, the intervention on behalf of Julianne was extended, and her prognosis remains guarded, as the circumstances involved early developmental difficulties with attachment and separation. However, because the child was relatively young (9 years old) at the time of treatment, there was a window of opportunity for change that would not be available in early adolescence. In the second family, the intervention was brief and the prognosis is relatively good, because early difficulties with attachment and separation did not exist. Furthermore, although the case was complicated by domestic violence, the youth, Robert, was older (14 years), approaching an age when teenagers are more receptive to the kind of self-reflection and insight that promotes successful treatment.

Julianne: A Case of Entrenched Alienation

Julianne, aged 9 years, was referred to our center because of her persistent refusal to visit with her father. The issue had become the subject of ongoing litigation. The father alleged that she had been "alienated by her embittered mother," and a custody change was proposed as the solution. Within minutes of first meeting the counselor, Julianne launched into a long tirade against her father. She began with a story (told in words that echoed her mother's) about how he once tried to drown her by taking her out in a leaky sailboat when she was a baby. She went on with a litany of complaints that she repeated whenever given the opportunity: "He never gives me my medicine for my asthma. . . . He lies all the time. . . . He's mean to me—he yells at me and hits me. . . . Once he abducted me. He locked me in the car and drove away real fast and I didn't get to see my mother for a whole day. He tries to buy my affections by giving me things but it's a trap. He just wants to get control of me and my mom. . . . I hate him! I never wanted to see him since I was a baby! It's so boring at his place—he just wants to do all of these stupid things like go to parks and children's museums and stuff, and the birthday presents he gives me are so dumb. . . . He never listens to what I want!"

Julianne's behavior when observed with each parent separately was strikingly opposite. With her father, she was anxious, angry, and conflicted; she treated him with disdain and rejected his many attempts to reach out to her and engage her in a mutual task of "draw-a-family." At the same time, she seemed hungry for his interest and attention. This ambivalence was expressed most clearly when Julianne would hit her father, at first playfully, as if enticing him to roughhouse with her; but then she would chastise him for hurting her. In turn, the father became indignant and somewhat officious. This interactive sequence concluded with Julianne calling her father a string of profane names. By contrast, Julianne demonstrated an extremely warm, dependent relationship with her mother. She was most solicitous of her mother's wishes in the mutual draw-a-family task, constantly sought her mother's approval for her efforts, and kept up a lively chatter that seemed designed to help keep her mother amused and interested in her.

Other observers (i.e., her teachers and day-care provider) gave Julianne a mixed review. They described her as generally sweet and compliant but perfectionistic. They also said she tended to be pseudomature, overly controlling with her peers, and easily crushed by the mildest criticism. During the extended litigation, she seemed anxious and depressed, had difficulty separating from her mother, suffered sleep disturbances and nightmares about being abducted, and was frequently asthmatic. Once she made her decision not to visit her father, she seemed much happier, and many of these overt symptoms of anxiety and distress disappeared. However, projective psychological testing (Rorschach) indicated that she was significantly depressed and markedly hypervigilant, distrustful, and guarded. She was highly attuned to the needs of others (low in egocentricity) and tended to construe the world in unrealistic ways. There was also much evidence of suppressed anger that could intermittently erupt in explosive episodes.

Julianne fits the profile of children who have experienced entrenched, highly conflicted custody disputes, together with early insecure (disorganized) attachments with their primary parent (Solomon et al., 1994; Solomon & George, 1996). She was an anxious, insecure child who had failed to achieve a complete psychological separation from her mother. Splitting was her major defense: she tried to keep a black/white, bad/good sense of herself and her parents. In this defensive system, her father (and herself with him) was all bad; her mother (and herself with her) was all good. During the mounting hostilities generated by the litigation, Julianne became increasingly anxious and fragmented whenever she dared to separate from her mother and consort with her father in any way. This rigid stance significantly undermined her ability to view other people in realistic ways. This split between the "all good, loving, protective, safe" mother and the "scary, dangerous, hateful, stupid" father was mirrored within her own self-structure. When Julianne was happy, in control, and masterful in ways her mother particularly valued, she postured in an assertive and decidedly pseudomature manner. When she felt unable to cope, out of control, and unable to achieve perfection, she became angry and upset, and projected her negative feelings and failures onto others, especially her "bad, hateful" father. She relied excessively on the presence of her mother to feel safe and whole, competent and good.

As is characteristic of these children, Julianne appeared to function better when she was in an alignment with her mother, refusing any contact with her father. Indeed, her strident stance in this ongoing battle between her parents was probably keeping her psychologically organized. This defensive posture was very fragile, however. It is common among such children that their intolerant, positivistic views and their sense of being wholly right and potent come from feeling themselves to be on the side of the angels in a "holy war." If the parental dispute dissipates and the spotlight is no longer on the child, this posture can easily break down. At this time, the shadow side emerges. No longer serving an important function for the parent, the child may become depressed and self-deprecating or take on a passive-aggressive, oppositional stance. It follows that these children are especially likely to have difficulties during adolescence unless given adequate therapeutic help. Specifically, relationships with peers are likely to become progressively more problematic, deepening these youngsters' depressive view of themselves. They can engage in risky behaviors (substance abuse, sexual promiscuity) as a defense against depression and difficulties with close relationships (as did Jason, in chapter 7). Alternatively, they can retreat from peer relationships and become increasingly isolated (as did Susan, in chapter 7).

The etiology of Julianne's disturbance in attachment and poor reality testing began with her early experience of both parents. The couple had never married, and their brief, chaotic relationship fell apart when Julianne was a toddler. From that point on, her mother was preoccupied with her own relationship difficulties with a series of men, some of whom were abusive to her. Emotionally, she was only intermittently and unpredictably available to her daughter. Julianne's early relationship with her mother was characterized by role reversal, in which the little girl quickly learned to caretake her mother to get her own needs met. Periodically over the years, when the mother was particularly anxious about her financial and emotional survival, she would withdraw from Julianne, who in turn became fearful her mother would abandon or lose interest in her.

To protect herself against these primitive fears of loss, Julianne tended to merge with her mother, incorporating her mother's views of the world. Consequently, Julianne shared her mother's every concern. All of Julianne's early fears were then recapitulated during the custody dispute, which, interestingly, was precipitated by two concurrent crises for the mother: her current lover deserted her, and Julianne's father stopped paying child support. At this time Julianne began to take on her mother's negative views of the father (and probably of men in general). It is important to note that the mother did not consciously indoctrinate her daughter into this stance. Compared with many angry mothers, this woman had been relatively accepting of the father's involvement in her daughter's life—that is, whenever he was meeting her own needs; at other times she was hostile toward him. The mother was naively incredulous of the child's more recent strident refusal to visit. It appeared, however, that Julianne had been a willing recipient of her mother's unconscious views. In fact, the child's symptomatic behavior, including her refusal to visit her father, probably fueled the interparental fight and, in a self-perpetuating cycle, helped entrench her defensive stance.

The father's role in this child's dilemma was obvious. First, from the time he left the household, he was only intermittently available to his daughter. During her preschool years, he responded in a passive-aggressive manner to the mother's shifting emotional and financial demands of him, by disappearing for months at a time. Though he did try to establish regular visitation when Julianne was older, she did not trust him to help her transition out of her enmeshed relationship with her mother. When Julianne became distressed during visits, he deepened her distrust of him by being rigid, controlling, and unempathic, all of which intimidated her. She perceived him as being particularly scary and dangerous when, on one occasion, he forced her into his car and drove away after an altercation that left the mother distraught and in tears at her front gate.

At the outset of counseling, it was important not to underestimate the strength of Julianne's feelings, fears, and convictions about her father. They had all the qualities of an intense phobia, which was not amenable to cognitive reasoning, and they involved primitive psychological defenses not easily amenable to treatment. When Julianne was forced by a court order to visit her father, with no therapeutic support and no protected setting, she became overwhelmed and disorganized by her anger and panic.

In terms of intervention, a coordinated family approach was needed, with all parts of this family and their helping agents (attorneys and therapists) cooperating as a unit. However, family therapy with mother, father, and child all present simultaneously was intolerable for Julianne. In this setting, it was not possible for her to make any move toward her father without feeling she was betraying and disappointing her mother. This child needed her own individual, protected relationship with a therapist—a private space in which she could gradually explore her separateness from her mother. The therapist then could also become a stepping stone (and buffer) for Julianne in relating to her father.

Both parents were seen initially in separate sessions by the same parenting counselor-mediator, who also maintained a close working relationship with the child's therapist. As with many of these enmeshed family conflicts, this couple had attempted conjoint therapy on a number of occasions, quite unsuccessfully. Any further attempts to do this kind of work were likely to escalate and deepen their conflict. Separate, concurrent sessions mitigated against their mutual projection of blame. The goal for each was to help them separate from the enmeshed conflict with each other and develop separate, parallel parenting relationships with their child.

The work with the mother began by helping her to understand why Julianne would benefit from resolving her relationship difficulties with father and learning to manage her altercations with him without fighting or fleeing. The counselor explained to the mother that both she and father were the cornerstones of this child's identity, that the parental conflict had fragmented and undermined Julianne's stable, positive sense of herself. The counselor described the difficulties that could be predicted for Julianne's future if these matters were not attended to. Furthermore, the counselor endeavored to connect these insights to the mother's awareness of her own troubled relationships with men and her longing to protect her daughter from making the same mistakes. She explained that Julianne could develop a more balanced view of her father only when she could view his strengths and weaknesses more realistically. This, in turn, would strengthen her ability to make accurate judgments in relationships with men, in general. Taking care to support her sufficiently and not to blame her for Julianne's difficulties, the counselor helped this mother to see how her own anger was also preventing her from viewing Julianne's father realistically.

At the same time, the mother was helped to protect Julianne from her own personal fears and worries, which this acutely sensitive and empathic child had so quickly incorporated, so that Julianne would not feel so burdened. This meant providing the mother with alternative sources of support. As this groundwork began to take hold, the mother was asked to actively support, even insist on, appropriate visits between Julianne and her father. She was also taught to reprimand Julianne for her disrespectful behavior toward him, such as hanging up the phone on him and calling him names. The mother was motivated to follow through with this work, because she was learning to trust that the parenting counselor-mediator was also working diligently with the father to help him respond empathically and appropriately to Julianne's more valid concerns. This support helped the mother to firmly correct the child's negative perceptions of the father's attempts to reach out to her: she told Julianne that her father was doing his best in the only way he knew how.

The work with the father involved having him back off from his request for primary custody and accept much less visitation time than he had requested at the outset. He also needed to learn how to be more empathic and less rigid and controlling with his daughter. The counselor encouraged him to continuously send his daughter the message that he loved her, and that he would always be there for her, no matter what happened. Julianne was invited to tell her father (first through her therapist, then through written messages, and finally in person) what she wanted from him as a father, and he was encouraged to listen and respect her wishes rather than imposing his own views of what she needed. As he responded to some of Julianne's material wishes (skating lessons, an allowance, birthday cards), she began to experience him as less intrusive and herself as more in control. The father was able to tolerate backing off on his demands when he began to understand more of the dilemmas that Julianne's early separation difficulties had created for her and when he was given overt appreciation for his positive efforts and good intentions toward his daughter. Unfortunately, however, although he intermittently acknowledged that his own angry, rejecting responses to his provocative daughter contributed to his alienation, he could not always contain himself. Progress in his relationship with Julianne was ultimately limited by his own explosive outbursts.

Therapeutic intervention with Julianne could not really begin until the parents settled into their own parental counseling and essentially agreed on the parameters of the intervention. Still hypervigilant and basically distrusting, Julianne was expectably resistant to forming a working relationship with the therapist in her individual therapy. She was highly controlling or uncooperative, and threatened to leave whenever the therapist did not proceed according to her way of thinking. The danger was that she would use her counseling sessions to protect her fantasies of omnipotence and to bolster her distorted view of her parents; and that the therapy would fail to touch her underlying depressive fears. On the other hand, she could not be confronted, challenged, or made to do what she was not ready to do.

The therapist proceeded very carefully by acknowledging Julianne's valid feelings about the manner in which her father had disappointed her, but without dwelling on them. The therapist then helped Julianne to surface and articulate her tremendous concern and compassion for her mother, her fear of her mother's not surviving emotionally and financially, and her worry about her mother's anger and unavailability. This was all couched in terms of "what a great kid you are for being so sensitive toward your mother, but how burdensome, and unfair it is for you to have these kinds of worries at your age." She was invited to "get on with your own life—have fun with your friends, work hard at school, enjoy your skating." In this way, the therapist supported Julianne's engagement in her own activities and peer relationships.

To protect the treatment, the therapist needed to maintain an empathic and equidistant stance toward both parents. At the same time, the therapist acknowledged for Julianne the intolerable nature of the ongoing mistrust, hostility, and fighting between her parents and helped her to identify the specific ways that she been affected. She maintained a balance between affirming Julianne's experience while gently challenging the absolute quality of her negative views of her father. In this way, the therapist loaned her own ego to the child and helped her achieve a more critical distance from both her parents. Over the course of this work with Julianne, the therapist used projective puppet plays, stories, role plays, and artwork to surface some of her deeper fears, as well as her rules and expectations about relationships (as illustrated in chapters 10 and 11).

The plan was to gradually reinstate Julianne's visitation with her father over a six-month period. The specific visitation arrangement at each time was arbitrated by a special master appointed to the case (see chapter 9) after consultation with all other professionals involved and as ordered by the court. Hence, the visitation order was not for the therapists or the parents to decide, but it was their responsibility to follow the court order. The father-daughter visits began in the therapist's office and progressed with considerable input from Julianne about what was tolerable for her. For example, she elected to accompany her father to dinner and took her cousin as a buffer. These visits progressed to longer day visits, again in the company of her cousin. The child's complaints about these visits were examined for what was rational and justified and what was not, and both parents were counseled accordingly.

Unfortunately, the father found it difficult to deal with his daughter's challenges to his authority and her stinging criticisms of his competence. He often retaliated or reinvolved the girl in his disputes with the mother. As a result, Julianne adamantly refused to stay overnight in her father's home. The situation was not helped when the father became impatient and angry with her, stopped visiting her for a couple of months, and then tried to reinstigate litigation to see her again. After this setback, it took several more months to normalize the day visits with his daughter.

This case illustrates how difficult it can be for all concerned parties to accept that the factors contributing to children's alienation have been a long time in the making and will be a long time in the mending. In some cases of parental alienation, too much damage has been done to repair the family relationships, or the parental conflict continues unabated, making a parental alignment the child's only relatively safe port in the storm. Young adolescents, in particular, may not be able to tolerate any kind of reunification efforts. If these youngsters are managing relatively well in other areas of their lives, they might need to have some respite from the visitation, and this respite might last for several years. Sometimes ongoing therapy can be insisted upon, in lieu of visitation. Here, youngsters tend to work through some of their issues indirectly by talking about their peer relationships. Therapists should not accept the task of parent-child reunification as the principal goal of therapy but only as a subgoal to that of helping the child get back on track developmentally. Most important, the goal of therapy should focus on the child's needs rather than on securing parents' rights.

Robert: An Acute Alienation Reaction

Robert was a 14-year-old boy whose parents had been separated for about two years. The marriage was marked by the father's verbal and physical abuse of his family and the mother's affairs with other men. The separation, initiated by the mother, was fraught with very high conflict. The father was rageful and threatening. He accused the mother of drug use and prostitution. There was possession snatching by both parents, continual litigation about property and support, and a major dispute over custody of the three children (Robert, 14; Alice, 13; and Tina, 11). A court-ordered custody evaluation resulted in the two oldest children living with their father at the south end of the city (so they could continue to attend their same schools and sporting activities) and the youngest living with her mother at the north end of the city. Since the parental separation, Robert had entered into "an unholy alliance" with his father and refused to visit with his mother or even talk with her on the telephone. He got into physical struggles with his mother and hit her on occasion. He had also been abusive with his two younger sisters.

This very large, sturdily built young man had the physique of a football player (he had been a star football player until he sustained an injury at the time of his parents' divorce). He had recently put on a great deal of weight, about which he was embarrassed. By court order, he was brought to counseling sessions by his father. Throughout the initial interviews, Robert's eyes kept brimming with tears and he struggled to keep them back. He was terribly ashamed of his inability to control himself. His verbal account of what was happening in his family was chaotic and incoherent (as was his father's story). He stumbled over his words and could barely complete his sentences. Only now and then, he would come out with a very strong, clear comment, such as, "My Dad looks at it this way. She [mother] is just doing this to get back at him!" These clear statements were obviously parroted versions of the father's polarized negative view of the mother.

To understand Robert, as well as his good progress in therapy, it is important to know that he had a loving, nurturing early experience with his mother. However, she became increasingly absent as he grew older, especially when she went back to work and the marriage deteriorated. The father's relationship with the boy had always been marked by bullying domination and intermittent physical abuse, as well as a great deal of love and caring. The father also derived considerable vicarious gratification from his son's sporting achievements. At the time of his parents' divorce, Robert could remember *nothing* negative about his father (neither the marital violence nor the abuse of himself); he could indicate only that if his father had been rough on him, it was probably because somehow he deserved it.

Robert's resistance to counseling was palpable, and he usually came late to sessions. Clearly angry and depressed, he proclaimed himself "bored, profoundly bored!" Attempts to talk about his feelings and his hitting his sisters were greeted with a defiant, "All kids hit . . . they always have in our family." The therapist noted that "hitting seems like an okay thing to do . . . that's true for your family, but it's not true for all families." Using information gleaned from interviews with both parents, she went on to comment that Robert had seen a lot of awful things that other kids haven't seen, like his father hitting his mother many times. She said he might not remember it, but he had been very brave: as a little boy he had thrown himself between his parents to stop them from fighting. It was possible he had prevented his mother from getting injured—maybe even saved her life.

Robert's eyes brimmed with tears again, and he mumbled that he did not want to remember: "All this counseling is no good . . . it only makes me more upset . . . all that is behind me now. Don't keep dragging it up." The therapist answered gently that it was not behind him, it was *in* him, and it came out in his bad dreams. It kept haunting him like a ghost, and she worried that it might come out and bother him years from now. For the first time, Robert looked a bit interested and queried, how could that be?

The therapist explained that in talking with people who had covered up their feelings and memories from the time of their parents' divorce, 10 or 15 years earlier, it was sometimes found that they now hit their own wives; or they got really depressed when they broke off with girlfriends, because troubled relationships reminded them of the past, of their own families. "The sad part is that we are likely to hurt the ones we love the most. For example, your dad really loved your mom a lot, and he hit her. There might come a time when you love someone a lot, and you might find yourself reacting in the same way, like from the past." The therapist went on to use the analogy of a broken arm, like the arm Robert had broken playing football. If the doctor had let it mend without setting the bone straight and putting it in a cast, he would have grown up with a crooked arm that didn't work right! It was the same with his feelings and bad memories. She told him she understood that he felt bad thinking about all this, that he would really prefer to stuff it away. More tears threatened to overflow, and Robert grabbed a handful of tissues. The therapist went on. "You don't trust me to help you. People have let you down. Especially you think your mom has let you down. You expect others to let you down."

It was at this point that Robert said, "I've let my Mom down. It's her birthday today and I didn't even call her!" In reply, the therapist told Robert that he was far too hard on himself. "You expect yourself to be Superman! You've done nothing wrong—and you're not to blame!" He mumbled that "other kids have it worse than I have." His therapist was skeptical: she told him she had seen a lot of kids and she thought Robert had it pretty bad. She believed he was worth spending time with in counseling. He was a sensitive, intelligent, caring teenager. He was also the one in his family who seemed to carry the most responsibility. Each of his sisters was taking care of herself, while he was looking after his dad and worrying about the money situation.

On the basis of this discussion, Robert agreed to continue with the therapy sessions and gave his explicit permission for them to talk about the kinds of fights he had witnessed between his parents and what had happened since the divorce, especially all the things his mother had done that upset him. During the next couple of sessions, using posttraumatic stress interviewing techniques (Pynoos & Eth, 1986), Robert reenacted specific scenes of violence between his parents that he remembered seeing. These were very traumatic incidences, in which his father became enraged and abusive, and the mother was victimized by his violence. When the therapist gave Robert a great deal of appreciation for his bravery and support of his mother, and for his compassion for his father's pain, the teenager was finally able to talk about these violent incidents and his moral outrage.

Although this boy was beginning to recall specific critical incidents about his family, he continued to find it difficult to use language to express his feelings and ideas, and to differentiate his own from those of his father. For this reason, he was invited to use the sandtray to create visual scenes that represented his view of his relationship with both parents. (The therapist explained that many people, even adults, could express their ideas better in art forms like music, lyrics, poetry, and sculpture than in words, and that using the sandtray was a way of doing this). In the subsequent four sessions, Robert produced an astounding series of sandtray scenes that very eloquently expressed his relationship with each parent separately and then both parents together.

The first, a scene at his father's house, involved his father as a superman with a large gun, venturing out with an army tank to visit the ape (the lawyer) and the "Evil Deistro" (the bank manager), both of whom were ensconced in a fortressed building surrounded by armed guards. In a corner behind a frail fence was a boy (Robert). His explanation of this scene was as follows: "Dad has to get himself all armored up, like with guns and tanks, when he goes out to see his lawyer and the bank manager. Then he comes home and we need protection 'cos he fires all his stuff at us." (The therapist commented that this showed excellent insight into his father's behavior, especially the way his father became stressed trying to cope with legal and money matters, and how that stress typically spilled over into his ranting and raving and bullying his kids.)

The next scene was at his mother's house. In one corner of the tray, he placed three babies (later identified as himself and his two sisters) who were "falling asleep, bored as heck, watching TV, and fighting with each other." In the center of the tray was a rendition of the Golden Gate Bridge and on the other side stood the skyscrapers of the city. He noted that while her kids were left at home, his mother was off in the city dancing with her friends all night; she came home really late and slept all the next morning. (When the therapist talked about how neglected, lonely, and unmothered kids feel in these situations, he answered simply, "You've got it!")

The next significant scene emerged through a gradual process of building and collapsing structures in the sand. "This is my Dad," he said, as he put together a precarious structure with the dominoes. He poured a little sand on the top and showed that, as the weight of the sand increased minimally, the structure collapsed (analogous to how likely his father was to decompensate under fairly minimal stress). The therapist then asked Robert to make a structure that represented himself, and he carefully built a much stronger base but showed that it became unstable at higher elevations, and that the top would collapse with the weight of added sand. Again the therapist admired his insight, especially the distinctions he was able to make between himself and his father, who had an extremely abused and neglected early life. Robert then talked about the particular kinds of things that were distressing and depressing for him.

Finally, Robert built two structures, both precarious (representing both his parents), that were separated by a thin card (which, he said, represented the lawyers). He kept pouring sand on the two buildings (his mother and father). His verbal commentary was as follows: "Both Mom and Dad are putting a lot of pressure, and pushing on both sides. . . . Both will try to last out to see who is going to make it through . . . who is going to cave in first?" He then showed that again and again, the father building collapsed first and more devastatingly. He continued, "Mom can rebuild . . . 'cos she has a strong family from behind. . . . Mom can always get more help from Grandma. Dad has no one, no one except us kids, and we only cost him more money and stress!" (At this point the therapist made the interpretation that, in his compassion and concern for his father, he has decided to support his father and help him hold up his end in the struggle for survival against his mother. Robert agreed.)

This is a truncated account of the important shifts in the brief therapy with this boy, which spanned about eight sessions. Gradually over the course of these sessions, his tears stopped. Robert expressed his ideas and feelings much more coherently, and as shown by the sandtray scenes, he was slowly differentiating himself from his father. His abusive behavior with his sisters ceased entirely. Over the space of about three months, Robert became receptive to telephone contact with his mother. He visited with her over the Christmas period, then gradually on a regular basis. The mother was carefully counseled as to how to respond to the boy's ambivalent overtures—a mixture of longing and hostility—and his testing of her commitment to him. The father was motivated to encourage the boy's contact with his mother; he was told that Robert was acutely depressed and needed the kind of nurturing that only his mother could give.

About 18 months later, Robert asked to see the therapist again. She was surprised and gratified to note that this boy had put himself on a healthy diet and lost all the excess weight he had gained during the divorce transition. He was now a strikingly good-looking young man with much improved self-esteem, but he was in somewhat of a crisis. He really wanted to live with his mother for a while, and he wanted to know how to do this without hurting his father deeply, and without his father becoming angry at him. It was only now that this boy could openly acknowledge and talk about his father's bullying domination, the intermittent abuse, and how really frightened he had always been of his father. After three more sessions, Robert made the decision to tell his father, and he made the transfer to his mother at the end of the summer vacation.

CONCLUSION

In conclusion, we offer a plea on behalf of children's rights and needs to have some choice in their destiny. Except where stated otherwise, we propose a presumption that the child should remain in the primary care of the person with whom she or he is more comfortable, unless there is clear and convincing evidence that the child is doing poorly in other domains of life. Such evidence might include emotional and behavioral problems like depression, conduct disorder, poor achievement and attendance at school, or significant difficulties with peer relationships.

When a child refuses visitation with a seemingly appropriate and reasonable parent, one can understandably feel miffed, frustrated, and rendered powerless by the child and angered at being foiled by what appears to be a pathological coalition between an aligned parent and child against the good judgment of the other parent, the involved professionals, and the authority of the court. In response, there is a tendency to become arbitrary, punitive, and coercive with the child. Losing sight of the delicate interweaving of the child's developmental tasks within the entangled web of parental conflict and each parent's preemptory needs and legal rights, one may be tempted to impose changes of custody and access arrangements on children that they are not well equipped to handle. This compounds their sense of powerlessness as persons in their own right. In so doing, we collude in the process of rendering children unseen and unheard in custody disputes that are fought fraudulently "in the name of the child."

PART III

INTERVENTIONS ON BEHALF OF CHILDREN OF HIGH-CONFLICT DIVORCE

Chapter 9

Building Multidisciplinary
Partnerships with the Court

A Spectrum of Dispute Resolution Services

THE INCIDENCE AND COST OF
HIGH-CONFLICT DIVORCE

What proportion of divorcing families are likely to need help in resolving disputes, and what kind of help appears to be sufficient for them to settle their disputes over their children? In the absence of any nationally representative study to date, estimates can be derived from relatively large studies of divorcing families in California, some of which are longitudinal (Depner, 1993; Duryee, 1991, 1992; Maccoby & Mnookin, 1992). In 70 to 80% of divorcing families with children, custody is uncontested or the issue is settled without the help of the court or its related services. Presumably, these parents make their own agreements or seek consultations with attorneys, mental health professionals, and private mediators to arrive at mutual decisions. The remaining 20 to 30 percent of divorcing families go to court, where they are joined by never-married parents disputing custody. (In California, about one fifth of the couples litigating custody have never been married.) Of those families in court, more than half settle in state-mandated mediation sessions; about one fourth settle after an evaluation that includes recommendations to the court; the remainder settle during the process of trial or their disputes are decided by a judge. (California law requires that all families attempt mediation before they can litigate their custody disputes.)

In terms of the public costs associated with divorce, these figures indicate that, on average, one fourth of all divorcing families seek the assistance of the courts. Almost half of those in court (or more than one tenth of all divorcing families) make up the highly conflicted subgroup that cannot settle their disputes in brief mandated mediation. Clearly, these families consume a disproportionately large share of the court's precious resources. This small subgroup use twice their share of family court counseling hours and, presumably, the majority of judicial time available for all custody hearings (Duryee, 1991, 1992). In addition, it is estimated that the children of these families are four to five times more likely to have emotional and behavioral problems of clinically significant proportions (Johnston, 1992a, 1994b). Hence they are likely to be over-represented among children receiving mental health services and to consume disproportionately those resources offered by the schools and the community.

Highly conflictual divorcing families make heavy demands on the energies of family law attorneys, mediators, custody evaluators, counselors, and even judges. Despite the increased attention they receive, these clients are more likely than any other group to be hostile and unappreciative of professional efforts. They may fail to pay assigned fees, allege bias on the part of court officers, and even try to report or sue professionals for malpractice. A very small minority of these vulnerable clients can become paranoid, volatile, and ominously threatening. Quite apart from their excessive demands for professional time, their behaviors are particularly stressful for legal and mental health professionals, and contribute greatly to staff "burnout."

The private financial costs to the families concerned can be prohibitive. These may include extraordinary legal fees, costs of custody evaluations and therapy for all family members, as well as expenses associated with psychological testing, supervised visitation and exchanges, or drug and alcohol monitoring. Time taken from employment to attend court hearings and to seek legal and mental health counseling reduces potential earnings, as does loss of productivity owing to emotional stress and preoccupation with the disputes. It is not unusual for men and women to become emotionally and financially destitute as a result of these struggles over custody.

What is the most troubling is that these families often do not seem to resolve their conflicts despite the increased attention they receive and the unusual amount of private and public resources expended on their behalf.

Instead, their children continue to be exposed to the constant stress and disruption of their parents' disputes, unremitting anger, and distrust. It is time to use the public and private resources already being expended in cost-efficient and clinically effective dispute resolution forums that will be more responsive, more humane, and more suited to the needs of these families.

THE NEED FOR INTERDISCIPLINARY PARTNERSHIPS WITH THE COURT

Making family separation and divorce less painful for children and parents requires a fundamental redefinition of the role of the court. Furthermore, it requires new multidisciplinary partnerships between the court and attorneys, mediators, and mental health professionals, to arrive at viable solutions. This calls for a corresponding shift in perspectives and functions among these helping professionals and a rethinking of their ethical obligations.

Currently, a number of assumptions about the role of the court in highly conflicted custody matters need to be questioned. First, family courts have been used primarily to make decisions for divorcing couples who cannot make their own—as if courts have some greater wisdom or special knowledge about what is best for children. Second, family courts have been induced to act in loco parentis for some highly conflicted families—as if courts had the capacity to monitor the day-to-day care of children. Third, the custody litigation process has been used primarily to determine which is the better parent and to relegate the other to a secondary, inferior status—as if it were appropriate for disputing parents to be publicly scrutinized and held to a higher standard of accountability than those in nondisputing divorces or intact families. Fourth, judges have been asked to take on and resolve family dilemmas that other professionals and the community at large have failed to resolve—cases that attorneys have failed to negotiate and mediators have failed to settle, for families that counselors and therapists have failed to help. Inexplicably, there is an assumption that judges have some special capacity to resolve the most difficult, the most complex of all family problems. Is it any wonder that family court assignments for judges are so unpopular, so often avoided, and usually staffed by rotating assignments to prevent burnout?

We submit that none of these functions should be primarily the court's responsibility. Rather, within its vested authority, the role of the family court should be one of leadership in bringing the issues, the parties, and their helpers to the table to determine the following: first, how fractured families can coordinate their resources and care for their children after the parents' separation; second, how families can be helped to protect, preserve, and reconstitute the positive aspects of the parent–child and other family relationships, wherever possible; third, how parents can resolve their ongoing disputes and deal flexibly with subsequent child rearing issues in a timely manner, during the years that follow the divorce; and fourth, how the community can help these families while they are raising their children (Wallerstein, 1991). Note that this reframing of the court's primary function entails a proactive rather than a reactive stance. Although the court can provide leadership in this set of tasks, it will require each of the helping professions to reorient their efforts to attain these goals.

From this new perspective, family law attorneys' primary role is not to strategically maneuver the presentation of evidence and evoke statutes and case law to win their clients' case—as if their clients were indifferent to the effects of a legal victory on the lives of their children and as if the need for an ongoing working relationship with the other spouse/parent were irrelevant. In this new kind of partnership, the family attorney's role includes counseling clients fully on their rights and responsibilities *as parents and co-parents*, and exploring deeply the ramifications of all the clients' actions not only on the clients' welfare but on the welfare of the children as well. The attorney can then responsibly and ethically advocate for their clients' more clearly defined interests. Most important, in every case the family attorneys need to draft unambiguous stipulations and court orders with sufficient detail to provide the kinds of external structures and constraints necessary for the family fragmented by ongoing conflict to be able to proceed with some semblance of order and safety.

Within a framework of collaboration, mental health professionals who undertake therapy with parents and children cannot pursue their work into the emotional lives of their clients in isolation from the legal decision-making process. Rather, some triage and coordination with other involved professionals are seen as necessary to ensure that clients are spending their money and emotional energy in the most effective way and to protect them from being fragmented by competing demands from professionals with different agendas. Most important, therapists who work in private, confidential settings with these families need to make sure they are working in concert with the other helping professionals involved by sharing their various perspectives and reaching consensus about clinical goals, prognosis, and intervention strategies.

From this new perspective, court administrators need to reexamine the cumbersome procedures by which families are bungled through the system when they cannot easily settle their differences. Costly delays, complex procedures, and bureaucratic demands exacerbate the stress for these most vulnerable of families. A common procedural system developing in some more forward-looking jurisdictions is to offer a spectrum of services beginning with preventive measures (such as parenting education and mediation) that are minimally intrusive and designed for the broadest population of families. Those who fail to settle through these means are then referred to progressively more intrusive treatments that link mental health interventions to the social control mechanisms of the court (such as custody evaluations, coparenting arbitration, and supervised visitation), as illustrated in Figure 9.1.

This procedural organization rests on the principle that family courts should provide no more intrusive intervention into the private lives of families than is sufficient for them to care for their children. This certainly seems to be an improvement on a one-service-fits-all mentality, yet many court staffs and administrators question whether it is the optimal approach. Do some families have to fail successively at each level of service before they get the kind of help they really need? Are there more efficient and less painful ways of matching families to the most effective kind of service? A different approach is to consider the array of services shown in Figure 9.1 as a range of available alternatives, with access governed by defined criteria of need (e.g., domestic violence or substance abuse problems, which signal the need for a specific combination of interventions).

A SPECTRUM OF DISPUTE RESOLUTION SERVICES

In the balance of this chapter, we describe trends in the provision of alternative dispute resolution services (with details about particular programs) that are summarized in Figure 9.1, including the essential character of each service, what kinds of interdisciplinary partnerships are needed with the court, what is known about good outcome effectiveness, and for whom each service is best suited. Since our focus in this book is specifically the highly conflictual subgroup, services for these families are examined in

FIGURE 9.1

Alternative Dispute Resolution Services
For Divorcing Families

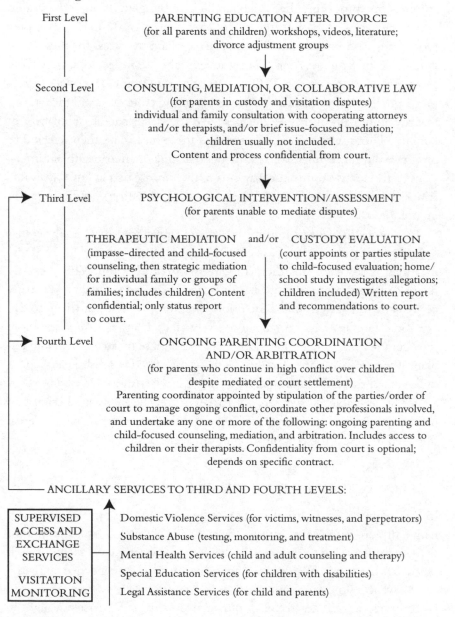

First Level — PARENTING EDUCATION AFTER DIVORCE
(for all parents and children) workshops, videos, literature;
divorce adjustment groups

Second Level — CONSULTING, MEDIATION, OR COLLABORATIVE LAW
(for parents in custody and visitation disputes)
individual and family consultation with cooperating attorneys
and/or therapists, and/or brief issue-focused mediation;
children usually not included.
Content and process confidential from court.

Third Level — PSYCHOLOGICAL INTERVENTION/ASSESSMENT
(for parents unable to mediate disputes)

THERAPEUTIC MEDIATION   and/or   CUSTODY EVALUATION
(impasse-directed and child-focused
counseling, then strategic mediation
for individual family or groups of
families; includes children) Content
confidential; only status report
to court.

(court appoints or parties stipulate
to child-focused evaluation; home/
school study investigates allegations;
children included) Written report
and recommendations to court.

Fourth Level — ONGOING PARENTING COORDINATION
AND/OR ARBITRATION
(for parents who continue in high conflict over children
despite mediated or court settlement)
Parenting coordinator appointed by stipulation of the parties/order of
court to manage ongoing conflict, coordinate other professionals involved,
and undertake any one or more of the following: ongoing parenting and
child-focused counseling, mediation, and arbitration. Includes access to
children or their therapists. Confidentiality from court is optional;
depends on specific contract.

ANCILLARY SERVICES TO THIRD AND FOURTH LEVELS:

SUPERVISED
ACCESS AND
EXCHANGE
SERVICES

VISITATION
MONITORING

Domestic Violence Services (for victims, witnesses, and perpetrators)

Substance Abuse (testing, monitoring, and treatment)

Mental Health Services (child and adult counseling and therapy)

Special Education Services (for children with disabilities)

Legal Assistance Services (for child and parents)

greater detail. Preventive interventions for the broader population of divorcing families (such as divorce education, mediation, and the practice of collaborative law) are mentioned only briefly, as background for innovative approaches with more troubled families.

Divorce Education

Recently, there has been increasing concern across the United States to provide the broad population of divorcing families with access to helpful information about divorce. (A national survey of every county in the country found that one fifth had educational programs for divorcing families, almost all of which were established during this past decade [Blaisure & Geasler, 1996].) The basic assumption regarding parenting education is that "knowledge is power," and that, with informed understanding, parents will be motivated and able to resolve divorce disputes more easily. In particular, there is a focus on providing parenting education for divorcing couples (which is clearly distinguished from therapy) about the needs of their children as well as how to minimize the stress of their own divorce transition, how to problem-solve and make decisions together, and how to provide a postdivorce family environment that will protect and promote their children's development (Lehner, 1994; McIsaac, 1994; Petersen & Steinman, 1994; Roeder-Esser, 1994; Schepard, 1993). Some jurisdictions have mandated parent education for all parents filing for divorce; some require it only when parents register a disagreement about the custody and care of their children at the time of filing. For other jurisdictions, it is still voluntary. Parenting education may be provided within the court, by community agencies in a separate setting, or by collaborative efforts between the two.

These programs vary greatly in extensiveness: almost two thirds offer a single session for parents only, and fewer than one fifth offer six or more sessions (Braver et al., 1996; Salem et al., 1996). Programs specifically developed for children, or for families including children, are rarer (Bolen, 1993; DiBias, 1996). Programs also vary in content: most likely to least likely topics covered are (1) the impact of divorce and parental behaviors on children; (2) parenting skills and conflict management; (3) legal issues such as dispute resolution, custody options, parental rights, and support obligations (Braver et al., 1996). Different methods of presentation are used (typically incorporating a range of media including reading materials, video, lectures, homework tasks, group discussion, and role playing). Most of these are group programs and can range in size from several parents at an evening meeting to weekend workshops with several hundred in attendance.

THE PRE-CONTEMPT/CONTEMNOR'S GROUP DIVERSION COUNSELING PRO-GRAM. Almost all educational programs are designed for the general divorcing population, although they may be attended by a significant number of highly conflictual parents ordered by the court to participate. The one exception is the Pre-Contempt/Contemnor's Group Diversion Counseling Program, in Los Angeles County, which is an educational program specifically designed for "parents who have high levels of conflict, are chronically in violation of custody and visitation court orders, and seek frequent court intervention" (Kibler et al., 1994). Frustrated with existing remedies such as probation, fines, and jail time for parents who do not comply with custody and visitation orders, the architects of this program aim to provide an alternative educational remedy for the family court similar to traffic school for those with driving infractions. The goals of the program are to provide parents with information about pertinent issues—the effects of divorce and parents' conflictual behavior on children, custody and visitation laws, the range of available child-sharing plans, the consequences of noncompliance with court orders—as well as to improve parents' skills in communicating and resolving their conflicts.

The program was designed for the ethnically diverse urban community of Los Angeles. It is offered on alternative months and continues for six consecutive weeks of one two-hour session each week. Security is provided by having bailiffs present during sessions, and precautionary measures are taken to prevent potentially volatile parents from meeting in hallways and parking lots. Both parents are required to attend by court order, stepparents and new partners are invited to join the group, children are not included. The three facilitators, who are gender and ethnically diverse, are dynamic and experienced instructors whose style is to make an emotional and passionate plea on behalf of the children, using a variety of media including lectures, videotapes, small and large group discussions, homework, and role-play exercises.

All referrals to the program are made by judges, and parents are court-ordered to attend. Many come unwillingly and resentfully, others with more grace and interest. Some are ordered back a second time or required to write a class paper on what they learned. The size of the group varies widely, depending on the number of referrals (25 to 75 at any one time). Information obtained in the groups is not kept confidential from the court process. However, in practice the only routine feedback is a certificate of completion provided to parents.

Each of the six sessions has a different theme. In the first, following introductions and establishing rules of conduct within the group, a didactic presentation is given on the historical aspects of custody, the roles of the different courts, and the emotional, legal, and economic processes of divorce. The session ends with the showing of a video emphasizing children's need for access to both parents. The second and third sessions focus on the developmental needs of children and the meaning of their symptoms of distress, and explore parenting plan options. The format is a combination of film and facilitated discussion. The later sessions (fourth through sixth) are devoted to providing information about conflict management and effective communication, and involve the parents in role playing the negotiation and mediation of conflicts. During these sessions, small groups of parents practice resolving non-divorce-related conflicts, and then in the last session, they attempt to resolve common custody and visitation disputes.

OUTCOMES OF EDUCATIONAL PROGRAMS AND CRITERIA FOR USE. A systematic evaluation of the Contemnor's program is currently being undertaken. Consequently, to date there are no clear indications for whom this is an effective intervention. In fact, probably because their widespread use is relatively recent, the outcomes and cost-effectiveness of all the different kinds of postdivorce parenting education programs have yet to be systematically evaluated or compared with one another. Published studies are rare (Arbuthnot & Gordon, 1996; Stolberg & Garrison, 1985). Some programs have gathered data on consumer satisfaction (Schepard, 1993).

Important unanswered questions include to what extent divorce education facilitates parents' capacity to settle their disputes more rapidly and in ways that benefit their children. Of special interest is the question of whether education is likely to be an effective primary *preventive* measure for the subgroup at risk for divorce impasses and ongoing disputes over child custody. For those families already entrenched in chronic disputes, it has been argued that information conveyed by parent educational programs will be selectively perceived and distorted in the service of the parents' own needs and their disputes with each other. Indeed, preliminary evidence suggests that the outcomes of brief psychoeducational interventions are poor (Pearson, 1996). Given the relatively low costs of group educational programs, compared with dealing with disputing couples on a case-by-case basis, there is an urgent need to evaluate the relative effectiveness of group interventions for families at impasse.

Mediation

Most U.S. states now have some provision for mediation of custody disputes by statute, court rule, or judicial referral. Mediation as originally conceived is the use of a neutral, professionally trained third party in a confidential setting to help disputing parents clearly define the issues, generate options, order priorities, and then negotiate and bargain differences and alternatives about the custody and care of their children after divorce. From an ideological viewpoint, mediation is clearly distinguishable from therapy and from litigation in its goals and methods (Folberg & Taylor, 1984; Kelly, 1983). In this dispute resolution forum, the assumption is that the mediator can attend to power imbalances between the parents, contain and deflect the emotional conflicts of the divorcing couple, and help them to become more rational, focused, and goal-oriented. Mediation has been widely advocated as the forum of choice because it empowers parents to make their own decisions, avoids unnecessary state interference in family affairs, and increases satisfaction and compliance with agreements reached. Children are usually not directly included in the actual mediation sessions, because it is believed that the decision making is primarily the parents' responsibility and that parents themselves will be able to best represent the needs of their children in the process. If the mediation is not successful, the information obtained during the process is generally not available to the court. (However, in 55% of counties in California, which mandates mediation for all custody and visitation matters, mediators are empowered to make recommendations to the court, a practice that has generated considerable controversy.)

OUTCOMES OF MEDIATION AND CRITERIA FOR USE. More than a decade of experience and a number of outcome evaluations have shown fairly consistent findings: 60% to 76% of mediated disputes result in agreements; of these, 40% to 57% are full or complete resolutions (Depner et al., 1994; Duryee, 1991, 1992; Emery, 1994; Kelly, 1996; Kelly & Gigy, 1989; Maccoby & Mnookin, 1992; Pearson & Thoennes, 1984; Slater et al., 1992; Sprenkle & Storm, 1983). These studies indicate the overall effectiveness of mediation for the majority of divorcing families in reaching agreements, with lower costs and less stress than are incurred by litigation. But it is not clear that mediation results in significant long-term benefits, in terms of enhanced parent and family functioning (Kelly & Gigy, 1989; Pearson, 1996).

The primary indication for a successful outcome in mediation is parents who, with the mediator's help, demonstrate the capacity to contain their emotional distress and focus on the children's issues. Mediating parents who can behave somewhat rationally with each other and have a history of parental cooperation tend to have more successful outcomes, compared with those who fail to mediate. Despite high levels of anger and conflict, these individuals can more easily distinguish their children's needs from their own and tend to acknowledge the value of the other parent in the child's life. It is generally asserted that brief mediation of divorce disputes, especially if offered early on, is an effective preventive measure, and mediation is the intervention of choice for tailoring access schedules to fit the needs of child and family.

It is important to note, however, that cases designated as "failures of mediation" have all the characteristics of high-conflict divorce, as we have defined it. The failures have been described as enmeshed and highly conflicted couples who are ambivalent about their separation and have severe psychopathology or personality disorders (Ehrenberg et al., 1996; Kressel et al., 1980; Pearson & Thoennes, 1980; Waldron et al., 1984; Walters et al., 1995). Moreover, it has been argued that mediation is inappropriate for many dysfunctional families with histories of chronic litigation, severe domestic violence, or allegations of child abuse and molestation (Germane et al., 1985; Girdner, 1990; Pearson & Thoennes, 1984). Poor mediation outcomes are generally predicted for parents who have rigid, highly divergent perceptions of their children's needs, which they tend to confuse with their own needs, and who harbor a pervasive distrust of each other's capacity to provide a secure environment (Pearson, 1996). In sum, high-conflict divorcing families have largely been identified by their failure to make effective use of traditional mediation methods that rely upon a rational decision-making process.

The Practice of Collaborative Law

Many family law attorneys are concerned about the financial costs and emotional suffering wrought by litigation and are seeking new solutions for their clients. One innovation is the practice of collaborative law, which rests on the shared commitment of both parties and their lawyers to reach a fair, honest, and sound divorce agreement without resorting to litigation in court (Marin Collaborative Law Group, 1995). The parties stipulate that they agree to give complete, full, honest, and open disclosure of all information, whether requested or not, and to engage in informal discussions and conferences for the purpose of reaching a settlement of all issues. All consultants retained by the parties, such as accountants, therapists, and appraisers, are likewise directed to work in a cooperative effort to resolve the issues.

Attorneys who enter into this kind of contract with their clients do so only if the other party is also represented by a lawyer bound by the same conditions and constraints. Such conditions require the attorneys involved to practice at the highest standard of integrity, negotiate in good faith, and withdraw as legal representative if the matter does go into court. Infractions of these standards of practice permit disqualification of the attorney and withdrawal from the process.

The benefits of collaborative law are thought to be several: First, unlike the practice of mediation, it retains the advocacy role of each attorney, whose responsibility is to advance the best interests of his or her respective clients. At the same time, it emphasizes cooperation between the parties, which is likely to benefit the children. The tension between advocacy and cooperation is thought to induce more creative thinking about how to produce a "win–win" situation for the parents. Furthermore, it avoids the high costs of litigation procedures, such as formal fact finding, depositions, preparation of briefs, filing of motions, and, of course, representation in court. Because the work products of the collaborative law process are not available for any other attorney who does not practice in this manner, and because the attorneys are not available as witnesses, consultants, or representatives in any related litigation, there is considerable motivation to settle the disputes outside of court.

Disadvantages include the lack of scrutiny and accountability when informal rather than formal legal procedures are used. Considerable costs may also be incurred in hiring another attorney and starting from scratch, if the collaborative process does not reach a resolution. To offset these possible drawbacks, stipulations for collaborative law may provide for the appointment of an arbitrator who will decide residual issues under dispute, including arguments about the manner in which the negotiations have proceeded.

OUTCOMES OF COLLABORATIVE LAW AND CRITERIA FOR USE. To date, no outcome evaluations of this approach are available. No indications for whom
this method is the best suited have been established.

Therapeutic Mediation

It seems evident that chronically conflicted parents are acting out deeper
personal and interpersonal difficulties when they cannot cooperate on behalf of their children and when they resist mediation, negotiate in bad faith,
and make repeated unrealistic demands in court. A more effective intervention in these cases must begin with an understanding of why these parents
are locked into chronic disputes. Utilizing such understanding, counselors
can devise strategic, focused therapeutic interventions to resolve the deeper
impasse, so that parents can make decisions more rationally. Moreover, with
an understanding of the developmental needs of the individual child, therapists can help parents to contain their own psychological agendas so that
they can focus on meeting the needs of their children.

IMPASSE-DIRECTED MEDIATION. Early versions of a therapeutic approach to
custody disputes (Milne, 1978; Waldron et al., 1984) were developed into
what is now referred to as *impasse-directed mediation* (Johnston & Campbell,
1988; McDonough et al., 1995). This service model is specifically designed
for high-conflict, bitterly litigating families, all of whom are referred by
family courts after failing brief issue-focused mediation or following custody evaluations and judicial orders.

There are three important ways in which impasse-directed mediation
differs from the more issue-focused mediation described above. First, in a
radical departure from what is viewed as a necessary distinction between
therapy and mediation, this approach brings these two interventions together. The rationale is that, until some of the underlying emotional factors that have converged to create the impasse are dealt with, these parents
cannot make rational, child-centered decisions. The diagnostic and counseling component is not provided in a separate setting, apart from the actual
negotiations, because an understanding of the impasse, the parents' dynamics, and the children's needs—all of which is gleaned during the counseling
phase—is invaluable in helping to choose negotiation strategies and building psychologically sound agreements.

Second, impasse-directed mediation is based upon a differential assessment of the divorce transition impasse (see chapter 1) and its immediate as well as potentially long-term effects on children. The assumption is that many parents in these embittered, intractable conflicts have little ability to protect their children from their own personal or spousal problems. Not only are their parenting capacities diminished at the time of the separation or divorce, but there is also the risk that parenting will be chronically compromised by the parents' own personal problems or by the ongoing conflict. Hence the goal is to educate and counsel these parents about the children's needs and also, in many cases, to undertake direct therapy with the children to help them cope with and manage their difficult family situations.

Third, the goals of impasse-directed mediation are to develop psychologically sound and satisfying child access plans, to help the family through its divorce transition, and to build a structure that can support the parents' and children's continued growth and development. The completion of the access agreement is not seen as an end in itself. Rather, it is secondary to and an outward symbol of the family's transition and restructuring process.

Impasse-directed mediation, as originally developed, is a confidential service provided outside the court in a private setting. The parties must stipulate that the counselor will not be asked or subpoenaed to testify in court. The only information provided to the court is whether or not family members have participated in the program. The only nonconfidential recommendation the counselor can give is that the family should return to court to resolve a specific issue if the process is unsuccessful in reaching a crucial agreement.

For the first part of the intervention, parents are seen separately for counseling, and then they are seen together for mediation, unless there is a threat of domestic violence. When seen separately, the parents do not have the guarantee of confidentiality; the counselor exercises discretion to use any information provided by one parent in counseling or mediating with the other. Children, however, are assured confidentiality from their parents. The role of the attorneys is to encourage their clients' participation and to draw up the stipulations that will protect the process. Collaboration between attorneys and counselors during the process is limited, confined to procedural matters (e.g., clarifying the need for a financial issue to be settled before proceeding with a custody matter, or vice versa). The attorneys also need to enter agreements into the court record or proceed to another dispute resolution forum with any residual issues that remain unresolved.

VARIATIONS OF IMPASSE-DIRECTED MEDIATION. Several variations of impasse-directed mediation have been developed. Initially, an individual family model was developed that comprised between 25 and 35 sessions. Subsequently, this model was compared with a group model in which five to eight families (including parents and children) were seen in a series of seven or eight multihour sessions (see Figure 9.2). There are four phases to both the individual and group models: (1) assessment, (2) prenegotiation counseling, (3) negotiation of a plan, and (4) implementation.

1. *Assessment.* During the assessment phase (six to eight hours), parents are interviewed separately and the child is seen individually in a play-interview. Next, each parent is observed in a separate, structured setting with the child, during which time they are asked to "draw a family" together. These clinical observations together with a history of the dispute and a history of each parent, the marriage, and its breakdown, and a developmental history of the child make up the information used to formulate a detailed assessment of the family impasse and its developmental effects on the child. (See Appendix: Guidelines for Initial Assessment of High-Conflict Divorcing Families.)

2. *Prenegotiation Counseling.* The prenegotiation counseling phase (12 to 16 hours) is when each parent, in separate sessions from the ex-mate, is prepared for mediation by the counselor, who strategically intervenes in the family impasse and attends directly to the child's needs. (In the single-family intervention, family members are seen in individual sessions; in the multifamily intervention, parents and child are each seen in separate, concurrently running groups with their peers.) The strategy here is two-pronged. The counselor helps each parent develop some awareness or insight into the impasse. If the parent is too emotionally or characterologically disturbed to benefit from direct counseling, intervention is directed at another element of the impasse (e.g., the parent's spouse, new partner, or extended network). The counselor also attempts to educate each parent about the effects of the conflict on the child. This ranges from asking questions that raise the parent's consciousness about the child, to directly counseling her or him, and, in the more extreme situations, to strongly advocating on the child's behalf. Insights gained from directly seeing the children in their own individual or group sessions provide compelling authenticity to the counselor's interventions with parents.

It is hoped that this two-pronged strategy will shift the parents' stance,

FIGURE 9.2

Flow Chart and Structure of Individual and Group Impasse-Directed Mediation

Phases	Court Referral	
I Information Gathering and Assessment	*Intake Center* ↓	
	Parents are informed about the service: Its counseling mediation nature and separation from legal proceedings are highlighted. A sliding-scale fee is assessed. ↓	
	Information-Gathering Interviews	
	One or two individual interviews are conducted with each parent and each child seen separately. Significant others are invited to participate in counseling. Standardized measures and questionnaires are completed. ↓	
	Strategy Conference	
	Service providers develop a dispute-specific assessment of each family and formulate an individual or group intervention plan. ↓ ↓	
II Prenegotiation Counseling Phase (Preparation for Negotiation)	*Individual Family Impasse-Directed Mediation Model*	*Multifamily (Group) Impasse-Directed Mediation Model*
	Each family member is seen in individual and, when appropriate, conjoint interviews.	Five to eight families of mixed sex and mixed custodial arrangements are seen together.
		Each family member is seen in his or her group; parents are seen separately from their ex-spouse.
	Length of service depends on the family's individual needs.	Four two-hour weekly parent groups are conducted.
		Four two-hour weekly children's groups are conducted; children are seen with their peers.
	One counselor mediator sees the entire family.	Two counselor mediators lead the parent group; one counselor conducts the children's group.
III Negotiation or Conflict Resolution Phase	Conjoint interviews are conducted (if appropriate) with parents to finalize plans and draft access agreements.	Three or four three-hour joint mediation groups are conducted with the two-parent groups combined; all three counselor mediators are present.
		One or two additional interviews are conducted with individual couples (if needed) to draft or finalize an agreement.
IV Implementation Phase	The last session reviews insights gained and settlements reached; referrals are made for counseling or to court. ↓	
	On-call Consultation A counselor mediator is available to the family for emergencies and continued mediation. ↓	
	Six-month and Twenty-four-month Follow-up	

so that they will be able to mediate more rationally. If this approach fails, the counselor helps the parents identify and explore the realities of their position (e.g., the laws of the land, what is possible and not possible to achieve in court, what they can realistically expect from the ex-spouse, and what their child is capable of handling). In providing this reality check, it is, of course, important for the counselor to avoid offering legal advice or imposing cultural biases. Under the shadow of these sobering realities, a realistic agenda for the actual mediation or negotiation session is prepared.

3. *Negotiation or Conflict Resolution.* The negotiation or conflict resolution phase is when specific disputed issues are resolved and a set of access agreements are developed. The divorcing couple are usually brought together for the first time (in conjoint sessions for the single-family model, or in a group of other parents for the multifamily model). Alternatively, "shuttle negotiation" is used when it is neither wise nor possible to bring parents together (e.g., when domestic violence is a concern). This is usually a fairly rapid phase (one or two sessions) and proceeds according to fairly straightforward mediation techniques, except that considerable attention is given to making the kind of agreements that will avoid setting off the impasse dynamics that have been identified in earlier phases of the work (Garrity & Baris, 1994; Johnston & Campbell, 1988).

4. *Implementation.* The implementation phase follows, during which time the counselor remains available to each family on an individual basis for emergency consultations (in the event of new or renewed conflict) and to help parents interpret, monitor, and modify their agreement.

BRIEF IMPASSE CONSULTATION. The initial model of impasse-directed mediation involved, on average, 27 hours for the individual-family service and 17 hours for the group service. While this was well within the range of what is considered short-term therapy, its cost was generally viewed as prohibitive for families with few resources and for publicly funded court-connected services. For this reason the initial model was adapted to a *brief impasse consultation* of three to five sessions (or about 10 hours per family). This brief version is similar to a confidential mini-evaluation (Mosten, 1992) and essentially involves the following: (1) a rapid assessment of the family's impasse and its impact on the child (interview with each parent and collateral contacts regarding the child, or a child interview/observation); (2) a feedback session in which there is a strategic reframing of the problem from the point of view of the child's needs, in a manner that parents can accept; and

(3) a redirecting session in which the couple is helped to agree on a procedure for resolving their impasse and meeting their child's needs over time.
The couple is then referred to community services for implementation of
the agreement.

OUTCOMES OF THERAPEUTIC MEDIATION AND CRITERIA FOR USE. In terms of
outcome effectiveness, two studies of high-conflict families referred from
the family courts ($N = 80$ and $N = 60$) who received this treatment indicated that about four fifths reached initial agreement and two thirds were
able to keep or renegotiate their own agreements regarding custody/access
and to stay out of court over a two- to three-year follow-up period (Johnston, 1993b; Johnston & Campbell, 1988; Johnston & Coysh, 1988). Group
and individual-family methods were equally effective in achieving these
agreement rates. However, the group method resulted in more cooperative
and less conflictual coparenting relationships, whereas the individual-family
method tended to result in better parent-child relationships. In terms of
economic feasibility, the group method was 40 percent more cost effective
in terms of counselor hours than the individual-family method (17 versus
27 hours). Court filings were reduced to one sixth of their former rates.

Another study ($N = 50$) compared the brief consultation model with
the longer individual-family model in a sample of low-income separating
families characterized by unfounded allegations of abuse and concerns
about abduction (Johnston, 1996). Both were equally effective at a nine-
month follow-up in increasing parental cooperation and resolving disputes.
Interestingly, these therapeutic services occurred in the context of vigorous
court intervention that included, where indicated, assessments, sanctions,
restraining orders, and visit supervision. This suggests that brief, strategic
therapeutic intervention into these most difficult custody disputes might
have the greatest effectiveness when paired with legal restraints and admin-
istered early in the legal process.

For which families, then, is impasse-directed mediation best suited? The
parents most likely to benefit are those who are moderately vulnerable to
loss and rejection, those who have experienced traumatic or ambivalent
separations, and those who are enmeshed in "tribal warfare" within the
larger social network. The approach may also be beneficial where children
are showing symptoms of distress or are at high risk because the parents are
too preoccupied with the fight to focus on their needs. On the other hand,
the service, although beneficial, may not be sufficient for parents with

more severe personality disorders. Such parents are less able to obtain or sustain a reasonable perspective, and their defensive processes and preemptory needs continue to disrupt any agreements or semblance of family stability. Moreover, the service is not appropriate where there is a need to investigate serious allegations of domestic violence, parental abuse of children, or other kinds of severe family dysfunction. In such cases, the confidentiality of the model is inappropriate because feedback needs to be provided to the court so that legal safeguards can be put in place to protect the family members.

Custody Evaluation and Recommendations

CRITERIA FOR USE. When attorney negotiations, mediation, and therapeutic interventions cannot resolve disputes over custody and care of children, mental health professionals are often called upon to offer expert opinions to the court as to how these disputes should be resolved according to the current legal standard, which is "the best interests of the child." Alternatively, when there are serious allegations of child neglect, abuse, or molestation, a case of disputed custody might be referred directly for custody evaluation. Compared with the other dispute resolution services described in this chapter, custody evaluation has a long tradition and has played an integral role within the adversarial litigation system. As such, it has been the subject of considerable scrutiny by forensic psychologists and psychiatrists as well as family attorneys regarding its purposes, methods, and standards of practice (Schutz et al., 1989; Stahl, 1994).

Rather than attempt to summarize the present "state of the art" of custody evaluation as it pertains to its role in litigation, we limit our commentary to highlighting how custody evaluation can be used as an alternative dispute resolution method in its own right. We argue that too often the adversary tradition of the courtroom dominates the goals of the evaluation. When this occurs, the process can take on the appearance of a pathology hunt, which often holds the litigating divorced parents to a higher standard of mental health than intact and nonlitigating divorcing families, and which may not be relevant to the child's actual needs and experience. For example, custody evaluations often employ standardized psychological tests (e.g., the Minnesota Multiphasic Personality Inventory) to search for psychological disturbances within the parents as individuals, with no acknowledgment that these tests provide little valid information about parenting capacities or the quality of the parent–child relationships (Hysjulien et al., 1994). Moreover, this focus on who is the "better" or psychologically healthier adult obscures the question of the child's unique concerns and developmental vulnerabilities. As noted by previous researchers (Wallerstein & Kelly, 1980), a parent defined by most measures as "personally competent" is most likely to be hardworking, achievement oriented, assertive, self-controlled, and independent but may not necessarily be receptive to the child's views and needs, which is a core characteristic of effective parenting (Baumrind, 1971, 1978) and a key predictor of positive outcomes of divorce for children (Kline et al., 1991; Tschann et al., 1989).

GOALS OF THE EVALUATION. A child-focused evaluation begins with the assumption that the child will have a postdivorce relationship with each parent over the long term, regardless of time spent together or whether that parent actually sees the child at all. As shown in the preceding chapters on child development, this is so because each parent is a central, archetypal figure in the child's inner psychological life and thus has a profound impact on the child's development. A child-focused evaluation that seeks to resolve disputes rather than identify the "most competent" parent will therefore (1) focus foremost on the child's needs and experience of each parent; (2) minimize the parents' sense of shame and exposure and acknowledge their competencies; (3) explicate the causes of and potential avenues for diffusing the parental conflict and its effect on the child; (4) evaluate each parent's current and characterological capacities to resolve the parental conflict and to meet the child's needs over time; and (5) identify which custody plan, therapeutic support, or arbitration structure is needed to support the child's development over the short and long term (Roseby, 1995).

Perhaps the greatest value of the evaluation report, if prepared from this perspective, is that it can provide parents with an integrated view of their child, who may be reinforcing the parents' divergent views by behaving differently in each home. At the same time, the evaluation can reflect to parents how each is being perceived, with more nuance and balance than their own distortions and projections of blame allow. Most important, a child-focused evaluation allows for vigorous advocacy on behalf of the child, whose needs, to this point in the litigation, may have been poorly understood by the parents themselves and by the court.

THE EVALUATION PROCESS. There are ways of setting up the evaluation process to maximize the potential for agreements, just as other procedures can maximize the conflict. Evaluators can serve the child most effectively if they serve as impartial experts appointed by the court, or by stipulation of both parties, and if they are provided with access to all family members. As described in chapter 1, disputes are likely to escalate when a therapist provides expert witness testimony regarding custody issues without specific knowledge of the child and all parties to the dispute. Disputes can easily become entrenched if an expert retained by one side pits his or her professional opinion against that of the expert retained by the other side, primarily because neither expert is likely to have access to full information about the family or the trust of all parties.

An explicit prior arrangement should be made regarding the manner in which the final custody report is disseminated and reviewed. Optimally, this arrangement will be made in writing and signed by both parties and their attorneys. The practice of having parents first learn the contents of the report from their attorneys, in chambers or in open court rather than in privacy with the evaluator, cannot be considered constructive in any sense. Rather, it reaffirms the win/lose structure of the litigation and is most likely to exacerbate the parents' sense of shame and helplessness. Giving parents the opportunity to review the report with its author provides a greater potential for diffusing the conflict and helping the parents to absorb what it has to say about the short- and long-term needs of the child.

If the evaluator's report is later contested by either party, rather than subjecting the family to the inordinate stress of multiple assessments, a second expert, appointed in the same manner as the first, can review the procedures, findings, and recommendations of the initial evaluator to determine whether they conform to professional standards, ethics, and scientific rigor (American Psychological Association, 1992, 1994; Association of Family & Conciliation Courts, 1994). A flawed evaluation can exacerbate the shame of vulnerable parents, which in turn escalates rather than diffuses the parental conflict. When the dispute is inflamed in this way, the children are often rendered vulnerable to ongoing parental hostilities long after the litigation ends. Optimally, an evaluator's competency should encompass clinical knowledge and experience in the diagnosis and treatment of chronically conflicted as well as well-functioning divorced parents and children, in addition to more general education, training, and experience in the areas of child and family development, child and family psychopathology, and the impact of divorce on children.

Within a litigation–conscious arena, evaluators can become more focused on protecting their own professional reputations and legal liabilities than on the needs of the family. Such self-interest can result in inappropriately exhaustive and intrusive assessments and reports. To ensure that all parties have similar expectations about what is to be accomplished by the evaluation and to avoid unnecessary intrusiveness and cost, it is helpful for the court to define the specific scope and purpose of the evaluation. Consequently, it may pinpoint a particular issue (e.g., which school the child should attend), and only if necessary does it need to encompass a complete family evaluation (e.g., psychological testing of all members, school and home visits, substance abuse assessments, child abuse and molestation investigations).

OUTCOMES OF EVALUATION. Studies of outcomes of the evaluation process indicate that the final court order is in accord with the evaluator's recommendations in about 85 percent of cases. In 70 to 90 percent of cases, after hearing the recommendations, the parties reach a negotiated agreement, which is then entered as a consent judgment (Ash & Guyer, 1986a; Maccoby & Mnookin, 1992; Simons et al., 1990). However, follow-up studies of families who have undergone custody evaluations show rates of re-litigation about twice those of families who settled on their own (Ash & Guyer, 1986b, $N = 267$; Hauser & Straus, 1991, $N = 700$). Altogether, these studies indicate that evaluations appear to be very effective in reaching a short-term settlement, but by themselves they may bring little relief for high-conflict couples and their children over the long term.

Monitoring, Enforcement, and Arbitration

Pervasive distrust and multiple, overlapping concerns about the ex-partner's parenting practices typify the high-conflict separating and divorced family. Recent studies comparing mandated mediation, ongoing custody litigation, and family abduction samples indicate that frequency of allegations among the three samples is as follows: *neglect* (38%, 48%, and 54%, respectively; *child physical abuse* (18%, 27%, and 38%, respectively); and *child stealing* (6%, 10%, and 20%, respectively). In addition, grave concerns were raised, again among the three sample groups, about exposing the child to the other parent because of one parent's *substance abuse* (36%, 65%, and 78%, respectively); *domestic violence* (65%, 79%, and 68%, respectively); or *criminal activity* (7%, 10%, and 46%, respectively) (Depner et al., 1992; Johnston, 1994b). Within the context of custody litigation, where there is a strategic advantage to presenting the opposing parent in a negative light, these allegations can be viewed with considerable skepticism, if not dismissed entirely. In some cases, the allegations do have some basis in fact, but critical incidents are often misconstrued or exaggerated by the negatively biased perceptions of the parties. In other cases, parents' concerns are clearly well founded, and the child is urgently in need of protection.

The danger lies in the court's failure to ensure that appropriate investigations are made into allegations of abuse, neglect, and domestic violence, and in not acting to protect the child and the victim parent in situations where it is warranted. These matters usually require not only judicial intervention but judicial case management and coordination of the numerous court actions, involvement of different courts (e.g., criminal and juvenile), and involvement of different professionals and community agencies outside the court (Edwards, 1993; King, 1993). Attorneys for parents and children must also counsel with and advocate for their clients and guard against potentially unwarranted violation of their clients' civil liberties.

When serious allegations are raised, and especially when they are supported by corroborating evidence (police, medical, and child care reports), it behooves the court to take precautionary protective measures during the interim period required to complete a more thorough evaluation. This may involve supervising or suspending visitation. If allegations are substantiated, custody and visitation court orders may include mandates for parents to continue with supervised access or exchange, to cooperate with drug and alcohol monitoring and treatment, to attend parenting classes, or to provide therapy for the child. Courts need to establish close working relationships with community agencies that provide these kinds of services and to establish clear and ethical procedures to govern sharing information and monitoring compliance with court orders.

Throughout the United States, a variety of court-related services with a coercive regulatory function have been developed to deal with cases in which there are not only ongoing disputes over visitation but also concerns about emotional, physical, and sexual mistreatment of children. These new services tend to rely less on parents' voluntary participation in educational, mediation, and therapeutic processes; rather, they increasingly depend upon monitoring, enforcement, and arbitration. In general, these are not confidential services: the information obtained may be relayed to the court.

COPARENTING COORDINATION AND ARBITRATION. This approach provides highly conflicted families with an appointed coparenting coordinator to help the parents make ongoing decisions about their children over the long term (Zibbell, 1995). This new kind of professional role has been developing in a number of jurisdictions across the United States and is variously named: *special master* (in California), *wiseperson* (in New Mexico), *custody commissioner* (in Hawaii), and *coparenting counselor* or *med-arb* (in Colorado). The role of the guardian ad litem is being expanded to include this function in some places. Either a mental health professional experienced with custody matters or a well-seasoned family law attorney may be used as a coparenting arbitrator. The common distinguishing feature of this new species is that the coparenting coordinator is usually, but not always, given some kind of arbitration powers by stipulation of the parties or by court order. In general, this is not a confidential service, and the appointed person may need to report to the court if his or her arbitrated decision is challenged in court.

Broadly speaking, there are two coparenting arbitration models: In the first, the coparenting arbitrator is called on to arbitrate only when the parents cannot settle a specific dispute. He or she acts solely as an arbitrator and does not perform counseling or therapeutic functions for the family. In many of these families, which are often identified by the extremity of their conflict and multiprofessional involvement, a child therapist or a confidential mediator is working with the family in an ongoing way. These other professionals or the parents themselves call in the coparenting arbitrator when a specific matter cannot be resolved. The advantage of this model is that arbitrators have a distinctly separate role from the other professionals. They are a private, neutral "court of appeal" who, over time, can develop a great deal of in-depth knowledge about the family and the trust of its members. The disadvantage is that it is more costly and cumbersome to add yet another professional layer to the family system.

In the second model, coparenting coordinators act as the parenting counselor, mediator, or child therapist in an ongoing way and exercise their right to arbitrate only when parents fail to agree on a specific matter. A variation on this theme is where the existing professionals in a case (e.g., therapists, mediators, special education teacher) form an *arbitration panel* and render a consensual decision on specific issues, whenever parents reach a stalemate. Whereas this second model may be more economical, role confusion, boundary questions, and ethical problems arise whenever professionals shift their primary functions.

For either model, certain commonalities apply: specifically, to institute a coparenting arbitrator in a case, an explicit, written contract with the parties, their attorneys, and other relevant persons involved with the family (e.g., therapists) is drawn up, signed by both parties, and filed in court. This contract should include the following elements: (1) how the arbitrator is to be chosen or appointed, and how he or she may be terminated; (2) the specific domains within which the arbitrator can make decisions and the limitations of his or her powers; (3) the methods of conflict resolution the arbitrator may use; (4) the procedure for bringing an issue before the arbitrator for a decision; (5) the permissible lines of communication by which the arbitrator may gather information; (6) who pays for the services of the arbitrator, and when and how; (7) how and when the arbitrator's decision is to be made a court order; and (9) the procedure for challenging the arbitrated decision in court.

It is obvious from this list of conditions that the stipulations can be complex, cumbersome, and costly to draw up, unless there is a body of local rules, procedures, and interprofessional support for the process. In some jurisdictions, boilerplate stipulations have been developed containing a number of optional clauses, which can be adapted for a specific family. In some states, family law attorneys and judges have been able to apply existing laws (e.g., the statutes on the use of special masters, in California) to empower the coparenting arbitrator. In other jurisdictions, new legislation may need to be enacted, or existing laws modified, to permit this kind of delegation of judicial authority and to define its limits. The successful establishment of coparenting arbitration procedures requires ongoing professional education, the development and monitoring of standards of practice, and close collaboration among all professionals involved. To date, the use of arbitrators has been a private, not a public, service, the fees for which are prohibitive to many families unless offered on a sliding scale.

OUTCOMES OF COPARENTING ARBITRATION AND CRITERIA FOR USE. To date, there is little information on outcome effectiveness with this relatively new model of intervention. One preliminary survey ($N = 166$) indicated greatly reduced litigation rates for these families in the short term, i.e., six court appearances per year as compared with about one fifth after the appointment of a special master (T. Johnston, 1994). Another survey showed very mixed reactions from clients ($N = 52$) about the helpfulness of coparenting arbitration, while professionals ($N = 37$) were much more enthusiastic about its benefits (Vic & Backerman, 1996). Many questions remain to be studied: How is the process being implemented, with what outcomes, and at what cost? Are clients' legal rights to due process sufficiently protected, and are families' psychological needs better served using this method, compared with litigation?

The coparenting arbitrator is thought to be useful in a number of situations. First, parents with severe personality disorders who become locked in immutable impasses and are chronically litigating may need this potentially coercive intervention to protect their children from the chaos. Second, in families where there is less character pathology but great difficulty making important mutual and timely decisions, this service should ensure better coordination between parents. Examples include situations in which infants and very young children require continuous reworking of the agreement because of their rapidly changing developmental needs, or where a child has special needs owing to a physical, mental, or emotional disability. Third, a coparenting arbitrator may monitor potentially abusive situations: where there are ongoing but unsubstantiated allegations of physical or sexual abuse of a child and where there is concern about intimidation and control by a violent parent. Fourth, a coparenting arbitrator may be useful when the intermittent mental illness of a parent (e.g., bipolar depression) requires monitoring so that appropriate adjustments can be made to the child's care and residential arrangements when the parent becomes symptomatic (Lee, 1989).

Supervised Visitation

These programs make up a rapidly growing new social service that has been developed in direct response to some kinds of intractable divorce disputes. Currently, there are more than one hundred such programs nationwide, brought together by a fledgling organization called the Supervised Visitation Network, which has drawn up standards of practice (Pearson & Thoennes, 1996; Straus, 1996; Straus & Alda, 1994). Largely staffed by trained volunteers or counseling interns and funded variously (and inadequately) by local, state, or charitable grants and advocacy groups (e.g., domestic violence agencies), these programs aim to provide a protected setting for visitation to occur between children and the noncustodial parent (Hess et al., 1992; James & Gibson, 1991; Stocker, 1992).

MODES OF SUPERVISION AND CRITERIA FOR USE. The supervision can take a variety of forms, and its extensiveness can vary over time. In the most extreme cases, the supervision may be part of a therapeutic intervention into the parent-child relationship and is undertaken by a trained counselor. When children are at high risk (because of a parent's psychological disturbance, substance abuse problems, history of emotional or physical abuse, molestation, serious domestic violence, or child abduction), visitation may occur only under the continual surveillance of a neutral third person in a closed setting. In situations of less gravity, supervision may be performed in an open setting (e.g., at a park or in the noncustodial parent's home) by family members or friends. When there is no direct threat to the child but a possibility of verbal or physical abuse between parents, the supervision may be limited to the time of exchange of the child, in a place that is safe and neutral to the parents and benign to the child.

EXPEDITED VISITATION SERVICES. One illustrative program is the Expedited Visitation Services (EVS) in Maricopa County, Arizona, which is designed to provide a rapid response to parents without legal representation who have problems gaining access to their children. Interestingly, its development was prompted by widespread controversy over the fact that payment of child support was enforced (e.g., by automatic wage withholding), whereas virtually no attention was being paid to noncompliance with visitation orders (Pearson & Anhalt, 1994). The process begins with a conference (lasting about two hours and including both parents) with an EVS officer (who has mediation training and experience in child support collection), within seven days after a request has been made by a parent. The outcome of this conference is either a mediated agreement that will then be court-ordered or a recommendation to the court that may be used as the basis for a court order. Typically, recommendations include elaboration and clarification of visitation orders or a request for enforcement and monitoring of the visitation.

The monitoring function, which is undertaken by a community agency, involves court-initiated telephone or mail contact with each set of parents to determine whether there were any problems with the visitation at regular or intermittent intervals. During the typical six-month monitoring period, parents who have allegedly violated orders may be summoned back to the EVS officer or to the court for a review hearing with the judge.

The initial goal of the EVS intervention is to establish "the visitation habit." The staff believes it is important to establish regularity and predictability by having families comply with a court order and that these efforts should precede attempts to have the couple communicate and explore the emotional roots of resistance to visitation. There is considerable sentiment that EVS fills a community need by providing rapid access to the court, eliminating visitation denial as a rationale for nonpayment of support, and offering low-income families a mechanism for resolving problems. Concerns have been raised, however, about the extent to which this program delegates authority to nonjudicial officers and potentially violates parents' rights to due process, and how orders might ride roughshod over the emotional needs of children who are anxious and phobic about visitation.

OUTCOMES OF SUPERVISED VISITATION. Formal evaluations of these programs to date are virtually absent (Abromovitch et al., 1994). Though supervised visitation is more likely to ensure physical safety, it is not yet clear how long it should be employed and how it should be structured for different types of family situations. Most important, it is largely unknown how well and under what conditions these structured environments nourish the parent-child relationship and benefit the child (Straus, 1996). Direct study of children's responses is rare, but preliminary data are promising (Lee et al., 1995).

CONCLUSION

This chapter has described an array of alternative dispute resolution services that attempt to provide more humane and effective forums for the resolution of family conflict, with special attention to those that target the most troubled families among the divorcing population. The structure of each model of service, the criteria for its use, the nature of the interdisciplinary collaboration required, the available outcome effectiveness data, and the connections between community services and the courts have been outlined. To make these services truly responsive to the needs of children within their disrupted families, the service providers must have an in-depth understanding of the development of children in these highly conflictual and violent environments.

Chapter 10

Clinical Work with Parents and Children of Families in Entrenched Custody Disputes

*I*n this chapter, we describe and illustrate counseling and mediation, and the phases of long-term coparenting coordination with families in seriously entrenched custody disputes. Principles and techniques for working directly with children are also shown. The therapeutic approach used here draws on neo-analytic object-relations theory and self-psychology (Hedges, 1994; Kernberg, 1976; Kohut, 1977; Masterson, 1985; Masterson & Klein, 1989; Singer & Salovey, 1993; Spence, 1982). However, there are a number of important ways in which these treatment interventions depart from most traditional therapies:

1. the degree to which the structured framework of the intervention provides a rule-governed process for managing the ongoing conflict
2. the way in which the active, directive, focused role of the counselor-mediator (CM) fashions and maintains a holding environment for the child in the fractured family
3. the ebb and flow of the family's high, positive expectations mingled with their pessimism and disappointment (i.e., their idealizing and de-idealizing transferences)
4. the way that the strong feelings and reactions of the CM (i.e., the countertransference) are used in the intervention.

The structured framework of the intervention is specified in the treatment contract or stipulation that parents sign at the outset. As explained in chapter 9, parents are usually asked to give consent for all information to be held confidential from the court, with the exceptions of any child abuse or threats of violence, for which reporting is mandated. It is understood that the CM can exchange information freely between parents in separate interviews but that the children's confidences will be privileged. The only kind of feedback parents receive about their child will be general clinical impressions, unless the child consents to the release of more specific information. In addition, clear expectations are defined as to the CM's having both a therapeutic and a mediation role, and about the need for the CM to have direct access to the child (or to the child's therapist). Rules are specified about how and what can be communicated to the court or special master (coparenting arbitrator) if one is appointed and how fees are to be divided (usually each parent pays his or her own fee and half of each of the child sessions). Parents are told that the child is always the focus of the interventions and that they, as adults, are always viewed in their roles as parents. In this respect, the intervention is similar to child guidance work.

Although there is nothing unique about the components of the intervention, their combination is unusual: It requires an understanding of how people defend against the loss and rejection inherent in divorce. It is also important to know how to work with personality-disordered people and with those who are made more vulnerable by the divorce and litigation. Understanding about family systems from a strategic and structural vantage point is essential, as is a thorough grounding in children's emotional and social development. Finally, mediation skills are needed to help parents make concrete decisions and parenting plans.

The time commitment required in working with these families is often startling to counselors new to this work; it is especially intensive during the beginning stages. For more severely conflicted families, the CM should budget three to five hours per family per week for the first two months or so and expect to deal with frequent crisis demands by telephone. This generally tapers off to about one or two hours per week for the succeeding two to six months. Intermittent or regularly scheduled follow-up sessions or telephone counseling usually follow after that period (one or two hours per month). The time demands for any one case will depend on the level of pathology in the parents as well as the schedule of litigation and, of course, on the parents' capacity to pay for the intervention. For chronically entrenched disputes of long-standing duration, we have come to expect that real structural shifts should occur within 18 months to two years after the onset of intervention.

THE PHASES OF THE INTERVENTION

There are typically several distinct phases in a successful intervention: (1) initial referral and contract formation; (2) assessment of the impasse and its effects on the child; (3) reformulation of the problem, challenge, and crisis; (4) working through and resolution; and (5) termination and follow-up.

Initial Referral and Contract Formation

The process begins with a strategic "dance," as each parent vies for position and advantage. The CM can expect to spend a great deal of time with phone calls from all parties, which may continue for a considerable period before the intervention can begin. It is especially important for the CM to keep a balanced perspective and maintain neutrality. Both parents must agree to proceed before any information gathering or counseling sessions may take place. The terms of the contract need to be carefully explained, preferably with written guidelines and consent forms. Other professionals involved with the family need to be informed and an understanding reached about their respective roles. At the outset, parents are usually seen separately, especially where there is extreme animosity and threat of violence; and each one is then scheduled to bring in the child for a separate play-interview and for a parent-child observation session.

Parents come to the intervention with a range of expectations and strong feelings, mostly negative ones. A few are searching for the miracle solution: they express their high expectations and excitement and may give the CM the sense that he or she will be their savior (which is highly gratifying but seductive). More commonly, parents are ambivalent, skeptical, distrustful, or even paranoid. Some feel quite hopeless and despairing, convinced that no one can help. They may appear exhausted by what feels to them like a life-and-death struggle. Others are highly focused and energized by the dispute. Almost all parents express fears that the CM will be duped by the other side.

Some of these parents have a utilitarian, exploitative attitude: "What can you do for me? Can I use you to get what I want?" Simply put, they are in search of an ally in the power struggle. Their unspoken agenda may include questions like "Can I use counseling to delay or avoid an outcome I don't want [e.g., an unfavorable court decision or a confrontation with my violence]?" They may see counseling as a way to prolong the marriage and deny that the divorce is occurring. It is important for the CM to tease out these various motivations and decide whether the case is a suitable one for confidential therapeutic mediation, or whether a custody evaluation or a coparenting arbitrator is needed instead (see chapter 9).

The professional needs to keep in check a number of unconscious or preconscious emotional responses and avoid acting out. For example, the CM might find herself being vague and nonspecific about the terms of the contract (e.g., whether reports will be made to the court); or the CM may be tempted to abandon some of the necessary structure as a concession to capture an ambivalent or unwilling client (e.g., agreeing not to see the child). Sometimes there may be a temptation to relinquish neutrality in favor of the less emotionally disturbed parent, backing away from the more disturbed. Or in response to his own fear, the CM may merge with the more disturbed parent, making unnecessary concessions to placate that parent and avoid the threat of violence. Occasionally, a CM may be seduced into trying to rescue one or both parents or the child to prove she is a more effective therapist than the string of mental health professionals that have preceded and failed.

CASE ILLUSTRATION: THE REFERRAL. The P family consisted of father (44 years), mother (36 years), and son, Dante (5 years). They were referred by their attorneys to our specialized counseling and mediation services for highly conflictual and violent divorcing parents. The attorneys reported that these parents had been separated for three years, after a brief marriage that both parents described as "unbelievably romantic" and "intensely passionate" at the beginning, but that "went sour pretty fast." The end of the marriage was marked by a series of struggles wherein Mr. P would physically restrain his wife from trying to leave him. The final separation was precipitated by one such violent incident, when Mrs. P fled to her mother's home. She filed spousal abuse charges against Mr. P, and he counterfiled parental kidnapping charges against her.

During previous unsuccessful attempts to resolve the custody dispute, the family were seen by two mediators and five different therapists. The court files indicated continual disagreements between these parents over money, child visitation, and the child's health care and preschool. Mrs. P had filed two child abuse reports against Mr. P, charging him with being inappropriately sexually and physically abusive with the child. Neither report was substantiated by Child Protective Services. Following a court-ordered custody evaluation, Mrs. P was reluctantly persuaded to accept a recommendation that the father have visitation with Dante (who was then 2 years old) every other day for several hours and one overnight each weekend. To allay Mrs. P's fears of physical abuse, all exchanges were to take place at the local police station. The parents had such vituperative arguments about each one's right of access to Dante at nursery school that the school asked them to leave. Mrs. P then had their son secretly admitted to a nursery school in another neighborhood, which prompted Mr. P to instigate another round of litigation in family court.

The entry of this couple to our service was preceded by long, elaborate negotiations by telephone, first with each attorney and then with both parents, regarding the contract for the counseling. Each parent made extensive inquiries about the CM's qualifications and experience, and especially about her attitudes toward fathers, joint custody, and battered women. She patiently answered each of these questions with professional candor. There were also arguments about the CM's access to previous therapists, who had confused the situation by disagreeing with one another and failing to coordinate their interventions with the family. Finally, the attorneys drew up, and the parents signed, a detailed stipulation wherein the CM was to assume the roles of both child therapist and coparenting coordinator for the family, with access to a designated special master who would have arbitration authority whenever the parents could not reach agreement around any specific issue.

In her initial interviews, Mrs. P frequently dissolved into tears as she voiced her extreme suspicion and distrust of both the CM and the process. Presenting as a timid, victimized woman, she described herself and her marriage mostly in the terminology of the battered women's movement. She appeared to be very frightened of Mr. P and believed him to be mentally unstable and emotionally, if not physically, abusive of Dante. At the same time, she appealed to the narcissism of the CM, who felt seduced by the challenge of proving that she was a more competent therapist than the long line of prestigious professionals who had tried before to help this family, and failed.

Mr. P was a highly anxious man who rambled on obsessively during his initial interviews. Typically, he arrived early for his sessions with copious notes, documents, tapes, and sundry pieces of evidence for the CM to review. Between interviews, he telephoned, wrote letters, or left long messages for the CM with further documentation of his claims. The CM experienced him as overwhelmingly intrusive, demanding, and controlling. At the same time, it was evident that he was extremely needy and became quite distraught if he felt the CM cut him off or misunderstood him. He required her constant validation. He was clearly humiliated by the accusations that Mrs. P had made against him for violence and the series of allegations of his sexual molestation and physical abuse of Dante. In defense, he tried to paint a picture of Mrs. P as a vicious, manipulative, unscrupulous woman who deliberately trumped up these charges to acquire custody. He refused to concede that she was frightened of him.

Assessment of the Impasse and Its Effect on the Child

Once the contract is entered into, the CM undertakes a thorough dispute-specific assessment of the divorced couple, giving special attention to any history of domestic violence in the spousal relationship from courtship to separation and including a brief synopsis of the early family history of each parent. An overview of the developmental history of the child is also obtained, with special attention to what the child has witnessed of the parental conflict/violence; what separations and losses the child has experienced, and at what age; the child's reaction to the parental separation/divorce; his or her relationship with both parents; and the child's symptoms of distress at transitions between parents as well as other emotional or behavioral problems (including somatic ones), school achievements, and peer relationships (see Appendix: Guidelines for Initial Assessment of High-Conflict Divorcing Families).

Most important is a formulation of the divorce impasse (see chapter 1) and its actual or potential impact on the child's development (as described in chapters 4 through 7). This is a very specific formulation of the intrapsychic and interactional disturbances within and between the adults and their effects on the parenting, the parent–child relationships, and the symptoms of distress, the defenses, and the coping style of the child. It is also important to consider how the child's disturbance and defensive adaptation is, in turn, contributing to the parental disputes. The CM may come up with a series of alternative hypotheses that will be carefully considered in designing the intervention. The idea is to formulate a strategic plan of attack: determining what elements of the impasse can be shifted and what has to be bypassed or diffused, and how this will be done. (For more details, see Johnston & Campbell, 1988.)

Typically, an "idealizing transference" develops during the assessment phase. The CM's empathic listening during the often intensely emotional individual interviews is experienced as validating each parent's perceptions, feelings, and reality. This kind of idealizing transference by the parents is valuable because it can reinforce the hope that the CM will be able to effect changes. The transference will be deepened by the CM's willingness to accept any documentation the parent wants to supply about the situation, including audio and video tapes, character references, and previous evaluations. In addition, the CM generally talks to any significant others, at the request of both parents. This leads to high, positive expectations on the part of the parents. The challenge is to meet the parents' needs to be acknowledged in these ways without relinquishing neutrality and inadvertently confirming their distorted views.

Some CMs can be seduced into wanting to gratify these idealistic fantasies during this "honeymoon" phase of treatment and will, with good but misguided intentions, hint at or promise what they cannot deliver. Others, who are more skeptical—because they have been down this road before—maintain a cool, dispassionate distance, an overly cautious, inscrutable stance experienced as nonsupportive and anxiety-provoking and that may even induce paranoia in the client. The optimal stance is to relate empathically to the feelings expressed by both parents and consciously withhold judgment about the accuracy of their perceptions, while emphasizing to both that there are two sides to every story and that problems such as theirs are often very complex. This stance is likely to be experienced as more understandable, if not reassuring.

CASE ILLUSTRATION CONTINUED: THE ASSESSMENT. A dispute assessment and history of the P family revealed the following impasse dynamics: Mrs. P was the eldest of five children in a family where the father was alcoholic and physically abusive. As a child, she survived the family chaos and her parents' divorce by merging with her victimized mother and taking care of her siblings. In this sense, she had not consolidated her own interpersonal boundaries and had difficulty feeling like a separate, viable person in her own right. Historically then, this woman had an insecure conception of herself that shifted with other people's conceptions of her. Not surprisingly, she was excessively dependent upon others to define her identity and her reality (for example, at the time of entry to our service, she had embraced the feminist ideological stance). As an adult, she tended to idealize others (lovers, therapists, psychic healers) and would initially submit herself to them but then, in the course of time, would experience panic, a loss of self, and a feeling of being engulfed and overrun. Her passive acquiescence inevitably turned to furious anger. She would then defensively split off from her "bad" angry feelings and project them upon the merged other. As she withdrew from the de-idealized relationship, she would then reclaim her "good" self.

Mr. P was an only child whose early years were marked by considerable doubt of his own competence and by insecurity about his masculinity (his father deserted the family when Mr. P was 2 years old). His smart, successful mother spent her time earning a living for the two of them, which left her young son feeling lonely and needy. Now, in his intimate relationships, Mr. P's obsessive and idealizing defenses, shored up by a rigid superego, were barely able to contain his sexual and aggressive impulses. These threatened to overwhelm him whenever he felt rejected or abandoned. In fact, Mr. P did not seem to feel that he was a real or valid person unless he was constantly receiving affirmation from others. In his amorous relationships, this man tended to give himself up to a joyous loss of boundaries and became experientially fused with his lover, involving perhaps a temporary psychotic break (indeed, he boasted to the CM about hallucinating in this manner during sexual intercourse with his wife).

Within the marriage, an impasse was formed because Mr. P's loss of boundaries and his demand for constant validation were terrifying to his wife, a woman who so easily allowed others to define her. She felt she was trapped in an abyss with a psychotic man whose aggression, sexuality, and power had no bounds! Their physical struggles that prevented her from leaving (or emotionally withdrawing) were symbolic of their individual self-struggles: hers to regain herself by separation, his to prevent loss of himself in isolation. Mr. P now desperately needed reunion with his wife to feel whole.

Externally, the impasse was solidified by the community of mental health and legal professionals, none of whom addressed the core disturbance in their interventions with this couple. Instead, a succession of professional people undertook investigation into the allegations and became unwitting agents for the couple's projections of the disowned aspects of self onto each other. While Mr. P's tenuous self-esteem was battered by the on-

slaught of allegations, Mrs. P's defensively distorted perceptions were rei-
fied by the investigation and litigation processes.

Unfortunately, the institutionalized polemic between the attorneys and
the adversarial court system established a fertile environment for the defensive splitting and projection of blame inherent in this couple's divorce disputes. Furthermore, the court, in its shortsighted wisdom—and backed by
misinformed mental health professionals—saw fit to encourage a visitation
arrangement that not only reinforced the struggle between the parents but
also placed their young child, Dante, squarely in the middle of the fight.

The impact of this couple's impasse on their capacity for parenting and,
in turn, upon Dante's development was profound. Five-year-old Dante
presented initially as a small, slightly built, tousle-haired child with a
charmingly warm manner toward adults (including his teachers and counselor). Much of his behavior seemed bent on winning and holding their interest in him (e.g., he was always presenting gifts to them, eager to please
and placate). He looked much younger than his age, and much of his play
was reminiscent of a younger child. He showed little interest in or capacity
for cooperative play with other children; at preschool he usually played
alone, or he hung around the adults, especially his parents whenever they
volunteered as teacher aides. Though he was perceived to be bright and articulate, his teachers indicated that he was neither emotionally nor socially
ready for kindergarten.

Mrs. P reported that her son had great difficulty separating from her,
whether going to his father or going to preschool. Most times she had to
pry him loose from her and push him through the door of the police station at transition times for the court-ordered visits. (She herself was visibly
frightened of even making eye contact with the father during these exchanges.) At preschool, Dante would "totally fall apart" when she was due
to leave and would become hysterical, clawing and attacking his mother.
At home, she often struggled with him over dressing, eating, and getting
ready to go anywhere. He would hold on to her leg or the furniture and
even hit her if she attempted to coerce him.

The child's inordinate separation anxieties had been engendered by repeated traumatic separations from an anxious, depressed, and frightened
mother, beginning when he was 18 months old. These highly distressful
separations were in part due to the visitation arrangements in place. Dante
responded to these arrangements with understandable ambivalence. While
he longed for a degree of autonomy from his mother, he had also learned

to fear separations from her. He was caught in a bind that made him angry as well as helpless, dependent, and terrified. Consequently, he became symptomatic in ways that further compromised the mother-child relationship: He clung to his mother and he also hit her. For the mother, this behavior vividly brought to mind Mr. P's controlling and intrusive treatment of her. At these times, Dante became the personification of her husband, and just as she had done in the past when her husband became demanding and abusive, she would try to retreat or escape from Dante by ignoring him or by locking herself in her room. This increased the child's panic at her abandonment and reinforced his self-defeating cycle of clinging dependency and rage.

Mrs. P was exquisitely attuned, however, to Dante's panic and fear at the time of his transition from her to his father. She interpreted his distress not as anxiety about being abandoned by her but as a valid response to an abusive and controlling father. Because she was bound by the court-ordered visitation arrangement, she felt totally helpless to protect him or send him on his way with soothing messages that he would be all right and that she would be there when he came back. Her attitude, in turn, interfered with Dante's ability to use his father as an alternative primary parenting figure.

Mr. P believed he had a very positive, close relationship with his son, and he proudly noted that the boy had no separation problems or behavioral difficulties with him, implying that obviously *his* parenting was superior to the mother's. In actuality, the child's perception of the father was partly based on the bad-mother-me state that Dante experienced as he separated from his mother and was partly borrowed from the mother's perception of the father as potentially dangerous. Dante's representation of his father, then, involved a somewhat primitive projection of a self that was potentially bad—frightening and unsafe. The father represented the powerful, separate *other* who must be propitiated; hence Dante tended to be charmingly passive and overcompliant with his father and with adults in general. Mr. P himself commented with a slight puzzlement that Dante was extremely eager to please him and was very fearful of any sign of his father's anger, even a mild reprimand. For example, in his anxiety to please his father, Dante (who had extremely finicky eating habits) would stuff his mouth with food and then gag. Overall, however, Mr. P was thoroughly delighted and charmed by his attractive son, who was so adult-focused, and he liked to parade Dante around his circle of work associates.

Dante's anxiety, his struggles for autonomy within his enmeshed, conflicted relationship with both parents, and his suppressed aggression were all expressed in somatic symptoms: he was bedwetting and asthmatic (especially at time of transitions); he periodically refused to eat or else gagged on his food; and he became inordinately involved in masturbation and sexual play with other children. These symptoms in turn triggered the mother's concern that the father was sexually abusing the boy. However, these concerns could not be substantiated.

A careful evaluation of the molest allegations indicated that although Mr. P tended to have poor emotional boundaries with his child, he was appropriately cautious about physical boundaries, largely because he was very aware that he would have to defend himself against continuing allegations of abuse from the mother. It would seem that Dante's sexualized behavior did not necessarily indicate sexual abuse but rather served specific psychological functions. It was self-soothing in that it helped him calm his chronic anxiety about being in this frightening family situation, and it was self-stimulating, enabling him to explore his own boundaries and to experience some pleasurable autonomy from his relatively unbounded, emotionally intrusive parents. (See chapter 5 for further discussion of these dynamics.)

Reformulation of the Problem, Challenge, and Crisis

As in other brief, focused therapies, the intervention proper usually begins with the therapist's redefinition or reframing of the problems and issues under dispute, one hopes in a manner that each parent can accept. This reframing may involve direct interpretation of the impasse and an explanation of what the dispute is doing to the child. Here, the leverage for change is generally the parent's concern for the child. Alternatively, it may involve some careful modification of the parents' views, using their primary defenses as leverage for change. For example, one may make an appeal to the self-interest of the parent as a leverage for change, using the fact that the parent has a vested interest in saving face and appearing to be more noble than the spouse. This cognitive reframing generally relieves anxiety; it makes rational what has been experienced as craziness. This kind of intervention works well at an intellectual or cognitive level; however, it is often difficult to know how much the family members have truly absorbed and understood psychologically. Most certainly at this point, the bulk of the hard work in producing emotional and behavioral change still lies ahead.

Here we comment on a rather radical departure from traditional approaches to psychotherapy: what is unusual in this approach is the degree of detail in the history taking, the focus on the child's subjective experience, and the way in which this information is used to make interpretations to the parents to heighten their empathic commitment to their child. What begins as a cognitive reframing is later revisited over and over again, at the dynamic level, in future sessions.

If the CM succeeds in being both accurate in interpretation and at the same time protective of the parents' vulnerabilities, the parents may be impressed and intrigued by the redefinition offered to them and by the depth of the CM's insight. When this happens, the idealizing transference is magnified. In some instances, the CM is experienced by one or more family members as the all-knowing, all-giving, omnipotent parent figure who is somehow going to fix everything. If this occurs, it might be important to actively discourage or modify the transference by interpreting it and predicting the potential for trouble ahead. This will prolong the CM's power to effect change. Alternatively, if the cognitive reframing is clumsy, inopportune, or experienced as an attack, the CM may be dismissed as naive, in which case he will be swept into the most troubled waters of the intervention—the rocky shoals of "challenge and crisis."

Sooner or later, following the reframing of the dispute, there almost invariably follows a period of acting-out by one or both parents, testing and challenging the CM and precipitating a crisis or a series of them. For example, one or both parents may act out by snatching or withholding the child, disputing or physically fighting at the transition between homes, or simply behaving as they always have, regardless of their new knowledge and the insights they have supposedly gained from the cognitive reframing. This acting-out behavior must be confronted and interpreted according to the CM's understanding of the impasse and its effects on the child. It is crucial that the CM be available to deal with this crisis period and be willing to work through it by firmly confronting any behavior that either hurts or fails to protect the child. At the same time, the CM defines principles and rules for ways in which situations like this have to be handled in future. (These principles or rules are the bases of the mediation agreements that will be drawn up later.)

During the crisis, there is generally a precipitous de-idealization of the CM: the parents may be bitterly disappointed, even hostile; they may charge the CM with naïveté, bias, unethical conduct, or ineffectiveness and failure, just as all others before this have failed them. They may become disillusioned and depressed about the chances of anyone's being able to help them. In the worst-case scenario, the CM can become a phobic object or the focus of their paranoid projections.

Countertransference feelings can be equally intense: the CM may feel anxious, defensive, and angry. Some counselors at this point abandon the case or defensively withdraw into a passive, compromised stance. Others act out in retaliation, becoming hostile and accusing the client of provoking the crisis. Alternatively, the CM may participate in the splitting and projection of blame by scapegoating the other professionals involved. Clinically, the CM may have the experience of absorbing the emotional responses that the distressed parent is afraid of owning (the projective identification), and this can be overwhelming. She may feel stupid, confused, incompetent, unethical, sly, greedy, bad—or all of these at once. One CM commented, "My brain felt like it was being sucked out with a straw!" Another said, "I felt slimy and dirty, and I wanted to take a shower." Yet another had disturbing dreams of being condemned for some unknown horrible crime.

Perhaps the most frightening aspect of this experience is that often both parents, not just one, are likely to be raging at the CM in this manner. Consequently, he can feel very vulnerable and likely to be annihilated by their fury. It is important for the CM to make use of consultations with an experienced and trusted colleague to tolerate and understand these powerful feelings. Indeed, this aspect of the work provides an essential access to the visceral, experiential sense of how children feel and what they potentially fear will happen if they assert themselves in any way in this dangerous place they inhabit.

Resolution of the crisis is critical to the successful treatment of a case. To become a real, separate person and not a "part-object" of the parent's idealized or de-idealized self, the CM must carefully, patiently, and persistently reiterate his position and point of view. Specifically, this means repeatedly focusing on the child's needs and experience, empathically reflecting the parents' own needs and feelings, differentiating each parent's needs from those of the child, and appealing to and validating the good attributes of each parent. At the same time, the CM continues to confront aspects of the parents' behaviors that are destructive to their children or to themselves. The idea is that the distressed parent (like the 2-year-old child with a temper tantrum) will try to destroy the CM; but the CM stands undemolished and undaunted, at which time she begins to be perceived as a separate and more real person (no longer an idealized part-object).

The CM's role is neither passive nor neutral; rather, it involves taking a strong, active, supportive, but confrontational stance with both parents, while advocating for the child's needs. The idea is to align with the "good parent" attributes of each parent and to gently but firmly confront them about their negative attributes. This involves supporting their valid perceptions of the other parent and withholding support for those that are invalid or cannot be confirmed. Disputing parents are often puzzled and even suspicious of the CM's active support for both sides. They think that he "speaks with a forked tongue," saying whatever each parent wants to hear. In actuality, the CM is not being inconsistent or contradictory but is painting a picture that each parent can tolerate and that is also part of a larger and more realistic, less negative and polarized view. Though the CM starts with two polarized partial positions, he tries to understand the whole, teasing out the shared reality so there will be less and less chance of saying to one parent something that would not be true to say to the other. It is this shared reality that the CM imparts to the child and the child can use for mastery. The narratives the CM later constructs for and with the children and sends home with the parents to read as bedtime stories become a metaphor for that shared reality.

The CM must be able to use her emotional reactions both selectively and therapeutically in this process. We have not found it helpful to be a passive-neutral recipient of the parents' rage and contempt. They will not learn anything if they are allowed to act out and project in this manner. Rather, they may become more frightened and chaotic, and the CM can indeed become ineffective and even supportive of their pathological defenses. The CM must consciously and selectively use his expectable emotional reactions as a confrontational mirror of the parents' outrageous or inappropriate behavior. To this end, the CM may openly convey shock, distress, outrage, and even anger in responding to these clients, but always with therapeutic wisdom and in moderation. Again, when countertransference feelings run high, consultation with another experienced professional can be invaluable. At all times, the CM must examine the motivation for her own observable stance and continually ponder the question "Am I helping these persons by my emotional response, or am I merely protecting myself from the manner in which they are narcissistically wounding me?" At the same time, the CM can limit the amount of hostility that has to be absorbed by insisting that he will not be sworn at or otherwise verbally abused. The CM should also feel free to tell hostile, accusing parents that they are being unfair, ungrateful, or unrealistic about the efforts being made on their behalf. In other instances, when reframing the issues and correcting the parents' distorted perceptions, the CM may express surprise, curiosity, puzzlement, or incredulity at the stance they are taking.

The consistent availability of the CM over the long haul is unquestionably an important component of successful treatment. Although clients have the right to withdraw at any time from the process, the CM needs to make it clear that she will remain available to them, provided they try to be fair, honest, and civil. Unrealistic hopes and fantasies, however, need to be confronted as such: the CM makes clear, over and over again, if necessary, what realistically can and cannot be done. The message to these families is that they will not be abandoned in their struggle. This is an unusual if not unique experience for many of these people, who indeed have been abandoned and negated repeatedly not only by their own early caretakers but, within recent memory, by therapists, attorneys, and other professionals.

One strategy that should be used with care is to join with parents in their level of intensity of emotional expression, so that the CM may indeed raise his voice at times or say something outrageous to get the parents' attention. For example, one of the authors once deliberately hyperventilated when a father told her of some extremely inappropriate action he intended to take with his sons. Her reaction riveted his attention and stopped his reckless tack. Indeed, there is likely to be a high level of drama at times with these people, and one needs to know how to take over the role of stage director of the play. We have speculated that the high level of drama and emotional intensity that these parents both generate and demand may relieve their feelings of existential emptiness, incipient depression, and fears of emotional death.

CASE ILLUSTRATION CONTINUED: REFORMULATION, CHALLENGE, AND CRISIS. The major intervention with the P family spanned a period of two years. After the treatment contract was signed and during the first two months (i.e., the assessment and early intervention phase), each parent and child was seen individually one to two hours per week. The crisis period of the intervention then lasted for about six months and was managed by two one-hour sessions every other week (including emergency telephone calls). The extended working-through phase required monthly meetings with each parent and child. After two years, the CM remained available to the family on an as-needed basis.

With Mrs. P, the initial task was gaining sufficient trust without allowing her to merge with and depend excessively on the CM (in other words, without precipitating an idealizing transference that would invariably result in disappointment, de-idealization, and rejection of the CM). Though the CM was warmly empathic about Mrs. P's fears, she was also quite rational and focused on specific facts (especially of the alleged domestic violence), which she obtained during a thorough history taking. The mother's concerns about her child were also carefully documented. A critical distance was established by acknowledging that, given her experiences with therapists and the court, Mrs. P had good reason not to trust and that she should continue to be vigilant and to maintain her guard. At the same time, the CM told Mrs. P that in their work together she would try to be extremely frank and honest with Mrs. P, and that she might offer perspectives Mrs. P would not like to hear, so as not to mislead her in any way. She also clarified that the CM's allegiance was solely to the child, not to either parent. Mrs. P then expressed her basic fear that the CM would be duped, controlled, manipulated, or seduced by the father. In reply, the CM chose to disclose some of her personal reactions to Mr. P by retorting rather dryly that he was "certainly not [her] type."

The first crisis in the intervention occurred when Mrs. P realized that, even after her full disclosure, the CM did not concur fully with her view that the father was a dangerous, violent, emotionally abusive man and that she should have full custody and he limited visitation. The CM frankly countered this stance by pointing out that Mrs. P was so frightened and debilitated by Mr. P, so phobic about him, that her own parenting of Dante had been seriously compromised. She noted that the mother's behavior was that of a seriously battered woman, even though the actual abuse was far less than many women in our program had experienced. Mrs. P had to agree that this was so. The CM then clarified that Mrs. P had a special vulnerability to her ex-husband, that he was triggering an inordinately phobic, poisonous reaction in her. Although it would have been possible to deepen this intervention into an exploration of Mrs. P's relationship with her own father as the origin of this vulnerability, the CM judged that this interpretation would be too threatening to Mrs. P's tenuous defenses and basic personality style. Instead, she chose to support Mrs. P's ego functioning by building on her healthy desire to be a good parent to her child. The

CM noted that Dante's angry, ambivalent separation struggles with the mother and the mother's reactions to Mr. P were both serious parts of the problem, and they needed to be corrected. The CM provided an analogy to the safety instructions in an airplane, where parents are told to put on their own oxygen mask before they try to do that for their child. In short, Mrs. P needed to rescue herself before she tried to rescue her child.

Given that the impasse between these parents had much to do with Mrs. P's need to secure her interpersonal boundaries and with Mr. P's urge to psychologically if not physically intrude in a way that made her feel threatened, the CM agreed that Mrs. P should have no direct contact with the father at all. The CM took on the responsibility of providing the protective barrier by sorting through all communications between them, rephrasing requests where appropriate, passing on necessary messages, and mediating child issues as they arose. The CM also assumed the responsibility of "monitoring" Dante's safety with his father and giving Mrs. P full feedback. Likewise, it was understood that Mr. P would be entitled to feedback about the progress of the mother's relationship with Dante. Once these arrangements were in place, Mrs. P was receptive to parental counseling on behalf of her son. The CM was then able to provide her with many concrete ideas about how to manage Dante's separation anxieties. Mrs. P's confidence in this process was greatly increased when the CM effectively managed the father during a series of challenges he made to her position of authority in the current situation.

Once Mrs. P began to feel more confident, the CM intervened with all the significant persons in Mrs. P's and Dante's network to produce among them a common perception and handling of the situation—a united front. This network included Mrs. P's attorney and the feminist psychologist who had diagnosed her as a battered woman (with them, the CM was extremely frank about the mother's problems in parenting); Dante's nursery school teachers (to coordinate the parents' involvement in his school); and the pediatrician (to agree on how to manage the treatment of Dante's asthma). Generating a united front in this way is often effective when parents have shifting views of the world and unstable relationships with others.

While Mrs. P was being seen in individual counseling sessions, intervention with Mr. P proceeded apace. Initially, this man felt driven to salvage his reputation and self-esteem. Both had been badly bruised by the series of allegations that Mrs. P had leveled against him. The CM accepted without complaint the numerous documents and evidence that he believed would vindicate him in her eyes. She also talked with everyone he wanted to testify on his behalf—including the custody evaluator, the previous therapists, the police officers at the local station, and, of course, Dante's teachers and pediatrician. However, the CM did not minimize or trivialize Mr. P's controlling behavior with his wife; rather, she discussed each physically violent event in detail, interpreted his motivations, and labeled his violence unacceptable and illegal. Interestingly, Mr. P had no difficulty admitting his actions when they were detailed in this manner.

There followed several crises, however, in which Mr. P challenged the authority and control exercised by the CM by making unilateral decisions about the visitation times. One Sunday, for example, he kept Dante with him without preplanning or permission. Several weeks later, he scheduled an airplane trip with the child at times he unilaterally decided upon, interfering with the mother's regular access arrangement. Furthermore, in spite of the CM's explicit requests that he not call her emergency number without good cause, he phoned at all times of the day and night, leaving long, inconsequential messages interspersed with unilateral and high-handed decisions about his access to his son at times that were convenient to him. To get this father's attention and to avoid his dismissing the problem, on each of these occasions the CM reacted in a dramatic manner: she was shocked, dismayed, offended, even angry at his inconsiderate behavior! In this way, she firmly confronted him on his acting-out and made a strong recommendation on behalf of orderly joint decision making that would provide Dante with much-needed regularity and predictability in both homes. Moreover, she insisted that Mr. P accord her more respect and consideration by tempering his unreasonable, preemptory demands. Over the months that followed, Mr. P also needed considerable parenting guidance, especially on how to put boundaries around his own emotional needs and provide for the needs of his 5-year-old child. Mr. P was immensely gratified by these discussions about himself and his son and responded well to this kind of intensive counseling.

During the first six months of work with both parents, a number of other structural changes were effected by the CM. The visitation arrangement was changed to accord with her recommendation that they alternate extended long weekends (five days to the father and nine days to the mother) to reduce the number of stressful transitions for Dante. The place of transition was also changed to the local nursery school (rather than the police station, which evoked any number of frightening fantasies for

Dante). With the input of the preschool and the counselor, the parents also agreed to keep Dante back in nursery school for another year. Following recommendations by the pediatrician, a plan was mediated to manage the child's asthma when he was being transferred from one to the other parent.

When there were disputes over finances, a separate mediator was employed, as this was not part of the CM's role with the family. When the mother sought the support of the counselor to move out of the area with Dante, the counselor explained how this child's fragile sense of himself as separate and autonomous from both parents had been developmentally delayed by the entrenched custody dispute, and that a consistent relationship with both parents was needed before he could manage a long-distance relationship with either one. Finally, the CM encouraged both parents to place Dante in nursery school daily and, a year later, in kindergarten. These opportunities allowed Dante to become more independent of his parents and gave them more time to devote to their own lives and professional interests. Within nine months, both parents were working for the major portion of the workweek, and expressing a good deal of pleasure in their individual achievements.

WORKING WITH THE CHILD. Decisions about when to initiate direct treatment for children of highly conflicted custody disputes and what kind of therapy is likely to be helpful must be made with considerable thought and care. There are not always clear answers to the many questions that arise, and each case must be considered on its own merits. For example, is child therapy the best way to allocate scarce family resources? Should the child be seen by the CM as part of the family intervention or assigned her own individual therapist? Should siblings be seen by the same therapist, and if so, when are conjoint sessions appropriate? How can one be sure that individual therapy for the child is well coordinated with the rest of the family intervention? Can the child benefit from individual therapy or would group therapy be more useful at this stage in the child's development? Should the intervention be short- or long-term, and what might one expect to achieve in each mode? What are the consequences if children revise their defensive processes when they continue to be in a malignant family situation? In short, what kind of therapy can one effectively conduct inside a domestic war zone?

More often than not, the need for therapy for the child is yet another hotly disputed issue between parents. Too often, the child is taken to therapy by one parent without the knowledge or consent of the other. Accepting a child for treatment under these conditions is highly questionable and may amount to malpractice, because the therapist will almost always be perceived as having aligned with one parent against the other. When this happens, the child's loyalty dilemmas are compounded, and the therapist then becomes one more party to the fight rather than a neutral person who can help the child move toward his own reality.

The intervention with the child is defined by several important parameters, some of which represent departures from more traditional psychotherapeutic work. First, the clinician functions as a "reality holder" for these children, who need help in comprehending and differentiating the external threats that are encompassed by real aspects of their family situation and their internal fears. Second, these children can rarely talk directly about their feelings and perceptions, at least not in the beginning. Instead, a therapeutic experience needs to be provided into which children can project their views of their interpersonal world, where their defensive distortions can be expressed and then revised. Third, therapeutic progress is constrained by the extent to which the child's capacity for basic trust has been compromised by early and chronic exposure to parental conflict and narcissistic parenting. Each of these three issues will be considered in turn.

Children of chronic custody disputes live in a chaos that is both overt and subtle; as a result, the child's experience is to be confused, disoriented, nonviable, ignored, misinterpreted, frightened, and overwhelmed by the chaos of the parental disputes and by the conflicting realities portrayed through the passions and fears of their parents. These children's intrapsychic fears have thus exploded into the real world and are being acted out by the parents. Consequently, their capacity to view the world realistically is rendered extremely problematic.

In direct work with children, the therapist presents a view of the world that begins to make sense for them. The child's reality can be confirmed through empathic attunement (gleaned from the therapist's knowledge and experience of both parents and a factual understanding of what is going on in both homes). In this way therapists lend their own ego functioning to children to help them make sense of their world and their feelings in very concrete and specific ways. The counselor may directly comment on the reality of the child's situation. More often the commentary is indirect; that is, the counselor uses narratives and dramatic plays (in stories and scenes that symbolize the family situation) to help children understand and reconfigure the internal scripts they have devised about family relationships. At the same time, the therapist stands as an ally and models, by her own neutrality and acceptance of them, how the child can have a respectful, caring relationship with both opposing parents.

Working through acute or chronic trauma requires access to the memory of particular experiences and the capacity to reflect on them. This is an unlikely condition for children whose experiences of trauma have been early, pervasive, subtle, chronic, and defensively distorted. These experiences have to be recovered at the perceptual level through (re)enactment of some kind. In therapy, this can be done through dramatic role play, puppet play, sandtray play, storytelling and dreams, and artwork (drawings and sculpture). Through these projective media the child's scripts and expectations about family relationships and the injunctions embedded within them can be surfaced and commented upon (sometimes directly but usually within the symbolism of the play). It is within the therapeutic safety of this projective play that the child can risk experiencing and differentiating his own feelings. This self-experience can be a prelude to the capacity for empathy; once the child begins to feel empathy for herself, she can develop real empathy for others.

The therapist's role in the child's (re)enactment is not passive. While the child is encouraged to take the lead and the therapist acts as a sensitively attuned enabler and follower, usually the child becomes stuck at some point and needs guidance to proceed. Some children are so constricted that they cannot play at all. Others become easily frightened and overwhelmed by their impulses and disrupt the play, or they become chaotic when certain themes emerge. Still others repeat the play over and over in an endless repetition-compulsion. A realistic and detailed understanding of the child's exposure to traumatic events and the associated developmental dilemmas, as well as therapeutic skill, is needed to determine if, when, and how to intervene within the child's impasse when it is expressed in projective play. The danger of intervention lies, of course, in imposing intrusive demands similar to those of the needy parents. The danger of nonintervention lies in abandoning these children in their struggle to cope. The therapist has the choice of exploring, clarifying, offering insight, or actually demonstrating (directly or indirectly through the symbolism of narrative or projective play) new solutions and ways of coping that will provide a way out of the impasse.

Throughout the work with these children, the therapist must reassess their capacity to use the therapeutic relationship as a reparative experience and developmental stepping stone. In the best of situations, the therapist becomes the new constant object whose predictable availability and attunement allow the child to revisit the possibility of internalizing this constancy. Too often the child's capacity for trust has been so compromised that the therapist is initially shut out, avoided, manipulated, or controlled by the child's profound need to maintain distance. While obviously there is no easy way to make a child more trusting, neither can the therapist passively accept being relegated to this limited and powerless position. Instead, the therapist might comment on what the child is doing: "You don't trust me to help you." Or the therapist might actively negotiate with the child for a more active participation: "You really want to be the boss today. You may sit in my chair and we will play cards for half the time, and for the other half, I need you to tell me some stories using these sandtray toys"; or "We will go into the other room and play basketball after we have done some things together. Would you like to do some drawings or play with the puppets today?"

Despite their desperate need for help, some children may not be amenable to individual therapy at all, because it is too threatening or they do not have the developmental capacity to make good use of it. As is discussed more fully in chapter 11, a therapeutic group experience may be far more useful to them. Alternatively, or in addition, one might consider creating a network of support and safety within their wider environment, where reparative situations and relationships will be consistently available to them. When resources permit, this might involve making and protecting opportunities for them to have drama, dance, art, or music classes. Families with more limited resources can enroll their children in scouting, school, or neighborhood sporting activities or Big Brother or Big Sister programs or simply support the child's involvement with favored family members, neighbors, and other interested adults. The point is to protect the children's access to adults who are especially and consistently attuned to their needs.

CASE ILLUSTRATION CONTINUED: WORKING WITH THE CHILD. During the first several months of their intervention, while the CM was attempting to deal with the challenges and crises of working separately with Mr. and Mrs. P and trying to coordinate their parenting, Dante was seen in his own individual sessions. Here, he was simply encouraged to tell stories using the sandtray materials. Through an analysis of his projective play, the CM was able to develop some ideas about the scripts that were governing his perceptions and coping responses. (See chapter 5 for a description of Dante's oedipal dilemmas as revealed in his play.) The CM's careful observations of Dante became leverage for her work with the parents. Thanks to this groundwork, she became a strong and compelling advocate for the child because she was able to communicate authentically how he was experiencing his parents' fight over him. Her understanding of Dante's experience also became the basis on which she made fairly specific recommendations to them, as described above. The only interventions that the CM made with Dante directly were supportive, affirming his feelings about how hard it was to go between homes and helping him understand the visitation schedule better.

After about six months of treatment, the parents settled down into a cooperative relationship and the new visitation schedule was in operation. At this point the CM determined that Dante's situation was stable enough for him to tolerate a deeper level of intervention, with especially designed stories about Robbie Rabbit, a smart little brown rabbit with long floppy ears and a cute white tail, who faces the dilemma of living in two burrows. (See Johnston et al., *Through the Eyes of Children: Healing Stories for Children of Divorce* [New York: Free Press, 1997].) These stories contained commentary tailored to Dante's family situation and incorporated scripts about family relationships that he had formed. They suggested new, more effective, developmentally appropriate coping responses to deal with his dilemmas. They also carried an indirect message to his parents, because Dante took home a copy to each house.

In the first story, Robbie Rabbit was fed up with hurrying back and forth from his mom's burrow to his dad's and decided to go on strike at his mom's place. He said no to everything, held on to the furniture, and ended up staying home in bed all day. Eventually, he got very tired and bored, and he grew thin and weak. He realized it was not at all fun to do nothing and decided to get up, go play with his friends, and return to school. (This story was a commentary on Dante's ambivalent struggle for control and difficulty in separating from his mother.)

In the second story, Robbie Rabbit was still moping and cross because his mom and dad couldn't live together. His beloved teacher, Ms. Teresa Rabbit, explained to him that his parents once loved each other, what went wrong, and how they decided to live apart. She told him how he could be like both his parents and live with and love them both. (This story was aimed at giving Dante a simple cognitive understanding of his family situation and permission to love and identify with both parents. Interestingly, it also provided the parents, especially the mother, with more understanding of why their marriage had failed.)

In the third story, Robbie Rabbit was shown to be spending more and more time with other little bunnies and less and less time with his parents. A refrain or mantra was developed: "I can do things by myself! No grown-ups allowed! Only kid bunnies!" (This story was meant to encourage Dante in his peer relationships and slowly decrease his dependence on his parents. During this time, the parents were encouraged to spend less time at his preschool.)

Although Dante was usually very constricted and refused to talk directly about his family situation, he responded with delight to these stories and often acted them out in the sandtray, embellishing them and adding postscripts. He also created his own stories, from which the CM drew more understanding of his needs.

Over the next six months and into his kindergarten year, Dante's behavioral adjustment markedly improved, his asthmatic attacks decreased, and he played more independently with his peers. His teachers remarked that he was achieving very well academically and was becoming well known for his extremely elaborate, creative stories and models. Both parents were giving him permission to be with the other parent. They helped him telephone when he missed the other and generally were more supportive, accepting, and even appreciative of each other's role in his life.

In general, Dante's ambivalent struggles for control and dependency with his mother became less frequent. However, one afternoon after school, he got into an altercation with his mother, who locked him out of the house (as a time-out). Furious, he kicked in a glass panel on the front door, cutting his leg severely. His mother was distraught; she screamed for help, called 911 (who dispatched ambulance and police), then called his father. Both parents met at the hospital and sat through the surgery while his leg was stitched. Dante was thrilled with having reunited them. Both parents were partially swept back into earlier memories of their love for each other, as they united in their efforts to help their child through this traumatic experience.

The CM was extremely concerned that Dante had developed a very dangerous script for reuniting his parents. Consequently, she devised a story in which Robbie Rabbit schemed to reconcile his parents with all kinds of tricks. Unbeknown to both, he plotted to have them talk to each other on the phone, invited them both to the same birthday party, feigned illness, and eventually hurt himself very badly before he succeeded in bringing them together. In the story, Ms. Teresa Rabbit commented on how badly he had hurt himself and how scared he was, and she suggested a better way to have them unite on his behalf. She proposed school as a safe place for both parents to come together to see Robbie Rabbit's class work and watch him play.

Dante responded to this story with particular pleasure. His parents began to meet regularly at his school, and on the very next occasion, they reported separately that Dante had seized each by the hand and led them triumphantly into the classroom, where he showed his parents his schoolwork. By this time, he was considered by his teachers to be achieving extremely well. Within a couple of months of this incident, the mother volunteered to set up a full joint custody arrangement with the father, on an alternating weekly basis.

Unfortunately, directing the parents to meet at Dante's school and having Dante provide them access to his school achievements backfired, as the parental disputes began to invade that previously neutral territory. During the following year, minor incidents of disagreement accumulated between the parents over sharing responsibility for his school lunch box, his winter jacket, and his homework as he moved between homes. Not coincidentally, when the CM went on vacation early in June, a major crisis and regression in family functioning occurred. Dante made a Father's Day gift for his dad that was taken home to his mother's place and somehow lost. Mr. P believed this was deliberate and warned (actually threatened) the mother that she was not to deliver Dante for the next visit until she recovered the gift. Mrs. P panicked and went into hiding for several days, which was a repetition of what Dante had experienced as a very young child! Finally, the substitute CM was called in and helped to quell the mother's anxieties by supervising Dante's reunion with his father on the usual schedule. After that summer, it was perhaps not surprising that Dante's school performance suddenly deteriorated. He resisted doing any work that might be co-opted into the parents' fight. He began scribbling again instead of writing clearly, as he used to do.

This led to another intervention using a Robbie Rabbit story in which Robbie became so bothered by his mother and father's arguing and fighting over his school performance and work products that he got "really mad and he decided not to write any more—from now on, he would just scribble!" Within this therapy session, Dante pretended to be Robbie by scribbling over several sheets of paper with great intensity, until the CM slowly and deliberately suggested that Robbie Rabbit resolve henceforth "to do his schoolwork only for himself, not for his parents, and so he decided to write beautifully again." As though in a trance and with obvious great pleasure, Dante then and there proceeded to write slowly and beautifully, as he was capable of doing. Subsequent attempts to redeem his school as a conflict-free zone for Dante were reinforced by his teachers, who took more responsibility for monitoring his progress. They also counseled both parents, especially the father, to provide the boy with more autonomy in his learning. It was especially important that the parents refrain from disputing over his transitional possessions—clothes, books, pets, and toys.

Working Through and Resolution

The working-through phase may continue to involve intermittent crises, especially with more characterologically disturbed parents or when the children's symptomatic behavior continues to reactivate the conflict between them. If so, the techniques remain as described above. The family may need to be referred to an arbitrator or returned to court to obtain a more structured agreement or a reality check on their unrealistic expectations about the kind of relief the court can provide.

In other respects, this phase involves a great deal of child guidance work and parent counseling, coaching for coparental communication with respect to the children, and, of course, monitoring parents' behavior and agreements. When elements of the core impasse recur, ongoing interpretation is offered and strategies are developed to help the parents cope without compounding the impasse. During this phase, a series of coparenting agreements are drafted that not only specify time-sharing arrangements but also define the principles by which parents are to treat each other and by which they can make good decisions about their child in a timely manner. These agreements may need to be formalized as court orders by stipulation, in which case they need to be passed on to the parents' attorneys, the child's attorney, or the special master or arbitrator (if there is one).

The CM's aim is to build a functioning organizational structure out of the family chaos. Initially, most elements of the structure lie within the CM, who acts, at the minimum, as a benevolent dictator and, at the utmost, as the charismatic center for parents and child. Gradually, a working group becomes organized as the role of each family member is delineated and stabilized. Later, a family constitution is drawn up, as these roles are codified into a set of principles and rules about how members are to treat one another independently of the CM, the coparenting arbitrator, or the court.

It is hoped that at this stage parents will view the CM more realistically as a concerned helper, a coach, and a benevolent (but human and fallible) person profoundly interested in their child and in them as parents, as well as someone who takes much pleasure in their child's growth and development and in their accomplishments as good parents. In the best of situations, the family members now know that the CM understands their history and their vulnerabilities but cares about them and values them despite their limitations. Most important, the CM continues to relate positively to both parents, thus providing a model for the child. The problems for the CM at this stage include managing his own boredom and frustration at the slow pace of change with the more characterologically disturbed people, which is manifested in the need to deal with the same old issues again and again.

CASE ILLUSTRATION CONTINUED: WORKING THROUGH. Although they had little contact with each other during the succeeding five years, Mr. and Mrs. P did communicate on essential matters and continued to use the CM to help them make joint decisions and develop cooperative plans for Dante. Although calling in the special master (arbitrator) was often raised as a threat when they could not agree, in actuality he was never employed in this case. It was enough for each parent to bargain under the shadow of what they believed the special master would arbitrate, which was usually anticipated for them by the CM. The security of having him in the background as a backup, however, seemed important to both parents.

As the parents settled into predictable routines and responses, Dante began to test his capacity for autonomy between the two of them by requesting changes in the schedule, which they accommodated. First, he decided it was boring to be with his dad and that he wanted to spend more time with his mom; later he reversed the arrangement, wanting more time again with his dad. Then he began to make more unreasonable requests, which neither parent would deny him. Dante was assuming a great deal of power in both families, especially with his father. It was important to help these parents put some limits on his control of their attention, time, and resources. The result was that both parents implied that the CM was to blame when they reached a compromise in mediation that Dante did not like. Dante became rather angry with the CM, feeling that she was dictating his life and that his parents and he had no input in decisions being made. At that time the CM decided to see Dante on a less frequent basis (since he no longer needed direct counseling) and encouraged his parents to assume full responsibility for the decisions made on his behalf. The parents also took some parenting classes that helped them to set firm, consistent limits and deal more easily with Dante's manipulativeness and intermittent passive-aggressive stance toward them both.

Termination and Follow-Up

In general, one does not really terminate with these families. Rather, the CM fades into the background, leaving behind, one hopes, the principles and knowledge that will be necessary to structure the family's ongoing interactions, until the child is able to psychologically and physically emancipate. To reduce their dependency on the CM, she may elect to see them less frequently, or to charge higher fees for follow-up appointments and telephone calls.

The question remains, How can these families continue to be helped if the initial CM cannot be consistently available to them over the long term? Unfortunately, many parents do not follow through on a new referral, and the most the CM can do is leave them with a good parenting plan and appropriate principles and parenting guidelines to follow. Or if it seems reasonable and the permission of family members is forthcoming, the CM may introduce a new CM into the picture and transfer the family through a series of conjoint sessions. Alternatively, in family and professional conferences, the emerging structure and process can be passed on to grandparents, teachers, or child care workers. These meetings should include a clear definition of what behaviors to flag for further help. Sometimes, the CM can suspend regular sessions for a period of months, or even years, and contract to do specific pieces of follow-up consultation at family milestones (e.g., at the child's entry into elementary school or adolescence). Another strategy is to offer them one or two final sessions to be kept "in the bank" for use in an emergency.

Optimally, the CM will remain ever-present for the child and for the parents as a realistically available person to consult in the event of renewed conflict, developmental changes of the child, or changes in life circumstances. Psychologically, the CM functions as the family conscience: a "superego" figure to whom each of the family members feels accountable on some level. Effective counselors doing this kind of work often become members of the divorced family's network, akin in their stabilizing influence to elders in the lives of families buttressed by close-knit extended family, tribal, or community ties. In sum, the counselor is like the old-time family physician or a "mental health pediatrician" who remains in contact throughout the child's growing-up years.

Chapter 11

Group Treatment of Children in Conflicted and Violent Families

$\mathcal{I}$n this chapter we present a group treatment model that was developed in the high-conflict project for school-age children who live in highly conflicted and violent divorced families (see Roseby and Johnston, 1997, for the model in manual form). The strategies that are described here can also be adapted for individual work with this age group. We also describe strategies that can be used in group or individual work with younger children in the 5-to-7-year age range.

COPING PATTERNS IN SCHOOL-AGE CHILDREN

As we noted in chapter 6, school-age children often seem to be compliant and well functioning in ways that mask their underlying vulnerability. These are, after all, youngsters who have learned to finesse a position that meets their parents' conflicting expectations to gain acknowledgment, acceptance, and protection. It should not be surprising then that by school age, many children have perfected the art of appearances. When we work closely with these children, however, we typically find a profound sense of alienation and isolation that lingers not too far below the surface. The children seem to manage this fragile interior by narrowing their perceptions, thoughts, and feelings to fit predictable, oversimplified, and invariant patterns. These patterns are organized around their profound need to maintain a sense of interpersonal predictability and control.

By school age, these patterns seem to consolidate as interior scripts (see chapters 3 and 6) that define the children's views of relationships and the particular role that each must play to sustain and control them. In the defensive world view that results, the children come to understand themselves and others in concrete terms that limit feeling, ambiguity, complexity, and spontaneity. These very human qualities are experienced as dangerous, because they might undermine the children's abilities to predict and control the interpersonal world. The children seem to give themselves very little room to stray from their defensive scripts. After all, they provide an invariant set of rules and expectations that protect them from the unpredictability of their most significant relationships.

DEVELOPMENTAL DIFFICULTIES
THAT RESULT FROM COPING PATTERNS

While these rules and expectations provide a sense of control, they also create and maintain interpersonal distance. In a sense, the children become locked in a protective prison of rule-bound behavior and perception that undermines their developmental progress and limits opportunities for new relationships that might support maturation and growth. This kind of defensive alienation can be particularly troubling during the school-age period, when children ordinarily rely extensively on friendships with their peers to mature into an increasingly complex and workable understanding of themselves, other people, and relationships. Of equal concern is that these vigilant children often resist engagement in individual treatment relationships. Their trust is very hard won and can take more time to develop than the family's financial or emotional resources sometimes allow. The group approach described here is an alternative treatment and potential bridge to individual work.

A RATIONALE FOR GROUP STRUCTURE

The children in our project responded to group intervention with a degree of ease and pleasure readily apparent from the outset. In part, this may have been because school-age children naturally prefer to use their age mates as a reference group when they can. When they discover that "I am not the only one" and that their story does not carry the shock value for others that it carries for them, their sense of shame and isolation lessens to a degree. The group becomes an alternative culture within which the children can learn from and about their peers. This is particularly important for youngsters who tend to control and avoid rather than form real relationships. The leader, in turn, can represent a benevolent adult who defines and supports a coherent moral order.

The group setting also permits an activity-oriented focus that is particularly appropriate for school-age children. Activities can be structured to allow participants to titrate their approach to painful issues as they freely select a balance between watchfulness and participation. The experience of making choices is particularly central for these children for whom control over feelings is a salient developmental and interpersonal issue. Group activities can also capture the children's imagination and provide a sense of pleasure that is all too often a foreign experience. For the group leader, the technical challenge is to maintain the group's serious therapeutic agenda without forestalling the children's enjoyment and real freedom to contribute to and modify the group experience.

The peer-oriented action of the group structure also provides these youngsters with a kind of unself-conscious strength in numbers. When that atmosphere takes hold, it seems to release the group from the need to anticipate and meet the expectations of those in charge. This kind of breathing room is particularly welcomed by children who have learned to survive the double-binding demands of their parents' conflict by focusing vigilantly on the needs of powerful adults. Because the group setting helps to release the participants from their hypervigilance, they tend to act out their interpersonal difficulties and articulate their inner concerns rather more openly than in individual interviews. Group leaders, therefore, can gain a reasonably accurate understanding of the children in a fairly brief amount of time. When group leaders have this kind of insight, they can represent the children's needs and concerns quite powerfully in collateral work with parents. This supporting work, which may be conducted individually or in psychoeducational groups, is essential to the effectiveness of the children's group approach.

Conflicted parents also seem more at ease with group rather than individual treatment as a starting point for their children. These parents frequently express the belief that sharing experiences with peers will help their youngster to feel more normal and less isolated. This belief, accurate in its own right, also seems to reflect the parents' hope that hearing about similar situations will help children see their own parents as less uniquely flawed because of their divorce and continuing conflict.

STRUCTURE AND MANAGEMENT
OF THE CHILDREN'S GROUP

The children's group model provides for 10 weekly sessions that are detailed in manual format (Roseby & Johnston, 1997). Older children (ages 10 to 12) meet for 90-minute sessions; younger children (ages 7 to 9) generally meet for one hour. Separate groups for these age ranges allow the leaders to tailor each group's tempo, activities, and discussions to its members' particular developmental capacities. The groups tend to range in size from five to eight participants and optimally include a balance of boys and girls. When siblings fall into the same age category, the decision to treat them together or separately rests with the clinician. In some cases, siblings can benefit from the comfort each brings to the other in the course of the group experience. In other cases, each child needs a separate place in which to find her own way forward.

The decision to use one or two group leaders depends on the availability of resources, the training and experience of the leaders, and the specific needs of the children in the group. Experienced single leadership can be successful, particularly with more mature groups. But the participants' level of acting-out is extremely difficult to predict. In the early phases of the intervention, these children often seem quite constricted and easy to manage. After several group sessions, though, many lower their guard, becoming less compliant and more active and expressive in the process. When this happens some children may act out in ways that interrupt the work and disturb the emotional tone of the group. At that point, co-leadership becomes most useful. One leader will be needed to support the disruptive child, while the other maintains the group's equilibrium. When there is doubt, co-leadership is therefore preferred. Discussion between co-leaders can also provide the children with a model of negotiation and conflict resolution between adults. At least one of the co-leaders should be an experienced clinician, while the other may be in training. In this way, the group can provide a service to the children as well as an apprenticeship to clinicians who wish to learn the model.

Whenever possible, each participant is evaluated as fully as possible before the group work begins. When time and resources permit, the evaluation is most useful when it includes family and individual interviews, behavioral checklists from parents and teachers, self-report, and projective testing of the children. This kind of information can help the group leader to understand each child as fully as possible in a relatively brief time. As a result, he can structure each child's experience in the group in a therapeutically focused manner and communicate credibly about their child with each parent.

A repeated assessment at the end of the group can provide the basis for developing follow-up treatment and support plans. For some children these plans may be limited to intermittent follow-ups, particularly if the work with the parents has been successful. Others seem to benefit from cycling through the group program two or even three times. Still others transition from group to individual treatment, bringing with them a clearer understanding of the therapeutic process, a more consolidated sense of the issues troubling them, and a more practiced access to the language of feeling. These achievements tend to reduce the children's defensiveness in a one-on-one therapeutic relationship.

The group work seems to be most effective when the leader is also the clinical case manager for the child and her family. In this multifaceted role the group leader conducts the initial and final evaluations, works with the child's parents individually or in psychoeducational groups, and sees the child and the family at structured intervals thereafter. When the group is co-led, the responsibility for these interventions can be divided, so that each child and family has the opportunity to develop a primary and continuous relationship with one of the leaders. In high-conflict situations, when both parents and children tend to be quite fragile, this kind of continuity can provide the level of support needed to anchor and maintain the work.

THEORETICAL FRAME OF THE CHILDREN'S GROUP

A central goal in the children's group work is to help them discover and revise the unconscious rules and expectations that govern their understanding of themselves, other people, and relationships. A second and equally important goal is to help the children access and tolerate a broader range of feelings as their scripted ideas begin to shift. To address these goals in a theoretically coherent way, we turned to a normal developmental model of interpersonal understanding (Selman, 1980). The model describes the way in which children's understanding of themselves, other people, and relationships ordinarily parallels their ability to move beyond their own subjective experience and point of view. As their ability to take on other perspectives increases throughout the school-age years, children's interpersonal understanding becomes increasingly realistic, complex, and flexible. Selman contends that children ordinarily mature in their interpersonal understanding quite naturally, as they grapple with the demands of friendship. It is here that children must learn how to make sense of and balance their own needs, feelings, and point of view with someone else's. As children meet these challenges they learn about the codes of moral conduct, that is, how to conduct themselves as individuals who also belong to a community.

Ironically, when children in high-conflict families defensively cling to their oversimplified and invariant scripts for understanding themselves and other people, the ordinary challenges of new relationships tend to deepen their constriction; it is the only response that feels safe. The group approach is designed to challenge this response in ways that the participants find safe, interesting, and pleasurable. Each session includes a progression of structured activities that address elements of this overall goal in four interrelated content areas. These include exploring the language and complexity of feelings; defining and understanding the self; defining and revising family roles, relationships, and rules of moral conduct; and dramatizing and revising family roles, relationships, and rules of moral conduct. In each domain the structure of the activity remains constant, while the focal content is generated by the group participants. This approach allows the leader to maintain a therapeutic focus while supporting the children's sense of individuality and personal agency.

EXPLORING THE LANGUAGE AND COMPLEXITY OF FEELINGS

Many children in highly conflicted families have little experience with using language to express their own emotions. In part, this is because feelings themselves often seem frightening and uncontrollable. Labeling feelings out loud can make them seem terrifyingly personal and real. This creates a significant bind, because words are an essential tool that children need to reflect on and communicate their own experience. Feeling words also represent the only intermediary step that can represent inner experience and delay action. This is a step that many of the children have neither practiced nor witnessed, so that feelings seem all the more uncontrollable to them. For these reasons, it is important to create an environment in which the symbolic expression of feelings is not only permitted and encouraged but especially valued.

Feeling-Color Charts

One of the first things that the leader and children create together is a feeling-color chart that is used throughout the group sessions. To circumvent the children's natural reticence, the leader introduces the task with a challenge: Can this group generate a longer list than the group that went before? Participants quickly become focused on the length of their list. The end result can be satisfyingly compared to the short list of feelings the leader has developed for the purpose. The feelings identified in this way tend to capture the children's concerns with surprising directness. One chart, for example, included words such as "frustererated," "faultred," "embaresst," as well as more familiar-looking words: weird, sick, unwanted, helpless, homesick, private, left out, resentful, confused, closed up, and stressed.

Once the list is complete, the leader helps the group assign a color to the words that seem to represent primary feelings that repeat in several forms; these may include variants of angry, sad, weird, and so on. Each word is then circled, underlined, or otherwise identified with its corresponding color. When this has been done, the group works on identifying appropriate blends of color for more complex emotions. For example, if *mad* is assigned the color red, and *sad* is the color blue, then the group may decide that *embarrassed* should be assigned a combination of red and blue because it represents these mixed feelings. Work on the chart provides the group participants with an opportunity to consider and discuss feelings in an atmosphere of pleasure and safety. The activity is also designed to introduce the group to the concept of blended and complex emotions. This idea is crucial for children whose thoughts, feelings, and ideas about people and relationships tend to be polarized and oversimplified. The chart remains in the group room for the duration of the program. It becomes a shared point of reference as children identify feelings (by name or color) in the rest of their work together. As they use the chart in this way, children learn to express multiple and often contradictory feelings without feeling obligated to acknowledge one and ignore the other.

Feeling-Thermometer Charts

In a related activity, the children complete a chart on which five or six thermometers are used to depict levels of feeling. The first task is to label each thermometer with a feeling from the color-feeling chart. That done, each child is asked to color each thermometer (using the color-feeling chart as a guide) to whatever level indicates the intensity of that feeling in a particular situation. Levels are labeled: None, Some, Pretty much, Very very much, and Totally. Typically, the leader identifies a situation that is commonly experienced and can be tolerated by the group. For example, the children may complete the chart to describe levels of feelings that they experienced coming to group that day, going from one parent's home to the other, or overhearing an argument.

Older groups can sometimes work with the direction to complete the chart according to how they feel "most of the time." The children may each choose to explain their chart to the group when it has been completed. One particularly constricted youngster explained, somewhat paradoxically, that she felt "mad" and "lonely" none of the time. She then acknowledged feeling "sad," "confused," and "worried" some of the time and "heartbroken" very, very much of the time. These kinds of responses illustrate the level of disclosure that tends to becomes the norm quite early in the group process.

At this point, each child is given the opportunity to charade a feeling from her chart. The group's task is to guess the feeling. The activity becomes more interesting and complicated when the charade is extended to include not only the feeling but the level of feeling. When the charade is successfully completed, the leader follows up by asking the child how the charade would change if the feeling level went up or down. The leader can then invite a nonjudgmental discussion of questions such as, Do people always show or act on their feelings? How does this change when the level of the feeling changes? What are some different ways for showing or hiding feelings? What are different words that people use for different levels of feeling? The intent here is to increase the children's tolerance for feelings by helping them understand that feelings vary in intensity and do not necessarily lead to action (e.g., anger is not always acted out as violence). The children can be helped to understand, for example, that it is possible to experience anger as crabbiness, irritation, or annoyance, before fury enters the picture. Fury, in turn, may or may not then explode into action. The point is further clarified as the leader repeatedly emphasizes the idea that feelings and behavior are distinct. Feelings, the leader stresses, are not a matter of choice. As a result, they cannot be controlled or judged as right or wrong. How feelings are acted upon, however, requires both choice and control. Action is a matter of right and wrong. It is here, in the domain of action, that children can begin to consider the question of moral conduct.

These tools and strategies that address gradations in children's feelings can be useful in individual therapy when children are using puppets or sandtray toys to work through their experiences. Puppets or sandtray figures can charade their feelings, while they literally hold and change feeling thermometers to show their level of feeling as they play out their parts. The extent of discussion and interpretation, of course, will depend upon timing and each child's capacity.

Masks

Working with masks can provide concrete ways for children to assimilate and practice the distinction between feelings (internal states) and action (external representations). The work begins on a positive note, as the leader suggests situations in which hiding feelings can be useful. Such situations might include "smiling as if nothing has happened when you are walking home with your friends and you have stepped in a dog mess on the sidewalk" or "looking like you don't care at all when someone teases you at school." These suggestions lead to others from the group and provide a natural transition into making masks. The masks, representing an "outside self" that can be used to hide or protect the "inside self," are later used in role playing. The role plays begin with an invitation from the leader, "Have you ever been in a situation when you have needed your mask?" Group participants typically respond with ease.

One 11-year-old boy, for example, described a situation in which his classmates had all flunked a test that he had passed. He used a sad mask to show how he behaved in the presence of his classmates. When the leader asked him to show the feelings beneath the mask, he moved out of sight of his "classmates" in the role play, tossed the mask in the air, and crowed exuberantly, "I passed! I passed!" An 8-year-old girl made a smiling mask that she used in every subsequent role play involving her bitterly conflicted parents and stepparents. When the leader asked her to show the feelings beneath the mask, the idea seemed to be so frightening that she could not release the mask from her hand. This child received a great deal of support from the leader for using her mask when she so clearly felt that she needed it.

These different levels of response can help the leader to assess the degree of constriction in individual children and define their treatment needs over the long term. As the children work with masks, they can begin to be more conscious of their inner life and how it might be represented in behavior. This new awareness introduces the possibility that they can make choices about how, when, and with whom to express themselves. The leader addresses the question of choice in the context of the role plays by asking each child to consider safe persons, places, or times when she might remove the mask and communicate how she really feels. For example, 12-year-old Mary made a smiling mask, without eyes, for a role play in which she was required to visit her father when she wanted to stay home with her mother. When prompted by the leader, Mary was able to show the furious face beneath the smiling mask to her "brother" in the role play. She affirmed that sometimes he seemed safe enough for her to be real with him in this way.

As they begin to practice and assimilate more flexible ways of achieving interpersonal safety and control, some children experience a degree of release from their inner constriction. At the same time, they begin to understand that other people have thoughts, feelings, ideas, and motives that may or may not be inferred from their behavior. For many of these youngsters, these new ideas can challenge their rigid and oversimplified patterns of understanding how people and relationships work. The resulting dissonance and interest can, in turn, catalyze new developmental progress. The more vulnerable children in the group seem to benefit most from observing other children's process. In so doing, they take in new words, concepts, and possible behaviors that become building blocks in later individual or group work.

DEFINING AND UNDERSTANDING THE SELF

Because children in high-conflict families tend to organize their experience in response to the needs and expectations of others, they often lose sight of themselves. As a result, they have difficulty identifying and supporting their own feelings, ideas, motives, and preferences. While this absence of self can masquerade as compliance during the school-age years, it will not serve in adolescence, when issues of identity press for resolution.

The issue of self-definition is first addressed when children are invited to imagine and then draw a private room to which they have exclusive access.

The room may be any size, shape, color, or location and may contain whatever the child wishes. Like much of the material produced in group, these inner rooms reflect the children's longing for protection and can be useful in diagnosis. Eight-year-old Karen, for example, drew a room that contained only a magic box. In the box were magic clothes that could transform her into an angel or a princess when she put them on. This chameleon-like defense is commonly observed in children like Karen, who have been exposed to serious and chronic violence. Her drawing not only clarified the defense but emphasized the inner emptiness that surrounded and maintained it. Eight-year-old Alan, who had also been exposed to violent fights between his parents, made a drawing that protected and empowered him in a different way. His room held floor-to-ceiling computerized gaming equipment and had so many electronic locks on the door that they took up half the page.

In subsequent sessions, the leader uses guided imagery to help the children to symbolically enter this inner space and use it as a safe place in which to identify private thoughts, feelings, or wishes. In one activity, for example, the leader guides the group members to their "inner room" and suggests that they find a gift there. Once the image is in place the leader asks: "What is your gift?" "Who sent it to you?" "Is there a note?" "What does it say?" Many of the children say that their gift is cash: "A million dollars so that I can buy my own car and my own house!" "A thousand dollars, so I never have to worry about money again." Often, the wish for unlimited money comes from children whose parents fight about child support. Once the children have identified their gift, they can add it to the drawing of their room. The addition, like others that follow, becomes a concrete way of representing the children's expanding self-awareness.

In a later session, the children use the room as a safe place in which to consider the future. First, they are invited to identify the year when they will reach age 21. This brings a measure of concreteness to the activity. Once done, the group members identify three private wishes or expectations for themselves at that age. These are written on apple-seed-shaped paper that is then "planted" (glued) in a pot in the drawing. The leader explains that these seeds will grow and change along with the children, in the safety of their private rooms. The wishes that the children identify in this way often reflect both possibility and vulnerability. Alan, for example, wrote, "I expect that I will be really smart and fat, and sit around and watch TV a lot, like my dad." The intent here is to introduce the children to their own potential for mastery. Once expectations can be articulated, they can be shaped. Naturally, the shaping cannot occur in a limited number of group meetings. The children's own expanding consciousness provides the catalyst for change over time.

The children seem to generalize from these "private room" activities in rather concrete ways. Parents frequently report, for example, that their children show a new interest in making plans for privacy in their homes. Sometimes the youngsters have their own rooms, and these are rearranged. Others work on creating private space wherever they can find it. Some parents have said that their children asked for lock boxes and diaries after this work began in group. Nine-year-old Katie's mother told us her daughter came home after being picked on by her friend Caitlin and said, "I just went into my private space to think about what to do." Katie's mother described this incident in a parent group meeting after hearing about the "private room" activities. She said, "Usually, Katie has a meltdown when Caitlin teases her. This was so different. I recognized it instantly . . . this was the most active position I had ever heard from her . . . so unlike her, I thought it came out of the blue . . . but it didn't."

Children in individual treatment often begin their explorations of boundary issues with similar metaphors. For example, in a treatment session in the early stages of individual therapy, one 8-year-old girl from a highly conflicted family spontaneously began to make a sign that read DO NOT ENTER WITHOUT KNOCKING. When the therapist asked whether she wanted this sign for her own room, she nodded, then made a second sign that read YOU MAY ENTER WITHOUT KNOCKING. This presented a natural entry point, which the child herself had offered, for the therapist to suggest that they might draw a private room and an open room. These drawings then became the basis for evolving discussions about what the rooms might contain, as well as how and why they might be different.

DEFINING AND REVISING FAMILY ROLES, RELATIONSHIPS, AND RULES OF MORAL CONDUCT

Children's unconscious scripts tend to be supported by rules and expectations that distort their understanding of family roles, relationships, and moral codes. Activities that address these issues are designed to raise questions about what is right, fair, and expectable in relationships, as well as to bring to the surface feelings that are associated with these concerns.

The younger school-age children begin this work by developing a list of "jobs" that are fair and appropriate for different family members. For children, jobs include role-defining behaviors such as "playing with friends," "learning in school," and "earning an allowance," while for parents, they may include behaviors such as "protecting the children," "earning money for the family," and "figuring out their own fights."

This kind of concrete clarification and the leader's affirmation can provide participants with alternative norms recognized within the community of their group. This new "moral culture" can be very reassuring to children who live with constant ambiguity about what is right and just conduct in family relationships. In a similar way, older children use discussion and consensus to codify a set of rules for relationships. In these discussions the leader introduces the group members to specific strategies for conflict resolution that may be practiced during role plays. For many of the group members these activities and ideas can be quite powerful and thought provoking.

Human Sculptures

In a related activity, the leader helps each group member to create a human sculpture using other group members (Satir, 1972). The sculpture represents each child's view of the way people in his family relate to one another most of the time. When the sculpture is completed, the child creates an ideal version that represents how members of the family would relate in a perfect world. Both sculptures are silently videotaped. The group then discusses the video with a sense of both distance and drama. During the discussion, the leader helps the children to identify the underlying script and the rules and expectations that sustain it. The leader's remarks generally take the form of admiring observations that protect the group member while helping her toward greater awareness; for example, "It seems as if you work very hard in your family, and that you have figured out that a good way to be safe is not to have feelings," or "I notice in this sculpture how carefully you have trained yourself not to make demands on anyone. That takes a lot of guts and hard work, because it must get pretty lonely sometimes." Having made these comments, the leader can begin to ask how this hard work feels.

The sculpture of the ideal family provides the children with an opportunity to review and revise their ideas about relationships and their role in the family. This second part of the exercise can evoke feelings of anger, sadness, and loss. These feelings deepen the work as well as the children's vulnerability. Some can use the experience to integrate feelings about their current situations, as well as to consider new ethics and ideals for the families that they might create as adults. Others barely tolerate the dawning of new thoughts and feelings, so the work must be carefully titrated and requires alert clinical judgment on the part of the leader at every step.

The level of vulnerability was very much apparent in 8-year-old Vic. This child had watched or heard his cocaine-addicted father beat his mother regularly and severely, until the parents separated at his age of 4. At the time Vic was in the group, his father was preparing to remarry. Vic stated that he liked his stepmother-to-be but worried about the fights between her and his own mother, who felt quite jealous of the new relationship. Interestingly, Vic had fueled the animosity between these two women by telling exaggerated tales about how badly his stepmother treated him and how rudely she spoke of his mother. He did this in an effort to reassure his mother (and himself) that she was good and that he was forever loyal. In his first family sculpture, Vic included his father standing behind his future stepmother, who was wagging a finger warningly at his mother. Vic placed himself on his knees between the two women. With one arm he pushed against his stepmother, holding her back, while with the other he cradled his mother's waist in a gesture of protection.

The sculpture suggests a script in which Vic assumed the role of mother's rescuer in a frightening and unpredictable world. This role is consistent with earlier interview material in which Vic recalled that he used to call out when his parents were fighting during the night, and this made his father stop beating his mother. The leader began the discussion of this first sculpture by noting how much work Vic was doing, and how strong he had to be. The leader also noted how much he seemed to want to love and care for his mother. Because these observations were consistent with Vic's view of himself, he tolerated them. When the leader asked Vic how he felt about the way his father treated his mother, or whether he felt tired from all the work he was doing, he shrugged without interest; he could not acknowledge feeling anything. When the leader asked him whether he might need a mask, however, he readily agreed. He said it would have to be "a pretty fierce one." Within this framework, all of the discussion took on a hypothetical distance; for example, "If you had your mask on in the sculpture could you ever take it off?" "If you did take it off, what would be underneath?" Here, Vic was able to acknowledge that he was a little worried about his mother, but he could not comment about his father's bullying in any direct way. When the leader asked Vic whether protecting his mother was a child's job, he promptly said it was. When the group members referred to the "job" list and eventually disagreed, Vic became confused.

The feelings evoked in this discussion were very hard for Vic to tolerate. He managed them by creating an idealized sculpture that included himself, his parents, and his brother. He positioned them with their arms around one another, fixed smiles on their faces. Vic's soon-to-be stepmother was laid out, dead at the family's feet, with a REST IN PEACE sign on her chest. This second sculpture clarified the inflexible limits of Vic's scripted ideas about relationships. He could not imagine feeling any real anger or disappointment toward his violent father or any realistic way to manage the ambivalence of liking the person who made his mother feel sad and angry. The sculpture represented the developmentally inappropriate and magical solution that his rigid internal script allowed; that is, he killed off his stepmother in the sculpture in much the same way that he tried to kill off his ambivalence and his anger in reality.

Vic tolerated only a limited commentary on his second sculpture; yet enough for everyone to agree he had found a good solution to the problem of having mixed feelings about his stepmother, and maybe others in his family as well. Paradoxically, this supportive agreement gave Vic the first inkling that he actually had a problem. The script he had developed for defining his role and relationships was no longer airtight. Other solutions might be considered. As with many vulnerable children, Vic began work in group that was to be completed in subsequent individual treatment. Here, the rigid rules and expectations that bound Vic's internal and relational life were slowly released, so that growth and maturation became possible once again.

Identity Shields

School-age children ordinarily begin their journey toward an autonomous identity by striving to become an idealized self based, at least in part, on identifications with idealized qualities in both parents. Children in high-conflict families, however, often have rigidly distorted or conflicting ideas about one or both parents and their relationship to each. As a result, their identifications tend to be distorted or conflicted as well. Some children, for example, identify with one parent so completely that the relationship is merged, while the other parent is rejected and vilified. The child's moral judgment is significantly compromised when this occurs, because this kind of splitting inevitably represents a degree of distortion in the child's understanding of who is good and who is bad. Other children do not see relationships as a resource at all. One of the goals of group work, therefore, is to help children articulate and reality-test their understanding of each parent and other family members, so that they can emulate persons or qualities more consciously. This work is conducted through the creation of an identity shield.

The leader begins by inviting the group to consider the path that lies ahead. Adolescence is on the horizon and they will go to high school, learn to drive, begin to date, and so on. The leader emphasizes that there will be new opportunities to make conscious choices about the kind of person they want to become as they move toward adulthood. The identity shield can help them to consider those choices now. At this point, each child receives a poster board on which a coat of arms or shield shape is outlined. The shield is divided into five sections. One section is assigned to mother, one to father, two to other significant people that the child designates, and the largest and lowest section is assigned to the child. Group members are then asked to consider which qualities in each person on their shield they most admire and would like to strive for as they go forward, and which qualities they would like to leave behind.

Once these questions have been considered and discussed, the children write or draw symbols of the qualities in each person that they have chosen to keep, within the appropriate section of the shield. They then draw or write the rejected qualities outside that section. The children sort out their own qualities in a similar fashion as they complete the self section. Finally, the shield shape is cut from the poster board, a process that leaves the chosen qualities intact while the discarded qualities fall away.

It is important for the leader to make clear to the children that the shield is not a prescription for "perfect" behavior. This would be neither realistic nor necessarily desirable. Rather, the shield represents an ideal, or moral compass, that can guide the children as they mature. The leader helps the children to avoid an overly simplistic and polarized ideal by encouraging them to find concrete and descriptive words for their shields.

With this in mind, we note that 10-year-old Jacob created a shield including his mother, father, grandmother, grandfather, and himself. His mother's section included the words "The way she supports me in what I want to do." Outside the section and excluded from the shield were the words "her smoking, fighting, and overprotectiveness." His father's section included "brains, mechanical ability, athletic ability," and excluded his "stubbornness and yelling." The grandfather's section included "warm, kind, fun, and neat to be around," and left out "slow to understand." Jacob included "warm, kind, and smart" in his grandmother's section and left "cooking and bad eating habits" on the periphery. Finally, from his own qualities, Jacob included "imagination, drawing abilities, good grades, and smartness"; he left out "hiding feelings, and shyness."

Talk Show Panels

In one of the final group sessions, children are given an opportunity to consolidate shifts in their understanding of roles, relationships, and rules of moral conduct by serving as an expert panel on families. The panel is videotaped and dramatized as a television talk show, with one child acting as host. Members of the panel give advice to children in high-conflict situations who send "letters" to the panel. The letters, developed by the leader, reflect specific concerns that have been identified by members during group sessions. The leader lends weight and seriousness to the task by explaining that many professional people (including counselors, judges, and lawyers) really want and need to hear the children, because they truly are experts at living in conflicted families. Letters for the panel might include the following types of questions: "Dear Expert: My mom is very mad at my dad and she says lots of mean things about him. This really hurts my feelings to have her talk about him in that way. I'm scared that if I say anything, she'll be mad at me. Is there anything I can do?" "Dear Expert: Sometimes I think that neither of my parents really wants me around. Got any ideas about that?"

Children whose issues are reflected in the question almost always choose to lead the panel in formulating a response. Typically, their answers urge the letter writer to consider the expectations being placed upon her and question whether these are fair and realistic for a child. The children also give advice about how to state clearly what is and is not a child's concern, as well as if, when, and how to talk to parents about difficult feelings. The groups generally respond to this work with a good deal of animation and intensity, and tend to require very little prompting from the leader. When the exercise is successful, it can generate a sense that the group has a shared sense of morality and competence that is particularly valuable for school-age children.

As children prepare to videotape their "panel of experts," they are also given opportunities to create and videotape commercial breaks for their talk show. Here, group participants tend to show enormous ingenuity in finding products in the group room to "sell." These can range from the pencils in their backpacks to the telephone on the desk. The nature of the product seems to be immaterial. What matters is the children's immense pleasure in cooperating to create a videotaped segment in a format they recognize and can address with the kind of irony and sardonic humor that typically emerges in this age group. This kind of play can be a powerful antidote to the intensity of the letter content that these "experts" must address. The play also consolidates the group's ability to affirm one another as competent and likable.

DRAMATIZING AND REVISING FAMILY ROLES, RELATIONSHIPS, AND RULES OF MORAL CONDUCT

Role Plays

Role playing is the central strategy in the group approach because it gives the children a constructive opportunity to act out their internal script. In so doing, the rules and expectations that support the script can be made conscious and accessible to revision. At the same time, feelings that have been bound in by the script can begin to surface as well. Children develop their perspective-taking capacities as they act out points of view other than their own. When this happens, they can begin to move beyond the subjectivity of their script toward a more normal pattern of interpersonal and moral understanding.

As with all the interventions in this group treatment model, the role-playing activity is structured to maximize the children's sense of safety and control. The leader begins by showing one of a series of stimulus pictures and asking whether the drawing reminds anyone in the group of something that happened to him or someone he knows. The stimulus pictures suggest situations that are common in high-conflict families. They are used to evoke the children's rules and expectations about what is right, fair, and expectable in relationships, as well as to jog memories of particular traumatic scenes they may need to work through. One picture, for example, shows a child being pulled by the mother on one side and the father on the other. The child in the middle appears to be stretched beyond endurance. In another, a child watches while a man and a woman argue. The man gestures threateningly at the woman with his fist, and the woman wags her finger angrily at the man.

Once a child volunteers a situation to role play, he or she is offered the role of director. As director, the child can exercise the kind of control she often needs to counteract the vulnerability embedded in the remembered experience. The director selects group members to play particular roles and gives the players their lines and positions. In addition, the director tells each player what his or her feelings are in the situation, as well as whether and how to show those feelings. The process of identifying feelings and associated behaviors for each player requires the child who is directing to move beyond the unconscious internal script. He or she has to articulate ideas about roles, relationships, and rules in a way that makes objective sense to others. Not surprisingly, this requires considerable facilitation by the leader, particularly in younger groups.

When the role play is complete, the leader asks the director for a revised version. For less constricted children, the revised version represents an opportunity to express long-held feelings, wishes, and fantasies about how relationships could or should be conducted. New strategies for conflict resolution may surface here as well. When the revised role play does reflect a higher standard of conduct than the first role play has shown, it is important for the leader to affirm what is fair and right in the revised version in a nonjudgmental way. The leader may say, for example, "You would like people in the family to talk to each other without swearing and cursing. That may be something that everyone in the first role play would also say they want to get better control of, when they have a chance to calm down."

Other children, who cannot tolerate too much self-awareness, tend to act out scripted solutions that help them avoid real perceptions, needs, and feelings entirely. When this happens, the leader can help the group to differentiate the kinds of solutions that reflect or manage feelings and the kinds of solutions that can be realistically and morally achieved in relationships. This kind of differentiation is particularly important when the revised role play contains fantasies of vengeful and empowering violence.

All the role plays are videotaped by a group member (the camera person of the day) and reviewed during snack time at the end of the session. Role playing, role switching, and video reviewing all provide the children with opportunities to experience and coordinate different and increasingly complex perspectives of the reenacted event. In so doing, the children gain an age-appropriate measure of distance and mastery.

―――――――

The following material illustrates the work of a child who had enough capacity to allow a shift from awareness to mastery within the context of his role play. Eleven-year-old Daniel was the object of a bitter custody battle that left both his parents furious and uncooperative in ways that often deprived their only son of their support and protection. Daniel tended to manage by intellectualizing most of his experience and avoiding any expression of his feelings. When the group was shown a stimulus picture of a child caught between two adults, Daniel chose to direct a scene involving a boy named Joshua: Joshua was at his father's house, and the father was busy at his desk. Suddenly, Joshua remembered that he had left his homework at his mother's house. In a panic, he asked his father to take him to get it. The father told Joshua that he was far too busy, and anyway, it was his mother's job to get his homework to him. Joshua then called his mother, who said she was too busy, also, and suggested that his father pick up the homework. Joshua ended up without his homework, feeling sad, angry, and worried about what would happen at school the next day. In the final scene, Joshua was at school. His teacher berated him about his homework as his classmates watched and giggled. Here, Daniel directed Joshua to act "embarrassed, and underneath you are furious!" This marked the end of the first role play.

At this point, the leader invited Daniel to recreate the role play according to his own wishes. In response, Daniel chose to role play the scene at school and took the part of the teacher himself. In this version, the teacher said to Joshua in a very angry tone, "This is not your fault, your parents are to blame. I want a conference with them!" Here, Daniel selected other group members to play the role of Joshua's parents. Daniel, still in the role of teacher, berated the parents furiously for putting their son in a terrible position.

Because Daniel was able to acknowledge his anger and mobilize his indignation, the leader used the videotape review to validate his feelings and perceptions about what was right and fair in the situation and to consider strategies for mastery. In the discussion, the leader invited the children to talk about what would happen if Daniel let his parents know how furious he really was. In flat tones that belied his pain, Daniel said he was sure that both his parents would not care much one way or the other if they knew his real feelings. The leader wondered gently whether Daniel had taught himself to avoid being hurt by their indifference by being indifferent as well. In this way, she identified both the *rule* (i.e., do not let your feelings matter to you) and the *expectation* (i.e., because they will not matter to others) that supported Daniel's script. Daniel, who tended to be verbose and argumentative, made no answer, except for making unusually direct eye contact with the leader. When the session was over, the leader asked for Daniel's permission to talk with his parents about the issues that had come up in the role play. After some planning about what to say and how to say it, Daniel acquiesced. The leader must choose an intervention based on an assessment of the needs and capacities of each individual group member and his or her family. In this case, the leader chose to follow up in the collateral work with the parents, because Daniel seemed prepared to focus on coping and because she knew that at least one of his parents had enough capacity to tolerate and respond to the feedback.

Nine-year-old Suzanne's role plays suggested a more serious and pervasive level of constriction. Her parents had been quietly unhappy before they separated, when she was 7. From that time on, Suzanne's father was uncharacteristically erratic in his behavior and on several occasions was physically abusive toward her mother. During individual sessions, when Suzanne was asked about her parents' separation and angry fights, she was quite passive and seemed unable to do anything but sift sand in an otherwise empty tray.

After five sessions in group, Suzanne was able to volunteer a revealing role play that she chose to direct and act out, playing herself. The role play began when a "very worried" Suzanne telephoned her mother because her father did not pick her up from school at the expected time. Suzanne's mother then arrived on the scene to take her home. A moment later, Suzanne's father arrived as well. The parents argued and the father, infuriated by the mother's interference, slapped the mother across the face. He then became upset and tried to apologize to the mother, who was crying. The mother yelled at him to leave her alone. This ended the first role play.

Suzanne could not tolerate any discussion of her own feelings in this role play but freely improvised a second role play in which she was Superwoman. In this role, Suzanne flew through the air, picked up her father, and deposited him in his own house. She then flew back to her mother, brushed her off, comforted her, and put her to bed. With this done, she flew off to her own activities and found her way back to her father's house when she was done. Superwoman/Suzanne needed no one. She could take care of herself and her parents with a power so great that it defied both gravity and reality.

This role play illustrates the unconscious scripted rules and expectations that defended Suzanne against her feelings of dependence, helplessness, and fear—specifically, that she could and should protect her mother, because she expected her mother to be too weak and vulnerable to protect her. At the same time, Suzanne could and should supervise her father, because he could not be expected to control himself. As is true for many girls in high-conflict families, Superwoman/Suzanne unconsciously believed that her undemanding goodness was the wellspring of her power. As long as these distorted perceptions and beliefs held sway, Suzanne could not move toward a more realistic understanding of herself, other people, and relationships.

When the group members discussed the video of Suzanne's role plays, her impossible predicament came sharply into focus. To provide support, the leader commented on Suzanne's bravery and effort. The leader also admired the second role play. Though she agreed that Suzanne would feel better if she could be powerful like Superwoman, she mused out loud that Superwoman might sometimes become very tired and maybe even a little irritated. Suzanne acknowledged that Superwoman did at times feel this way. The group then focused on what could, in fairness, be expected of most children and whether they could, in fact, manage and protect themselves and their parents. For Suzanne, this represented a beginning shift toward greater awareness of her own needs and feelings.

Without corresponding shifts in her family or extended opportunities for further working through, Suzanne's burgeoning awareness could lead only to anxiety or depression. In this case, the leader worked with both parents to help them understand their daughter's constriction and her underlying feelings of helplessness. She held follow-up sessions between Suzanne and her father, in which they developed written agreements about how he would express his anger in the future. She worked with the mother to mobilize her capacity to protect and nurture her daughter more effectively. The leader also recommended a period of individual work for Suzanne, who was a child with many miles yet to go.

These role-playing strategies can be adapted to individual work when children become directors of their own role plays using puppets, sandtray toys, and other symbolic figures. The clinician works to identify the child's script in much the same way as the leader works in group. At the same time, the individual treatment relationship allows the clinician to help the child bring the script to the surface more slowly and therefore more clearly and completely than was possible in the group work. Feelings that arise along the way can be worked through at whatever pace the child can tolerate. Finally, when the family is stabilized or when the child is strong enough, revisions of the rules and expectations that support the script can become the focus of dynamic as well as cognitive changes.

STRATEGIES FOR YOUNGER CHILDREN

While the group structure clearly fits the developmental needs of school-age children, we continue to explore the efficacy of a group approach for the preschool- and kindergarten-age range. In this section, we describe a number of activities that have been successfully used in clinical trials with 5- to 7-year-olds, which can also be adapted to individual treatment (Roseby, 1994). Some of these activities address issues that also concern school-age children, but in a different way. Others address the core developmental difficulty for these youngsters described at length in chapter 4, the struggle over psychological separation and the defensive good-mother-me/bad-mother-me split that results. In this defense, which is organized against fears of abandonment, the good-mother-me contains aspects of the self that mirror and soothe the primary parent without separating from him or her. Feelings that support autonomy or connection with the other parent are contained as aspects of the bad-mother-me. Over time, this defensive fragmentation mitigates against self-expression, authenticity, and agency in any relationship. It is the organizing heart of the rigid patterns of feeling, thinking, and perception that are targeted in the group interventions for school-age children.

Exploring the Language and Complexity of Feelings

In a variant of the color-feeling charts that the school-age groups use, the younger children work with a leader-prepared chart that shows six "feeling faces": happy, angry, surprised, sad, confused, and scared. The children learn the feeling word for each face and can then point to the face on the chart to communicate their feelings in subsequent group sessions. Using pictures and limiting the number of feelings helps the children become familiar with the strategy so that they can participate fully and with pleasure.

Group members are also given a set of 18 feeling faces of their own to explore gradations in levels of feeling. The 18 faces include three happy faces, one small, one medium, and one large; three angry faces, one small, one medium, and one large; and so on. An alternative or addition to the feeling faces is to have the children agree on an animal they associate with each of the six feelings. For example, a lion may be associated with 'angry,' while a mouse may be associated with 'scared.' These kinds of pictures are readily available in children's coloring books. They can be made into different sizes by using photocopy reduction and enlargement.

Once each child has a set of animals or faces, she cuts them out and, by attaching each one to a straw, ends up with 18 "feeling lollipops." These can be marked with a color that the child selects to identify his set. These sets of animals or faces are then used for feeling charades. For example, a child may hold a medium-size happy face on a feeling lollipop behind his back. The child charades the feeling, then asks the group to guess the feeling, as well as how much of the feeling he is depicting: small? medium? or large? After the group guesses, the child may show the feeling lollipop.

These sets of feelings may also be used to develop more complex feeling words. One little boy, for example, called a small lion "mad," a medium-sized lion "furious," and a large lion "guider furious" to express his different levels of feelings. Feeling lollipops can be proffered nonverbally to express feelings during group activities. They can also be used to identify feelings in others by allowing the children to offer them to puppets, who do most of the role playing for this age group.

Clarifying Fragmentation and Exploring Integration: Bunny and Koko Meet Max

These youngsters tend to be defensively organized around "good" and "bad" aspects of themselves and, not surprisingly, understand others in a similarly concrete and polarized way. This activity is designed to make the split more concrete so that the children can begin to work with the possibility of integration. The leader introduces the work by explaining that some children come to group and say that their own feelings are very, very small, even invisible (this is a reference to the good-mother-me that is undifferentiated from the primary other). Other children come to group and say that their feelings are so big that they feel like they have a "wild thing" inside. Sometimes their wild thing is secret, sometimes not (this is a reference to the bad-mother-me striving for autonomy and self-expression, often in a frighteningly exaggerated way). The leader then introduces the children to two new and permanent group members. These are Bunny, a pink-and-white rabbit puppet that represents the good-mother-me, and Koko, a gorilla puppet that represents the bad-mother-me. Once the children have met the puppets, the leader introduces a boy puppet who represents the integrating figure. He is Max, the hero of the children's book *Where the Wild Things Are*, by Maurice Sendak (1963).

The leader reads the book aloud, in which Max gets into trouble with his mother and is sent to his room. From there, he travels to where the wild things are, dancing and singing with the raucous yellow-eyed creatures until he is tired and longs for home. Although the creatures beg him to stay, Max looks them firmly in the eye and tells them "No!" He then sails home to his own room, where he finds his mother has left his supper, which is still hot. After the reading, the Bunny puppet is identified as one who *never* feels like a wild thing and the Koko puppet as one who *always* feels like a wild thing.

These three puppets—Bunny, Koko, and Max—anchor many of the subsequent group activities. In one session, for example, the leader stages an argument between Bunny and Koko about who is right and who is wrong. Bunny calls Koko a bad, wild creature. Koko calls Bunny a scaredy-cat. Max is called in to arbitrate and tells them, "It's not bad to have a lot of wild feelings, but it's not so good to keep them all inside. You have to do some of both. When I need to get wild, I have a lot of fun, like Koko. When I'm getting too wild, I calm my wild self down and then I want to be more like Bunny. I guess I'm like Koko *and* Bunny: I'm a bunmonkey!" (Roseby, 1994).

Mastering Separation

Because these younger children are fundamentally anxious about separation, it is essential to allow them to work through some of their fears about making transitions from one parent to the other. This is done through role plays the children conduct with the puppets, against a backdrop of poster board scenery that shows Mom's house, school, and Dad's house. Group members may select Max, Bunny, or Koko to express their changing feelings and possibilities for mastery at different points in the role play.

Six-year-old Catherine, for example, described how her mother woke her up and told her it was her day to go to Dad's house. She used Koko here, because she felt furious and stubborn about having to make this visit in midweek. Catherine also used Koko at school, because she got into trouble all that day. However, she used Bunny at Dad's house, because she was scared to tell her father that she had gotten into trouble at school. The leader then used Max to explore how a bunmonkey might make the transition. Interestingly, Catherine herself provided some affirmation about the possibilities for integration that might come from this kind of work. While the leader was working with Max, she spontaneously began to stuff Koko's backpack with feeling faces. When the leader asked her about this, she said, "Well, this is how Koko could borrow a bit from Bunny, and he wouldn't scare himself so much—you know, like Max, a bit of both." With this possibility established, this child was able to revise the role play, using Max to talk through feelings that Koko had acted out in ways that felt both frightening and uncontrolled.

These younger children tend to respond to these and other activities involving Bunny, Koko, and Max in ways that suggest the puppets do capture essential aspects of the child's experience. Representing the fragmentation and integration so that they are both concrete and compelling seems to be a key ingredient in reaching younger children.

PSYCHOEDUCATIONAL GROUPS FOR PARENTS

The lasting value of children's experiences in groups depends in large part on the effectiveness of collateral work with their parents. Here, the goals are to heighten the parents' capacity to perceive and respond to their children's needs, separately from their own, and to enhance their motivation to make decisions and agreements that will protect the children from further conflict. These goals can be addressed quite effectively when the children's group leader also convenes psychoeducational groups for parents at intervals during the program.

In this format, the leader can provide the parents with information about the effects of conflict in general and then translate these general issues to the more specific concerns of individual children. In a sense, these meetings resemble group parent-teacher conferences in which the teacher (leader) describes the curriculum as it pertains to the needs of the class (group) and then focuses on the strengths and weaknesses of the individual student. In the psychoeducational group, as in the parent-teacher conference, the leader's direct experience of the child makes him or her credible to the parent. We emphasize that, in this dual role, it is important for the leader to protect the child's confidentiality. This means the leader is free to discuss his or her impressions of the child's needs, concerns, and coping style, but does not directly quote the child or share writings or drawings produced in group, without the child's permission.

Psychoeducational group meetings are convened at the beginning, in the middle, and toward the end of the children's 10-week program. To maximize parents' attendance, the meetings are scheduled to follow the children's sessions, and child care is provided. Scheduling also permits highly conflicted parents to participate separately. A child's father, for example, might attend parent group meetings scheduled for the first, fifth, and ninth week of the program, while the child's mother might attend during the second, sixth, and tenth week.

The work begins with education. Here, the leader establishes the commonality of the parents' experiences with chronic conflict and provides information about its effects on children in general. A working metaphor can provide an effective framework for understanding. For example, the child's sense of self can be likened to a tapestry that cannot be woven into a whole design without the horizontal (mother) and vertical (father) strands to hold it in place. Even when one or both kinds of strands are of poor quality, they cannot be ripped away without unraveling the whole design. Always, it is the whole design that must be strengthened.

Once this kind of a working frame of reference is in place, the leader describes subtle signs of distress in children of different ages and explains why some youngsters seem to show no signs at all. This explanation focuses on how children learn to "keep from unraveling inside" by becoming guarded and overcontrolled in their efforts to maintain appearances and predict what will be required of them. Here, the leader particularly emphasizes the ways in which children's efforts to achieve safety and control can leave them feeling as if they are not completely real, and unable to form authentic relationships with anyone.

With this information on the table, the leader can begin to help parents understand how these coping efforts can undermine children's self-esteem and limit their ability to mature in their understanding of themselves, other people, and relationships. This provides a foundation for explaining how a working agreement between parents can support the children by releasing them from loyalty binds and providing them with a predictable environment that will protect their involvement in life beyond the conflict and outside the family.

Once the leader has communicated these general points, the individual children become the focus of discussion. The leader frames his or her comments as observations, which the parent is invited to confirm or interpret differently. In discussing a child's need to maintain appearances, for example, the leader may say, "I've noticed that both Jane [your daughter] and John [your son] try really hard to get things perfectly right. It seems as if it's hard for them to take risks. For instance, one of them had trouble making a drawing without using a ruler and lots of erasing. I wonder if it's hard for them to make mistakes. Do you [the parent] notice this in your child? What do you make of it?"

This approach can help the parent focus on the child without undermining her parental authority or competence in the group. Parents' responses to these kinds of questions often lead to discussions of the causes of the child's difficulties. Some parents begin to see themselves and their role in the conflict more clearly when they recognize themselves in others' points of view. Others benefit from feedback that group members provide with the kind of directness and authority that comes from shared experience. When this happens, it is the leader's responsibility to maintain a safe and constructive tone in the group discussion.

Throughout the parent meetings, the leader also helps the parents to anticipate and support the kinds of changes taking place in the children as they work in group. This is particularly important, because a number of children do become more curious, assertive, and even rebellious as they find their own voice. These shifts can be difficult for parents to tolerate and manage appropriately, without information and direction from the group leader.

For some parents, their experiences in the psychoeducational group are enough to leverage their disengagement from the conflict and their commitment to developing and honoring coparenting agreements. This kind of outcome depends on the capacity of the parents to assimilate information about their child as an individual and to gain insight into their own role in the conflict. More vulnerable parents generally benefit in a more circumscribed way, achieving (though not always maintaining) a limited degree of insight and a conceptual framework for understanding conflict and its effects. This framework can become the foundation for additional work in therapeutic group mediation (see Johnston and Campbell, 1988, for a more extensive description of this approach) or in individual sessions.

A NOTE ON SERVICE DELIVERY

These group approaches for children and families can reach the broadest range of children, in a cost-effective manner, when they are offered in easily accessible and familiar settings such as schools, after-school programs, or neighborhood centers. This kind of service delivery represents a departure from traditional clinic-based approaches and presents new opportunities for cooperation among the professionals both outside and within the service site. In some collaborative models, professionals from a mental health agency may provide the services directly. In other cases, mental health professionals who have experience with the group model may train on-site clinicians to run the groups themselves. Bringing services to the children's own communities may go some way toward repairing their damaged trust in the power of connection.

Guidelines for Initial Assessment of High-Conflict Divorcing Families

GUIDELINES FOR PARENTS' ASSESSMENT

I. *General Impressions*

Appearance, behavior, ways of relating to interviewer; who referred; major concern in coming for service. In recording interviews, use the client's own words and describe nonverbal behavior as much as possible.

II. *Dispute-Specific Assessment of Family*

a. Describe issues between parents under dispute, length of dispute, precipitating factors, and attempts at solution. Include the stage of property and financial settlement.

b. Describe role of stepparent (and significant others, including extended kin, friends, therapists, attorneys) in agitating, moderating, or resolving interparental disputes.

c. Describe role of child in the interparental disputes. Include child's reactions to witnessing conflict/violence, child's understanding of content of conflict, child's involvement in conflict, or attempts at resolution. How central is this child in the parental disputes?

d. If relevant, describe a typical incident of physical violence between parents. Note precipitating factors (if any): who initiated first act of violence; response of the partner; escalation (if any); presence of third party (especially children); physical and emotional consequences; calls for help and response of third party. Note especially involvement of drugs and alcohol by either party to the violence.

III. Historical Material

- Socioeconomic status and background; occupational and economic history
- Ethnic background of parents
- Maternal and paternal history
- Family constellation with sibling series and position; significant losses; grandparents' marital history
- How parent sees own childhood; the best and most difficult times; significant relations with siblings; major pertinent events and illnesses; note especially any history of violence between parents and history of child abuse
- School and social adjustment, extracurricular activities, friendships, dating
- Work history
- Psychiatric history, therapy, hospitalizations, etc.; any evidence of long-standing psychological illness or acute exacerbation of symptoms immediately prior to or since separation
- Marital history
- Previous marriages or extended liaisons
- Premarital or extramarital pregnancies
- Courtship: How parents met, length of courtship, reasons for marriage and expectations
- Age of each parent at marriage; at birth of first child
- Course of marriage; sexual adjustment; separations; sources of conflict and of gratification; major events and stresses, including work history and any significant shifts

IV. Divorce History

- Events leading to marital failure; when and why did marriage begin to fail? Was there a third party? Intensity of conflicts; how much physical violence?

- Emotional response—parents and children, any significant others; how and what children were told; how spouses prepared each other for separation; circumstances of separation; child's understanding of situation
- Parents' central affective response to the divorce experience; psychological consequences of separation
- Major defenses and coping mechanisms mobilized by each parent (separately or in alignment with one or more children)
- Who actually made the decision to separate; who filed the petition of dissolution

V. Description of Child and Child History

- Pregnancy
- Attitudes to becoming pregnant; history of miscarriages, etc.
- Parental reactions and neonatal history; child's early temperament.
- Parental practices—recreations, leisure, disciplines, closeness, etc. General parenting role—who did what; was there a primary parent?
- Special stresses—birth or death or separation (before this separation) from a parent, grandparent, or sibling; moving.
- History of illnesses and accidents
- Hospitalizations and/or surgery: age, how long in hospital, reaction to the hospital experience
- Congenital conditions, medication
- School history
- Age began kindergarten
- Reactions to leaving home, any school phobia
- Grades skipped or repeated
- Academic performance—special learning difficulties
- Adjustment to teacher, peers, group (especially reactions to conflict situation)
- Ability to work independently
- Special behavior problems, acting-out, truancy
- Difficulty doing homework and how handled
- Extracurricular activities
- Changes since separation/divorce
- What behavioral changes have occurred?
- What attitudinal changes have occurred?
- What emotional/psychological changes have occurred?

VI. Assessment of Parenting Ability

- What is parent's attitude/feelings for child (e.g., guilt, resentment)? Any particular psychological meaning of child to parent?
- What is the style of the overt relationship with the child (e.g., conflict-laden, cooperative, distant, warm)?
- What is the quality of the more unconscious relationship (e.g., identification with child, needs child for scapegoat, for nurturance)?
- To what degree does parent cognitively understand child's needs? Comment on perceived and real understanding.
- To what extent is parent sensitive to child's needs (e.g., intuitive understanding, actual awareness of needs, real and perceived)?
- What is parent's ability to cope with child's needs, real and perceived?
- What is parent's usual style of coping with child demands (e.g., avoid, deflect, ignore, punish, impatience, desperation)?
- Overall estimate of parenting; characterize type/style of parenting (e.g., benign neglect, overprotective, "good enough," very competent, loving, etc.)
- Critical incidents. Please note reported or suspected child abuse, physical, psychological, sexual, incest, etc.

VII. Assessment of Parent-Parent Relationship

- What are the feelings of each parent for the other (e.g., bitterness, rage, mixed)?
- How intense are these feelings?
- Amount of parental friction/fighting/hostility/conflict?
- Resolution of the divorce/disputes
- To what extent does parent still think/obsess about the marriage/divorce/spouse? How much yearning for past?
- Estimate how resolved feelings are for spouse.
- To what extent does parent yearn to be married; to remarry?
- To what extent has parent established a separate life (e.g., new friends, new relationships, job, education, hobbies, etc.)?
- Estimate of amount of contact/communication between parents
- What is the content of this communication (e.g., child issues only; child issues/ex-spouse's family/discuss their feelings for each other; whether they have sexual relations)?
- Critical incidents. Please note any present actual or threatened physical violence, instances of abuse, etc.

VIII. Current Environment and Family Situation

- Composition of immediate and extended family: who is living with whom, and where
- Work situation; financial situation
- Physical setting—home and neighborhood—note changes and social mobility
- Sleeping arrangements
- Custody and visitation arrangements
- How were these arrived at?
- Child's reactions to going to and returning from each parent's home
- Visiting and its ambiance, routines, discipline, etc.
- Sibling relationships
- Family activities: as a family; degree of social isolation or contact with the community
- Extent of external supports—extended families, social contacts, etc., for parents and children

GUIDELINES FOR CHILD ASSESSMENT

I. General Impressions

- General topics discussed
- Affect expression and control during interview
- Subjective response to child
- What did the child talk about?
- What did the child play with (e.g., drew, then played with dolls)?
- What was the content of the child's play or fantasy expression (e.g., created family of four with dolls and had them go through a normal day, with one little girl doll getting into trouble and getting punished by mother doll; with father doll disagreeing but doing nothing; or drew pictures of brightly colored butterflies, etc.)?
- What was the central fantasy theme and/or preoccupation of the play or of what child talked about?
- What was the style of the play or verbal communication (e.g., obsessive, repetitious, scattered, intense/concentrated, joyous, etc.)?
- Three wishes: What did child say and/or do, and how did he or she react?
- What was the child's predominate mood in the session (e.g., unhappy, needy, wistful, anxious)?

- What affect was expressed/observed in the session, and how intense was it (e.g., anger, fear, worry, love)?
- How was the affect expressed or reflected (e.g., child threw animal; or in the drawings; or little girl doll expressed verbally, etc.)?
- To what or whom was the affect directed?
- How much control does the child show/feel re expression of affect (e.g., out of control, wild, desperate; anger is tightly controlled; child in control of affect; uses to manipulate parent, etc.)?
- Conscious awareness of loneliness, pain, anxiety in self, siblings, and parent

II. Specific Reactions to the Divorce/Parental Disputes/Abduction

- Child's response to and experience with the separation/divorce/abduction (from child's viewpoint)
- Affective response; thoughts, fantasies, and behavioral responses
- Child's understanding of the separation/divorce; how child understands the various or conflicting explanations; private ideas regarding divorce/abduction
- Child's perception of marriage; relationship to parents over course of time prior to separation
- Guilt or fantasied responsibility regarding causing divorce/parental disputes/abduction; degree of relief or anguish over separation from and reunion with parent; any fantasies or statements indicating physical or sexual abuse prior or subsequent to parental separation/abduction
- Child's response to conflict and violence:
- Child's understanding of parents' disputes and memory of violent incidents
- Emotional and behavioral responses to discussing parental discord/violence (amount of denial, avoidance, anxiety, anger; assignment of blame; use of fantasy)

III. Child's Relationship with Parents and Others

- Quality of attachment to both parents:
- Specific material regarding loyalty conflicts/temporary or ongoing allegiances; avoidance of preferences
- Current relationships with each parent, siblings; any unusual alignments or special conflicts

- Empathy for parent; to what extent does this child feel parented?
- Child's response to parent's distress or psychopathology
- Supportive figures and activities currently available and used; degree to which child has turned for support to extrafamilial figures, particularly teachers and peers; relationships with grandparents and other extended family members

IV. Child's Reactions to Current Visiting/Custody Arrangements

- Visitation or custody patterns as perceived by the child; child's desires regarding custody and visitation
- Ambiance of the home (or homes) as perceived by the child; response to custodial parent working outside the home; availability of the parent(s) psychologically; which parent child perceives as supportive; reversal of roles with parent

V. Coping and Symptomatology

- Defensive and adaptive resources employed to deal with stress; coping strategies
- Changes or presence of acute symptomatology; exacerbation or return of chronic symptoms; evidence of regression
- Premature sexual activity; pseudomaturity; drug/alcohol use; delinquent behavior

VI. Child's Attitudes and Participation at School, with Peers, and in Extracurricular Activities

- From child's perspective, how well he or she gets on with peers; how many friends; pride in school/sports achievements and pleasure from participation

FORMULATION OF THE IMPASSE AND ITS IMPACT ON THE CHILD

- What prevents the family from settling the dispute?
- *External Components*—e.g., extended family, significant other, and legal provocation of the dispute; economic hardship or sociocultural factors that help lock the impasse
- *Interactional Components*—e.g., polarized, negative images of the ex-spouse; ambivalence about separation; special psychological signif-

icance of child; adaptive and defensive use of each other, which creates the impasse

- *Individual Components*—e.g., intrapsychic conflicts and needs of individual members, psychopathology; or special needs of the child (such as illness or disability)
- What is the impact of the dispute and the impasse on the child? Evaluate to what extent the dispute and the impasse are related to child's symptomatology; assess the potential effects on the child's development if the dispute/impasse is not resolved
- What strengths and resources are available within the family and their social system to help resolve the dilemma (e.g., relevant parenting capacities, availability of others, capacities of the child, etc., and the possibility of mobilizing these)?

References

Abelin, E. (1975). Some further observations and comments on the earliest role of the father. *International Journal of Psychoanalysis, 56*, 293–302.

Abromovitch, R., Jenkins, J., & Peterson-Badali, M. (1994, July). Evaluation of the supervised access pilot project. Study prepared for the Ministry of the Attorney-General, Toronto, Ontario, Canada.

Acredelo, L., & Goodwyn, S. (1996). *How to talk to your baby before your baby can talk.* Chicago: Contemporary Books.

Ahrons, C. R. (1994). *The good divorce: Keeping your family together when your marriage comes apart.* New York: Harper Perennial.

American Psychological Association (APA) (1992). Ethical principles of psychologists & codes of conduct. *American Psychologist, 47*, 1597–1611.

American Psychological Association (APA) (1994). Guidelines for child custody evaluations in divorce proceedings. *American Psychologist, 49*, 677–680.

Anthony, E. J., & Cohler, B. J. (1987). *The invulnerable child.* New York: Guilford Press.

Arbuthnot, J., & Gordon, D. A. (1996). Does mandatory divorce education for parents work? *Family & Conciliation Courts Review, 34*, 60–81.

Ash, P., & Guyer, M. J. (1986a). Child psychiatry and the law: The functions of psychiatric evaluation in contested custody and visitation cases. *Journal of the American Academy of Child Psychiatry, 25*, 554–561.

Ash, P., & Guyer, M. J. (1986b). Relitigation after contested custody and visitation evaluations. *Bulletin of the American Academy of Psychiatry and the Law, 14*, 323–330.

Association of Family & Conciliation Courts (AFCC) (1994). *Model standards of practice for custody evaluations.* Madison, WI: AFCC.

Baumrind, D. H. (1971). Harmonious parents and their preschool children. *Developmental Psychology, 4*, 99–102.

Baumrind, D. H. (1978). Parental disciplinary patterns and social competence in children. *Youth & Society, 9*, 239–276.

Berger, J. (1988). Directions in expectation states research. In M. Webster, Jr., & M. Foschi (Eds.), *Status generalization: New theory and research* (pp. 450–476). Stanford, CA: Stanford University Press.

Berk, R. A., Berk, S. F., Loseke, D. R., & Rauma, D. (1983). Mutual combat and other family violence myths. In D. Finkelhor, R. J. Gelles, G. T. Hotaling, & M. A. Straus

(Eds.), *The dark side of families: Current family violence research* (pp. 197–212). Beverly Hills, CA: Sage Publishing Co.

Bibring, E. (1961). The mechanism of depression. In P. Greenacre (Ed.), *Affective Disorders* (pp. 13–48). New York: International Universities Press.

Blaisure, K. R., & Geasler, M. J. (1996). Results of a survey of court-connected parent education. *Family & Conciliation Courts Review, 34,* 23–40.

Blos, P. (1967). The second individuation process of adolescence. *Psychoanalytic Study of the Child, 22,* 162–187.

Blos, P. (1970). *The young adolescent.* New York: Free Press.

Bolen, R. (1993). Kids' turn: Helping kids cope with divorce. *Family & Conciliation Courts Review, 31,* 249–254.

Bowlby, J. (1969). *Attachment and loss, vol. 1: Attachment.* New York: Basic Books.

Bowlby, J. (1973). *Attachment and loss, vol. 2: Separation.* New York: Basic Books.

Bowlby, J. (1980). *Attachment and loss, vol. 3: Loss, sadness and depression.* New York: Basic Books.

Braver, S. L., Salem, P., Pearson, J., & DeLuise, S. R. (1996). The content of divorce education programs: Results of a survey. *Family & Conciliation Courts Review, 34,* 41–59.

Bretherton, I., Ridgeway, D., & Cassidy, J. (1990). Assessing internal working models of the attachment relationship. In M. Greenberg, D. Cicchetti, & E. M. Cummings (Eds.), *Attachment during the preschool years: Theory, research and intervention* (pp. 273–308). Chicago: University of Chicago Press.

Brown, M. W. (1942). *The runaway bunny.* New York: Harper & Row.

Burgner, M., & Edgcombe, R. (1972). Some problems in the conceptualization of early object relationships: Part II: The concept of object constancy. In R. S. Eisler, A. Freud, M. Kris, & A. J. Solnit (Eds.), *The psychoanalytic study of the child, vol. 27,* pp. 315–333. New York: Quadrangle Books.

Bushman, B. J., & Cooper, H. M. (1990). Effects of alcohol on human aggression: An integrated approach. *Psychological Bulletin, 107,* 341–354.

Carlson, B. E. (1984). Children's observations of interparental violence. In A. R. Roberts (Ed.), *Battered women and their families* (pp. 147–167). New York: Springer.

Cath, S. H., Gurwitt, A. R., & Ross, J. M. (Eds.) (1982). *Father and child: Developmental and clinical perspectives.* New York: Basil Blackwell.

Clewar, S., & Riven, B. (1991). *Children held hostage: Dealing with programmed and brainwashed children.* Chicago: American Bar Association.

Coates, S. (1990). Ontogenesis of boyhood gender identity disorder. *Journal of the American Academy of Psychoanalysis, 18,* 414–438.

Davies, P. T., & Cummings, E. M. (1994). Marital conflict and child adjustment: An emotional security hypothesis. *Psychological Bulletin, 116,* 387–411.

Dell, P. F. (1989). Violence and the systemic view: The problem of power. *Family Process, 28,* 1–14.

Depner, C. E. (1993). *Research update document E: Highlights from the 1991 California family court services snapshot study.* State-wide Office of Family Court Services, Administrative Office of the Courts, San Francisco, CA.

Depner, C. E., Cannata, K., & Ricci, I. (1994). Client evaluations of mediation services: The impact of case characteristics and mediation service models. *Family & Conciliation Courts Review, 32,* 306–325.

Depner, C. E., Cannata, K. V., & Simon, M. B. (1992). Building a uniform statistical reporting system: A snapshot of California family court services. *Family & Conciliation Courts Review, 30,* 185–206.

Deutsch, H. (1945). *The psychology of women, Vols. I & II.* New York: Grune & Stratton.

DiBias, L. (1996). Some programs for children. *Family & Conciliation Courts Review, 34,* 112–129.

Dobash, R. E., & Dobash, R. (1979). *Violence against wives.* New York: Free Press.

Dodge, K. A., Bates, J. E., & Petit, G. S. (1990). Mechanisms in the cycle of violence. *Science, 250,* 1678–1683.

Dodge, K. A., & Somberg, D. R. (1987). Hostile attributional biases among aggressive boys are exacerbated under conditions of threat to the self. *Child Development, 58,* 213–224.

Duryee, M. A. (1991). *Demographic and outcome data of a court mediation program.* Final report to the State-wide Office of Family Court Services, Judicial Council of California, San Francisco, CA.

Duryee, M. A. (1992). Mandatory court mediation: Demographic summary and consumer evaluation of one court service: Executive summary. *Family & Conciliation Courts Review, 30,* 260–267.

Duryee, M. A. (1995). Guidelines for family court services intervention when there are allegations of domestic violence. *Family & Conciliation Courts Review, 33,* 79–86.

Edgecombe, R. (1976). Some comments on the negative oedipal phase in girls. *Psychoanalytic Study of the Child, 31,* 35–61.

Edwards, L. (1993). A comprehensive approach to the representation of children: The child advocacy coordinating council. *Family Law Quarterly, 27,* 417–431.

Egeland, B., Jacobvitz, D., & Papatola, K. (1987). Intergenerational continuity of parental abuse. In J. Lancaster & R. Gelles (Eds.), *Biosocial aspects of child abuse.* New York: Jossey-Bass.

Egeland, B. Jacobvitz, D., & Sroufe, L. A. (1988). Breaking the cycle of abuse. *Child Development, 59,* 1080–1088.

Ehrenberg, M. F., Hunter, M. A., & Elterman, M. F. (1996). Shared parenting agreements after marital separation: The roles of empathy & narcissism. *Journal of Consulting & Clinical Psychology, 64*(4), 808–818.

Eissler, K. (1958). Notes on problems of technique in the psychoanalytic treatment of adolescents: With some remarks on perversions. *Psychoanalytic Study of the Child, 15,* 223–254.

Elkind, D. (1967). Egocentrism in adolescence. *Child Development, 38,* 1025–1034.

Emery, R. E. (1988). *Marriage, divorce and children's adjustment.* Newbury Park, CA: Sage Publishing Co.

Emery, R. E. (1994). *Renegotiating family relationships: Divorce, child custody and mediation.* New York: Guilford Press.

Erikson, E. H. (1963). *Childhood and society.* New York: Norton.

Esman, A. (1989). Borderline personality disorders in adolescents: Current concepts. *Adolescent Psychiatry, 16,* 319–336.

Exner, Jr., J. E. (1990). *A Rorschach workbook for the comprehensive system,* 3rd edition. Asheville, NC: Rorschach Workshops.

Exner, Jr., J. E., & Weiner, I. B. (1982). *The Rorschach: A comprehensive system, Vol. 3: Assessment of children and adolescents.* New York: Wiley.

Fast, Irene (1979). Development in gender identity: Gender differentiation in girls. *International Journal of Psychoanalysis, 60,* 443–453.

Fast, Irene (1984). *Gender identity: A differentiation model.* Hillsdale, NJ: Analytic Press.

Fast, Irene (1990). Aspects of early gender development: Toward a reformulation. *Psychoanalytic Psychology, 7* (suppl.), 105–117.

Flavell, J. H., Fry, C., Wright, J., & Jarvis, P. (1968). *The development of role-taking and communication skills in children.* New York: Wiley.

Folberg, J., & Taylor, A. (1984). *Mediation: A comprehensive guide to resolving conflicts without litigation.* San Francisco: Jossey-Bass.

Freud, A. (1958). Adolescence. *Psychoanalytic Study of the Child, 13,* 255–278.

Gardner, R. A. (1987). *The parental alienation syndrome and the differentiation between fabricated and genuine child sex abuse.* Creskill, NJ: Creative Therapeutics.

Gardner, R. A. (1992). *The parental alienation syndrome.* Creskill, NJ: Creative Therapeutics.

Garrity, C. B., & Baris, M. A. (1994). *Caught in the middle: Protecting the children of high-conflict divorce.* New York: Lexington Books.

Germane, C., Johnson, M., & Leman, N. (1985). Mandatory custody mediation and joint custody orders in California: The danger for victims of domestic violence. *Berkeley Women's Law Journal, 1*(1), 175–200.

Giles-Sims, J. (1983). *Wife battering: A systems theory approach.* New York: Guilford Press.

Gilligan, C. (1982). *In a different voice: Psychology theory and women's development.* Cambridge, MA: Harvard University Press.

Gilman, I. S. (1980). An object-relations' approach to the phenomenon and treatment of battered women. *Psychiatry, 43,* 346–358.

Girdner, L. (Ed.) (1990). Mediation and spousal abuse. Special issue of *Mediation Quarterly,* 7(4).

Glick, P. C. (1988). The role of divorce in the changing family structure: Trends and variations. In S. A. Wolchik & P. Varody (Eds.), *Children of divorce: Empirical perspectives on adjustment* (pp. 3–34). New York: Gardner Press.

Gordon, D. E. (1988). Formal operations and interpersonal and affective disturbances in adolescence. In E. D. Nannis & P. A. Cowan (Eds.), *Developmental psychopathology and its treatment: New directions for child development.* San Francisco: Jossey-Bass.

Greif, G. L., & Hegar, R. L. (1993). *When parents kidnap: The families behind the headlines.* New York: Free Press.

Grillo, T. (1991). The mediation alternative: Process dangers for women. *Yale Law Journal, 100* (April), 1545–1610.

Hanks, S. (1992). Translating theory into practice: A conceptual framework for clinical assessment, differential diagnosis and multimodal treatment of maritally violent individuals, couples and families. In E. Veino (Ed.), *Intimate violence,* pp. 157–176. Washington, DC: Hemisphere Publications.

Hauser, B. B., & Straus, R. B. (1991, March). Legal and psychological dimensions of joint & sole custody agreements. Paper presented at the 68th Annual Meeting of the American Orthopsychiatric Association, Toronto.

Hauser, S. L. (1991). *Adolescents and their families.* New York: Free Press.

Hedges, L. E. (1994). *Remembering, repeating and working through childhood traumas.* Northvale, NJ: Jason Aronson.

Hess, P., Minton, G., Moelhman, A., & Petts, G. (1992). The family connection center: An innovative visiting program. *Child Welfare, 71,* 77–88.

Hetherington, E. M. (1972). Effects of father absence on personality development in adolescent daughters. *Developmental Psychology, 7*(3), 313–326.

Hetherington, E. M., Cox, M., & Cox, R. (1982). Effects of divorce on parents and children. In M. E. Lamb (Ed.), *Nontraditional families* (pp. 223–288). Hillsdale, NJ: Lawrence Erlbaum Associates.

Hewitt, S. K. (1991). Therapeutic management of preschool cases of alleged but unsubstantiated sexual abuse. *Child Welfare, 70*(1), 59–67.

Hodges, W. F. (1991). *Interventions for children of divorce: Custody access and psychotherapy*, 2nd edition. New York: Wiley.

Hoppe, C. F., & Kenney, L. M. (1994, August). A Rorschach study of the psychological characteristics of parents engaged in child custody/visitation disputes. Paper presented at the 102nd Annual Convention of the American Psychological Association, Los Angeles.

Horney, K. (1967). *Feminine psychology.* New York: Norton.

Hysjulien, C., Wood, B., & Benjamin, G. A. H. (1994). Child custody evaluations: A review of methods used in litigation and alternative dispute resolution. *Family & Conciliation Courts Review, 32*, 466–489.

Jaffe, P., Wolfe, D., & Wilson, S. (1990). Children of battered women. *Developmental clinical psychology and psychiatry, vol. 21.* Newbury Park CA: Sage Publishing Co.

James, B., & Gibson, C. (1991). Supervising visits between parent and child. *Family & Conciliation Courts Review, 29*, 73–84.

Johnston, J. R. (1992a). *High-conflict and violent parents in family court: Findings on children's adjustment and proposed guidelines for the resolution of disputed custody and visitation.* Final report to the Judicial Council of the State of California (Grant #891826), San Francisco, CA.

Johnston, J. R. (1993a). Children of divorce who refuse visitation. In J. H. Bray & C. Depner (Eds.), *Nonresidential parenting: New vistas for family living* (pp. 109–135). Newbury Park, CA: Sage Publishing Co.

Johnston, J. R. (1993b). *Developing preventive interventions for children of severe family conflict and violence: A comparison of three models.* Technical Report of the Center for the Family in Transition, Corte Madera, CA.

Johnston, J. R. (1994b). *Prevention of parent or family abduction through early identification of risk factors. Stage I, Part B.* Final report to the Office of Juvenile Justice & Delinquency Prevention, Department of Justice, Washington, DC.

Johnston, J. R. (1996). *Prevention of parent or family abduction of children through early identification of risk factors. Stage II, Part B.* Final Report to the Office of Juvenile Justice & Delinquency Prevention, Department of Justice, Washington, DC.

Johnston, J. R., & Campbell, L. E. G. (1988). *Impasses of divorce: The dynamics and resolution of family conflict.* New York: Free Press.

Johnston, J. R., & Campbell, L. E. G. (1993a). A clinical typology of interparental violence in disputed custody divorces. *American Journal of Orthopsychiatry, 63*, 190–199.

Johnston, J. R., & Campbell, L. E. G. (1993b). Parent–child relationships in domestic violence families disputing custody. *Family & Conciliation Courts Review, 31*, 282–298.

Johnston, J. R., & Coysh, W. S. (1988). *Evaluation of preventive services for divorcing families. Part I: Parents' functioning; Part II: Children's functioning.* Technical Report of the Center for the Family in Transition, Corte Madera, CA.

Johnston, J. R., Gonzalez, R., & Campbell, L. E. G. (1987). Ongoing post-divorce conflict and child disturbance. *Journal of Abnormal Child Psychology, 15*, 493–509.

Johnston, T. (1994). *Summary of research on the decrease of court involvement after the appointment of a special master.* Paper presented at the Special Masters Training Conference, Palo Alto, CA.

Jordan, J. V. (1993). The relational self: Implications for adolescent development. In S. C. Feinstein (Ed.), *Adolescent Psychiatry* (pp. 228–239). Chicago: University of Chicago Press.

Kagan, J., & Lamb, S. (Eds.) (1987). *The emergence of morality in young children.* Chicago: University of Chicago Press.

Kalmuss, D. (1984). The intergenerational transmission of marital aggression. *Journal of Marriage & the Family, 46,* 11–19.

Kalter, N. (1977). Children of divorce in an outpatient psychiatric population. *American Journal of Orthopsychiatry, 47,* 40–51.

Kalter, N. (1990). *Growing up with divorce: Helping your child avoid immediate and later emotional problems.* New York: Free Press.

Kalter, N., Riemer, B., Brickman, A., & Chen, J. (1985). Implications of parental divorce for female development. *Journal of American Academy of Child Psychiatry, 24*(5), 538–544.

Kaufman, J., & Zigler, E. (1987). Do abused children become abusive parents? *American Journal of Orthopsychiatry, 57,* 186–192.

Kegan, R. (1982). *The evolving self: Problem and process in human development.* Cambridge, MA: Harvard University Press.

Kelly, J. B. (1983). Mediation and psychotherapy: Distinguishing the differences. *Mediation Quarterly, 1,* 33–44.

Kelly, J. B. (1996). A decade of divorce mediation research: Some answers and questions. *Family & Conciliation Courts Review, 34,* 373–385.

Kelly, J. B., & Gigy, L. (1989). Divorce mediation: Characteristics of clients and outcomes. In K. Kressel, D. Pruitt, & Associates (Eds.), *Mediation research: The process and effectiveness of third-party intervention,* pp. 263–299. San Francisco: Jossey-Bass.

Kernberg, O. (1976). *Object relations theory and clinical psychoanalysis.* New York: Jacob Aronson.

Kibler, S., Sanchez, E., & Baker-Jackson, M. (1994). Pre-contempt/contemnors group diversion counseling program: A program to address parental frustration of custody and visitation orders. *Family & Conciliation Courts Review, 32,* 62–71.

King, D. B. (1993). Accentuate the positive—Eliminate the negative. *Family & Conciliation Courts Review, 31,* 9–28.

Kirkpatrick, M. (1990). Thoughts about the origins of femininity. *Journal of the American Academy of Psychoanalysis, 18*(4), 554–565.

Kline, M., Johnston, J. R., & Tschann, J. M. (1991). The long shadow of marital conflict. *Journal of Marriage & the Family, 53,* 297–309.

Kohlberg, L. (1981). *The philosophy of moral development.* San Francisco: Harper & Row.

Kohut, H. (1977). *The restoration of self.* Madison, CT: International Universities Press.

Kohut, H., & Wolf, E. S. (1978). The disorders of self and their treatment. *International Journal of Psychoanalysis, 59,* 413–424.

Kressel, K., Jaffe, N., Tuchman, B., Watson, C., & Deutsch, M. (1980). A typology of divorcing couples: Implications for mediation and the divorce process. *Family Process, 19,* 101–116.

Lampel, A. K. (1996). Children's alignment with parents in highly conflicted custody cases. *Family & Conciliation Courts Review, 34,* 229–239.

Lapsley, D. K. (1993). Toward an integrated theory of adolescent ego development: The "new look" at adolescent egocentrism. *American Journal of Orthopsychiatry, 63,* 562–571.

Lax, R. F., Bach, S., & Burland, J. A. (Eds.) (1986). *Self and object constancy: Clinical and theoretical perspectives.* New York: Guilford Press.

Lee, C. D., Shaughnessy, J. J., & Bankes, J. K. (1995). Impact of expedited visitation services, a court program that enforces access. *Family & Conciliation Courts Review, 33,* 495–505.

Lee, M. (1989). *The use of special masters.* Paper presented to the State-wide Conference for Family Court Services, San Diego, CA.

Lehner, L. (1994). Education for parents divorcing in California. *Family & Conciliation Courts Review, 32,* 50–54.

Lerman, L. J. (1984). Mediation of wife abuse cases: The adverse impact of formal dispute resolution on women. *Harvard Women's Law Journal, 7,* 57–113.

Lewis, D. O., Lovely, R., Yeager, C., & Femina, D. D. (1989). Toward a theory of the genesis of violence: A follow-up study of juvenile delinquents. *Journal of the American Academy of Child & Adolescent Psychiatry, 28,* 431–436.

Lewis, M. (1992). *Shame: The exposed self.* New York: Free Press.

Lund, M. (1995). A therapist's view of parental alienation syndrome. *Family & Conciliation Courts Review, 33,* 308–316.

Maccoby, E. E., & Mnookin, R. H. (1992). *Dividing the child: Social and legal dilemmas of custody.* Cambridge, MA: Harvard University Press.

Mächtlinger, V. J. (1981). The father in psychoanalytic theory. In M. Lamb (Ed.), *The role of the father in child development,* 2nd edition. New York: Wiley.

Magana, H. A., & Taylor, N. (1993). Child custody mediation and spousal abuse: A descriptive study of a protocol. *Family & Conciliation Courts Review, 31,* 50–64.

Mahler, M. S., Pine, F., & Bergman, A. (1975). *The psychological birth of the human infant.* New York: Basic Books.

Main, M., Kaplan, N., & Cassidy, J. (1985). Security in infancy, childhood, and adulthood: A move to the level of representation. In I. Bretherton & E. Waters (Eds.), *Growing points of attachment theory and research.* Monograph of the Society for Research in Child Development (Serial No. 209).

Marin Collaborative Law Group (1995). Principles and guidelines for the practice of collaborative law. Unpublished manuscript. Available from P. H. Tessler, 16 Buena Vista Avenue, Mill Valley, CA 94941.

Martin, D. (1987). The historical roots of domestic violence. In D. J. Sonkin (Ed.), *Domestic violence on trial.* New York: Springer.

Masterson, J. (1985). *The real self: A developmental, self, and object relations approach.* New York: Brunner/Mazel.

Masterson, J., & Costello, J. (1980). *From borderline adolescent to functioning adult: The test of time.* New York: Brunner/Mazel.

Masterson, J., & Klein, R. (Eds.) (1989). *Psychotherapy of the disorders of the self: The Masterson approach.* New York: Brunner/Mazel.

McClenney, L., Johnston, J. R., & Wallerstein, J. S. (1994). Adjustment to divorce as a function of prior trauma and perceptions of the marital relationship. Technical Report of the Center for the Family in Transition, P.O. Box 157, Corte Madera, CA 94976.

McCord, J. (1988). Parental behavior in the cycle of aggression. *Psychiatry, 51,* 14–23.

McDevitt, J. B. (1975). Separation-individuation and object constancy. *Journal of the American Psychoanalytic Association, 23,* 713–742.

McDonough, H., Radovanovic, H., Stein, L., Sagar, A., & Hood, E. (1995). *For kids' sake: A treatment program for high-conflict separated families (Parents' group manual).* Family Court Clinic, Clarke Institute of Psychiatry, 250 College Street, Toronto, Ontario, M5T 1R8 Canada.

McIsaac, H. (1994). Orientation to mediation in Portland, Oregon. *Family & Conciliation Courts Review, 32,* 55–61.

Miller, D. (1978). Early adolescence: Its psychology, psychopathology, and implications for therapy. In S. C. Feinstein (Ed.), *Adolescent psychiatry* (pp. 434–447). Chicago: University of Chicago Press.

Milne, A. (1978). Custody of children in a divorce process: A family self-determination model. *Conciliation Courts Review, 16,* 1–16.

Mnookin, R. H. (1985). Divorce bargaining: The limits of private ordering. *University of Michigan Journal of Law Reform, 18,* 1015–1037.

Mnookin, R. H., & Kornhauser, L. (1979). Bargaining in the shadow of the law: The case of divorce. *Yale Law Review, 88,* 950–997.

Mosten, F. S. (1992). Confidential mini-evaluation. *Family & Conciliation Courts Review, 30,* 373–384.

Mueller, C., & Pope, H. (1977). Marital instability: A study of its transmission between generations. *Journal of Marriage & the Family, 39*(1), 83–94.

Munsch, R. (1986). *Love you forever.* Willowdale, Ontario, Canada: Firefly Books.

Newman, L., Harrell, A., & Salem, P. (1995). Domestic violence and empowerment in custody and visitation cases. *Family & Conciliation Courts Review, 33,* 30–62.

Pearson, J. (1996). Child access projects: An evaluation of four access demonstration projects funded by the Federal Office of Child Support Enforcement. *The Center for Policy Research,* Denver, CO 80218.

Pearson, J., & Anhalt, J. (1994). Examining the connection between child access and child support. *Family & Conciliation Courts Review, 32,* 93–109.

Pearson, J., & Thoennes, N. (1980). Mediation project—An update. *The Colorado Lawyer Family Law Newsletter,* 712–721.

Pearson, J., & Thoennes, N. (1984). Final Report of the Divorce Mediation Research Project, *Association of Family & Conciliation Courts,* Research Unit, 329 W. Wilson St., Madison, WI 53703.

Pearson, J., & Thoennes, N. (1996). Supervised visitation: Survey of service providers, Denver, CO 80218.

Petersen, V., & Steinman, S. B. (1994). Helping children succeed after divorce: A court-mandated educational program for divorcing parents. *Family & Conciliation Courts Review, 32,* 10–26.

Piaget, J. (1979). The intellectual development of the adolescent. In A. Esman (Ed.), *The Psychology of adolescence* (pp. 104–108). New York: International Universities Press.

Pope, H., & Mueller, C. (1976). The intergenerational transmission of marital instability: Comparisons by race and sex. *Journal of Social Issues, 32*(1), 67–72.

Pynoos, R. S., & Eth, S. (1986). Witness to violence: The child interview. *Journal of the American Academy of Child Psychiatry, 25,* 306–319.

Ricci, I. (1997). *Mom's house/dad's house: Making shared custody work.* 2nd edition. New York: Simon & Schuster/Fireside Book.

Roeder-Esser, C. (1994). Family in transition: A divorce workshop. *Family & Conciliation Courts Review, 32,* 27–49.

Roseby, V. (1994). A group treatment manual for preschool and kindergarten-aged children who live in highly conflicted, violent or separating families. Unpublished manuscript.

Roseby, V. (1995). Uses of psychological testing in a child-focused approach to child custody evaluations. *Family Law Quarterly, 29,* 97–110.

Roseby, V. (in press). Conflicts in gender and sexual identity in children of high-conflict divorce. In T. Cohen, H. Etezady, & B. Pacella (Eds.), *The vulnerable child, Vol. 2.* Madison, CT: International Universities Press.

Roseby, V., Erdberg, P., Bardenstein, K., & Johnston, J. R. (1995). Developmental psychopathology in children in high-conflict families: Attachment, personality disorders and the Rorschach. Paper presented at the Society for Research in Child Development, March, Kansas City, KS.

Roseby, V., & Johnston, J. R. (1997). *High-conflict, violent, and separating families: A group treatment manual for school-age children.* New York: Free Press.

Roseby, V., & Wallerstein, J. (1997). Impact of divorce on school-age children: Assessment and intervention strategies. In P. Kernberg & J. Bemporad (Eds.), *Handbook of child and adolescent psychiatry.* New York: Brunner/Mazel.

Ross, J. (1982). From mother to father. In S. Cath, A. Gurwitt, & J. Ross (Eds.), *Father and child,* pp. 189–203. Boston: Little, Brown.

Rutter, M. (1987). Psychosocial resilience and protective mechanisms. *American Journal of Orthopsychiatry, 57,* 316–331.

Sagatun, I. J., & Barrett, L. (1990). Parental child abduction: The law, family dynamics, and legal system responses. *Journal of Criminal Justice, 18,* 433–442.

Salem, P., Schepard, A., & Schlissel, S.W. (1996). Parent education as a distinct field of practice. *Family and Conciliation Courts Review, 34,* 9–22.

Satir, V. (1972). *Peoplemaking.* Palo Alto, CA: Science and Behavior Books.

Schank, R. C., & Abelson, R. P. (1977). *Scripts, plans, goals and understanding.* Hillsdale, NJ: Lawrence Erlbaum Associates.

Schave, D., & Schave, B. (1989). *Early adolescence and the search for self: A developmental perspective.* New York: Praeger.

Schepard, A. (1993). Educating divorcing and separating parents. *University of Michigan Journal of Law Reform, 27,* 133–227.

Schutz, B., Dixon, E., Lindenberger, J., & Ruther, N. (1989). *Solomon's sword: A practical guide to conducting child custody evaluations.* San Francisco: Jossey-Bass.

Schwartzberg, A. (1980). Adolescent reactions to divorce. *Adolescent Psychiatry, 8,* 379–392.

Schwarz, E. D., Kowalski, J. M., & Hanus, S. (1993). Malignant memories: Signatures of violence. *Adolescent Psychiatry, 19,* 280–300.

Selman, R. L. (1980). *The growth of interpersonal understanding.* New York: Academic Press.

Sendak, Maurice (1963). *Where the wild things are.* New York: Harper & Row.

Silver, J. M., & Yudofsky, S. C. (1987). Treatment of aggressive disorders. *Psychiatric Annals, 17,* 365–405.

Simons, V. A., Grossman, L. S., & Weiner, B. J. (1990). A study of families in high conflict custody disputes: Effects of psychiatric evaluation. *Bulletin of the American Academy of Psychiatry & the Law, 18,* 85–97.

Singer, J. A., & Salovey, P. (1993). *The remembered self: Emotion and memory in personality.* New York: Free Press.

Slater, A., Shaw, J. A., & Duquesnel, J. (1992). A consumer evaluation of mediation and investigative services: Executive summary. *Family & Conciliation Courts Review, 30,* 252–259.

Solomon, J., & George, C. (1996). The effects on attachment of overnite visitation in divorced and separating families. Paper presented at the Biennial Meeting of the International Conference on Infant Studies, Providence, RI.

Solomon, J., Wallerstein, J. S., & George, C. (1994). The effects of violence on infant-parent attachment in divorced and separated families. Paper presented at the 13th International Congress of the International Association for Child and Adolescent Psychiatry and Allied Professions. July, San Francisco.

Spence, D. P. (1982). *Narrative truth and historical truth: Meaning and interpretation in psychoanalysis.* New York: Norton.

Spero, M. H. (1990). Portal aspects of memory overlay in psychoanalysis: An object relations contribution to screen memory phenomena. In A. J. Solnit, P. G. Neubauer, S. Abrams, & A. S. Dowling, *The psychoanalytic study of the child, vol. 45* (pp. 79–106). New Haven, CT: Yale University Press.

Sprenkle, D. H., & Storm, C. L. (1983). Divorce-therapy outcome research: A substantive and methodological review. *Journal of Marital & Family Therapy, 10*, 239–258.

Springer, C. (1991). Clinical work with adolescents and their parents during family transitions: Transference and countertransference. *Clinical Social Work Journal, 19*, 405–415.

Stahl, P. (1994). *Conducting child custody evaluations: A comprehensive guide.* Thousand Oaks, CA: Sage Publishing Co.

Stern, D. N. (1985). *The interpersonal world of the infant: A view from psychoanalysis and developmental psychology.* New York: Basic Books.

Stocker, S. M. (1992). A model for a supervised visitation program. *Family & Conciliation Courts Review, 30*, 352–363.

Stolberg, A. L., & Garrison, K. M. (1985). Evaluating a primary prevention program for children of divorce: The divorce adjustment. *American Journal of Community Psychology, 13*, 111–124.

Straus, M. A. (1979). Measuring intrafamily conflict and violence: The conflict tactics (CT) scales. *Journal of Marriage & the Family, 41*, 75–86.

Straus, R. (1996, May). A summary view of supervised visitation in the United States. Paper presented at the Annual Meeting of the Association of Family & Conciliation Courts, San Antonio, TX.

Straus, R., & Alda, E. (1994). Supervised child access: The evolution of a social service. *Family & Conciliation Courts Review, 32*, 230–247.

Terr, L. (1988). What happens to early memories of trauma: A study of twenty children under age five at the time of documented traumatic events. *Journal of the American Academy of Child & Adolescent Psychiatry, 27*, 96–104.

Terr, L. (1990). *Too scared to cry.* New York: Basic Books.

Tomkins, S. S. (1978). Script theory: Differential magnification of affects. In H. E. Howe, Jr., & R. A. Dienstbier (Eds.), *1978 Nebraska symposium on motivation, vol. 26.* University of Nebraska Press.

Tschann, J. M., Johnston, J. R., Kline, M., & Wallerstein, J. S. (1989). Family process and children's functioning during divorce. *Journal of Marriage & the Family, 51*, 431–444.

Turkat, I. D. (1994). Child visitation interference in divorce. *Clinical Psychology Review, 14*, 737–742.

Vic, M. H., & Backerman, R. (1996, March). Mediation/Arbitration: Surveys of professionals and clients. Paper presented at the Boulder Interdisciplinary Committee on Child Custody, Boulder, CO.

Waldron, J. A., Roth, C. P., Farr, P. H., Manor, E. M., & McDermott, Jr., J. F. (1984). A therapeutic mediation model for child custody dispute resolution. *Mediation Quarterly, 3*, 5–20.

Walker, L. E. A. (1984). *The battered woman syndrome.* New York: Springer.

Walker, L. E. A., & Edwall, G. E. (1987). Domestic violence and determination of visitation and custody in divorce. In D. J. Sonkin (Ed.), *Domestic violence on trial: Psychological and legal dimensions of family values* (pp. 127–152). New York: Springer.

Wallerstein, J. S. (1991). Tailoring the intervention to the child in the separating and divorced family. *Family & Conciliation Courts Review, 29*(4), 448–459.

Wallerstein, J. S., & Blakeslee, S. (1989). *Second chances: Men, women and children a decade after divorce.* New York: Ticknor & Fields.

Wallerstein, J. S., & Kelly, J. B. (1980). *Surviving the breakup: How children and parents cope with divorce.* New York: Basic Books.

Walters, M. G., Lee, M. S., & Olesen, N. (1995, March). Rorschach findings about parenting capacities of parents in protracted custody disputes. Paper presented at the Society for Personality Assessment, Atlanta, GA.

Widom, C. S. (1989). Does violence beget violence? A critical examination of the literature. *Psychological Bulletin, 106,* 3–28.

Winnicott, D. (1960). Ego distortions in terms of true and false self. In *The maturational processes and the facilitating environment,* 2nd edition (pp. 140–152). New York: International Universities Press.

Winnicott, D. W. (1971). Transitional objects and transitional phenomena. In *Playing and reality* (pp. 1–25). New York: Routledge.

Zeanah, C. H., & Zeanah, P. D. (1989). Intergenerational transmission of maltreatment: Insights from attachment theory and research. *Psychiatry, 52,* 177–196.

Zibbell, R. A. (1995). The mental health professional as arbitrator in post-divorce child-oriented conflict. *Family & Conciliation Courts Review, 33,* 462–471.

Bibliography

Buchanan, C. M., Maccoby, E. E., & Dornbusch, S. M. (1996). *The divided child: Adolescents' adjustment after divorce*. Cambridge, MA: Harvard University Press.

Cappell, C., & Heiner, R. B. (1990). The intergenerational transmission of family aggression. *Journal of Family Violence, 5*, 135–152.

Carlson, R. (1981). Studies in script theory: 1. Adult analogs of a childhood nuclear scene. *Journal of Personality & Social Psychology, 40*, 501–510.

Caspi, A., & Elder, G. H. (1988). Emergent family patterns: The intergenerational construction of problem behavior and relationships. In R. Hinde & J. Stevenson-Hinde (Eds.), *Understanding family dynamics*. New York: Oxford University Press.

Cherlin, A. J., Furstenberg, Jr., F. F., Chase-Lansdale, P. L., Kiernan, K. E., Robins, P. K., Morrison, D. R., & Teitler, J. O. (1991). Longitudinal studies of effects of divorce on children in Great Britain and the United States. *Science, 252*, 1386–1389.

Cicchetti, D., & Aber, L. A. (1980). Abused children—abusive parents: An overstated case? *Harvard Educational Review, 50*, 244–255.

Cummings, E. M., & Cummings, J. S. (1988). A process-oriented approach to children's coping with adults' angry behavior. *Developmental Review, 8*, 296–321.

Cummings, E. M., & Davies, P. (1994). *Children and marital conflict: The impact of family dispute and resolution*. New York: Guilford Press.

Cummings, J. S., Pellegrine, D. S., Notarius, C. I., & Cummings, E. M. (1989). Children's responses to angry adult behavior as a function of marital distress and history of interparental hostility. *Child Development, 60*, 1035–1043.

Depner, C. E., Leino, E. V., & Chun, A. (1992). Interparental conflict and child adjustment: A decade review and meta-analysis. *Family & Conciliation Courts Review, 30*, 323–341.

Emery, R. E. (1982). Children of parental discord and divorce. *Psychological Bulletin, 92*, 310–330.

Emery, R. E. (1989). Family violence. *American Psychologist, 44*, 321–328.

Esman, A. (1980). Adolescent psychopathology and the rapprochement phenomenon. *Adolescent Psychiatry, 8*, 320–331.

Fantuzzo, J. W., & Lindquist, C. U. (1989). The effects of observing conjugal violence on children: A review and analysis of research methodology. *Journal of Family Violence, 4*, 77–94.

Finkelhor, D., Gelles, R. J., Hotaling, G. T., & Straus, M. A. (Eds.) (1983). *The dark side of families: Current family violence research.* Beverly Hills, CA: Sage Publishing Co.

Forsstrom-Cohen, B., & Rosenbaum, A. (1985). The effects of parental marital violence on young adults: An exploratory investigation. *Journal of Marriage and the Family, 47,* 467–472.

Furstenberg, Jr., F. F. (1994). History and current status of divorce in the United States. *The Future of Children, 4,* 29–43.

Furstenberg, Jr., F. F., & Nord, C. W. (1985). Parenting apart: Patterns in childrearing after marital disruption. *Journal of Marriage and the Family, 47,* 893–904.

Gelles, R. J., & Cornell, C. P. (1985). *Intimate violence in families.* Beverly Hills, CA: Sage Publishing Co.

George, C., & Main, M. (1979). Social interactions of young abused children: Approach, avoidance and aggression. *Child Development, 50,* 306–318.

Girdner, L. (1986). Family mediation: Toward a synthesis. *Mediation Quarterly, 13,* 3–8.

Green, A. H. (1987). Generational transmission of violence in child abuse. *International Journal of Family Psychiatry, 6,* 389–403.

Grusznski, R. J., Brink, J. C., & Edleson, J. L. (1988). Support and education groups for children of battered women. *Child Welfare, 67,* 431–444.

Grych, J. H., & Fincham, F. D. (1990). Marital conflict and children's adjustment: A cognitive-contextual framework. *Psychological Bulletin, 108,* 267–290.

Hauser, B. B. (1985). Custody in dispute: Legal and psychological profiles of contesting families. *Journal of the American Academy of Child Psychiatry, 24,* 575–582.

Hernandez, D. J. (1993). *America's children: Resources for family, government, and the economy.* New York, Russell Sage Foundation.

Herrenkohl, E. C., Herrenkohl, R. C., & Toedter, L. J. (1983). Perspectives on the intergenerational transmission of abuse. In D. Finkelhor, R. J. Gelles, G. T. Hotaling, & M. A. Straus (Eds.), *The dark side of families: Current family violence research* (pp. 305–316). Beverly Hills, CA: Sage Publishing Co.

Hershorn, M., & Rosenbaum, A. (1985). Children of marital violence: A closer look at the unintended victims. *American Journal of Orthopsychiatry, 55,* 260–266.

Herzberger, S. D. (1983). Social cognition and the transmission of abuse. In D. Finkelhor, R. J. Gelles, G. T. Hotaling, & M. A. Straus (Eds.), *The dark side of families: Current family violence research* (pp. 317–329). Beverly Hills, CA: Sage Publishing Co.

Hoff, P. M. (1994). *Parental abduction: How to prevent an abduction and what to do if your child is abducted* (4th ed.). Washington, DC: National Center for Missing and Exploited Children.

Horowitz, M. J. (1988). *Introduction to psychodynamics: A synthesis.* New York: Basic Books.

Hughes, H. H., Parkinson, D., & Vargo, H. (1989). Witnessing spouse abuse and experiencing physical abuse: A "double whammy"? *Journal of Family Violence, 4,* 197–209.

Hughes, H. M. (1988). Psychological and behavioral correlates of family violence in child witnesses and victims. *American Journal of Orthopsychiatry, 58*(1), 77–90.

Jaffe, P., Wilson, S., & Wolfe, D. (1986). Promoting changes in attitudes and understanding of conflict resolution among child witnesses of family violence. *Canadian Journal of Behavioral Science, 18,* 356–366.

Johnston, J. R. (1990). Role diffusion and role reversal: Structural variations in divorced families and children's functioning. *Family Relations, 39,* 405–413.

Johnston, J. R. (Ed.) (1992b). *Violence and hate in the family and neighborhood.* ERIC Clearinghouse on Elementary and Early Childhood Education, University of Illinois at Urbana, Champaign.

Johnston, J. R. (1994a). High-conflict divorce. *The Future of Children, Children and Divorce, 4(1),* 165–182.

Johnston, J. R. (1995). Research update: Children's adjustment in sole custody compared to joint custody families and principles for custody decision making. *Family & Conciliation Courts Review, 33,* 403–414.

Johnston, J. R., Baris, M. A., Breunig, K., & Garrity, C. (1997). *Through the eyes of children: Healing stories for children of divorce.* New York: Free Press.

Johnston, J. R., Kline, M., & Tschann, J. (1989). Ongoing postdivorce conflict in families contesting custody: Effects on children of joint custody and frequent access. *American Journal of Orthopsychiatry, 59,* 576–592.

Kline, M., Tschann, J. M., Johnston, J. R., & Wallerstein, J. S. (1989). Children's adjustment in joint and sole physical custody families. *Developmental Psychology, 25*(3), 430–438.

Kroger, J. (1989). *Identity in adolescence: The balance between self and other.* New York: Routledge.

Lerman, L. J. (1984). Mediation of wife abuse cases: The adverse impact of formal dispute resolution on women. *Harvard Women's Law Journal, 7,* 57–113.

McCloskey, L. A., Figueredo, A. J., & Koss, M. (1995). The effects of systemic family violence on children's mental health. *Child Development, 66,* 1239–1261.

McKay, M. M. (1994). The link between domestic violence and child abuse: Assessment and treatment considerations. *Child Welfare, 73,* 29–39.

Patterson, G. R., DeBaryshe, B. D., & Ramsey, E. (1989). A developmental perspective on antisocial behavior. *American Psychologist, 44,* 329–335.

Pearson, J., & Anhalt, J. (1992). Final report: The visitation enforcement program's impact on child access and child support. The Center for Policy Research, Denver, CO 80218.

Pearson, J., & Thoennes, N. (1988). Divorce mediation results. In J. J. Folberg & A. Milne (Eds.), *Divorce mediation: Theory and practice* (pp. 429–452). New York: Guilford Press.

Roseby, V., & Johnston, J. R. (1995). Clinical interventions with children of high conflict and violence. *American Journal of Orthopsychiatry, 65,* 48–59.

Rosenberg, M. S. (1987). Children of battered women: The effects of witnessing violence on their social problem-solving abilities. *Behavior Therapist, 4,* 85–89.

Santrock, J. W., & Warshak, R. A. (1979). Father custody and social development in boys and girls. *Journal of Social Issues, 35,* 112–125.

Schank, R. C. (1982). *Dynamic memory: A theory of reminding and learning in computers and people.* Cambridge: Cambridge University Press.

Sedlak, A. J. (1988). The effects of personal experiences with couple violence on calling it "battering" and allocating blame. In G. T. Hotaling, D. Finkelhor, J. T. Kirkpatrick, & M. A. Straus (Eds.), *Coping with family violence: Research & policy perspectives* (pp. 31–59). Beverly Hills, CA: Sage Publishing Co.

Shiono, P. H., & Quinn, L. S. (1994). Epidemiology of divorce. *The future of children, 4,* 15–28.

Steele, B. F. (1986). Notes on the lasting effects of early child abuse throughout the life cycle. *Child Abuse & Neglect, 10,* 283–291.

Straus, M. A., & Gelles, R. J. (1988). Has family violence decreased? A reassessment of the Straus & Gelles data. *Journal of Marriage & the Family, 50,* 281–291.

Straus, M., Gelles, R., & Steinmetz, S. (1980). *Behind closed doors: Violence in the American family.* Garden City, NY: Anchor/Doubleday.

Wallerstein, J. S. (1985). Parent-child relationships after divorce. In E. J. Anthony & G. H. Pollack (Eds.), *Parental influences in health and disease* (pp. 317–347). Boston: Little Brown.

Westen, D. (1991). Social cognition and object relations. *Psychological Bulletin, 109,* 429–455.

Wolfe, D. A. (1987). *Child abuse: Implications for child development and psychopathology.* Newbury Park, CA: Sage Publishing Co.

Zaslow, M. J. (1989). Sex differences in children's response to parental divorce: Samples, variables, ages and sources. *American Journal of Orthopsychiatry, 59,* 118–141.

Index

Also of Interest from The Free Press——

High-Conflict, Violent, and Separating Families: A Group Treatment Manual for School-Age Children

VIVIENNE ROSEBY AND JANET R. JOHNSTON

"This manual is a rich resource for both novice and experienced leaders who work with school-age children in groups. Role-play exercises, drawing, and fantasy imagery activities encourage children to verbalize their feelings, even as they distance themselves from their parents' conflicts, and develop hope about future relationships." —Nancy Boyd Webb, DSW, Fordham University Program in Child and Adolescent Therapy, and author of *Play Therapy with Children in Crisis*

1997 ISBN: 0–684–82769–7

Through the Eyes of Children: Healing Stories for Children of Divorce

JANET R. JOHNSTON, KAREN BREUNIG, CARLA GARRITY, AND MITCHELL BARIS

Written by leading authorities on child psychology and divorce, this book is a valuable and much needed tool for parents and professionals who work with children struggling with family breakup. Relying on imagination and metaphor, the original stories and illustrations in this unique anthology provide a safe and effective way to help children understand and cope with their parents' separation and living apart. For generations, stories have been a foundation for teaching children. *Through the Eyes of Children* continues that tradition and allows children the chance to recover and heal from divorce.

1997 ISBN: 0–684–83703–X

Impasses of Divorce: The Dynamics and Resolution of Family Conflict

JANET R. JOHNSTON AND LINDA E. G. CAMPBELL

"Battles over children take place on many fronts, but custody is the critical campaign. . . . Johnston and Campbell have thrown themselves into the midst of such divorce feuds as mediators, clinicians, and investigators. In doing so they have produced a book that is timely, insightful, and practical. . . . The uninitiated will be horrified by the insightful portrayal of the destructive maneuvering carried out in the name of the 'child's best interest.'" —*Contemporary Psychologist*

1988 ISBN: 0–02–916621–7